Leisure

LEISURE: LIFESTYLE AND LIFESPAN

Perspectives for Gerontology

MAX KAPLAN, Ph. D.

1979   W.B. SAUNDERS COMPANY / Philadelphia / London / Toronto

W. B. Saunders Company: West Washington Square
Philadelphia, Pa. 19105

1 St. Anne's Road
Eastbourne, East Sussex BN21 3UN, England

1 Goldthorne Avenue
Toronto, Ontario M8Z 5T9, Canada

Library of Congress Cataloging in Publication Data

Kaplan, Max, 1911–

Leisure, lifestyle and lifespan.

Bibliography: p.

1. Retirement—United States.   2. Social work with
the aged—United States—Case studies.   3. Gerontology.
4. Leisure—United States.   I. Title.

HQ1064.U5K36   301.43′5′0973   78–74892

ISBN 0-7216-5272-7

Leisure: Lifestyle and Lifespan: Perspectives for Gerontology   ISBN 0-7216-5272-7

Last digit is the print number: 9 8 7 6 5 4 3 2 1

This book is dedicated to

R. PYRON AND CONNIE CONNALLY

and to

the memory of my parents,

HENRY AND SARAH

Preface

Both professional and personal elements have entered into the preparation of this volume. The contract for its writing came within a few weeks of my 65th birthday; precisely 25 years had passed since undertaking leisure studies at the University of Illinois; just ten years ago I had left Boston for a free-floating assignment at the University of South Florida, from which the Leisure Studies Program emerged; and finally, the completed manuscript for this volume was mailed to Philadelphia a few weeks after mandatory "retirement" at a time when this volume argues that age is increasingly useless as an index of uselessness.

This convergence of private memories and views are intertwined with social changes that affected many millions like myself who were sons and daughters of immigrant parents, grew up in the depression that *was* a depression (the motto of our college class was "WPA: Here we come"), started a working career as a social worker for $30 per week, than raised a family over the decades through World War II, Korea, Vietnam, inflation, TV I (black and white) and TV II (color), and saw Charlie Chaplin pictures the first time around.

Our generation saw the birth of Social Security. I served as a consultant and participant in the White House Conference on Aging both in 1961 and 1971. Increasingly, education, business, and labor unions, as well as the federal government, began to notice the older generation. More important, the elderly themselves have begun to defy "ageism" by taking the initiative in transforming attitudes about them. They have learned from power struggles and identity "crises" of the blacks and women, and they have started to realize that they cannot wait for others to improve their lot. To insure personal growth rather than accept a philosophy and policy of atrophy or empty existence they must themselves assume creative leisure roles, develop programs through political action, and transform agencies and facilities of their communities. This book hopes to prepare gerontologists more carefully for meeting the elderly on the common ground of retirement as a new personal condition and leisure as a new social role.

Sections 1 and 2 present the facts and arguments of the volume. Section 3 considers several "environments" for leisure roles, as in the community or the center. Section 4 then considers several types of activity experiences, for each provides a unique expression of leisure roles. Since this work is addressed primarily to gerontologists, Section 5 is devoted to programming, counseling, and training policies.

Issues, concepts, questions, approaches, and illustrations are stressed throughout, rather than recipes for action or organization. The appendices provide more detailed discussions or supplementary material to those found in the text. Bibliographies for such a volume are inherently difficult, for the parameters of "leisure" are not clear, even to professional scholars of the field; yet, an attempt is made.

Of those to whom I am indebted for listening and responding in one way or another, my students should be noted, both in the University of Southern Florida and in settings of the University of Southern California, North Carolina, Arkansas, as well as in lectures in many parts of the world. Ms. Susan Loring, editor at W. B. Saunders Company, has been helpful and understanding. Others to whom a debt is owed will be found scattered throughout the text or in footnotes. The invisible presence has been Barbara; her own professional and personal creativity has eased and enriched my own "lifestyle" immeasurably. Final stages of the volume were completed in the friendly environment of Salisbury State College on the eastern shore of Maryland, where two former Florida colleagues have created an innovative Department of Leisure Studies—K. Nelson Butler and C. Phillip Bosserman.

Contents

Roles

INTRODUCTION

The position taken here is that "leisure" is a social role in retirement, with unique circles, functions, rewards, and attitudes towards one's "self." This argument results from the knowledge that work is not the entire role during one's productive years, for it is performed along with such roles as, for instance, friend, father, citizen, Presbyterian. Our time in history is one during which the work role itself has become increasingly modified with the reduction in annual work hours, and, simultaneously, when opportunities for leisure have expanded in both the public and private sectors.

These are the themes of the first section. Even as this volume was being prepared, major national changes were in the wind. Congress, by healthy margins, was passing legislation to eliminate mandatory retirement for federal employees and the magical number "65" for other workers. Maine had removed its age limits, the state of California was considering a scheme to reduce unemployment by more "leisure sharing," the President's wife had convened a special conference on problems of the aging, and Vice President Walter Mondale had acquired a deserved reputation in dealing with problems of the elderly.

Some statistics in Section 1 will soon be outdated, but in the direction of a further accentuation of leisure and a further rethinking and restructuring of work-nonwork patterns. That those Americans over 65 will expand their political power and effectiveness is a safe projection, and that their social roles as elderly will, therefore, invite ongoing discussion and analysis, are the bases of this volume.

CHAPTER 1

The Concept "Social Role"

This volume treats the social roles of retirement and leisure, and discusses how these types of roles intersect. Thus, there are three overall conceptions that must be considered: "social role," "retirement," and "leisure." Their interrelationships are partly a response to and partly a cause of various social changes in our period of history. Any reader who is looking for easy methods for organizing a leisure or recreation program is forewarned: such principles, policies, and programs which become explicit in Section 5 will emerge only after considerable analysis that may often be detailed, but always relevant.

Rigor in this study of the elderly is needed as much as when dealing with medical, economic, housing, or other concerns. Perhaps it is needed even more in this area. For geriatric, economic, and social welfare disciplines are well established; "leisure studies," however, is not even accepted in many policy or theoretical quarters, whether among laymen or scholars. Reasons for this will be amplified later, as some history of this study is traced. We turn here to the concept "social role."

The "role" concept is borrowed from the theater. Someone, as *actor,* "plays" the part of a villain, a hero, a lover—that is, he tries to convince the audience by his skills, at least for the duration of the performance. Some actors are so convincing that, like the comedian Jack Benny, the image of the "key role" (in his case, good-hearted but stingy) becomes an off-stage image as well. "Is he really like that?" is a common topic of conversation about stage figures, yet the training of the actor emphasizes the distinction between the separate "realities" and the professional's task of remaining in constant, objective control over his every action and emotion on stage.

3

The transference from this world of make-believe to the world of "real" social relationships would seem to come easily. In life itself there are, on the one hand, you and I and Miss Jones in the next office, made up of flesh and blood and heart. But each is also a "social construct," or an artificially conceived functionary. I am a professor; you are my department chairman; Miss Jones is a secretary. Not all professors or university chairmen or secretaries are alike, but each of these "roles" is far more like each other than are those of a random number of people on the street. This is true simply because each society, or such parts of it as "schools," "factories," and "fire stations," decides what it wants "teachers," "workers," and "fire fighters" to do. The "social role" is ascribed—defined in good part—for Mr. Brown or Miss Jones, and becomes part of his or her training in school or on the job.

In practice these realities often overlap as to "ourselves" and our roles. For example, in medical schools, there will be found students who wear unused stethoscopes around their necks, not for utility, but as a symbol of who they are—or intend to be, and engineering students may be seen with slide rules that are unnecessary at the time. Thus, we take on not only the skills of the profession we hope to join, but also the attitudes, symbols, superstitions, gestures, and even the ideological credo that later will identify us as a loyal part of the group.

On the surface, then, it appears that there is *one* of us as a "person," but *many* roles that we each play "on the stage of life": as father, husband, worker, congregant, American, Kiwaniian, Republican, friend, golfer, and so forth. Perhaps we come closer to the truth by seeing ourselves as a kind of one-person consortium or as a perpetual, integrative process. One moment we put on a robe, the court clerk announces us, everyone stands, and we sentence the prisoner to jail. An hour later we are having informal conversation with a friend (perhaps he was a "judge" earlier in the day, with a robe to provide the proper symbolism). One morning Mrs. Brown is praying in church, acting as she is supposed to according to the traditions of her church; in the evening, she is a member of a home "audience," being entertained by a TV show. The daytime "judge" is in trouble when he confuses his role with being a "husband" at home and orders his wife around; Mrs. Brown may be disappointed if she expects to be entertained in church.

It is an amazing ability that we all develop for moving from one social role to another easily, without losing our bearings. One clue to our success is that we usually build much of our "balance" or identity around one or two *key roles*. For most of us work is the key role. All else is given shape from our work, such as whom we marry, where we live, and our social level. The retiree has lost this center or core of identity; what replaces it? These are central issues to readers of this volume, for the profession of gerontology emerges from this transition.

Here we must clarify the term "social role" more fully. Students of social psychology will explore the various technical distinctions that consume the energies of academia; the differences are concerned especially with a degree of emphasis on the relative influences of the society or environment vis-à-vis the "libido" or other terms for the person as an autonomous being.

For our purpose we will rely on the concept of social role that was developed by the eminent sociologist, Florian Znaniecki.[1] Influences of this thinker will be found throughout this volume.

The concept of "social roles" rests on the interaction between two or more persons and is, therefore, opposed to the view that there is an innate psychological "active tendency" or "essence" of the person acting alone. This interaction extends into social relations and eventually into complex social systems. One of the principles that I shall consequently employ is that retirement is not a mere withdrawal from work roles but, rather, that retirement—even if seemingly devoid of positive "content"—becomes a complex set of *new* relationships for the retiree. The job of recreation and leisure leaders is not to find *substitutes* for work, for *retirement has a dynamic and meaning of its own.* Our task is to build on the nonwork complex we call "leisure" and to help the retiree to raise it to its maximum usefulness within the framework of his enlarged skills and tastes.

Another major concept that Professor Znaniecki emphasized was humanism, or more technically, the concept of a "humanistic coefficient."[2] Again, this was used to counteract the tendency then prevalent among sociologists to imitate the methods of natural scientists. The phenomena of relationships must be seen by the scientist as they are experienced by the participants, not as they fall into neat theoretical formulae. The "humanistic coefficient" will be reflected later in our concept of leisure; it leads to a major conclusion of this book—namely, that a leisure or recreation "program" best emerges from a knowledge of *people,* and not from values or techniques introduced from the outside in the form of *programs.*

Another major principle in this approach to social roles is that the interaction within a group—indeed, the very nature of a social group—results from the relationships of the particular roles played in the situation, rather than by an interaction between whole persons. This contradicts the notion, still heard in some quarters, that a social group is merely a collection of total "persons." If, however, we understand what Znaniecki called the "selective bond" between individuals that brings them or keeps them together, we confront the

---

[1]Florian Znaniecki, *The Method of Sociology.* New York: Holt, Rinehart & Winston, 1934. For other discussions of social role, see: R. E. Park and Ernest W. Burgess, *Introduction to the Science of Sociology.* Chicago: University of Chicago Press, 1921; G. H. Mead, *Mind, Self and Society.* Chicago: University of Chicago Press, 1934; E. T. Hiller, *Social Relations and Patterns.* New York: Harper & Row, 1947; C. H. Cooley, *Human Nature and Social Order.* New York: Charles Scribner's Sons, 1922; Ralph Linton, *The Study of Man.* New York: Appleton-Century-Crofts, 1936; Werner Sombart, *Der Bourgeois.* Munich: Duncker-Humblot, 1913; Sir James George Frazer, *The Golden Bough.* New York: Crowell Collier and Macmillan, Inc., 1922; Stefan Czarnowski, *Le Culte des heros.* Paris: F. Alcan, 1919; Georg Simmel, "The Sociological Significance of the Stranger," *Introduction to the Science of Sociology,* pp. 322–327; Roberto Michels, *Political Parties.* New York: The Free Press of Glencoe, 1949; Herbert Spencer, *Principles of Sociology.* New York: Appleton-Century Crofts, 1877; Pitirim Sorokin, *Society, Culture and Personality.* New York: Harper & Row, Publishers, 1947, chapter 19; and Hans Gerth and C. Wright Mills, *Character and Social Structure.* New York: Harcourt, Brace World, Harbinger, ed., 1964.

[2]Znaniecki, op. cit. pp. 43–49.

real possibility of discovering new bonds or potential areas of relationships without a radical change of the people in their wholeness. We thus come to the dynamics of innovation and growth by persons.

Znaniecki's theoretical summaries arose from the specific studies of such roles as peasant, peasant housewife, farm laborer, industrial worker, unemployed worker, child, pupil, soldier, teacher, artist, and man of knowledge. The sociologists R. E. Park, G. H. Mead, E. T. Hiller, and E. W. Burgess have developed aspects of the similar concept *personal roles.* Ralph Linton, the anthropologist, is widely quoted for his theoretical formulation of role. Pioneering studies of specific roles were Sombart's *Der Bourgeois,* Frazer's analysis of priests and kings in *The Golden Bough,* Czarnowski's work on the hero, Simmel's on the stranger and the poor, and Michels' on the political leader. Herbert Spencer had already outlined a theoretical basis for the study of social positions and functions in his "Professional Institutions" and other portions of his voluminous writings.

"From the sociological point of view," wrote Znaniecki, "the primary matter about an individual is his social position and function, and this is not a manifestation of his nature, but a cultural system he constructs with the help of his milieu, seldom creating, usually copying it from ready models." This theory of the social person deals with the positions he occupies and the functions he performs in his social environment, "each involving definite rights and obligations, which in most cases are attached to similar positions and functions. . . ."[3]

Between the person and the *social circle* that participates with him in the action, which may range from the collection of snails or Rembrandts to a love of dogs or the game of canasta, there exists a common value. Whatever the political, recreational, social, economic, religious, or educational value may be, singly or in combination, the performance of a role implies a reciprocal relationship. There can be "no active banker without clients, no practicing physician without patients, no reigning king without subjects, no child-in-the-family without other family members."[4]

Obviously, then, since in a complex society the person engages in various pursuits with a number of groups (as father, citizen, golfer, worker, or friend) he enters "into as many reciprocities as there are customary, expected duties and functions which he performs."[5] Inasmuch as particular roles may require specific abilities and skills, or are restricted to certain ages, sexes, or races, the person becomes conscious of "his own self" as a psychological entity and how others regard him. "In every Western language there are hundreds of words denoting supposed traits of 'intelligence' and 'character,' and almost every such trait . . . is positively or negatively valued, either in all persons or in persons performing certain kinds of roles."[6]

[3]Florian Znaniecki, *The Social Role of the Man of Knowledge.* New York: Columbia University Press, 1940, p. 120.
[4]*The Social Role of the Man of Knowledge,* p. 117.
[5]Hiller, op. cit. p. 338.
[6]*The Social Role of the Man of Knowledge,* p. 16.

The *function* that the person performs within his circle corresponds to needs of the group. Our concern as analysts may be with the origin and changes of that function or with the training that prepares the person for its completion or its relation to functions performed by others within the group.

The last component of the social role is the totality of rights and privileges given to a person by his circle: rights that may concern his bodily existence (such as possibility of movement, protection from injury, or occupation of certain places), his material economic rewards, his social standing, his reputation, or the range of his choice of women. This totality is called *status,* or *prestige.*

In sum, the social role includes the presence of: (1) a social circle; (2) the attitudes of the person toward himself, toward others, and toward the reaction of others to him; (3) the functions he performs; and (4) his status. It is taken for granted that the total situation implies the presence of common values and a pattern of norms or standards of behavior.

Since the role is not a mere static datum about an individual but a process or dynamic system of relationships, some problems that face the sociologist who undertakes the analysis of a specific role may include the following:

1. "Its components may be variously interconnected in the course of its performance."[7] Thus, has the subject under consideration emphasized one of the components above the others? Has he been content to follow patterns already established for his role, or is he an innovator in one respect or another?

2. It is "the connection between the individual and his social milieu, which is the main object of interest."[8] How is the role of the person related functionally to others that he plays within his circle; how does a person's participation in one role affect his simultaneous participation in others?

3. Most of the patterns "which have evolved during the history of mankind can be studied in the course of their becoming and duration."[9] Under what conditions has this role originated? How have prevailing codes and sanctions perpetuated or changed it? How has the educational system been utilized for these purposes? In the presence of diffusion of role patterns, what has been the influence on the role of such factors as "borrowing from neighboring cultures, travel, trade, migration, colonization, conquest, dissemination of book lore,"[10] and the like?

4. "The possibility of reaching such general conclusions about all social roles and more specific generalizations about social roles of a certain kind— such as the role of peasant, priest, merchant, factory worker, or artist—point obviously to the existence of essential uniformities and also of important variations among these social phenomena."[11] What, then, are the conclusions that *this* role suggests as applicable to other patterns?

---

[7] Ibid. p. 17.
[8] Ibid. p. 13.
[9] Ibid. p. 19.
[10] Ibid. p. 20.
[11] Ibid. p. 18.

This approach, therefore, is not a study of the individual; it is distinctly a sociology rather than a psychology precisely because its chief concern is with the connections of the person with the dynamics of group activity. Hence, there is no basic difference between role theory and the theory of groups. Role already implies group structure, group needs, training by the group, responsibility to the group. Indeed, Znaniecki defines the group itself as a synthesis of social roles.[12]

To summarize, a study of individual social roles means that we study a group interaction from the view of the actor, but a view and a function already patterned toward those of others. The role does not arise in vacuo, but from historical or functional needs present in the society. Its presence is a manifestation of those conditions and a realization of one type of solution. For example, to study the origins of the *hazan,* the singer of the Orthodox Jewish service, we need to see how the professional precentor arose from the notion that everyone is near God and capable of approaching him.[13] This democratic Judaic idea, in turn, grew out of the priesthood traditions of Assyria, Egypt, and Babylonia. Whether one begins with the history and works inward toward the present role, or starts with the role and goes outward wherever the problem demands, is largely a question of what reaches the heart of the problem posed more clearly and quickly.

THE "ELDERLY" AS A SOCIAL ROLE

In applying this theoretical outline to our subject, an immediate issue arises: are we talking about the social role of the "elderly," the "retiree," or both simultaneously? "Elderly" refers to a condition in *relationship to,* while "retirement" refers to a condition of *withdrawal from;* the word "elderly" has no meaning unless there is a concept of "youngerly,"—i.e., childhood, youth, middle age. Obviously, the number of years has nothing to do with it; in a study of New York City junior high school students, the perception of who is "old" ranged from 19 to 91 years! However, an "elder" is a *role.* As Webster's *New World Dictionary* (1974) notes,[14] an elder may be an older person with some authority or dignity in a tribe or community, an officer in an early Christian church, a minister in some Protestant churches, an assistant at

---

[12]F. Znaniecki, "Social Groups as Products of Cooperating Individuals," *American Journal of Sociology,* May 1939.

[13]A. Z. Idelsohn, *Jewish Music in Its Historical Development.* New York: Tudor Publishing Co., 1944. For several studies of roles of musicians, see S. Chaneles, *The Concert Pianist: The Study of the Social Roles and Functions of the Artist in American Society.* Ph.D. (sociology), New York University, 1960. Mic. 60=5274, DA 21; 8,2395; A. Ellison, *The Composer Under Twentieth Century Political Ideologies.* Columbia University, Ph.D., 1950. K. P. Etzkorn, *Musical and Social Patterns of Songwriters: An Exploratory Sociological Study.* Ph.D. (sociology), Princeton University, 1959. Mic. 60=4983, DA 21; 5,1281. D. J. Nash, *The American Composer: A Study in Social Psychology.* Ph.D. (sociology), University of Pennsylvania, 1954. DA 14, 879. C. C. Onion, *The Social Status of Musicians in Seventeenth Century France.* Ph.D. (history), University of Minnesota, 1959. Mic. 59=5084; DA 20; 6,2238.

[14]Cleveland and New York: World Publishing Co.

Communion, or a member of the Melchizedek priesthood in the Mormon Church. Obviously, some retirees are not old, and some elderly persons are not retired.

Of the several definitions of "retiree," one that most closely approximates the vernacular use is he or she "who has retired from work, business, etc." Of course, we "retire" to sleep and we "retire" the baseball batter, but the prominence of the work dimension in our lives is evident in the dictionary use above. A more inclusive single statement would be that a retiree is one who withdraws, temporarily or permanently, from any sphere of activity, interest, or commitment.

Because we emphasize the work role, to withdraw from the job is often interpreted, even by gerontologists, as the negation of all roles. Hence, we often relate loneliness or boredom among retirees to the "loss of role." Yet, as noted earlier, we all have numerous roles at any time in our lives. What actually happens, then, is that the retiree faces the task of transforming or readjusting the *relationship* of his roles. The diminution or elimination of the work role is less dramatic (or to some, less traumatic) than it would have been several centuries ago. Indeed, retirement itself is an innovation of the past century and, even within that time span, a reduction from about 70 to about 40 hours of work weekly represents a lifetime reduction in work hours from 140,000 to 80,000.

"Play," since the classic analysis by Johann Huizinga, is not a meaningless, frivolous, empty-headed experience, but a category of actions that can penetrate law, education, art, or other "serious" areas.[15] The retiree is in the favorable and historically unusual position of using a bulk of time (10 years in retirement × 50 weeks × 5 days × 8 hours = 20,000 hours!) in which to "play at" civic affairs, adult education, travel, or anything else.

As to the "teaching" component of the elderly in retirement, this derives from the fact that implicit in being an older person—not necessarily an elder in church—is that he becomes a model, image, or reminder to the younger generations of what is in store for them. This modelling can take explicit forms: (1) by teaching, as in the case of retirees who teach their peers in special classes—as in Cleveland, New York, San Diego, and elsewhere; (2) by serving as examples of ongoing vitality, as in the cases of Picasso, Casals, or Arthur Rubinstein; or (3) by transmitting their understanding from a sheer accumulation of experience, as in the advice of the parent to the child.

It will be useful here to apply Znaniecki's four components to the leisure role as it takes on new dimensions from the supplementation of time that was formerly used in work.

1. Social Circle. Upon leaving the work role this may, and often does, become enlarged. If one moves to a different community "making new friends" may, in fact, be a motivation and a fruition. In work one is often limited in friendships owing to the restraints of time and the network of social contacts related to the work, especially when the work may remove one from a

---

[15]*Homo Ludens.* Boston: Free Press, 1950.

broad base of persons with other backgrounds, as in the case of a lumberjack or farmer.

2. Functions. Upon leaving the work role these are seriously modified, as the overwhelming dominance of the job—with all of its psychological and social ramifications—is now replaced by the role of amateur painter, gardener, traveler, student, fisherman, or golfer. Unless one form of leisure dominates (for instance, the person who moves to a retirement community largely because of its golf course) the common experience of the retiree is that he confronts roles in bits and pieces: Monday night is club, Tuesday he fishes part of the day, and so on. The cumulative impact may be boredom, a sense of disorganization, alienation or, on the positive side, a sense of freedom, adventure, variety, joy, and release from the routine of the work years.

There is no conclusive evidence that the individual who concentrates on one or a few leisure roles is happier than one who takes the smorgasbord approach. One factor is the length of time since one has left work. There are also other variables, such as curiosity, the living or family situation, the presence of alternatives to choose from, or one's threshold for new experience.

3. Rewards, Status, Esteem. The major "reward" of work, aside from psychic satisfactions, remains that of income. There is, of course, a relationship: those with better incomes generally report more "satisfaction." It is the income in the retirement period that concerns us here, for retirement as well as work life relies in part on the economic base. Inflation has made matters worse; in its report to the Senate Committee as of 1976, the Special Committee on Aging noted:

> Older persons have half the income of their younger counterparts. In 1975, half of the families headed by an older person had incomes of less than $8,057 ($14,698 for families with under-65 heads); the median income of older persons living alone or with non-relatives was $3,311 ($6,460 for younger unrelated individuals).[16]

The Committee noted that a sixth of the elderly had incomes below the official description of poverty, a proportion that showed a decided improvement with recent increases in social security benefits. The black elderly are particularly in need. According to the National Center for Black Aged, 50% of the black elderly were poor in the urban areas, and 66% in rural areas. On all counts, as these comparisons were made, the black group had half the income of whites. Further, 23% of the blacks had no liquid assets and, among those who move into public housing, "63% of elderly black families moved from substandard housing . . ."[17]

Setting aside the financial rewards of a job, we come here to the various studies that have been performed concerning "job satisfaction." The general conclusion, not surprisingly, is that: (1) many workers, especially those who are not in professions or occupations in which they have real control over their actions, are unhappy in their work; (2) the higher-salaried jobs that require

---

[16]Senate Committee on Aging, U.S. Senate, Pt. 1, Developments on Aging; 1977. April 27, 1978, p. xvi.
[17]National Center on Black Aged, Fact Sheet, (undated), 1725 De Sales St., N.W., Washington, D.C.

the most preparation bring the highest personal satisfactions, and are most esteemed by the general society; (3) persons who come out of jobs that were highly structured, as in the military and business, have more difficulty in the transition period upon retirement than those who leave teaching, medicine, or other professions which allow more flexibility in decision making and the use of time.

In our utilitarian society, the status of older persons or retirees is not high. It is this image of uselessness that is a major problem for many retirees, especially in the transition period. We do not assume that the child is "useless" because it makes no direct contribution to the economy. Instead, we say that the child is "preparing" to contribute to the society. As to the elderly, the traditional (especially Germanic) view is to say that they have made their contribution, and no more is expected of them; the growing view, as in the U.S.A., is that the elderly now have a choice of living on the past or of continuing to grow and contribute. To the degree that the second alternative becomes the norm for the remaining life span of the elderly and their image by the rest of society, the status of the "third age" will rise in the decades ahead.

4. "Self."   Related to the previous paragraph is Znaniecki's last component of social role. The transformation and enlargement of the leisure role for the elderly is far more than the arrangement of time. The eight hours each Monday to Friday that one has spent working will somehow be filled. On the simplest level one can sleep more, or take more time for such tasks as getting the daily newspaper or eating. The concept of "self" is very much tied in with that of "ageism," a negative view of the elderly which will be discussed later (Chapter 5). Since such conceptions are deeply engraved in the collective psychology, a more likely source of change in attitude about oneself will come from the importance attributed to the *activity* in which the older person engages. For example, in recent years there has been a remarkable growth in the arts in the U.S.A. and Canada; education as a lifelong process has gained support; the civil rights and the women's liberation movements have renewed interest in volunteering for social reform. As increasing numbers of older persons become involved in these or other actions that carry general approval, the "selfhood" of the elderly will become more affirmative. It may be that the source of change in attitude about the leisure role of retirees must originate among them, just as women have been going through the process of accepting their own worth as a prelude to social action.

As to the general society the leisure role is, of course, enlarging for all of us, even those still engaged in the productive stage of our economy. Reasons for this emanate both from the attractions of leisure and the reduction of work to an instrumental level. Further, within that 20,000 hours (assuming a 50-week workspan for 40 years), as the next chapter will note, the emphasis on work has diminished psychologically.

The absence of work obligations for the retiree enlarges opportunities for other activities which may, on the surface, appear to be fragmentary, such as reading the newspaper or visiting a friend, but all of these in composite now become a major preoccupation, a reflection of values and a beneficiary of talents. Like the roles of the child, which are *to play and to learn,* the new "leisure roles" of the elderly retiree are *to play and to teach.*

One of the major debates for gerontologists in the transition has been about the "disengagement" theory, forwarded by Elaine Cumming and William Henry in their conclusions (1961) of studies in Kansas City.[18] According to them, role activity decreased in retirement as part of the normal and successful aging process; the release from past roles was accompanied by a lowering of "psychological energy." Both retirement and widowhood, accordingly, are societal sanctions for disengaging and, therefore, to increased freedom from social norms. The best situation is one in which the attitudes of the society and the retiree coincide. Much debate in professional circles followed the Cumming and Henry publication. To help clarify the issues, Arnold M. Rose observed what the theory does and does not say:

> It is not a hypothesis which states that as people get older, they are gradually separated from their associations and their social functions. . . . Nor does the theory of disengagement state that, as people become physically feebler or chronically ill, they are thereby forced to abandon their associations and social functions. . . . Finally, the theory of disengagement does not say that because older people tend to have reduced income in our society, they can no longer afford to participate in many things. . . [The] theory of disengagement is that the society and the individual prepare *in advance* for the ultimate "disengagement" of incurable, incapacitating disease and death by an inevitable, gradual, and mutually satisfying process of disengagement from society.[19]

The assumption of the present volume is neither an affirmation nor a denial of the Cumming-Henry theory, but rather that retirement roles—as leisure itself—is, or can be, a positive adaptation to a new lifestyle. The role in retirement, as we have seen, is composed of circles, functions, rewards, and perceptions of the "self." Rather than "disengagement" or its opposite concept, "activism," the present approach might be described as one that emphasizes *transition.*

Following Section 3 (Environments) there will be a summary analysis of the various social roles for the elderly within the national culture, the retirement community, senior center, nursing home, and library. A comparable analysis will follow Section 4 (Activity Experiences), with emphasis on components of the roles that enter into the character of the phenomena we call aesthetic, civic, intellectual, mass media, physical, social, spiritual, and touristic.

---

[18]Elaine Cumming and William E. Henry, *Growing Old: The Process of Disengagement,* New York, Basic Books, 1961.

[19]A. M. Rose, "A Current Theoretical Issue in Social Gerontology," *The Gerontologist,* 4:46–50 (1964) quoted by Jerry Jacobs in "An Ethnographic Study of a Retirement Setting," *The Gerontologist,* 14:483–487 (December, 1974).

Freedoms

INTRODUCTION

Leisure as a new social role is recognizable mainly by its freedoms, which is why it is the most difficult of roles. There are few precedents, there are numerous resources that need to be explored and integrated, and there are myths about free time that need to be overcome.

Section 2 is consequently devoted to freedoms *from* and freedoms *for.* Obviously, retirement is freedom from work. Many do not want to retire, for one reason or another, and would not apply the term "freedom" to their new situation. The freedoms *for* to be discussed are less obvious. Since this is a volume for gerontologists, those in which they have taken part are areas for policy, program building, counseling, or research.

Chapter 4 is addressed to freedom from the medical and social sciences just at a time when these fields have become seriously interested in the elderly. I do not intend to deny the contribution they have made and will continue to make in the understanding or treatment of illness or attitudes connected with aging. Yet this is where the rub lies; they are, as general fields, inclined to overextend the connecting links of aging with present-day realities. As the biological model deals with the body and underplays the mind and other sources of health, so the social sciences deal with data about *what is* and underplay the potentials of *what could be.* Neither field does so with pretensions of doing otherwise; such limits are an integral part of their traditions. There are no plots to be dramatically exposed. A call for freedom from the medical and social sciences is an open invitation for gerontology—already an eclectic discipline—to venture freely into other forms of knowledge as it seeks out new visions and versions of mature adulthood.

Freedom from social and political ageism is more concrete. It is not difficult to do a content analysis of motion pictures, TV, or other mass media to discover the prevalent social attitude about the "poor, ill, inactive elderly." These attitudes, integral to an industrial youth-oriented society, have played into the hands of the private sector of our economy, making jobs for younger people, and easing the life of comptrollers and personnel officers who can plan their labor costs more precisely. The political or public sector—as in government and education—have fallen prey to the same numbers game of "65."

CHAPTER 2

Decline of the Work Role

The importance of work as a key role in history is taken for granted everywhere. As the scholar Sebastian de Grazia summarized this post-Reformation view, work is not only the "right and moral thing to do," something that is "good for you, a remedy for pain, loneliness, the death of a dear one, a disappointment in love. . . ."[1] As a layman notes the matter in a less romantic light:

> Work gives order to life. . . . Through work, man finds his own level . . . The house in which we live and all its conveniences . . . the food we eat . . . and the clothes we wear . . . these, and infinitely more, do we receive and give through the common bond of work . . . if it is honest work, performed with all the pride, skill and integrity of the worker, then the world will be a better place because of it.[2]

Our daily activity reflects this attitude in our speech habits with such words as "homework, busywork, workbooks, workouts, workshops, workhorses, school work, work or task forces, works of art, workrooms, worksheets, workups, classwork, work schedules, make-up work, boardwork, remedial work, course work, committee work."[3]

Thus the concept of the "Puritan work ethic" has had a powerful impact in both economic and theological circles. Its essence is that hard work will lead one to heaven; it has been both a social counterrevolutionary influence (work rather than revolution) and a personal motivation (work as the mainspring of character).

In the literature on leisure it has become popular to note the decline of the work ethic by pointing to lower numbers of working hours through the week, year, or lifetime. I have also followed this path in former writings.[4] Here

---

[1]*Of Time, Work and Leisure.* New York: The Twentieth Century Fund, 1962, p. 15.

[2]Max Kaplan, *Leisure: Theory and Policy.* New York: John Wiley and Sons, 1975, pp. 278–279.

[3]William Harper, *Play Factory Advocate.* Emporia: Kansas State University, 1974.

[4]Max Kaplan, *Leisure in America: A Social Inquiry.* New York: John Wiley and Sons, 1960, Chapter 3; *Leisure: Theory and Policy,* op. cit. Chapter 12.

15

we will go back somewhat: (1) to relate the attachment of the "old old" to work values and of the "new old" to other values; (2) to raise questions about the validity or mythology of the "work ethic"; (3) to relate the discontinuity of work values in retirement to the growth of what I shall call "bulk time"; and (4) to show that the work ethic has declined with the loosening of class lines.

THE "OLD OLD" AND WORK VALUES

There is a difference between what may be termed the "old old" and the "new old." It is more than an arbitrary year—such as 80—within the segment of the elderly. Rather, it is an historical difference. The "old old" are those who, regardless of chronological age, were born and raised abroad. The major migration wave to the U.S. took place in the 30 years before World War I. Those who arrived about 1910 and were 20 years old are now (1979) 89. True, there are only 1.9 million persons over 85 in the U.S.A., but it is to them that much welfare was directed (they were in their 40's during the Depression); it was in their generation that legislation arose that moved us ultimately toward Social Security, OAO (Office of Aging), and the gerontological profession.

The "new old," by now the large majority of those over 60 or 65, were born in the U.S. Their aspirations were more than getting settled or raising their children to be "Americans"; indeed, if we take the "new elderly" as those who were youths in the period when television came, the 15-year-olds of the mid-1940's will be 55 in the early 1980's. This is the generation to which gerontology should now be addressing itself; it is a group that has been raised in a time of more freedom in decision making. More important, the "new old" grew up in a world where time itself was a value. Recreation (for work) gave way as a value toward creativity (in living). The new generation of elderly grew up in more urban and therefore more secular environments. The religious component of the work ethic was less influential than it had been among farm generations.

IS THERE A WORK ETHIC?

A second explanation for the decline of the work ethic arises from some doubt as to whether it really existed in the first place. Rather, did this ethic serve as a convenient mythology for the industrial age? For if work per se is a fundamental motivation, why does it need a theological rationale? Why is a heavenly reward necessary? And, indeed, a reading of English history in the early decades of the Industrial Revolution indicates that villagers and farmers did not flow to Manchester, London, or Liverpool to reach heaven sooner, nor did they hurry to the factories in response to a work "instinct." They went to make money. Even with this earthly reward, some had to be recruited or dragooned by force and false promises.

There is a more serious objection to the view that the work ethic is our primary value or drive; it is, after all, a means. Heaven represents the end. Can work be both means and end? This logical fallacy has been repeated endlessly, yet the paradox exists. Further, what is heaven? A 40-hour week, or any number of hours? The fuzzy concept of heaven, accepted with little elaboration, is that in heaven there is no work, and the chosen are forever free to gambol, converse or, in Sebastian deGrazia's articulation of the Greek view of *paidia,* to be led to "beauty, to the wonder of man and nature, to its contemplation and its recreation in word and song, to be serenely objective . . ."[5] Let us submit a more realistic hypothesis, more in line with the evidence all around us: *the primary value of mankind in industrial societies is leisure.* This is what work permits and frees us to do. In preindustrial societies there is a difference, for then one's work is holistic: the whole farm is cultivated, whole shoes and whole dresses are made. The preindustrial worker does not find himself in an assembly line, with fragmented responsibility and only a fragmented car fender to guide through a machine process under technology's Saint Taylor.

Has anyone ever heard of AFL-CIO contracts that call for union members to volunteer their labors on a Saturday? Yet we all know of persons who do seek out volunteer tasks on weekends and during vacations and years of retirement. In the Peace Corps we find persons of all backgrounds, ages, and ethnic origins who are giving several years of their lives to serve other cultures. A Gallup poll of the late 1960's revealed that retirees would be willing—60% of the sample—to give four hours per week to community activity, if the tasks were significant, and if they were asked.

Why, then, has the myth of the work ethic persisted? It helped ease the way for the worker, making life more bearable. It also provided a useful myth for the industrialist-manager, making his own "workaholic" preoccupation in a competitive situation more bearable and honorable, and it served as a rationale for a "growth ethic" as a basis for industrialization. One element of the case for capitalism was a common view in our country that under communism there was no incentive to work, and hence the "peasants" could never develop a complex technological society. Sputnik put that myth to final rest.

The worker takes off on a Friday to do his "thing" as soon as he can. This holds true not only for the American worker; even in Japan, perhaps the classic contemporary illustration of the work ethic, employees who formerly returned to the workbench on a boring weekend are now asking for more free time. A Center for Leisure Development was begun there in 1972, funded by big business and government. The myth of the work ethic has served the business community. Yet its leaders are in a position to leave work at odd times, and flexible work patterns have always been theirs to enjoy. This is one reason why upper echelon executives have consistently reported a high level of satisfaction in their work, but they continue to wonder aloud why their employees, although well paid, are not as captivated by the jobs they perform in a more structured time frame.

---

[5]deGrazia, op. cit. p. 15.

TRANSITION TO BULK TIME

A third factor in the diminution of the work role is not only the emergence of more free time but its restructuring into various forms of bulk time: longer weekends, vacations, and retirement periods. Obviously the nature of one's work directly influences the leisure of an individual—the income level it provides, the demands made on one's energy and health, the residential location permitted by the job, the degree and nature of requisite skills, the time structure, and the types of satisfactions.

The retired person perceives all these factors in retrospect. Someone who has retired only a few months ago is perhaps more strongly influenced by prior work habits and attitudes than he will be after some years, but his background as an engineer or metal worker will never completely be erased. Yet, since the pioneering research at the Western Electric Company decades ago, studies of work motivations and satisfactions point out the human or social elements of the working situation—relating to other people, performing a function, obtaining a response, contributing to a task, and so on. The absence of these constitutes a serious void upon retirement. What becomes the reality of retirement is the absence of a schedule, a job, and a social apparatus, all at once.

Two kinds of time constructs then come into play. One is the sudden confrontation with bulk or block time—whole days, weeks, months, years; the other is a more gradual realization of one's life stage, or the "third age," in which there emerge new images of oneself. These new time constructs are, therefore, both subjective and objective realities; they are the ultimate uniqueness of retirement and the basis for the sociopsychological considerations in leisure programming. Both can be a personal heaven or hell—a source of freedom and emancipation, or a deprivation and emotional loss. Leisure need not produce a substitute on the same time dimension as work, although some community center schedules for the elderly match the traditional working day. Leisure that capitalizes on the bulk time of retirement builds on its new freedom; one illustration is the provision for classes that extend over weeks rather than the terminal activities of only a few hours.

Bulk time has, for many persons, become both a reality and an aspiration. It is a contiguous or continuous arrangement of minutes, hours, days, and weeks realized through the shorter working day, longer weekend, vacation, sabbatical, "leave of absence," and retirement. When, in 1926, Henry Ford declared a five-day work week for his employees, a revolution in aspirations began toward the two-day rest as a natural right. Riva Poor has documented the recent interest in the three-day weekend, an interest abetted by federal legislation that moved various holidays to guarantee all of us at least five such weekends.[6]

By the 1970's, millions of American workers enjoyed three weeks of paid

---

[6]*4 Days, 40 Hours: Reporting a Revolution in Work and Leisure.* Cambridge: Bursk and Poor, 1970.

vacation. The UAW-Ford negotiations of 1976, accompanied by a strike, included the demand for more free time. Although the expanded number of jobs was the spoken rationale, left unsaid but well understood was the additional desire to break the monotony of repetitive work. The union, reflecting the current feelings of auto workers, did not request a guarantee of overtime.

What seems to come of this is a tendency toward *miniretirement* periods, indeed, for many such periods over the years. We have here an example of differences between the "old" and the "new" retirees; the latter should, on the basis of built-in, accumulated miniretirements, have less difficulty in adjusting to bulks of retirement time. The "new" retiree became an adult at a period in American life when the leisure ethic became popular.

From a physiological and social point of view, the older person differs markedly from the young person, the woman, or the black, in that a period of many years has passed to bring him or her to the present point. The accumulation of years is, in fact, the major uniqueness of this generation. In some societies there was the additional factor of being held as the wisest before the accumulation of printed history or folk tales.

The Social Security Act of 1935 set the age of 65 as the dividing line (62 for women) by copying the German social welfare practice going back to the 1880's (when its workers had a life expectancy of 40). These ages were later changed to 62 and 60 and, with legislation introduced in 1978, were being modified toward no limit for federal workers and 70 for those in private industry. If the general age for voting and finishing school is seen roughly as around 20, then a numerical pattern follows:

	Education	Work	Retirement	
0	@ 20 years	@ 40 years	@ 15 years	85

In a Santa Barbara conference in 1967, the gerontologist Alex Comfort was supported by prominent research biologists in arguing that if they were granted sufficient funds to study the aging process, they could raise our life expectancy to 95 by the end of the century. Even discounting such confidence, it is likely that in the decades ahead the relationship above, 20:40:15 years, will show a larger amount of retirement years as life is extended, as more workers leave their work in younger years, and as Social Security extends its benefits. A rough guess is that by 2000 A.D. the line could appear as:

	I	II	III	
	Education	Work	Retirement	
0	@ 20 years	@ 30 years	@ 35 years	85

Thus, the average adult over 20 of today may have more total leisure than work time to confront over a lifetime. Adding a further difficulty to the analysis is the trend toward removing or diminishing the lines between I, II, and III, as in the lengthening of vacations and the introduction of sabbaticals.

U.S. Steel now provides 13 weeks paid sabbatical to workers every fifth year of employment; the tradition of a half year off for seven years of service is found in many universities. The proposal has been made that *all* workers should be entitled to sabbaticals, paid for by the federal government. France now has a federal law whereby every worker who requests it is given several weeks a year to attend adult education sessions, with the employer bearing the cost. Other nations, notably West Germany, have moved in the direction of "flexitime," whereby employees are responsible for doing their job in any arrangment of time that fits personal moods or family convenience, and that integrates with the work patterns of colleagues.[7]

An extension of flexibility within the work week, or year, is the flexible *life* pattern. With the inevitable growth of cybernation and more sophistication by both management and labor, annual work contracts may give way to lifetime career choices, so that a relatively young person who now takes for granted the possibility of lifetime financial planning (mortgages, insurance policies, etc.) will as easily enter into a flexible scheme of alternating work and sabbatical blocks of fixed time. The modification of pension plans in the late 1970's will facilitate a change of jobs as an integral component of lifetime planning.

The import of all this is that not only will the proportions of years in stages I, II, and III be altered, but the divisions *between* them will become fuzzy in the wake of work/nonwork flexibilities.

Even now a problem for both public policy and gerontological counseling is the development of bridges between the stages from education to work (I-II) and between work and retirement (II-III). Recent thinking is also concerned with the transition from late life to death.

CONTINUITY AND DISCONTINUITY OF WORK VALUES

The "old" issue was a valid one, whether or not one's work values led the worker in a natural way toward retirement. The issue is by no means eliminated, and among the current beliefs is that those in professions can normally expect an easier transition to retirement than persons leaving business. The "new" issue, if we move toward the gradual elimination of life stages in a sequence, is the gradual *fusion* of "work" and "leisure" values. Again the professions offer a model, for in essence such people do not make clear distinctions between work and nonwork. While it may be an exaggeration to say that they don't know if they are working or not, it is safer to conclude that the satisfactions they derive from work and leisure are substantially the same. Robert J. Havighurst had concluded this to be the case in such matters as sociability and the feeling of being needed by others.[8]

---

[7]Bernhard Teriet, "Arbeitzeit und Arbeitsvolumen in der Bundesrepublik Deutschland 1960–1975," *Mitt Ab*, 1 (1977) "Der Jahresarbeitszeitvertrag—ein Arbeitskonzept der oder mit Zukunft?" *Analysen und Prognosen*, (Nov. 1976) "Phased Retirement—New Task for Personnel Management," *Mensch und Arbeit*, 2(1977).

[8]"The Significance and Content of Leisure Activities from Age Forty to Seventy," Cleveland: Gerontological Society, 1957; "Leisure and Lifestyle," *American Journal of Sociology*, LXIV, No. 4 (Jan. 1959), pp. 396–404.

What seems to be developing now is that an increasing number of persons are seeking the kind of work that provides them with a lifestyle they seek. The data is particularly clear for younger workers who, once maintenance needs are met, prefer the kind of jobs that are "interesting" and "significant."[9] Further, once employed, they prefer more free time than more income. Fred Best has explored this issue more fully than anyone in the U.S.A. In Table 2–1 he presents a fascinating response to the three choices of patterning of time over the lifespan. These replies were collected between July and September, 1976, from a questionnaire given to 150 employees: 51 manual (road construction) workers, 7 service workers, 36 clerical workers, and 52 professional and managerial workers. Two questions were asked: "Which of the life patterns described above do you think most persons would prefer?" and "In your opinion, which of the life patterns described above would be best for the overall well being of society?" Thus, while most seemed to think that others in the society would prefer the present style of life, over 67% chose one of the two cyclic life plans. Although Best does not suggest this, it seems apparent that this contemporary thinking is more characteristic of workers living and working in the city.

Further, the facts from his other studies based upon larger samples clearly indicate the desire of the younger generation for more time rather than more income when they are faced with this choice as workers:

> . . . the nature of income-time trade off preferences within the United States of the mid-70's may be substantially different from anything we have known in the past. Over the last two decades American workers have eschewed reductions in the work week in favor of "lump" units of free time such as long weekends and vacations.[10]

The "new old" of the late 1970's and 1980's have already been introduced to this kind of thinking. For example, over 15 million Americans moved into the southern states during the 1960's; the more comfortable lifestyle in the South may afford a smoother transition to retirement than a sudden move into Florida or Georgia when one has remained in the North throughout the work life.

An additional tendency, still new to much of American business and industry, is the concept of "progressive retirement," by which the worker— usually a high echelon figure—is given a month or more to become active in some community activity; this period is increased over a period of several years.

---

[9]"Flexible Work Scheduling Beyond the Forty-Hour Impasse," in Fred Best, ed., *The Future of Work*. Englewood Cliffs: Prentice-Hall, 1973, Chapter 9, pp. 93–99; Fred Best and Barry Stern, *Lifetime Distribution of Education, Work and Leisure: Research, Speculations and Policy Implications of Changing Life Patterns*. Washington, D.C.: The George Washington University, Institute for Educational Leadership, 1976; "Work Sharing and the Desire of Employed Workers for More Free Time," California Legislature, Senate Select Committee on Investment Priorities and Objectives, *Leisure Sharing*, Testimony, November 1, 1977.

[10]Fred Best, P. Bosserman, and B. Stern, *Income-Free Trade Off Preferences of U.S. Workers, a Review of Literature and Indicators*, summary and updated report based on *Changing Values Toward Material Wealth and Leisure in the United States*, HEW, Contract P00-75-0221, Washington, D.C.: HEW, Assistant Secretary for Education, Jan. 1976.

Table 2–1 PERSONAL PREFERENCES AND OPINIONS TOWARD ALTERNATIVE LIFETIME PATTERNS*

LIFE PATTERNS CHOICES	PERSONAL 1ST CHOICE	VIEW OF OTHERS' PREFERENCES	BEST FOR SOCIETAL WELL BEING
A. *Straight Progression from School to Work to Retirement:* A life pattern in which all schooling and pre-work training is accomplished in youth or early adulthood, where one works full time with limited annual vacations during middle adult years, and enters full time retirement sometime after age 60. Thus school education is restricted to youth, work to middle adulthood, and free time to old age.	21.2%	37.1%	22.5%

Diagram of Option A:

```
0   10  20  30  40  50  60  70
┌─────┬──────────────────┬─────┐
│/////│                  │█████│
└─────┴──────────────────┴─────┘
   ↑          ↑              ↑
Education    Work       Retirement
                        (Free Time)
```

| B. *Most Schooling in Youth with Several Rotations Between Work and Free Time Throughout the Remainder of Life:* A life pattern in which most schooling and pre-work training is accomplished in youth or early adulthood, where one primarily works full time during middle adulthood but with extended periods away from work (for example 6 months) every 5 or 6 years, and increases the proportion of free time in later years until complete retirement in late 60's. Thus maximum retirement would be exchanged for extended free time periods in mid-life. | 37.7% | 37.7% | 41.7% |

Diagram of Option B:

```
0   10  20  30  40  50  60  70
┌─────┬───┬───┬───┬───┬───┬─┬──┐
│/////│   │   │   │   │   │ │██│
└─────┴───┴───┴───┴───┴───┴─┴──┘
   ↑       ↖↑↗      ↑  ↑↑↖↑
Education  Work     Free Time
                  & Retirement
```

*From Fred Best and Barry Stern, *Lifetime Distribution of Education, Work and Leisure: Research, Speculations and Policy Implications of Changing Life Patterns.* Washington, D.C., The George Washington University, Institute for Educational Leadership, December, 1976, unpublished.

In summary, the new attitude toward work is to view it as part of the continuum of life. Its purposes and its satisfactions are not, ipso facto, separated from other values. Work is a part of the total lifestyle and, without interfering with its pragmatic purposes—making the car, farming the land, teaching the class—the elements of leisure are brought in: a library is created

Table 2–1 PERSONAL PREFERENCES AND OPINIONS TOWARD ALTERNATIVE LIFETIME PATTERNS (*Continued*)

Life Patterns Choices	Personal 1st Choice	View of Others' Preferences	Best for Societal Well Being
C. *Basic Schooling in Early Youth with Continuous Rotations Between Education, Work and Free Time Throughout the Remainder of Life:* A life pattern in which basic education in essential skills (reading, math, etc.) ends early, where most persons leave school periodically starting in mid-teens for limited periods of work, and then finish high school and other education in the course of lifelong rotations between work, school and free time. Thus time spent for education in youth and time spent for retirement in later years would be reduced in exchange for extended periods of education and free time during the middle years of life.	29.8%	15.2%	25.8%

Diagram of Option C:

| D. No Answer | 11.3% | 10.0% | 9.9% |

for the factory worker, rotating exhibits of sculpture are found in some Danish plants or, among Zenith workers in the U.S., teams of employees decide what they will accomplish that day. The impact of these fusions is that one lives an integrated life, so that derived from the work ethic are the satisfactions of accomplishments, skills, response, and the feeling of being useful, and from the leisure ethic such satisfactions that come with spontaneity, the satisfaction of adventure, and the exploration of new experiences and persons.

Aside from whatever gains such a lifestyle brings, the transition to full retirement is easier, and quite natural. Simultaneously, such an emerging lifestyle for larger segments of the population reduces the contrast between work and nonwork. Retirement, ideally, would not exist in such an ideal, for the concept of "work" would have been replaced by the Biblical term "works" or the contemporary concept of "commitments."

CLASS CHANGES AND THE WORK-ETHIC MYTH

Finally the work ethic, or its myth, is declining because of the loosening of social class lines. Now that the middle class has access to the energy and the services that only yesterday were the prerogative of the rich, it also adopts the mental attitudes of the wealthy. It is not necessary for us to follow Veblen's thesis in every respect; his major point remains useful: the value of leisure as a status symbol.[11] Whether the larger car is bought to imitate the rich or because it is a better car need not be argued; in spite of inflation, large cars continue to be bought, energy crises and presidential exhortations to the contrary. Only federal legislation on limits upon gasoline consumers will limit the size of cars.

With the car, the highway, the football bowls, and the TV specials comes also a growing ease with time in bulk. And bulk time feeds an upper-class ideology; it makes no difference whether the worker is blue- or white-collar. The urge for leisure is color-, class-, and collar-blind. These days, on an individualistic and democratic level, the term to use and the process to watch is *lifestyle*. Here, too, we put our finger on leisure itself as a new social role—the heart of the potential meaning of retirement.

---

[11]Thorsten Veblen, *Theory of the Leisure Class*. New York: Macmillan, 1912.

CHAPTER 3

Rise of the Leisure Role

The social role of leisure goes back to the factors that led to the ascendancy of leisure. There are several large areas that can be explored in this quest—the physical, intellectual, aesthetic, social, and civic. Cutting through these areas are an infinite number of activities, from helping one's church to reading a book. The task for the elderly in relation to leisure is easier than that required of the young person in finding his work for, at the retirement stage, one has a lifetime of developed tasks and varied experiences upon which to draw. At 20, in choosing whether to go into law, banking, or teaching, no one has yet had extensive, tangible experience in any of those fields. Compare this with the retiree who, in deciding whether he wants to put his time into fishing, travel, or painting, may already have done all three over many years.

The role of leisure may have elements from the past, or it can move into new experiences. In retirement one has the time to probe and test, both himself and the experience. Since fishing, travel, or painting will probably involve different colleagues, the retiree has the option of interacting with different types of persons. And in each, as Znaniecki has observed, he attaches himself to the others to form social groups that are unified by the single bond of common interest. In conversation more than in other activities we can reveal more of our total selves. These advantages contribute to the quality of variety and freedom in leisure: the freedom to move into the experience, remain in it for a flexible period, and get out when one desires.

We can assume that the ongoing pursuit of an activity entered into voluntarily is satisfying, that it is based on a pleasant expectation and subsequent recollection. The "pleasantness" need not be reduced to laughter, for it may include the time that goes voluntarily to see *Hamlet* or *Gone With The Wind*.

Nor need leisure be identified only with receiving sensations, as in sports or the arts. One can, of course, sing, act, run, play a game. Does the singing, composing, or writing have to be superficial? Is amateurism the same as dilettantism? Many important Russian composers, including Rimsky-Korsakov, were "amateurs"; scientific inventions and important books have come from "free time" preoccupations. Thus, intensity and depth can characterize the leisure role.

25

There is a common association of leisure with relaxation, not only emotionally but normatively, yet the norms or rules of a game can be rigorous, as can be the demands of an art. There must be a large population of persons who are more concerned with the "rights" and "wrongs" of their golf game than with their work habits.

Opportunities for personal growth and service to others are also consonant with the leisure role. Perhaps together they spell out the most radical departure of contemporary leisure from conceptions of the past. When work was the primary time-consuming activity, and the myth of the work ethic was unchallenged, leisure—or any nonwork activity—took a secondary place. Recreation was, in truth, "re-creation"—for more work. Leisure could not be thought of as a positive, affirmative force except in the therapeutic sense. That day is past. The myth, since it was believed, had power, like primitive magic; if one was *supposed* to feel less guilt if his leisure was "deserved" from prior hard work, then he *did* feel better about his leisure.

Finally, echoing the "humanistic coefficient" that Znaniecki insisted upon as the sine qua non of sociology, no single activity (attending an exhibition) or complex of activities (art) can be identified as "leisure." Its content can literally be anything, and as we review the activities of retirees later in this volume, their variety will be one of the pleasant aspects of the review.

Thus, we can say that the *leisure role is one that consists of relatively self-determined activity–experience that falls into one's economically free time roles, that is seen as leisure by participants, that is psychologically pleasant in anticipation and recollection, that potentially covers the whole range of commitment and intensity, that contains characteristic norms and constraints, and that provides opportunities for recreation, personal growth, and service to others.*[1]

These elements need not all be present at any time; some can be more prominent than others, and *any* experience or activity may be seen as leisure by the participant. Further, although this construct of elements is sufficiently cohesive to distinguish leisure from religious, economic, or political activity, there will be overlapping from one to the other. For instance, in throwing a basketball, a player may cross himself, although he is not in church; in the work place, one may read a newspaper, knowing full well that this is not a library or a living room.

ORIGINS OF THE NEW LEISURE

Given this conception of leisure as our major working tool, we have yet to ask how leisure has reached its prominence in our time. A lifestyle of leisure has traditionally been the characteristic symbol of the rich and the nobility. Work, for the upper classes, was not the way of finding salvation—the means was power. And wealth, in the feudal tradition, was not the fruit of work; even today, in some of the upper class clubs in Chicago and Philadelphia, the

---

[1]Max Kaplan, *Leisure: Theory and Policy.* New York, John Wiley and Sons, 1975, p. 26. Reproduced by permission of the publisher.

wealth that has been earned (worked for) does not hold the same prestige as that which has been inherited.

The "rich" and the "super-rich" of whom Lundberg writes are not the subjects of the contemporary new leisure.[2] That phrase is attached to the middle and lower social and economic levels. These are the segments that have derived new freedoms from industrialization, urbanization, unionization, and secularization. These four, in an historical convergence, arose from movements to which we attach such names as Marx, Freud, Darwin, Gompers, and Henry Ford. The workers, not the upper classes, had fallen victim to the work ethic, but the power of collective bargaining put that ethic to rest in fact if not in lip service. Gradually the rewards that labor obtained went beyond a greater share of the economic pie into a sharing of free time. Economic history here intersected with the theological adoption of Saturday as the Judaic Sabbath, or seventh (last) day of the week, and Sunday as the Christian analogue, the first day of the week. Had Christianity emerged historically from the Moslem tradition and calendar—with Friday as the day of rest—would there have evolved a "weekend" of eventually two adjoining days? In Iran even now, Thursday and Friday constitute the official weekend, so the question may be an idle one. In the western world, at least, the goal of unionization became the 8-8-8 formula, with eight hours each for work, sleep, and "living," but on a weekly chronology of 40 hours or the five-day week. This was a twentieth century realization, supported by possibilities for upgrading productivity through machines and downgrading theology through a growing scientism. This convergence has been expressed in the statement, "The surrender of this support (from church ideology), together with the inherent depersonalization of work through advanced industrialization, were the twin forces that provided the ideological foundation for contemporary leisure."[3]

Along the way there were other, more mundane developments that brought the possibility of more free time to the common man as an aspiration and a guilt-free right. In the 1970's, as we dart across the nation's double highways and turnpikes with our fast cars, the memory of mud roads and vulnerable tire tubes of the 1920's is not far from the consciousness of millions of our present retirees. The 70-year-old of today was mature then, and can testify to the change in lifestyles brought about by both material and social changes. Whether born abroad or in the U.S.A. (the "old old" or the "new old"), the transformation was dramatic. New lifestyles reflected the new technology and the new attitudes. But more than memory or history are the stuff of our present concerns.

IMPLICATIONS OF THE LEISURE ROLE

There are implications from the prominent role that leisure plays in the lifestyle of our elderly. First, we return to the role itself, and again the

---

[2]Ferdinand Lundberg, *The Rich and the Super-Rich*. New York: Lyle Stuart, 1968.
[3]Kaplan, op cit. p. 359.

distinction between "old old" and "new old" comes into play. For those who grew up when the mythology of the work ethic was in full control, a transition to the leisure role can be difficult. The attitude that grew out of commitment to work was unsympathetic to "idleness," "relaxation," "fun," or "amusement." These were interim experiences at best, and tools of the Devil at worst; in either case, they had to be earned through work. Retirement within such an ideology is difficult, and to be opposed. It lacks the possibility of positive valuation. Little skill or thought needs to be put into such leisure except, as Veblen pointed out, for those who did not need to work. For them, the "leisure class" as distinct from the "working class," nonwork was the norm, and skills were developed to become experts at it. The rich retiree was anomalous in the England of the nineteenth century, for he had always been retired; it took no new effort to be a club member in one's seventh decade of life when he had been there for three previous decades.

A second difficulty in the retirement role under the theological preindustrial ideology was that aspect of the leisure role that permits "the whole range of commitment and intensity." The phrase was only applicable to work. Who, in such a period, goes into a serious consideration of arts? Women, of course, for men's work must be productive. The "amateur" is not to be taken seriously by the art world; if he pretends to seriousness, he is a dilettante.

Finally, the opportunities for personal growth and service to others are not central to the preindustrial or outdoor leisure philosophy and social role. Indeed, they are suspect. Only children's play is useful for growth, for the child is a miniature adult and play is an instrument of social control by elders.

For the "new old," leisure carries all the opposite connotations. Anything can be leisure, and that includes intensive, challenging, and creative activity. Heaven has become more attainable through leisure, for it is no more reserved for workaholics; one can write poetry and become deified, or serve the public community and become privately canonized. The ascendancy of leisure, for this postindustrial mind, is not a victory of hedonism but a realization of Aristotle's vision that true freedom would come when looms could weave by themselves. Leisure is, after all, more an attitude than an activity—an attitude that takes freedom seriously, out of the polling booth as well as in.

The "new old" were born in this country, and are more inclined than their parents to be relaxed with gadgetry and comfort. These they accept automatically, without guilt and with considerable expertise. Planes no more intrigue them, and television in color is by now natural. These forms are now giving way to a questioning of utility: comfort for what? As soon as that question is posed, maturity sets in.

Leisure has not ascended to the topmost level because hedonism has taken over, but because the material base is so broad that hedonism has become diminshed in importance as other values become available in a society of many alternatives. For example, Disney World confronts a crucial question for all "advanced" societies: can such a region, blessed with sun and sand, also be enriched with mind and heart? Can sports coexist with sonatas, spring baseball with opportunities for adult education?

For if coexistence is possible—more, if it is natural—in such a region, heaven has, indeed, been relocated for the eclectic in mind and mood. An examination of this balance (or imbalance, if that proves to be the case) could become a primary mission of agencies that study leisure in such regions. The South (or "sunbelt") provides an enormous regional laboratory. Florida, for instance, with less than nine million permanent residents, plays host to over 25 million tourists per year. The financial gain runs into the billions, but the philosophical and social issues boggle the imagination. Of course, the ascendancy of leisure in a state like Florida applies to all ages.

The "new old" move into retirement as these recent gains become evident. The chicken-egg circularity takes over: (1) new attitudes contribute to this expansion; and (2) the expansion precipitates new attitudes. Put another way, a lesson that Robert Moses never learned in crisscrossing Long Island with highways is that more cars require more highways but, concomitantly, new highways encourage new cars. Those among us who turned 70 in the 1970's were already 40 in the 1940's and thus fully aware of the electronic miracles that matured in that war and postwar decade. They then lived through the Korean and Vietnam conflicts. William Manchester has depicted those decades in dramatic detail.[4] Mainly, they had seen us enter the space age. When one retires in the 1970's he has already been thrilled at an Armstrong putting his foot down on the moon, and the glories of science are somewhat jaded. He does not know, and hardly cares, whether he is flying across the country in a jumbo jet at 400 miles per hour or at 500—or is it 600?

While commercial TV has by far attracted greater interest than public channels among the elderly, public stations have devoted proportionately larger portions of their time to discussions or portrayals of the elderly. Cable TV, potentially a highly useful tool by which any group of citizens can reach the public, has not been used. We make a mistake, however, in associating the ascendancy of leisure for the contemporary generation of elderly with time units or dollars. To repeat, it is the new depth of intensity and the range of opportunity that are the more crucial indices, together with the shedding of guilt feelings through the secularization of leisure.

In summary, leisure can be characterized as a construct of elements that can be injected or found in any activity. Thus, leisure is not limited to defined activity; it is a social role and a social process whose elements spill over into other institutionalized situations such as education, religion, work, and politics. Conversely, leisure absorbs elements that are derived primarily from other areas, such as from the arts (the element of expression) or from work (the element of discipline, as in a game of golf.)

Since the ascendancy of leisure is primarily a reflection of the rise of the middle classes and the common man, gerontology is concerned with the democratization, not the "elitization" of leisure; this does not imply a "midcult" or "mass cult" in standards but, on the contrary, the exploration of

---

[4]*The Glory and the Dream.* New York: Bantam Books, 1974.

potential depth among all persons. This exploration takes place on the level of activity-experience and in new dimensions of time.

The clock, as Woodcock has noted, was a major symbol of industrial society.[5] It still remains a possession of the majority of older persons by force of habit, or by the need to structure one's time to pills or to Lawrence Welk. In Williams Park, St. Petersburg, we have asked people what time it is, and recorded how many had watches, and how far they were in error if they had to guess the time. Comparisons were made with young people. We found that 85% of older males had watches, compared to 48% of males in their 20s; 52% of older women had watches, but only 39% of young females. When it comes to guessing time, young girls were wrong an average span of 47.04 minutes, and older women were wrong by less than 27 minutes.

Time, wrote the philosopher Kant, "is not an independent substance nor an objective determination of things . . . but the form of inner sense, that is, of the perception of ourselves and our inner state. . . ."[6] A new set of issues is emerging when the constants of this "form of inner sense" are less constant. Work was one such constant; television programs are another form of constant. There is also a relation of time to type of activity. We know, for example, that a more complex activity requires more attention, is usually more interesting, and seems to go quicker than a simple activity. Boredom, conversely, emerges from the dearth of anything absorbing. On the perspective of weeks, months, and years, we react to rhythms of events, and create rituals and ceremonies to mark time periods.

Already it is clear that the dollar becomes less useful with inflation as the hour becomes more useful; with the dollar we can buy less, as all the elderly know who live on savings. The "trade-off" of time for income will be influenced by this imbalance, and now requires a new attempt in social science to create new models of time perception and evaluations. In respect to this issue we are perhaps where psychology was before Freud. Gerontology would seem to offer a potential home for such research.

The outermost parameter of time will be not months or years but one's full lifespan. The flexibility of work life will be aided by lifetime work and nonwork plans and contracts, as well as by the new federal laws delaying or suspending mandatory retirement altogether. The guaranteed annual income, in one form or another, will probably have become an academic matter by the end of the century. As I have noted in other writings, it should be possible to establish "hour banks," permitting the borrowing of bulk periods of time for travel, education, or any other private purpose with the same kind of collateral on which we can now borrow money.[7] New combinations of labor,

---

[5] George Woodcock, in A. Naftalin, ed., *An Introduction to Social Science*. New York: J. B. Lippincott, 1953, pp. 209–212.

[6] Immanuel Kant, "Transcendental Aesthetic," in E. E. Harris, ed., *Fundamentals of Philosophy*. New York: Holt, Rinehart and Winston, 1969, Section II, Chapter 29.

[7] Kaplan, op. cit. pp. 289–291.

management, and government will develop, in response to cybernation and to aspirations for more free time. Phillip Bosserman and Juanita Kreps have proposed various work and nonwork options, based on daily, weekly, monthly, and yearly frameworks.[8] Labor unions will increasingly press for lifetime contracts. Retirement itself may change drastically in its meaning as a concept, goal, destiny, fear, or even as a chronological fruition of work.

---

[8]Phillip Bosserman, "Implications for Youth," pp. 131–163 and Juanita Kreps, "The Allocation of Leisure to Retirement," (Appendix) in Max Kaplan and Phillip Bosserman, eds., *Technology, Human Values and Leisure.* Nashville: Abingdon, 1972.

CHAPTER 4

Freedom from the
Medical and Social
Sciences

The social and biological sciences have much to teach us in the field of social gerontology, yet there can be no mature social gerontology until it goes beyond what these disciplines have to say. In that sense gerontology, and therefore the elderly whom it represents, will achieve a new freedom; leisure is an especially central area for such freedom. That is the essence of this chapter.

DEMOGRAPHIC REALITIES

The directions of population growth have made it essential for the field of demography to turn its attention to the elderly. A journalistic phrase calls it "the graying of America." As *Newsweek* pointed out in its special section of that name of February 28th, 1977, the situation goes back to the baby boom of 1947 to 1957, when 43 million children were born who by now make up a fifth of our total population. They will be middle-aged by the 1980's and 1990's. In 1977, we had 23 million between the ages of 35 and 44; this segment will reach 41 million by the year 2000, and will constitute the retirees of the first two decades of the new century. Putting it another way, in 1977 we had 23 million over 65, or 3 million more of this age group than in 1970; the number will swell to 31 million by 2000, and to 52 million in 2030 A.D. Figure 4–1 notes the dramatic growth in the proportion of persons 65 and over, from the year 1900 to the present, and into 30 years of the next century.[1]

Among the 28 million Americans over the age of 60—13% of the total population—62% are under 75; 1.9 million are over 85; 700 are over 100

---

[1]Data given here and below taken from *The Graying of Nations: Implications*. Hearing before the Special Committee on Aging, U.S. Senate, 95th Congress, Nov. 10th, 1977. U.S. Gov't. Printing Office, Washington D.C., 1978, 99–586.

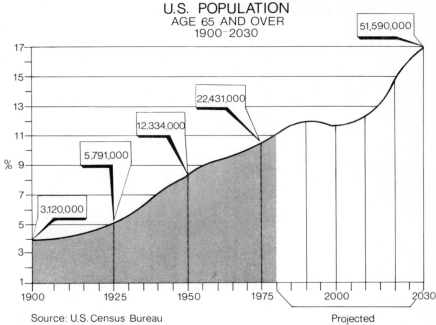

U.S. POPULATION
AGE 65 AND OVER
1900-2030

Source: U.S. Census Bureau   Projected

AGE GAUGE – Chart shows the percentage of the American population 65 and older from 1900 to 1975, with predictions for 1980 to 2030.

Figure 4-1.

years old. It is the total, the 13%, that suggests some significant change in our population picture, leading to the prospect of drastic social, economic, and political changes over the next quarter century.

The Washington Post, in William Chapman's similar report, "The Graying of America: a Portrait" (April 17, 1977) noted:

Aspirin is advertised as much as an arthritic pain reliever as a headache remedy, Campbell's Soup produces "Soup For One," aimed at the elderly living alone. There's the return of the cruise ship, a vessel once thought obsolete but now revived, in part, to attract the retirees' trade travel. Big automobiles remain popular because the middle-aged and older buyers like solidity and comfort, not raciness and glamour.

Thus, while we recently heard much about the necessity for mandatory retirement at age 65 (or younger) to provide jobs for younger people, the solutions to the distribution of work, and income, now go in other directions. More older persons want to have a second career, and agitation is mounting for the removal of mandatory retirement. An anti–age discrimination law was passed in Maine in 1977 that permits state employees a lifetime career. Along the way, especially with the undoubted growth of cybernation, most workers will be freer from their jobs. Part of the population may shift from the standard work week to a partial work week, with a two- or three-day week, or five days of four hours a day. Eventually, we may see a major shift in which people over 55 can move toward a gradually lower level of involvement, with real retirement, or total leisure, only after 75.

It is small wonder that Social Security administrators are deeply immersed in population projections. The increasing burden on the system is evident: in 1945, the ratio of workers to retirees was 31 to 1, but now, with about 33 million persons receiving social security, the ratio is 3 to 1; by the year 2035 there will be less than two persons at work for every retiree. This proportional change is caused, in part, by the sheer increase in the proportion of older persons, for since 1900 the total U.S. population has tripled while the number of those over 65 has increased seven-fold. Every day in the year the nation gains 400 persons in the 65+ column, as 3600 die and 4000 celebrate their birthdays.

The national proportion of those over 65 will increase as follows by the end of the century:

Year (A.D.)	Millions– Both Sexes	% of All Ages
1975	22.40	10.5
1980	24.52	11.0
1990	28.93	11.8
2000	30.60	11.9

There are differences according to race. Counting both sexes, the increase of elderly in the period 1975 to 2000 A.D. will be 33.5% among the whites and 63% among the blacks.

Because women live longer, the sex ratio among the elderly in 1975 was 13.2 women to every 9.1 men. If we break this sex ratio into age segments for 1975:[2]

Of those 65 to 74 years .... 130 women to 100 men

74 to 85 years .... 176 women to 100 men

85 and over .... 217 women to 100 men

The proportion among all persons over 65 in 1975 was 144 women to 100 men; thus, among the more than 60,000 marriages annually with bride or groom over 65, men had a clear advantage in range of choice.[1] The same holds true among the thousands of elderly—no one knows the number—who have lived together without the marriage ritual, to get around the backward provisions of Social Security; new Social Security regulations signed by President Carter toward the end of 1977 ended the need for this practice.

Where are these older persons? There are nine states in which 12% or more of the residents are over 65; Florida is at the top, with more than 16%. In 1898, so the story goes, a Cleveland physician made the statement that the healthiest place he knew of for older persons was St. Petersburg; thus began

---

[1]Data given here and below taken from *The Graying of Nations: Implications.* Hearing before the Special Committee on Aging, U.S. Senate, 95th Congress, Nov. 10th, 1977. U.S. Gov't. Printing Office, Washington D.C., 1978, 99–586.

[2]Pt. I, Developments in Aging: 1977. Special Committee on Aging, U.S. Senate, 95th Congress, 2nd Session, Report 95–771, April 27, 1978, p. xxi.

a migration that has not yet run its course, so that by the year 2000, Florida may anticipate that one of every three residents will be over 65.

About one quarter of all 65+ persons live in three states: California, New York, and Florida. Arizona and Nevada claim a large number of elderly who migrated from other states. Vance Packard's *The Stranger* was a popularized study of dramatic mobility in our living patterns.[2] This applies to the elderly as well; 20% report they have moved in the past five years, 12% from somewhere in the same county, and 37% across state lines. Of course, the ownership of a car helps the tendency toward a change in residence. In 1972, 58% of household heads who were over 65 owned a car, compared to 88% among the 35 to 44 age group. Where the older couple had an annual income of $15,000, 92% owned one or more cars. Nevertheless, in both the rural areas and among the poorer elderly in the cities, transportation continues to be a serious problem in providing leisure opportunities.

As to living arrangements, about nine of every 100 older persons live in a household headed by a younger person, usually the son or son-in-law; the proportion is high among older blacks. Only five of every 100 over 65 live in nursing homes or similar institutions.

A SOCIAL SCIENCE MODEL

Population data of the kind found above is, of course, basic to any study of the elderly. Social sciences have very much to say concerning other dimensions of age segments. This volume has already considered the social role concept; although Znaniecki's formulation was applied here, all scholars in the psychosocial field have dealt with role in their discussions of personality, socialization, and group formation.

An example of another aspect of role theory will serve to illustrate a major contribution of social scientists to our subject. For this I turn to the anthropologists Robert and Rhona Rapoport and their work *Leisure and the Family Life Cycle*.[3] This volume marks a pioneering contribution to family studies for our understanding of leisure, and policy formation for related services. The Rapoports, codirectors of the Institute of Family and Environmental Research in London, were joined by anthropologist Ziona Strelitz in this study funded by the Leverhulme Trust.

Their purpose is explicit: "to suggest a perspective that supplements rather than replaces the perspective of social class and social change . . . This is the perspective of the human life cycle."[4] The life cycle concept, basic to family studies, has strangely been underexamined by students of leisure.

The concept of "need" is rejected as the basis of such social changes, as are the reduction and new flexibility in work hours, the turn to qualitative aspects

---

[2] Pt. I, Developments in Aging: 1977. Special Committee on Aging, U.S. Senate, 95th Congress, 2nd Session, Report 95–771, April 27, 1978, p. xxi.

[3] London: Routledge and Kegan Paul, 1975.

[4] Ibid. p. 14.

of life, the "leisure explosion," and the "palpable mass demand" for more of the same. Rather, three interrelated "lines" of influence are proposed: the planes of work, family, and leisure. The unique combination of this "triple helix" at the critical time of transition (the "unfreezing" of established patterns) provides the character of individual lifestyles at any point of life. Each of these life-line strands undergoes a "career" that affects other strands, and is rooted in a threefold dimension of motivations: *preoccupations* (mental absorptions), *interests* (ideas and feelings about what people want), and *activities* (spheres of action). Applied to young people, for example, the authors view some preoccupations as autonomy, stimulation, boredom, and work; interests can be seen as "doing one's thing." Characteristic activities are arts and crafts, dancing, mountaineering, and making music. From this analysis, they argue for the public policy that allows for "the development of interests appropriate to a given phase and situation, but also for the more generalized development of resourcefulness . . . to be able to adapt continuously and cultivate new interests."[5]

The Rapoports, who rely largely on case studies, have suggested in their views on policy the difficulty of American sociological and psychological positivism. Political and social policy must deal with what *should be*, for policy is a response to *problems*. Social problems, on the other hand, can have no "solution" without a concept of when a "no problem" condition exists. Crime and poverty, for example, start with a vision of social and economic "order" and "control." What are these visions? Fortunately, social science enters into the governmental policy process from its analysis of what the situation is; unfortunately that is not enough, for the amoral or "objective" view of social sciences—even if a legitimate approach for social science—is short of what is needed to work with the elderly. It is the gerontologists' responsibility to go farther, and move into the areas of social *values*. Yet so strong is the current hold of social science over gerontology that goals or values are underdeveloped. The scientist's view of *what is* has become accepted by the gerontologist with what *could be*. We have an analogy here with the social science surveys conducted by the commercial mass media—we are told that this is what American viewers want because this is what they choose. Obviously they can only choose from the programs provided for them.

In the courses of training, the graduate student of gerontology is given the sociological and psychological perspective. Research is recited, data are reported, but philosophy and history are absent. Freedom from the social sciences is not to reject but to go beyond them. The principles presented in Section 5 will do this.

THE BIOLOGICAL MODEL

A comparable situation exists for gerontology in relation to the biological sciences. The biological model, like that of the social sciences dealing with

---

[5]Ibid. p. 28.

aging as an increasing handicap, is incomplete because the medical profession which necessarily uses this model knows little about physical, mental, or emotional health. As Robert Butler has noted, many physicians are themselves guilty of what he calls "ageism," and psychiatrists have not displayed a major interest in the elderly.[6] The sociological and psychological methods, valuable as far as they go and indispensable as they are for understanding, are unwilling or unable to relate to other disciplines, especially those that deal with values, goals, wishes, and aspirations. The difficulty is a common one when the exigencies of research require a narrowing that is essential for accuracy and operational feasibility yet, once accomplished, falls far short of needed scope and range. An example is the report by DeCarlo of a 20-year study of twins that involved numerous scholars of the Psychiatric Institute. In this report a crucial matter was the criteria of "successful aging." Social gerontologists may judge for themselves the total inadequacy of the criteria adopted:

Good successful aging—able to carry on daily routine and absence of more than mild illness which would not impair one's daily routine; absence of chronic brain syndrome; and psychological test scores above half of a sigma from the subject's mean score (7 + .5s);

Fair successful aging—moderate incapacity to carry on daily routine as a result of past or present illness; mild chronic brain syndrome; and psychological test score between half a sigma below and above the subject's mean score (± .5s);

Poor successful aging—presence of marked debility or incapacitating illness; severe chronic brain syndrome; and psychological test score below half a sigma from the subject's mean score (<−.5s).[7]

Thus, at a time when the "new elderly" are increasingly involved with advantages of mental and bodily *health* on the one hand, and with the search for new roles in retirement through *growth* as persons, social gerontology finds itself in a crisis: how can it take advantage of biological and social approaches but at the same time go beyond them toward considerations and goals of ongoing development and services?

The medical, or geriatric, direction must necessarily deal with the body—of any age—as a machine that is born, grows, and dies. "Aging," by that route, implies a progressive deterioration. Obvious signs are known to every layman (wrinkles, slower walk) and to every physician ("diseases of old age" and "senility").

Yet a review of what biology and related sciences tell us has prompted a new look at what one might call *scientific semantics*—that is, facts do not always speak for themselves; it is the perspective that counts toward a meaning of the facts. For the student of leisure, these new tendencies are all important, for leisure activity and attitude are heavily dependent upon the *perception* of physical change as well as on the actual change.

---

[6]*Why Survive? Being Old in America.* New York: Harper and Row, 1975.

[7]T. J. DeCarlo, "Recreation Participation Patterns and Successful Aging," *Journal of Gerontology,* 29 (1974), pp. 416–422.

BIOLOGICAL CHANGE: AGING

There are theories of aging, but a surprising lack of unanimity within the life sciences. A recent summary of such theories lists them under the title of "wear and tear," "homeostatic imbalance," "accumulation of metabolic waste," "autocommunity," and "cellular aging." The difficulty, as Kimmel has noted, is the precise relation of something called the "aging process" as a physiological, social, and psychological phenomenon to the effects of disease.[8]

Otherwise, if these different variables are not disentangled, we are easily misled into equating aging with disease . . . as if sick, old people are the only kind of old people there are. If we make that error, then we not only overlook the old people who are quite healthy, but also we do not know whether the characteristics of the sick, old people result from their advanced age, their illness, or from the interaction of both.[9]

Every student of gerontology is aware of research into the characteristic acute and chronic diseases and impairments of older persons. Dr. Ruth Weg has summarized the matter as follows:

Older persons do become more vulnerable to disease: they are twice as likely to be physically disabled and to require hospitalization as younger people. There is an increase in morbidity and mortality with age. Cardiovascular disease, cancer, and cerebral accidents, the nation's three major chronic diseases and killers, have their greatest impact in severity and number among older persons. Those causes of illness and death that have come to be associated with old age undoubtedly have their etiology in young adult years, and frequently are diagnosed in the middle years.[10]

Dr. Robert Butler has commented:

It is obvious that the old get sick more frequently than the young, and 86 per cent have chronic health problems of varying degree. These health problems, while significant, are largely treatable and for the most part do not impair the capacity to work.[11]

Yet, as pointed out by Dr. Morton Ward, medical director of the Philadelphia Geriatric Center, often the elderly do not get regular physical check-ups; they often wait until they are actually sick before seeing a doctor, "because when they feel lousy they consider it part of getting old." Or, as the Center's assistant director, Dr. J. J. Cohen added, "You can't blame all illness on old age. Too many things have been brushed under the rug with the comment, 'You're old, what do you expect?'"[12]

Perhaps a balanced conclusion is that of Dr. Austin B. Chinn of the Andrus Gerontology Center:

It is true that there is no strict parallel between the development of disease as we understand it and the passage of time, and there is even less parallel between the

---

[8]Douglas Kimmel, *Adulthood and Aging: Interdisciplinary Developmental View*. New York: John Wiley and Sons, 1974, pp. 352–356. Reproduced by permission of the publisher.
[9]Ibid. p. 357.
[10]Ruth B. Weg, "Changing Physiology of Aging: Normal and Pathological," in D. S. Woodruff and J. E. Birren, eds., *Aging*. New York: Van Nostrand, 1975, p. 232.
[11]Butler, op. cit. p. 4.
[12]Lee Linder, Associated Press, December 20, 1977.

existence of illness and the passage of units of time. Good health, meaning the absence of disease and illness, therefore has a connotation which goes far beyond the meaning of youth and most certainly may be included as a resource for a portion of any age group. Indeed, if this were not so, disease and illness would be synonymous with advanced age, and all old people would be so afflicted to a proportionate degree of their years. On the other hand, to say that anatomical and physiological changes in many phylogenic species do not occur associated with the passage of time, would be equally in error. Some of these changes are associated with disease, influence it, and are in turn influenced by it. However, most scientists believe the processes are different even though there may be a degree of interdependence.[13]

Finally, the Senate's Special Committee on Aging has reported a national sample of the noninstitutional elderly population in 1973: 68% reported their health as "good" or "excellent," 22% as "fair," and only 9% as "poor." Less than 18% reported that chronic illness limited their mobility, even though 80% reported some chronic condition. Only 5% were confined to their homes, and far fewer (1%) were bedridden. Of every 100 persons interviewed, 83 reported no hospitalization in the previous year.[14]

Below is a brief summary of general conclusions on the relation of aging to those physical factors that seem especially relevant to leisure participation.

Sensory Losses. Although some loss of seeing and hearing occurs, the older person is more likely to wear glasses than to require a hearing aid. Cost and attitude both play a role. One estimate on the decline of sight is that the retina of a 60-year-old male receives about 30% of the light received by a 20-year-old. However, the decline starts early—for most males at 32, for females at 37.[15]

Dizziness. The vestibular functions relate to our sense of balance in maintaining an upright posture. There is common report of dizziness among older persons; one study found this condition among 81% of men and 91% of women over 63, with some correlation to heart failure among the more acute cases. Research on this has so far not been extensive.

Slowing. "Behavior of the older adult, whether it is perceptual, associative, or motor, tends to be slower than might be expected in a young adult . . ."[16] However, one explanation is that the slowness is due less to a decline of motor activity than to the reaction time, "since once a response fully occurs, it occurs smoothly and is carried out rapidly."[17] Related to this issue is the matter of "pacing," a situation in which someone performs a task according to a time plan or speed determined by someone else. The English psychologist, A. T. Welford, has concluded that older persons are more likely to feel harassed in a

---

[13]"Physiology of Human Aging," in J. E. Birren, ed., *Contemporary Gerontology: Issues and Concepts.* Los Angeles, University of Southern California, 1970, p. 50.

[14]*Developments in Aging: 1976, A Report of the Special Committee on Aging,* U.S. Senate, S. Res. 373, March 1, 1976, Part I, pp. XIX–XX.

[15]R. A. Weele, "Retinal Illumination and Age," *Transactions of the Engineering Society, London,* 26 (1961), pp. 95–100.

[16]James Birren and Jack Szafran, "Behavior, Aging and the Nervous System," in James Birren, ed., *Contemporary Gerontology: Issues and Concepts.* Los Angeles: Gerontology Center, University of Southern California, 1970, pp. 295–297.

[17]Ibid. p. 297.

paced situation;[18] "Overall," added Professor David Schonfield of the University of Southern California, "the evidence suggests that time pressure increases learning difficulties for older groups, makes them more susceptible to interference, and probably provides emotional disturbance."[19]

Intelligence, Learning, Memory. In this area there is a mixture of psychological or experimental knowledge and social attitudes. Just as serious doubts have emerged in recent years about the premises and techniques of IQ and other tests given to children, even more serious doubts can be raised about the status of older persons. The definition of "intelligence" becomes more crucial, for while delineations can be made in reference to the mastery of new concepts with children, the intelligence of older persons may be seen as a matter of how one applies a lifetime's experience to new situations. Yet, the ways in which the retiree reaches decisions—where to live, what to do—do not lend themselves to traditional measurements. Indeed, is a comparison of intelligence or memory across generations any more valid than comparisons between different cultures or historical periods? To the degree that the tests are useful, they show some advantages for the elderly:

> Results of standardized tests suggest that certain functions rise in scores with advancing age. Results of vocabulary measurement show, for example, that the healthy adult will generally know more words after he increases in age, i.e., with advancing age the individual accumulates more experience.[20]

What "experience" does is to enlarge the vocabulary a person may need in such situations as undertaking a new job, the kind of vocabulary accumulation that standardized tests leave untouched. As the issue relates to leisure, the ability to enter into new experiences depends upon attitudes and other personality components that are not measured by simple tests.

Some further difficulties are noted by one of the pioneers in measuring changes of intelligence among adults, Professor K. Warner Schaie of the University of Southern California.[21] He has pointed to the need for *longitudinal* studies in order to take into account the differences in life experiences, and the problems inherent even in such data. (Longitudinal studies have been made by Bayley, Lewis Terman, and others.)

> We do not know to what extent changes in the behavior of individuals are done strictly to age and to what extent they were caused by some environmental event which occurred during the interval between our measuring points . . . on the crystallized abilities there is very little change in intellectual function for an individual throughout adulthood . . . in functions that do not require speeded response or are affected by the slowing of reaction time within the individual, there are nevertheless marked differences in performance level between successive generations. For practical purposes, this means that although many old people are functioning at least as well as they did

---

[18]*Aging and Human Skill.* London: The Nuffield Foundation, Oxford University Press, 1958.

[19]Birren and Szafran, op. cit. p. 368.

[20]Ibid. p. 298.

[21]"Age Changes in Adult Education," in D. S. Woodruff and J. E. Birren, eds., *Aging.* New York: Van Nostrand, 1975, pp. 111–123.

when they were young, still the young of today function at a much higher level than those who were young 50 years ago.[22]

Some skills possessed by the older person may now be obsolete, but new skills can be acquired. In its 1972 Dubrovnik conference, the Center for Social Gerontology of Paris developed a number of discussion panels, among them one concerning "innovations" among the elderly. Its conclusions are relevant:

There exists a wide and concrete body of evidence that older persons can be successfully exposed to activities and experiences which for them are innovations, as in the Scandinavian folk high schools, in adult education programs of many countries, and in a wide range of activities such as travel, making physical objects, education, the arts, and so on.[23]

GENERALIZATION ON PHYSICAL CONDITIONS

We conclude, then, that physical changes *by themselves* cannot serve as the basis for a leisure direction for the elderly; there are younger persons, in and out of hospitals, who are in wheelchairs or beds. In all cases, including the elderly, such a situation opens other possibilities for programming. The deaf and blind have rightly insisted that their potential for participation is undermined by stereotypes of the "normal." Similarly, factors of aging go far beyond the physical, and must be placed within the context of the total change.

Further, as in every other matter affecting the elderly, there is a self-evident danger in generalizing about a group of 23 million persons who cover a 30-year span. The range or scope of differences among them, in matters of health or in anything else, is perhaps larger than among other groups of over 20 million individuals.

As a whole, recent studies confirm the fact that older persons are generally in good health, but assume that they, as individuals, are "exceptions." Program administrators have accepted this and other myths, such as their inability to learn or to be useful to society. Leisure programs are, therefore, often geared to their incompetencies with the objective of keeping them occupied. This is an easy way out for the program, and raises few objections from the recipients. Many nursing homes can get away with a television set instead of a recreation program, thus nurturing the myth. Still other programs are entirely terminal, so that activities are ended at the time they are carried out, with little concern for future continuity.

The contemporary approach, as applicable here as it is to children, is to build educational and recreational programs on the basis of strengths and possibilities rather than on limitations.

---

[22]Ibid. p. 120.

[23]*Leisure and the IIIrd Age,* Third International Course of Social Gerontology, International Center of Social Gerontology, Paris. Dubrovnik, May 15–19, 1972. Committee, "Can Retirement Bring About New Forms of Behavior?" p. 182.

Our conclusion is that the social sciences, as they are conceived for the most part in the American academic view, cannot provide a full basis for social planning or policy because of their amoral positions in the totality of human knowledge. Gerontology cannot move forward until it moves frankly toward philosophy, aesthetics, and value theory. The present enchantment with social sciences, however, tends to prevent this.

The biological model, on the other hand, is one of devolution or progressive decline. This approach, entirely useful for geriatrics, lends itself to mythology as much as the nineteenth century perversion of Darwinian evolutionary theory for political and colonial purposes, based on the utilization of his idea of "survival of the fittest."

If we take the position that leisure for the elderly represents a new existence, freed from past limitations and mythologies, the functions of leisure are entirely open-ended. The purpose of our knowledge is to provide for the elderly the freedom of new possibilities, not to lock them into boxes of statistics about the way things are.

But the need for freedom goes beyond these disciplines. Another level, equally important, involves social and political attitudes. Here we deal with a freedom for the elderly of attitudes held by themselves.

CHAPTER 5

Freedom from Social and Political Ageism

Alongside other prejudices, Dr. Robert Butler has spoken of "ageism":

Ageism can be seen as a process of systematic stereotyping of and discrimination against people because they are old, just as racism and sexism accomplish this with skin color and gender. Old people are categorized as senile, rigid in thought and manner, old-fashioned in morality and skills. . . .[1]

He later added that:

Ageism is manifested in a wide range of phenomena, both on individual and institutional levels—stereotypes and myths, outright disdain and dislike, or simply subtle avoidance of contact; discriminatory practices in housing, employment, and services of all kinds; epithets, cartoons, and jokes. At times ageism becomes an expedient method by which society promotes viewpoints about the aged in order to relieve itself of responsibility toward them. At other times, ageism serves a highly personal obejctive, protecting younger (usually middle-aged) individuals—often at high emotional cost—from thinking about things they fear (aging, illness, and death).[2]

A spicier version of ageism was provided by Maggie Kuhn, founder of the Gray Panthers:

You know, all of us are supposed to be alike: crotchety and cranky, our brains shriveling up, and our sex organs withering away. That, of course, is nonsense. Many of us are livelier and smarter than ever. And as for sex, I'm afraid it's our adult children who are the prudes and who pass on myths about "dirty old men" and "dirty old ladies."[3]

One disturbing fact about ageism is that many older persons are themselves believers in it. Another fact is its acceptance in medical, political, intellectual, and even gerontological circles. Universities, for example, fall

---

[1]Robert Butler and Myrna Lewis, *Aging and Mental Health; Positive Psychosocial Approaches.* St. Louis: Mosby, 1973, referred to in R. Butler, *Why Survive? Being Old in America,* p. 12.

[2]*Why Survive? Being Old in America.* New York: Harper and Row, 1975, p. 12.

[3]Quoted by George Michaelson in "Maggie Kuhn: Gray Panther on the Prowl," *Parade* (Dec. 18, 1977).

victim to practices of mandatory retirement at 65, in spite of the pronounced shortage of senior professors to work with graduate students. A third fallacy is the dumping of many millions of persons into one image.

An attempt to refute ageism by listing older persons who have been highly creative (Verdi, da Vinci, etc.) is not useful, and produces the expected backlash—they were the "exceptions." Instead, we will examine here several theories of life stages, settle on "lifestyles" as a useful concept, and finally turn to the political process as the most useful method for escape from the ageism myth and its serious consequences.

Erik H. Erikson has been the most influential exponent of the psychological content of life stages. In a *Daedalus* issue devoted to the theme of adulthood, he presented a brilliant interpretation of the psychoanalytic symbolism suggested by Ingmar Bergman in his film *Wild Strawberries*.[4] A retired physician, Dr. Isak Borg, journeys to Lund for honorary services by his professional colleagues. From the detailed analyses of various sequences in the play (the dream, the decision, the strawberry patch, passengers, midday, the last examination, new life, the celebration, and evening), Erikson reviewed the principles that determine "a succession of life stages," familiar to readers of his major writings. The stages that Erikson used in his model were infancy, early childhood, play age, school age, adolescence, young adulthood, maturity, and old age. The principles that dominate "old age" are "Integrity vs. Despair, Disgust, Wisdom." His formulation of wisdom is "the detached and yet active concern with life itself in the face of death itself, and that it maintains and conveys the integrity of experience, in spite of the decline of bodily and mental functions."[5]

Crucial to students of leisure for the elderly is Erikson's phrase, "the integrity of experience," for the approach of leaders in community center and nursing home situations has often been to create frivolous programs. Rather than building on the strengths of a lifetime of experience, "fun and games" are often the only content that is provided. This practice of underrating the elderly may come in part from a tradition of recreation and in part from the underestimation of the skills, needs, and aspirations of the elderly. Indeed, the conception of wisdom can become a guiding principle for a mature leisure for mature persons with only a few modifications: *leisure for the elderly can be viewed as a concern with life itself, maintaining and even deepening the integrity of experience, in frank recognition of the changes in bodily and mental functions.* This, of course, contradicts ageism on a most fundamental level.

A second useful analysis of the interrelationships of life stages comes from the Confucian view of adulthood as a "process of becoming":

the idea that one's life on earth can and should be differentiated into discrete modes of existence and is, in essence, a preparation for an afterlife does not seem to have occurred in the Confucian tradition either. The emphasis instead is on the

---

[4]Erik H. Erikson, "Reflections on Dr. Borg's Life Cycle," *Daedalus,* 105, No. 2 (1976), pp. 1–28.
[5]Ibid. p. 23.

process of living itself. The maturation of a human being is viewed as an unfolding of humanity in the world. For without self-cultivation as a continuous effort to realize one's humanity, biological growth becomes meaningless. Adulthood, then, is "to become a person."[6]

The Western gerontologist will recognize in this Oriental view the parallel to a "developmental" theory of aging, but with a deeper symbolism than the one provided by a pragmatic social science. Erikson's view of "growth" into wisdom and the Confucian principle of "becoming a person" both parallel the Western social science accent on a *developmental* approach to aging rather than the more static, *genetic* view of life. From the standpoint of leisure studies, the question emerges as to whether leisure holds the potential for older persons of serving as a source of values that can contribute to an ongoing *growth*. Can leisure experiences be useful not only to those who are satisfied with passing the time through hopefully interesting or entertaining experiences, but also to those who seek ways of remaining mentally and emotionally receptive and growing?

Further, these concerns into the phases of life suggest that the older phases, by whatever name, are crystallizations of that which occurred before. The European concept of the "third age" has much to commend it, notably a simultaneous concern with stages I and II; furthermore, the concept does away with such loaded terms as senile, old, senior, and Golden Ager. A sense of *continuity* is a more accurate and strategic concept than *decline*.

The guiding principle that emerges from such a view is that *leisure can provide for the older person a clue and instrument for a concern with the ongoing adventure of living—the joy of the journey itself.*

A third classification as a basis for relating leisure to the family life cycle comes from the Rapoports who speak of adolescence, young adulthood, the established phase, and retirement.[7] A further subdivision is presented for the last phase as "preretirement" (55 to 60/65), "retirement" (60/65 to 75), and "old age." The preoccupation for all is the attempt to achieve a "sense of social and personal integration"; the major determinants of leisure activity for all are education, income, and health.

Anticipation, as the major concern of the "preretired," may take on different forms, such as "denial, inconsistent behavior, and the wish to hasten the process by retiring early." Calling upon the research of other scholars, the Rapoports have noted the sex imbalance that may now occur, as husbands and wives often drift apart in their interests, the awakening of closeness to relatives, intergenerational ambivalence, as grandparents "may wish to visit, play with their grandchildren, go on outings, and give them treats, but not to take responsibility for them," and the anxiety for men of an existence without a familiar pattern of work. In the preretirement phase, "A key issue for leisure

---

[6]Tu Wei-Ming, "The Confucian Perception of Adulthood," *Daedalus,* 105, No. 2 (1976), p. 109.
[7]Robert and Rhona Rapoport, *Leisure and the Family Life Cycle.* London: Routledge and Kegan Paul, 1975.

provision, is how to counteract the stereotype that older people are disadvantaged, disabled, incapable of cultivating new interests and building new life styles for later life."[8]

Realignment is the essence of the "retirement" phase. Again drawing on their own research in the Institute of Family and Environmental Research as well as on scientific literature, the Rapoports summarized the general characteristics of retirement: problems of unpreparedness; of money, health, housing, and social relationships; and the validity of both the "engagement" theory[9] and the "disengagement" theory.[10] In this phase the issue of leisure is a departure from the work ethic without psychic loss. The Rapoports noted the advantage of retirement communities (not found in England, but increasingly common in the U.S.A.) in which the collective ethos of enjoyment helps to undo the effects of earlier conditioning.

Life before death is the predominant theme of "old age." Some of its characteristics are psychological and physical distress, increasing loneliness, feelings of rejection, and adverse comparisons with earlier stages of their lives (such as declining mobility). "In this last period of life before death, old people cling to things they know, their treasured objects, environment, people and memories."[11] There is no doubt that this phase of life has been the one most ignored by leisure students who deal with the elderly.

What the Rapoports are here emphasizing is a sense of transformation in arriving at a summit of life, the acceptance and recognition of it as mature persons. *Leisure can provide the instrument for this security in accepting what we are at the final stages of life.*

LIFESTYLE: STAGES VS. SIMULTANEITY

From Erikson, the Rapoports, and the Confucianist view of "becoming" we have reminders that, whatever the process or nature of life's phases, to grow older can have many meanings. The biological reality is accompanied by the social and psychological reality. Yet there is a relatively new term in contemporary life, lifestyle, that suggests a horizontal differentiation interspersed with the vertical concept of aging; its principle seems to be *choice*. What is lifestyle, and what is its relation to the concepts of accumulated experience, wisdom, becoming, or the several stages that are noted by the Rapoports? How does one's lifestyle run through the various stages (Erikson), the method of adventuring or becoming (Confucianism), and the adaptation to finalities (Rapoports)?

"Lifestyle," according to Webster's *New Collegiate Dictionary* has only one definition, "an individual's typical way of life."[12] Style, we are told, is a "mode

---

[8]Ibid. p. 284

[9]R. S. Cavan et al., *Personal Adjustment in Old Age,* Science Research Association, Chicago, 1949.

[10]E. M. Cumming and F. W. Henry, *Growing Old,* New York, Basic Books, 1961.

[11]Rapoports, op. cit. p. 312.

[12]New York: G. & C. Merriam, 1976.

of expressing thought in language"; "manner or tone assumed in discourse"; a "distinctive or characteristic manner." Perhaps the subtle difference is between these methods of expressing *typicality* and the additional image of style as "overall excellence, skill or grace in performance, manner, or appearance." "He lives in style" is a judgment, beyond the prosaic comment of his "typical way of life."

The use of "lifestyle" wavers between these two emphases: (1) the judgment of a way of living that goes beyond the expected, comparable to such observations as "She lives an interesting life," and (2) "This is the way she lives." The term *meaning* adds a dimension to these terms. When we say, "John's life has meaning," we have said more than "John lives."

Two propositions emerge from this: (1) "meaning," "style," "distinctiveness," etc., can be recognized as *a part of* the lives of the elderly, the middle-aged, or the young; or (2) the "meaning" can come from *outside* one's present life, and derive from the interplay of factors in one's life that are usually identified with other ages or stages. In short, the term "act your age" permits meaning in life at any stage because it implies a certain predictability of activity, whereas the Auntie Mame type of person confounds us by the apparent "inconsistency" or confusion of the stages to which Erikson and the Rapoports refer.

Certain kinds of play are identified with ages; hopscotch and shuffleboard provide immediate examples. What seems to be happening now is that leisure's symbolism, especially regarding age, is weakening. Shuffleboard has never been popular with the young, but other activities have broken the age barrier. Tourism is one example—increasing numbers of elderly travel, and only the cost prevents more of it. Areas of experience once clearly reserved for the young—learning, active sports, sex, the learning of arts—are now age-blind. On the other hand, patterns that were once identified with the elderly are increasingly attractive to the young: living on the farm, communal modes of living, or storytelling (for instance, the new appeal of TV soap operas to the college generation).

Apparently we have a contradiction here in contemporary thought about the personality of the older person. On the one hand, we tell him, build on the strengths of your age (especially, your accumulated experience) and, conversely, we urge him to be free to do things that vary from the stereotypes of age—"you can do anything."

The solution revolves around the word, *meaning*. In stages I and II, the person is growing up and working. Each stage has its obvious meaning. The child-youth-student is learning and growing; she is future-oriented; education is her main commitment. This does not deny the validity of childhood as an end, but the child who dies has, we all agree, not "lived out" her life. The child is a classic case of *becoming;* we talk freely of "investing" in the child's future on a collective basis. For example, a common complaint of villages is that they have put out tax money to educate young people who then migrate to the city, which—quite accurately—gets much of its work force for nothing.

Similarly, the middle or work years have their implicit meaning: raising the children, moving along in one's career, participating in community, and so on. Its meaning, more than for children, comes from *present orientation*. Its depth comes from fullness at the time. Of course, there is a forward look, such as having grandchildren. But the meanings are already sufficient. By the time one has reached 50, he has experienced joys and sorrows, successes and disappointments. Further, and here we come to the crucial point, the meanings have come from either: (1) our confrontation with hopes, dreams, fears, tensions, that are implicit in daily life; or (2) from tensions that we have artificially created for ourselves.

The second is well illustrated by our attachment to sports, as spectators or as participants. Viktor Frankl, the eminent Viennese psychoanalyst and founder of logo-therapy, argues against the principle of homeostasis—that is, that sports serve an "inner equilibrium." Frankl maintains that man is always concerned with the world outside of himself in what he called the "self transcendence of human existence." In this quest for relationships, we do not avoid tensions, unless we are mentally ill; as in the case of sports, we *search for* and deliberately put ourselves into situations of tension. Many of our day-by-day lives are humdrum and boring. We attach ourselves to the fortunes of the Yankees or the Green Bay Packers. "In fact," said Frankl, "if an individual is not challenged by any tasks to complete, and thus *spared* the specific tension aroused by such tasks, a certain type of neurosis . . . may occur."[13]

The middle years can provide a balance of tension types, those from one's own life and those introduced into life by the TV screen or sports. Leisure, representing the latter half of the equation, rests on a base of ongoing reality of work and domestic and community relationships.

In the third age, retirement, the balance is distorted. Work, and even domestic relationships, are often missing. The lifestyle is deeply affected as work experience is lacking. A dimension of actual or potential tensions, and therefore, of meanings, is lost. And yet, the philosophy of recreation leaders often plays directly into this situation, with activities that are overly simple, terminal, and that fail to equal the former depth of work commitments. No wonder that "neuroses" set in, from boredom and lack of meaning.

Finally, the nature of tensions is that in a healthy profile of life they are resolved. We can see this in the theatre. Act I introduces the character and the situation, Act II creates conflicts, and Act III resolves them—differently (as in the difference between tragedy and comedy) but usually with some finality. The problem of leisure for the elderly is, therefore, *to provide the instrument for meaning through the presentation of tensions, in programs of challenge and complexity.*

One final observation at this point—the tensions, as we will see later, can come from one of many leisure pursuits, as in physical, aesthetic, intellectual, social, or civic forms of activity. But meaning through leisure is often associated with anticipation, expectation, preparation and fruition; in short, it is *future oriented.* Inherently, the anticipation of a resolution is ipso facto the major element of orientation to the future. Looking ahead to the principles of

---

[13]In O. Grupe et al., eds., *Sports in the Modern World—Choices and Problems.* Berlin, Springer-Verlag, 1973, p. 27.

later chapters, we confront a dual obligation in this regard, to assist the elderly in both terminal and in ongoing task-oriented, tension-creating leisure actions. The first are necessary to provide early satisfactions, especially with new activities, while the latter are required for setting projections through a process that moves along in time. Bingo and ceramics provide respective illustrations.

We must not delude ourselves by the word "tension." It does not coincide with illness, strain, a tightening, a cause for concern. When the potential author sends a manuscript to a publisher, he has added an element to his life, one that he created, that raises the question, "Will it be published?" This is tension in the sense that it has been used here. When one gives a party and hopes that the invited guests will come and enjoy themselves, this is tension of a small sort.

In summary, then, our look at the personality of the elderly has brought together the principles of: (1) growth and wisdom; (2) adventure and becoming; (3) adaptation; and (4) meaning. These are not new; however, their applicability to leisure for the elderly has not been common. Together they provide elements of happiness for older persons. They provide some categories to which we can later address the matter of the *functions* of leisure; they move a conception of personality forward from a static, descriptive term to a dynamic, ongoing *process*.

POLITICAL REALITIES

The tendency is to assume that a "process" is something that has happened to us; the realities of a dynamic society invite us to participate in creating the process. Political action is one means for action, affecting not only our objective *conditions* as segments of the population (such as women, minorities, children, elderly, handicapped), but also the images that are held about us and by us.

Unfortunately, the "lifestyle" image we have pictured above is largely an ideal; "ageism," as described by Dr. Butler, still largely prevails. It takes too long for traditions and thought patterns to change. Fortunately, the "graying of America" takes place when other submerged groups are exercising their latent power. The political arena has become their battleground, and we have already seen important legislative and court action on such matters as mandatory retirement, Social Security inequities, and age discrimination in jobs. All these judgments will have direct impact on leisure of the elderly, both psychologically by easing their minds and actually by providing direct programs.

The parallel groups to which freedom for the elderly is related are women and blacks, Several characteristics apply to all these groups in greater or lesser degree:

1. An unwillingness to accept and to act by the perceptions held of them by others; thus, in respect to traditions of their appositions—men, whites, and younger people—each is now a problem group.

2. A developing skill in creating power for social and political action for themselves.

3. An ability to learn from each other how to use this new power in establishing goals, in attracting attention from an apathetic public, press, or politician, and in organizing their skills.

4. A counterpart group in other parts of the world, albeit with different cultural nuances.

5. An increasingly distinctive literature, with sets of culture heroes, and recognized spokesmen (spokespersons).

However, essential differences also mark these groups:

1. In the degree of militancy, whether in the 1960's or in projections for the 1990's. The elderly, for example, are less inclined toward dramatic action, although Maggie Kuhn's Gray Panthers provides an exception.

2. The elderly presently attract sympathy in the press and political arena but relatively less in social welfare benefits than, say, the blacks.

3. By definition, "youth" and "elderly" represent a change in status and expected behavior *during their lifetime*. This raises, for public purposes, the issue of stages/ages, and legalistic/social definitions. In contrast, sex and color are constants.

4. The society is more likely to recognize the differences between women as individuals than it is for blacks and elderly. The latter two are viewed falsely as homogeneous groups.

One reason for pointing to this trio of population segments is that each group may become a new source of creative vitality in the decades ahead, in such areas as social thought and the arts, assuming that social marginality seems to be one factor toward creativity.

Second, all these groups have been caught up in the nebulous cause-and-effect relationships that have delineated social change since the turn of the century: the growth of cities and suburbs, a loosening of class lines, expanding education, explosion of television, major wars, medical advances, space explorations, fewer working hours per year, more automation and computerization, mechanized homes, growth of government, a broadened material base of goods and services, inflation and unemployment, Watergate and Vietnam, and a national mood of cynicism and pessimism evident in such areas as Watts more manifestly than in Westchester, but which is widely present everywhere.

As to politicization of the elderly, western Europeans have already had a considerable impact, according to a summary for the *New York Times* (December 4, 1977) by Jonathan Kandell. The thousands of social clubs for older persons are increasingly run by them. Over half the real estate of France is controlled by those over 60, and 55% of all corporate stocks. Contrary to the U.S. moves for removal of mandatory retirement, in Italy, France, West Germany, Spain, and elsewhere the move is toward earlier retirement. By 1980, 33 retirees will be found in the Europe scene for every 100 workers, compared to 20 in the U.S. The political impact of the older segment, combined with the need to find jobs for those under 25, led to legislation in France in June, 1977, permitting persons to retire at 60 and receive 70% of their last salary for five years, after which time normal pensions take effect.

For the United States, several broad directions may be detected:

1. Normal political activity among the elderly, as among anyone, embedded in such political actions as statements by the parties during campaigns. 95% of the elderly voted in the 1976 presidential election.

2. The ongoing work on the federal level of the Special Committee on Aging, U.S. Senate, the many state legislative committees and, most directly, the Office of Aging within HEW: more recently, the Institute for Research on Aging, headed by Dr. Butler.

3. Programs of such organizations as the American Association of Retired Persons (AARP) and the National Retired Teachers Association (NRTA), which emanate from the elderly themselves and are, in part, geared to influencing legislation.

4. The more militant Gray Panthers is already 8000 strong. It is concerned with a catalogue of issues from transportation to bank policies, medical reforms, and images of the elderly on television. Such activity is good involvement for the elderly, aside from its impact. As Ms. Kuhn notes, "It beats Geritol."

These issues coalesced at the White House Conferences on Aging, held in 1961 and 1971. Major attention has been, in both cases, toward obtaining financial security, improving pension plans, providing better health, and housing. However, a listing of sessions ("forums") for the 1971 meetings in Washington revealed a wider set of issues: education, employment and retirement, facilities, programs, and services, housing, income, physical and mental health, planning and government, research, training, transportation, and aging and rehabilitation.

Thus, "social roles," "recreation," and similar matters have not been ignored on the political front. The important recommendations of the 1971 Conference that are relevant to our topic are given below:[14]

RECOMMENDATION 1. Society—through government, private industry, labor, voluntary organizations, religious institutions, families, and older individuals—must exercise its responsibility to create a public awareness of changing life-styles and commitments in a continuous life cycle. Together they should discover and implement social innovations as vehicles for older persons to continue in, return to, or assume roles of their choice. These innovations should provide meaningful participation and leadership in government, cultural activities, industry, labor, welfare, education, religious organizations, recreation, and all aspects of volunteer services.

RECOMMENDATION 2. Program efforts to meet role problems and to create new role opportunities should be designed to serve all segments of the older population. Priorities should be determined according to local and individual needs; special effort must be made to include persons who might otherwise be excluded—the impoverished, the socially isolated, the ethnic minorities, the disabled, and the disadvantaged.

RECOMMENDATION 3. Society should adopt a policy of preparation for retirement, leisure, and education for life off the job. The private and public sectors should adopt and expand programs to prepare persons to understand and benefit

---

[14]*Post-White House Conference on Aging Reports, 1973,* and *Final Report of the Post-Conference Board of the 1971 White House Conference on Aging–June 1973.* Subcommittee on Aging of the Committee on Labor and Public Welfare and the Special Committee on Aging, United States Senate. Washington, D.C.: U.S. Government Printing Office, 1973, pp. 527–556.

from the changes produced by retirement. Programs should be developed with government at all levels, educational systems, religious institutions, recreation departments, business, and labor to provide opportunities for the acquisition of the necessary attitudes, skills, and knowledge to assure successful living. Retirement and leisure-time planning begin with the early years and continue through life.

RECOMMENDATION 5. Public policy should encourage and promote opportunities for the greater involvement of older people in community and civic affairs and for their participation in formulating goals and policies on their own behalf as a basis for making the transition from work to leisure roles. Society should reappraise the current life-style sequence of student-worker-retiree roles and promote role flexibility.

RECOMMENDATION 9. It should be the responsibility of the federal government, in cooperation with other levels of government, to provide funds for the establishment, construction, and operation of community-oriented, multiservice centers designed for older citizens. Industry, labor, voluntary and religious organizations should assist in the planning and implementation.

Social and political ageism can be viewed as the unofficial and official expressions or forms of prejudice. If, as noted earlier, the four elements of "social role" are (1) social work, (2) function, (3) reward, and (4) "self," the second—function—is most directly damaged in relation to older persons. The attempt to free themselves from ageism is, for the elderly, a move to be free to do more than they are now permitted by the general society and by governmental rulings. Until recently, almost *all* elements of society, as if in a grand conspiracy, combined against the elderly. The rationale was quite the opposite, paying lip service to the "well-earned rest" of older workers. More accurately, industrial society has concluded that the rationale is, in fact, loss of efficiency. The hard realities are that those in positions of power—businessmen, industrialists, politicos—are fundamentally and congenitally unconcerned with arguments about the psyche of the elderly, their "need to be needed," or similar arguments. Just as the television industry would present Hamlet every night and radio would feature the Ninth Symphony if thereby they could peddle more pills, so industry would eliminate mandatory retirement if it were convinced that its profits would increase. Growing contributions from the private sector toward social security have had this impact. As in the issues of civil rights for blacks and economic equality for women, the lessons have obviously not been self-evident to industry and business; they learn the hard way that the economic deprivation of black workers not only deprives them of an untapped labor force, but also carries an enormous tax bill for welfare, crime, and subsidy for public services in slum areas. Ageism, of which mandatory retirement is only one manifestation, must be shown to be costly to the economy and potentially undermining to the political system. Together these demonstrations may not completely change social attitudes. Yet, as in the area of race attitudes, studies have indicated that change in residential patterns would not have emerged except through law.

Legal and economic changes concerning the elderly of far-reaching importance are on the horizon, before the end of the century. The major new political force will be the elderly themselves.

CHAPTER **6**

Freedom for Creative Lifestyles

We return to the "social role" concept to complete these introductory chapters. What is needed is a national vision for realizing the ultimate potential of older persons in our culture. As the basis for this vision, we have presented a view of social role that includes:

Social circle: one's immediate environment.

Functions: what one does.

Status: position, rewards, esteem.

Self: image of oneself.

This is a social-psychological concept, for it subsumes both the individual and the group.

Yet even groups as collective units—family, play groups, church congregations, residents of a community—have "roles." For example, members of the Boston Symphony Orchestra have their own "reputation" or image, rewards, or rights that belong to no other group in the city, special functions to perform, and a "circle" of persons whom they serve. Indeed, one of the habits which a retired member of such a group retains is a psychological identification with the prestige of his former association. For example, I have brought to my university seminar as a guest speaker a gentleman who spent his working lifetime with the Ringling Brothers, Barnum & Bailey Circus. Retired for the past 20 years, he spoke with great pride of "our" travels, "our" act, "our" Circus, as he exhibited "our" pictures, played a record of "our" band, and proudly showed a letter stating his membership in the circus Hall of Fame. Our friend was the one who was responsible for cleaning out the lion cage after its act.

Beyond the circle of groups whose reputation is reflected in us, we function within wider circles of institutions—not our family but Families, not our congregation, but the Church and, finally, we are increasingly affected by national and international currents. All this is elementary, but restated merely to remind us that the fate of the older person is increasingly interlocked with historical trends, national legislation and traditions, state policies, or by the inclusive term *culture*.[1] There are, indeed, no lines that clearly demarcate one level of influence from another. Let us observe some of the outward or larger levels and move inwardly to our subject.

SOME PROJECTIONS AND GOALS

This book was begun a few months before the advent of the Carter administration, and was finished when its directions of leadership were quite well crystallized. Already there have been trends and the formation of new attitudes; the present administration has met them head-on, starting with energy and peace proposals. Within six months of its active life, it started to reorganize the welfare system. What transpired in those early months will perhaps be outdated on the day of our publication, yet several trends seem reasonably clear and, in some matters, inevitable.

1. The Carter regime which, barring unforeseen political upheaval, will be in office until the symbolic year of 1984, has already confronted the need for a broader financial base for Social Security in legislation of December, 1977. One of the results will be to permit the retiree to keep more earned money in addition to the income from Social Security. This will encourage older persons who can work to do so, solving for them the problem of isolation and providing a feeling of usefulness. The roles of "worker" and "retiree" will be blurred—itself a welcome development.

2. This national policy converges with two additional social attitudes on the part of the middle-aged; (a) a desire for more nonwork time, noted in the last chapter, hopefully without loss of income but with a willingness to forfeit overtime pay if given the choice; and (b) the growing concern of the middle-aged and middle classes that taxes are an increasing burden for a larger proportion of the elderly. All these feelings and legislative responses will, in my view, inevitably lead to the flexibilities in work patterns discussed earlier (Chapter 2), spread over a work life whose length is increasingly a matter of personal choice. This is also a time during which the "new old" find themselves in a national economy of abundance, just as the "old old" were in an economy of scarcity. In spite of the "work ethic" that underlies the Carter administration's positions, its humanitarian posture is one that seeks to help those who are in legitimate need—among them the elderly who are forced to bear the inflationary costs of daily living and mounting hospital fees. This will serve as relief to the middle-aged, but will buttress the argument and the inevitable trend toward lifetime work without mandatory retirement and a guaranteed annual income, in several variations. Both will fortify the economic position of the elderly, enabling them to afford more expensive forms of leisure, such as travel, and thus enlarging their variety of leisure roles.

3. We must be cautious, on the other hand, against a Babbittry that sees

---

[1]Pitirim Sorokin, *Society, Culture and Personality: Their Structure and Dynamics.* New York: Harper and Brothers, 1947, pp. 345–356.

only positive aspects for older persons. Ageism, like sexism and racism, is not eradicated by one administration or in one decade. That which is ultimately confronted is an accumulation of social attitudes and forces that have been fed by such factors as growing urbanism and changes in family life. No one set of solutions can be trusted to rectify the accumulated "human condition." However, if any one pressure group in our democracy has primary responsibility, it is the elderly themselves. Their ultimate freedom is *from their own surrender to ageism.* History may eventually show that such a permanent revolution by the elderly had its seeds sown in the 1970's.

The responsibility and professional commitment of those gerontologists, recreational workers, or others who are concerned with leisure activities and experiences must be to function from the assumption of this revolution. If they perform in this atmosphere of social change and commitment only by *responding* rather than by *participating,* then they are playing it safe and abdicating their responsibility. The new directions for the profession are twofold: (1) to overcome the attitudes of the community and society (which may include the nursing home or hospital director and the head of the Senior Center); and (2) to overcome the apathy of the elderly and their disbelief in themselves.

These broad lessons have been learned by the black minority, roughly equal in size to the post-65 minority. In both cases the greatest foundation for national action and social revolution has been the changing cultural character of American life, changes that affect all ages and segments. These changes, to a larger extent than before, can be brought into a framework of national planning. In recent years there has emerged a confidence in such planning from the success of the postwar economies of West Germany, Japan, and the European Common Market. In all those nations, all parties, left or right, have recognized the necessity for planning, both short and long range. Such technologies as computerization and the disciplinary advances of macro-economics are now available.

Perhaps most dramatic have been the attempts by the Third World nations to take advantage of these new techniques under the guidance of many United Nations agencies. Basic to all such plans—for transportation, communications, industrialization, environmental control, etc.—is the need for statements of objectives. As Gunnar Myrdal argued years ago in *An American Dilemma,* and more recently in *An Asian Drama,* a basic policy (whether for resolving black-white or Western-Asiatic differences) must set out the goals of all parties and then seek a reconciliation of existing differences. In other words, the West cannot impose its values upon Asia, or buy an allegiance to its values through military or even economic contributions.[2]

In our present case there can be no intelligent discussion of the elderly unless we present a vision of *their* goals, evaluate these against the value structure of the culture, and then assess the gaps. What the preceding dis-

---

[2]Gunnar Myrdal, *An American Dilemma.* New York: Harper and Brothers, 1944, Vol. 2, pp. 1041–1064; *Asian Drama, an Inquiry into the Poverty of Nations.* New York: Pantheon, 1968, Vol. 1, Chapter 2, pp. 49–69.

cussions of these introductory chapters have suggested is that these times of change are uniquely appropriate for a restatement of goals. Change *itself* has become a value; boldness, not meekness, is providing the basis for the goals.

We can begin the search for objectives by stating the general "needs" of older persons. Secondly, we can turn to more immediate issues concerning leisure. From this composite we should then have established some policy positions for legislation or social action and, simultaneously, a set of criteria that can be applied to types of activity experiences to be discussed in Section 4, and to types of environments noted in Section 3.

"NEEDS" OF THE ELDERLY

The functions of leisure activity experiences for older persons cannot be arbitrarily isolated from their general needs as people. Leisure, after all, is not a "therapy" which, like drugs, can be rationally prescribed and accurately measured for its impact—"eight degrees of activity is prescribed for Mr. Jones' loneliness, from 3 to 5 P.M. on Tuesday." Play, in its broadest sense, is a human right, on the same level as food, health, air, shelter, and the freedom to move.

Some years ago, based on the thinking of Clark Tibbitts, the Institute of Gerontology of the State University of Iowa listed the following "needs and drives" of the elderly in respect to leisure:[3]

  a. Need to render some socially useful service.
  b. Need to be considered a part of the community.
  c. Need to occupy their increased leisure time in satisfying ways.
  d. Need to enjoy normal companionships.
  e. Need for recognition as an individual.
  f. Need for opportunity for self-expression and a sense of achievement.
  g. Need for health protection and care.
  h. Need for suitable mental stimulation.
  i. Need for suitable living arrangements and family relationships.
  j. Need for spiritual satisfaction.

More recently Jacqueline Sunderland, director of the National Center on the Arts and Aging, presented a list of purposes served by the arts for elderly persons—a list that also seems to apply to other activities:[4]

Proceed through life continuously experiencing a sense of accomplishment and resultant self-esteem.

Aid in developing an appreciation for a wide range of sensory, intellectual, emotional, and aesthetic experiences.

Teach one how to cope with hostile environments by means of new understanding, attitudes, and skills.

Improve the general mental and emotional health by providing the tools for greater individual personality growth.

---

[3]Institute of Gerontology, Iowa City: University of Iowa, 1960.
[4]*Older Americans and the Arts; A Human Equation.* Washington, D.C.: National Center for Older Americans and the Arts and the John F. Kennedy Center for the Performing Arts, 1973, p. 1972.

Aid in establishing various new kinds of mutually stimulating social relationships.

Teach one to relate more easily and rewardingly with members of other groups, thus fostering more productive and humane societies.

Present possibilities for constructive social action.

Some general observations of my own were submitted in a 1960 essay:[5]

1. There is a "need" for a person to be needed, rooted, wanted—in short, "to belong. . . ."
2. Conversely, there is need for every person to be distinct from others. . . .
3. There is the possibility of combining leisure functions . . . Some leisure, more than others, offers a wide dimension of function. . .
4. There are some leisure activities which . . . serve additional persons of the society at the same time that they serve the participant.

My conclusion, then as now, is that: (1) any activity experience can serve many purposes; and (2) the same human "need" can be served by many forms of leisure or, as Havighurst has demonstrated, that different leisure activities can have the same significance for different persons.

In the following discussion both directions will be pursued. A scheme of "leisure functions" will be outlined, noting their special relevance to the elderly. Then, in Section 4, we will discuss categories of leisure to suggest a variety of objectives attainable by each.

My 1975 volume presented a series of "tensions" or "alternatives" that penetrate society as a whole. Leisure, it was suggested, differs from religion, marriage, or other insitutions in that it provides the possibility of resolving these tensions:

> Movement—rest
> Freedom—discipline
> Play—entertainment
> Sociability—isolation
> Construction—distraction
> Self-growth—recreation
> Self-worth—self-defeat

These were labeled "latent functions" of leisure.[6] The issue, in dealing with people of various interests and backgrounds, is to start with people, not programs, and especially not with specific activities. For example, loneliness is a major complaint.

On the construct above loneliness would appear within the category of "sociability—isolation." For all of us, there are times when we want to be left alone, and other times when we hunger for someone to say "hello." Innumberable ways can be found whereby someone can move from one end of this continuum to the other, from attending an art exhibit to joining a club. The responsibility of the leader is: (1) to know the people and their concerns; (2) to know what choices are open to them in their particular setting (nursing home, neighborhood, community, etc.); (3) to know whether the objective conditions

---

[5]Max Kaplan, *Leisure in America: A Social Inquiry*. New York: John Wiley & Sons, 1960, p. 27.

[6]_____, *Leisure: Theory and Policy*. New York: John Wiley & Sons, 1975, pp. 146–163.

(health, income, place of residence, etc.) are favorable or can be modified; and (4) to provide the necessary information and leadership for the realization of the program. Each depends on a knowledge of people. As will be shown later (Chapter 15), the ICL program in San Diego did not originate with courses, but with a group who felt the need for mental stimulation. The arts program in Boston University started when it was realized that one need of older persons—a "future orientation"—can be served through creative experience in the arts. John Putnam's groups went through a process of self-discovery in conversations by which they began to know each other; the result turned out to include a tree inventory as part of a conservation program.

Yet we cannot be naive. The reality of the community, the family, hospital, community center, or nursing home is that a range of "equipment" or "facilities" already exists: here is a family room, a beach, a shuffleboard court, a golf course, a TV set, a movie theatre, a park. These cannot remain unused until the sophisticated leader, by intuition or after reading this book, proceeds into discussions and investigates the "needs" of his people! They will already be using such facilities, for better or for worse. The leader-gerontologist can adopt several strategies to combine the obvious ("manifest") and the underlying ("latent") functions of activities with the needs of people:

1. *We can become more sensitive to the full range of potential functions that can be served through a given type of activity.* For example, a trip to another community can be enriched with information about the place to be visited, the opportunity to meet some of its residents or leaders, and so on.

2. *Having recognized that certain needs exist* (such as for intellectual exchange) *among our groups and that various opportunities are already present in the area* (such as courses for adults), *we can help to bring them together.* What may be needed is knowledge, or transportation, or the development of some skills.

3. When needs are clear, we can invent or organize leisure opportunities to help serve the desirable functions.

LEISURE: ITS OWN END

Having said all this, I propose now to examine leisure, not as an instrument in the tradition represented above, but as an end in itself. The arts will come to mind, as will sports, prayer, or even work. Each of these can be discussed instrumentally—arts for "self-expression," sports to "build character," prayer to achieve "salvation," work to "maintain" oneself, etc.—or they can be seen as self-fulfilling in themselves, as in the phrase "art for arts' sake." Certainly, the newer field of leisure deserves the same dualistic analysis. Let us first approach the subject from a common sense level, and then examine some sociological positions on "structural-functional" analysis. To the degree that there is good reason for gerontology to leave the instrumental view of leisure, it will have freed itself of a long tradition. The question remains, lastly, as to whether there are policy advantages in the view that leisure has its own characteristic essence.

In November, 1976, Mr. Gary Gilmore, who had already spent 18 of the previous 21 years in prison, was sentenced to death by a Utah jury for several murders. Given the choice of hanging or being shot, he chose the latter. His lawyer appealed the case to obtain a sentence of life imprisonment for his client. Gilmore fired his lawyer; he preferred death "like a man" over life behind bars. The case came to the Supreme Court where the judges heard Gilmore and granted his wish, to be shot by a team of five men on a Monday. The Governor postponed the execution until the next Wednesday so as to give the Board of Pardons the final judgment. Gilmore called the Governor's action "cowardly." (Several dozen citizens, meanwhile, had applied to be one of the team of killers—pay for the job, $175.) In January the official killing took place, amidst considerable notice in all the mass media, on editorial pages, and in classrooms. Among those opposed to the death penalty, the fight to make other official killings illegal continues.

In view of this episode, we may reread Abraham Maslow's category of basic human needs. The first is "survival."[7] This apparently did not apply to Mr. Gilmore, age 28, and not, apparently, to millions of young people, in all nations, at all times, who have volunteered in wars to help preserve "freedom," or whatever the cause of the day, conscious of risking their health, limbs, and life. What normal father would not risk his life to pull his child from the fire? What occurs in many hospitals was announced publicly on November 27th, 1977 by a hospital in Brisbane, Australia; every year five or six brain-damaged patients are permitted to die without notification of relatives, by removing life-supporting devices. "This hospital," read the policy, "does not believe in condemning people to life."[8]

If, then, the most basic of all human "needs"—survival itself—is open to questions, conditions, or circumstances, then how secure can we be in proclaiming that there are "needs" of a lower order? One problem in cataloging "human needs" is that, like an inventory of "instincts," the list never ends. Thus, if we apply the "needs" approach to the elderly, even more confusion results.

No one could object to the lists of needs of the elderly presented earlier. The lists read well, the items sound familiar, and they provide a good question for a university examination. Yet, even assuming their validity, would the lists change substantially if applied to younger people? Are there any priorities in the lists? Would anyone care to "weigh" the various items in any order, for evaluative purposes—10 points for number 1, 5 points for number 3? Do they apply to all older persons—to the lady next door, 84 years old, who needs no one except her dog, and is completely content with her soap operas?

The suspicion arises that if we try to justify "leisure" for the elderly according to the *functions* it performs in response to needs X, Y or Z, then we will be in for conceptual difficulties, problems of evaluation, policy traps, and false programmatic expectations.

---

[7] A. Maslow, *Motivation and Personality,* New York, Harper, 1954.
[8] New York Times, Nov. 27, 1977.

The assumption for leisure activity experiences for the elderly, and indeed for *all* age groups, is simple and direct. Play, expression, leisure, relaxation—whatever one cares to call this dimension of being fully human— is no more and no less important than food, sleep, work, friendship, love, or life itself. All these can be integral parts of larger purposes: the "full" life for some requires books; for others a cocktail before dinner; among many teen-agers life loses its meaning unless the phone rings constantly during mealtime, or a date develops for every weekend.

The truth is that several million elderly will finish this week without having heard what *I* would consider a "good" piece of music—yet they will somehow survive, and quite well.

Leisure is everything and it is nothing; there are no magic formulas by which specific activities serve specific functions. Placing a TV set in front of someone serves and influences the desires, habits, or patterns that are derived from the culture. We want TV sets or cars only when we have heard of such things, not in 1875 but in 1975. Wants or desires can be stimulated, influenced, curbed, or modified, for an individual is affected by what David Riesman has called "inner" directions (relatives, priests, traditions) or by "other" directions (current fads, mass media). The peculiar strength for the older person is that leisure can at once provide the satisfaction of what I have called "exploration" and "immobility." One simultaneously can see the world and remain in his chair. Let us examine this miracle more closely in reference to these conflicting "wants" of movement and stability that have always af-fected mankind.

As noted above, any form of leisure can have several functions at the same moment for one person or different functions for a number of persons. The "latent functions" of leisure, hidden beneath the surface, fall into a set of potential dichotomies that seem to confront individuals everywhere. The precise form or relative attraction of these pairs comes from one's situation, including family, subcultures, community, and the general culture.

Each of the leisure forms to be discussed in Section 4 falls into more than one of these pairings; for instance, the *physical* can go under "movement— rest" and "play—entertainment," *social* under "play—entertainment" and "sociability—isolation," and *intellectual* under "construction—distraction" and "self-growth—self-respect." Yet the point to be emphasized is that the desire of any of us to be alone or to be with others is not a manifestation of universal needs but derives from moods or momentary desires which various types of leisure can satisfy; conversely, engaging in specific types of leisure, such as reading, can intensify or underscore our desire to remain uninter-rupted by others.

Just as there is no universal need to eat three meals a day, the rigid schedules that are sometimes seen in retirement communities, hospitals, and nursing homes ignore the flexibility of natural moods. We will see, in a few chapters, the inevitable tension that always exists in such institutions between the mood or individuality of tastes and the organizational principles or prac-tices of the totality. I will note then that the recreational program may seek as one of its objectives some balance or compromise. But, equally important, is the recreation leader's role in affecting the actions of older persons toward greater quality among the leisure alternatives.

THE AMERICAN OUTLOOK

It would seem that the democratic ideal and the thrust of American life are hospitable to the realization of all these goals for the elderly. Below are some unique aspects of our national life for the directions and attitudes of leisure among our elderly.[9]

American leisure patterns reflect the history of a nation that grew up without a rigid carryover of the European or feudal principles or systems.

This political advantage may, in fact, have been a disadvantage for the elderly who, under feudalism, had a strong place in the family. Yet most of our elderly are of the "middle class," a postfeudal segment. Thus, the goal of "availability" is more naturally served today than it was formerly.

Leisure patterns in America have been related to the heterogeneity of our population—a factor that, in turn, is a part of the immigrant waves.

This statement applies more to the "old old" among us. We will see, for instance, that the multiple purpose Senior Center is a direct outgrowth of the Settlement House that began in the immigrant decades. Furthermore, the most successful of these, such as the 92nd Street Jewish Center in New York City, serve all generations and a wide range of interests; it knows how to provide leadership and how to involve its clients as coplanners.

It was as hard workers that our immigrants came to this country. . . .

Thus, the "old old" were the workhorses of America, before the era of strong labor unions. A vision for the future may speak of material growth, but will be achieved in higher proportion through technology and cybernation—not by hard work but by having sophisticated control over machines and processes.

The rise in mass literacy . . . becomes a . . . key element in the leisure of this country.

This, in turn, becomes one basis for taste discrimination as a goal and a potential for those who designate themselves as members of Toynbee's "creative minority."

The social class levels of participants in community transformation are undergoing radical changes, creating new areas for significant leisure involvement.

The growing importance of volunteerism on the community level will be noted in Chapter 14. Creative leadership as a leisure goal is, therefore, not

---

[9]These characteristics of American patterns are taken from my 1975 volume (op. cit.), Chapter 11.

limited to younger people; leisure roles for the elderly can be a goal for volunteers among the elderly.

. . . the private business sector . . . has become a more and more important factor in . . . activities, attitudes, and tastes for leisure.

From this arises broader alternatives for the elderly, such as commercial TV, but also a disinterest for levels of taste and a complete lack of involvement by the elderly.

. . . the public sector has also grown as a major instrument for leisure. . . .

Here, indeed, is the major variable in innovative facilities and techniques for programs of leisure affecting all ages, including the elderly. The nonprofit motive is the surest guarantee for innovative effort. Networks of local, state, and federal funding are already operative, and will multiply in new combinations or reinforcements.

A growth has been evident in the artistic life of America. . . .

This becomes one of the more fruitful areas of "personal growth" among participant elderly, of volunteerism for those who wish to be close to the scenes of action, or of becoming members of the public.

The conclusion that arises, then, is that from these conditions and trends in our national life, reinforced by the new-found freedom that our elderly are exercising in their own behalf, a vision for the elderly can realistically be grounded in the goals already noted. In the broadest statement of these possibilities, we can now see in America *a set of favorable trends, conditions, and self-aspirations among the elderly for the attainment of leisure goals that will contribute directly to their own health, longevity, happiness, intellectual growth and other needs, as well as enable a contribution to creative forces in such institutions as family or education and to all levels of government.*

Environments

The new roles, freedoms, activities, and lifestyles of the elderly take place in concrete settings or environments where people gather for certain purposes at certain times and under certain rules or control: in someone's home, community center, hospital, church, park, retirement village, or even in the street. To some degree an individual has some control as to the where and how, as in the community center, but in the general community a person has less to say.

This section intends to look at several of these settings, to see what each offers to the older person or retiree. Each provides the "social circle" discussed in Chapter 1. The participant responds to each setting, and the nature of this interplay between person and environment helps us to see how the "self" is perceived.

The danger in such an inventory of settings is that we may fail to view the transitions that occur—physically, psychologically, emotionally—in moving from one setting to another, from home to church, to restaurant, to shopping mall, to a friend's home—all within the leisure context. There may be different functions and rewards in each, yet there is an easy flow, even from the greater to the lesser degree of formality. Not until the 12-nation study of leisure (Chapter 7) was attention given to this matter of *sequence* of activities, except for private studies within the television industry where the sequences are from one type of program to another.

A related issue is that of moving back and forth from familiar to nonfamiliar activities—that is, from situations of security to innovation or personal adventure. One difficulty in using attendance statistics is that they often ignore a record of repetitions. Was it the first or the tenth visit? Is the repetition caused by the nature of the content or the security in expectations?

Extending from this issue of transitions from one type of activity to another is the issue of the value of promoting "networks" or linkages between activities and facilities. For example, municipal recreation departments have not generally been associated with travel facilities. Again, where a corporation like Del Webb constructs several retirement communities in various parts of the country, should the resident be able to move from one to the other to suit his moods and needs of climate? As the text notes, England has moved towards thinking in terms of networks, and in engaging personnel who can adapt to the integration of services within the community.

CHAPTER 7

The National Culture

Almost two decades after publication, Robert Havighurst's chapter that compares "life beyond family and work" in western societies remains the most comprehensive treatment of the subject.[1] The more recent and comprehensive study of 12 nations, edited by A. Szalai, does not deal with retired or older persons.[2] Following a summary of Havighurst's material, this chapter will note some more contemporary sources for comparative data, and present some comments about the importance of regional or national culture upon the elderly.

Havighurst uses "social role" as his basic analytic tool, defining it quite similarly to that found in Chapter 1. The roles he considers for the elderly are those of citizen, club or association member, church member, friend, student, and participant in leisure time activity. Before the industrial revolution such a study would have been useless for, in all Western society people worked as long as possible, and then lived "quiet, secluded lives." As he notes of the elderly in such a society, "They are not a recognizable social group or a recognizable social problem."[3]

In both the economy and the family older persons became visible as industrialization and urbanization set in. Thus, social policies were introduced that pertained especially to the elderly. A short history of such policies was given in a three-volume project of the Inter-University Training Institute (16 participating universities), found in all gerontological libraries.[4] Data was presented for Sweden, Denmark, Switzerland, West Germany, the Netherlands, Great Britain, France, and the United States. Thus, we need only note some of Havighurst's observations and data pertaining to leisure activities.

---

[1]Robert Havighurst, "Life Beyond Family and Work," in E. W. Burgess, ed., *Aging in Western Societies.* Chicago: University of Chicago Press, 1960, Chapter 9. Recent reports on aging in Scotland, Romania, the USSR, Czechoslovakia, Norway, France, the Netherlands, Japan, Denmark, and Sweden in *The Graying of Nations: Implications,* Hearing, Special Committee on Aging, U.S. Senate, Nov. 10, 1977.

[2]Alexander Szalai, ed., *The Use of Time: Daily Activities of Urban and Suburban Populations in Twelve Countries.* The Hague: Mouton, 1972.

[3]Havighurst, op. cit. p. 302.

[4]James E. Birren, ed., *Handbook of Aging and the Individual: Psychological and Biological Aspects.* 1959, Vol. 1; Clark Tibbitts, ed., *Handbook of Social Gerontology; Societal Aspects of Aging.* 1960, Vol. II. Chicago: University of Chicago Press. E. W. Burgess, ed., *Aging in Western Societies,* 1960, Vol. III. Chicago: University of Chicago Press, 1960.

Sweden looked favorably upon activity for older persons. "Hobby rooms" in retirement homes were common; home arts and crafts were encouraged. The elderly actually increased their interests in reading, gardening, travel, and the arts.

In Denmark, as of the 1951 data, time "dragged" for only 9% of the elderly, and went "easily" for 82%; Copenhagen residents did more card playing, walking, and listening to the radio than rural and town people. Most activities were carried over from former years, yet as many as 55% started walking after their working years, 15% began needlework, 10% began reading or music listening, and 18% began card playing. "Hobbies" were pursued less than in Sweden.

Swiss elderly continued to do simple work around the home, such as caring for animals and pets. Much card playing went on. Time was a burden for many retirees in the cities.

West German retirees were likely to be creatures of habit, continuing their free time activities from earlier years. "It is expected that older women will do handiwork and that older men will sit and talk with their friends."[5] It was reported (1956–57) that, in the Ruhr region, many older people were involved in raising small animals, especially goats. Gardening also had a high rating.

Clubs for older people were popular in the Netherlands. Radio was heard regularly by 35% of the elderly, with 36% of listeners preferring church broadcasts and 28% choosing the news.

As to the British elderly, Havighurst concluded:

there is no clearly defined role . . . . The upper-class person has been more or less leisured all his adult life and is expected to go on fairly much as in the past. The working-class man is expected to be tired and to be happy with little or nothing to do. For the middle-class man the expectations are even less clear. Women of the working class or the middle class are expected to go on keeping house as usual.[6]

Compared to the leisure of younger people, the elderly tended to diminish their activities and remain closer to home.

The French elderly were inclined to take life more easily than in earlier years, and represented a strong contrast to those of other western countries. France had the lowest retirement age, 60, although pensions go up with retirement. Almost a third reported economic distress, at least in the late 1940's and early 1950's. Yet, as a whole, with the largest proportion of elderly among the western nations, "there seems to be less feeling that old age is a problem . . ."[7] Leisure surveys reported an emphasis on such inactive pursuits as socializing and gardening. The elderly read less than younger adults.

RECENT CHANGES: OTHER CULTURES

An updating of the above material can be made immediately for all nations alike: the greatest change has been in the introduction and wide use of

---

[5]Havighurst, op. cit. p. 321.
[6]Havighurst, op. cit. p. 333.
[7]Havighurst, ibid. p. 335.

television. Even as Havighurst was writing, the reality was overtaking the data available to him, for in western Europe the number of TV sets was increasing from 2 per thousand inhabitants in 1950 to 77 in 1960 (in the U.S.A., from 70 to 310 in the same period). The distribution of TV sets per 1000 inhabitants in various nations for 1969 was as follows:[8]

Sweden	401
U.S.A.	399
Great Britain	284
West Germany	262
Denmark	250
The Netherlands	223
Belgium	207
Norway	207
France	201
Switzerland	184
Luxembourg	183
Austria	173
Italy	170
Spain	167
Ireland	153
Yugoslavia	76

This was reflected, of course, in the personal uses of television for leisure of those fortunate countries and families who had access to sets then and who, simultaneously, enlarged their available hours for watching.

We will see, in Chapter 16, the extensive use of TV by the elderly in the United States and Canada. Our own observations in both eastern and western Europe suggest a comparable use by the retirees of those regions in proportion to their available free time, ownership of sets or access, and shorter air schedules per 24 hours.

A second revolution in the leisure of all eastern and western nations was the expansion of travel for persons of all ages, especially in private cars. One American noted a distinct rise in the number of cars in Budapest over a short period.[9] Her impressions were supported by a report in the *New York Times* of August 7, 1977: "The novelty on the highways of Western Europe this summer is the quantity of motorists from Hungary and Czechoslovakia . . ." They joined the large trailer trucks from Bulgaria and Rumania that had been pounding the East-West routes for years, and the small cars of "guest workers" from Greece, Turkey, and Yugoslavia who went back and forth between their jobs in the West and their home villages.

The Socialist nations differ among themselves in their commitment to Marxism as well as in patterns of living, which reflect the cultural and historical differences even within regions of Yugoslavia and the USSR. Yet a common theme to all of them is economic security—what the American thinks of as the political price they pay. One Russian summed it up in this statement given to Hedrick Smith:

---

[8]Bernard Mueller, *A Statistical Handbook of the North Atlantic Area*, New York, Twentieth Century Fund, Table IV–12, p. 103.

[9]Dr. Barbara C. Kaplan spent long periods of time there in 1974 and in 1977.

We know life here is not as good as it is in America, that your best workers make three and four times as much as ours and your apartments and homes are bigger than ours. But we don't have to save for unemployment here. I bring home my pay, give it to Lyuba and she organizes the household. What do I have to worry about? There is enough money. You make much more than I do. But you have to save. You have to have reserves because any time you can become unemployed and you have to worry about your retirement. Not me. I never have to worry. I have a specialty. I can walk out of my institute and get another job in my specialty and I will make the same money . . . I don't have to worry about the future, and you do.[10]

Smith described the reality behind this security in his detailed account of life under the Soviets. The average pension, for example, was 40 rubles ($53) per month, which is below the poverty line for that society. "In practice," he noted, "many grandmothers and grandfathers have a cushion because they live with their grown children and many also continue to work after legal retirement as low paid watchmen, cleaning ladies, elevator operators, coat clerks, or maids—and the government encourages them to do so. But, after all, that is not retirement."[11]

I have seen elderly women in such places as Sofia and Warsaw carrying large loads of goods to sell, having come to the big city in the early hours of the morning, and every street bazaar from Debrecin in Hungary to the Old City in Jerusalem has its numbers of old and very old, as active as everyone else in the economic exchange and sociability that marks such events. Yet, as a leisure specialist in Budapest pointed out, we cannot transpose the standards of poverty or need from one culture to another, especially from West to East.

Some contemporary conditions in western Europe will serve to supplement Havighurst's study, in addition to the changes in mass media use and the increase of travel possibilities. In the work of Rhona and Robert Rapoport we obtain an authoritative picture of the present status of older persons in England. They noted that, from 1911 to 1971, the proportion of Britons over 65 rose from 5.4% to 13.2% of the population. There, as well as in the U.S.A.,

The conception that older people wish to continue working needs revision except in a minority of cases. They wish to be "occupied" and to have the companionship as well as the income an extra job provides. But the more general wish is to be able to enjoy a satisfying personal life—a wish that is more difficult for them to realize than many may have envisioned.[12]

Yet, even for a society where individualism is an image held by outsiders, the isolation of the elderly was less than the stereotype suggested. For example, while 80% of older persons in the U.S.A. lived within an hour's drive of at least one child, 90% of the British had this advantage. One difference that is directly concerned with leisure patterns was the recent development in England of community networks, integrations, or "composites" of leisure services. "Parks, baths, libraries, etc., were all seen to add up to an encompassing sphere . . . which, to be effective, should not be diffused among a string of

[10]Hedrick Smith, *The Russians.* New York: Ballantine Books, 1976, p. 90.
[11]Ibid. p. 91.
[12]Robert and Rhona Rapoport, *Leisure and the Family Life Cycle.* London: Routledge and Kegan Paul, 1975, p. 272.

departments."[13] The first such network began in 1968 in the county borough of Teeside; here, as well as in other communities since, the composite administration has covered the arts, sports, and other interests, and has included a unified control over urban open spaces (such as parks, playgrounds, water facilities, golf, ski slopes), open rural facilities (such as picnic areas, riding paths), and indoor facilities (meeting rooms, craft shops, libraries, sports halls, museums, concert halls and theatres).[14] The uniqueness of this trend for England's elderly was that it diminished the need for referrals from one agency to the next, and increased the flow of information to the elderly about what was available to them.

The West German pension system goes back three centuries, when only poorer persons were covered. All workers have been covered since 1968. The relation between work and leisure for all ages was most uniquely indicated in the larger number—about one third—of all workers who enjoyed a "flexitime" pattern. This has permitted the employee—with controls that depend on the type of enterprise—to work in his own choice of hours.[15] Even before this contemporary time structure, the use of free time by workers had been marked by the wide popularity of *vereins* (specialized clubs for men, meeting frequently), considerable biking, and the popular beer parlor. In recent years Germans have been seen all through the continent as tourists in buses, private cars, and motorcycles.

France provides a more detailed picture of changes since the Havighurst report. According to a report in the *New York Times* of June 14, 1976, France's 7 million elderly constituted about 13% of the population (they will become fully one third of the total by 2000 A.D.). Most of these had pensions, but more than 2 million elderly depended on financial help from relatives, government payments of about $5 a day, or subsidies covering about 40% of the rent in a private dwelling. Medical care, of course, was free. At work is the French person's fierce individualism and independence. Old people there often go to extremes to live alone, outside an institution, thus increasing the likelihood of mental depression.

One new policy to counteract this independence was the creation of 8000 clubs to provide home services for half a million elderly in the next few years. Most of these services will be for women, who outnumbered elderly men in France by six to one.

A study of four of these clubs in Paris was reported by a research team in 1975.[16] The motivations for attending were essentially social: to find companionship and something to do. Some who attended had lost their ability to cope with the world. The clubs' potentials were limited, but stimulation was their major contribution. They were limited in material resources and leadership.

---

[13]Ibid. p. 328.

[14]Ibid. p. 329.

[15]Bernhard Teriet, "Arbeitzeit und Arbeitsvolumen in der Bundesrepublik Deutschland, 1960–1975," *Mitt AB* 1 (1977); "Der Jahresarbeitszeitvertrag—ein Arbeitskonzept der Oder mit Zukunft?" *Analysen und Prognosen,* 11 (1976). "Gliding Out: the European Approach to Retirement," *Personnel Journal,* 57 (July, 1978), no. 7, pp. 368–370.

[16]Claudine Donfut, "Vacances: Loisir du 3ᵉ Age?" *Gerontology,* 20 (Oct. 1972), Paris: CNRO, Documents d'Information et de Gestion.

In 1973, Professor P. Vellas, dean of the University of Toulouse, opened the first "white-haired" university within the Faculty of Social Sciences. He wrote then: "I decided to approach the problems of the older generation from the public health angle, using the available resources of the university to strengthen a sense of moral and physical well being among elderly citizens."[17]

According to the newspaper account more than 400 older persons immediately applied. Music from Bach, Beethoven, and Chopin began some seminars, leading into the contemporary sounds of Louis Armstrong and Lionel Hampton. Trips were arranged to model farms, factories, research laboratories, and archeological sites. An art exhibition was presented, with works by 300 students. By 1975 about 20 "Third Age Universities" had been created in France, with such activities as yoga, swimming, walking tours, conferences, debates, art exhibitions, research, volunteer services in communities, and discussions of international issues.[18]

A leading scholar of leisure and the elderly in France, Claudine Donfut, has reported on vacations of the elderly in France.[19] In comparing vacation patterns among the elderly, she defined "vacation" as a "minimum of four day-long stays away from the usual residency, aiming at no professional ends, and due to no health reasons."[20] The time distribution of vacations indicated that the elderly of France liked to take vacations at the same time of the year as younger persons.[21] The data on destinations for all countries indicated that the elderly usually preferred to visit relatives on their vacation. Aside from this, the French elderly chose the seaside less than younger people, and went instead to the countryside. Over the years the proportion of elderly who took vacations has risen, with more "nomadic" behavior. The vacation behavior of the elderly showed a "regressive tendency" in expenditures among over 32% compared to their preretirement vacations, for health as well as financial reasons.[22] Donfut presented a significant table of vacation activities which showed that in relation to their normal patterns the French elderly engaged primarily in outdoor pursuits, especially walking (20% more), and had very little interest in cultural or social activities.[23] There was nearly a complete absence of creative or artistic activities during vacation, although a trend toward "discovery" tours was seen.[24] Contrary to the impression that older persons do not change their patterns of earlier years, Donfut noted that many elderly took their first vacation within their retirement years ("neo-vacationeer").

In view of the summary to be presented in Chapter 20 on travel among

---

[17]Dispatch by Rosette Hargrove, *American Statesman,* Austin, Texas, November 9, 1973.

[18]Dr. J. P. Tisseyre, "Le Troisieme Age, une etape decisive avant la vieillesse," in *Troisieme Age: Vivre ou Survive?* Paris: Arthaud, 1975, p. 21.

[19]"Vacances: Loisir du 3ᵉ Age?" in special number *Gerontology,* 20 (Oct. 1972), Paris: CNRO, Documents D'Information et de Gestion.

[20]Ibid. p. 24.

[21]Ibid. p. 26.

[22]Ibid. p. 56.

[23]Ibid. p. 72.

[24]Ibid. p. 74.

the elderly, Dr. Donfut's survey of tourism among the French elderly will be interesting. Much of what she found in a questionnaire study falls into the pattern of "institutionalized" tourism mentioned in Chapter 20. The selection of Corsica was largely a response to advertising. Little interest was shown in wanting to meet the people of Corsica. The plane ride was a new experience for 85% of the elderly; up to that time fear and a conservative attitude ("not at my age!") had determined their travel; married couples encouraged each other. Thus, for the elderly—no doubt in other countries as well as in France—the mode of travel was as decisive as the destination. This, as far as a trip to Corsica was concerned, eliminated those most fearful of change, and the less healthy; the enticements were a variety of reasons such as to forget one's worries, find social companionship, leave the everyday drudgeries, and "live like the rich." Following the holiday, the plane trip remained as the most striking memory, with warm recollections of excursions on the island, and the comfortable residence—somewhat different than they had anticipated. All wished to repeat the experience.

Leaving the western European cultures, two other cultures will be briefly discussed for their attitudes toward the elderly, Israel and China.

Israel

Israel served as host of the International Gerontological Society in the summer of 1976, where delegates heard about policies for the retired there. Many of the early pioneers there are of Golda Meier's time, giving way now to a new generation of citizens. The "open door" policy brought Jews from all over the world, no matter what their health or economic situation. As a result great burdens were placed on the welfare system. Adjustment to a new culture was difficult for those who arrived in their later years, especially those from the Near East and North Africa. Responsibility for the aged was given to the Joint Distribution Committee, part of the Jewish Agency. A network of homes for the elderly was created, called "Malben"; many of these are now operated by local communities. These offered many services and prepared persons to move into the community after some preparation, which included obtaining a working knowledge of Hebrew. Increasingly, the care of the elderly is taken over by such groups as Histadruth, the large and powerful confederation of labor unions, through its Health and Welfare Funds. A home for those from central Europe was supported from funds amassed by property confiscation in West Germany during the Hitler years. An example of the uniqueness of the cultural confrontations for older migrants has been the home of the "Bucherines," persons from a Persian province which became part of the Soviet Union. In Israel they share the Judaic culture in the broadest sense— more specifically, a common religious heritage. The "program" in such a residence has been geared heavily to education in the new society. This motivation, in the midst of an already dynamic society, has provided a level of cooperation and learning experiences that minimize the need for "keep busy" programs along traditional recreational lines. As one American visitor observed, Israel faces a universal dilemma: "segregating the aged into subcultural patterns, integrating them into communal life and evolving a new role socially and emotionally acceptable to them and society."[25]

China

A second culture that has undergone dramatic revolutionary change is China under the People's Republic. Its policies for the elderly are noteworthy. The following report is based on a visit there in 1972 by a clinical psychologist from Los Angeles, Dr. Yung-huo Lin.[26] She began by quoting from a letter of Anna Louise Strong in 1965, explaining why she chose to live in Peking at an advanced age. The controversial and distinguished liberal journalist wrote:

> What, especially, does China offer to old age? (1) China gives us special respect and privileges . . . Courtesy to the aged is part of China's way of life; (2) China gives us the choice of a new career . . . On this basis my creative work and social life flourish; (3) China's way of life mixes the generations, with consideration for the needs of all . . . sounder than the retirement homes of California; (4) China has increased my expectancy of life . . . from contact with a social life of great vitality and progress.[27]

Dr. Lin's observations confirmed this. Four of every five persons lived in communes in the rural areas, "—a miniature state," not unlike the Israeli kibbutz. From its production profits, each commune created its own facilities such as schools, hospitals, and meeting halls, and provided full care for those unable to work. No one, health and strength permitting, was eliminated from field work in the harvest season. Life in any of the ten cities with a million or more inhabitants has been characterized in recent decades by modern apartment buildings with gardens, parks, school, clinics, and child care centers. Facilities have been constructed to provide the greatest participation in educational, recreational, social, political, and health programs, so as to form a self-sustaining nucleus community.

Men can retire at 55, women at 50, a policy dating from the period of lower life expectancy, before the revolution. Everyone, of course, was working for the government. Aged party members and Army veterans retired at full pay; others, with less than 15 years of work, obtained retirement benefits of 50% of their salary—if 20 years, 70% of the salary. Work was guaranteed for life if the person was able and desired to continue working. One person was quoted from a taped interview: "We cannot retire. We have to transmit our skills to the younger generation. It is our responsibility to hand down our cultural heritage. Besides, we really enjoy our work and are happy that we are needed."[28]

[25]Sidney Entman, "Aging in Israel," Jacksonville, *River Garden News,* 1971, p. 3.

[26]Yung-huo Lin, "Retirees and Retirement Programs in the People's Republic of China," in *Industrial Gerontology.* Washington, D.C.: National Council on the Aging, Spring, 1974.

[27]Ibid. p. 81.

[28]Ibid. p. 81.

A professor was quoted:

Whether one retires or not depends on his individual needs and health and the extent to which his particular skill is needed . . . by and large, one's life becomes easier as he grows older. He is freer to do things that are meaningful to him and contribute to his own sense of worth and excellence.[29]

The general Chinese view frowns upon "doing nothing," or idling away one's time. In spite of guarantees for all childless old of food, clothing, shelter, and medical care, Dr. Lin observed that austere living is general. As to leisure, she wrote:

Recreation—museums, amusement parks, cultural entertainments, movies and sports events—are usually provided at low cost by the community. Public bus and train fares are greately reduced for the elderly. The Chinese believe in physical fitness; young and old alike practice Tai-Chi-Chuan and other exercises on the sidewalks or in the people's parks early every morning. Under the motto, "Serving the People," retirees are involved in many social services. At the Arts and Crafts Center in Peking, an old craftsman said, "In the old society, we were exploited and discarded. Now we are here to create and produce artwork for our country. We cannot work as fast as the young people and our hands are no longer strong and steady, but our experiences are rich and invaluable, and our ideas continue to flourish!"[30]

The Chinese also worked on such tasks as teaching agricultural skills or in high school workshops, caring for the children of working parents, and tutoring, somewhat similar to American retirees involved with such federal programs as Score or VISTA. In cities, older persons wore yellow armbands and helped police direct traffic (reminders of Boston and St. Petersburg, Florida!), to "remind litterbugs to keep the streets clean, settle disputes among pedestrians, and guide tours through various national shrines!"

James Reston, the *New York Times* columnist, was quoted at the close of Dr. Lin's account to the effect that in China there was not time for the elderly to "settle down and relax; . . . One is constantly reminded here of what American life must have been like on the frontier a century ago . . ."

THE ELDERLY IN THE AMERICAN CULTURE

After this review of several nations, the American reader will be interested in Havighurst's observations about the American elderly in the report quoted earlier; the comparison with the present may suggest whether the data as a whole remains fairly true. In the U.S.A., noted Havighurst, an "active use" of time is favored, with relaxation permitted "as long as it does not seem like vegetation." Yet very few live up to this role approval. In the "Prairie City" study, for example, the average retiree

Has some active recreations which he carries on individually or with others. Still has time on his hands, however. May play indoor or outdoor games—bowling,

---

[29]Ibid. p. 81.
[30]Ibid. p. 81.

croquet, shuffleboard, golf. Writes letters, may read widely. Crochets, knits, quilts, gardens, does crossword puzzles, works on collections.[31]

In the city studied, 30% were in "passive" recreations, and 7% were "vegetating." Those better off economically had more activity. On the national level, the conclusion was that "the American public expects old people to enjoy their leisure if they know how to do so."[32]

On the international level in western societies, Havighurst concluded that the elderly became less active with age—physically, socially, mentally, and therefore in their leisure. Little demand for intellectual activity was revealed by the studies. American elderly of the middle classes probably travelled more than their peers elsewhere. Finally, "The possibility of gaining ego-support through a more stimulating use of leisure appears to be good and is being applied vigorously in Great Britain and the United States especially."[33]

America's homogeneity as a culture may be said to date from as late as the 1930's; before that the different traditions among us emanated from population origins. There were 5,200,000 immigrants in the decade 1881 to 1890, over 3,600,000 in 1891 to 1900, almost 800,000 in 1901 to 1910, and another 10 million by 1930—a total of over 27 million, or 22% of our total population as the fourth decade of the century began. But these immigrants, and especially their children, took on the ways of the New World. Since then immigration to this country has been less than a half million per year. The homogeneity of the past 50 years is derived from a synthesis of both pluralism and ethnicity that our democratic system has permitted; our differences are rooted not as much in origins as in the internal influences of regionalism, social classes, occupations, and education.

As part of the Bicentennial in 1976 the National Endowment for the Humanities provided a summary of issues for nationwide discussion in schools, clubs, etc., and several of the major headings reflected the foundation of our values: "A nation of nations," "The land of plenty," "Certain inalienable rights," "Life, liberty, and the pursuit of happiness." With all our differences suggested by these topics, there has evolved a general "culture"—a set of broad characteristics—that by now affects all our elder citizens. There is disagreement as to what these national themes or values are, yet as one reads the literature of national psychologies, the cultures stand out from each other. Examples come to mind from what Barzini has written about Italy, Gramont about France, Michener about Spain, Benedict about Japan, Sampson about England, or Mead about the United States. Robin M. Williams has listed the major value orientations of our country as achievement and success, activity work, moral orientation, humanitarian mores, efficiency and practicality, progress, material comfort, equality, freedom, external conformity, science and secular rationality, nationalism-patriotism, democracy, and individual personality.[34]

---

[31]Havighurst, op. cit. p. 347.
[32]Ibid.
[33]Ibid.
[34]Robin Williams, *American Society: a Sociological Interpretation.* New York: Alfred A. Knopf, 1951, Chapter 11.

The anthropologists Kluckhohn and Kelly have defined *culture* as "that complex whole which includes knowledge, belief, art, morals, law, custom, and any other capabilities and habits acquired by man as a member of society."[35] What Max Lerner has written about us applies to the perceptions of the elderly, perhaps even more so than to younger persons because more of them have lived in other parts of the world:

> For good or ill, America is what it is—a culture in its own right, with many characteristic lines of power and meaning of its own, ranking with Greece and Rome as one of the great distinctive civilizations of history.[36]

This takes us back to the concept of "ageism" from Chapter 5, for it is clearly rooted in the values which, in their infinite interactions and amalgams, make up our culture. Twenty years ago the perceptive Max Lerner related this negative attitude to the culture as clearly as anyone has since that time:

> The most flattering thing you can say to an older American is that he "doesn't look his age and doesn't act his age"—as if it were the most damning thing in the world to look old. There is little of calm self-acceptance among the old, of the building of the resources which give inner serenity and compel an outer acceptance . . . One finds nothing like the Japanese reverence for ancestors or the valuation the Chinese set on the qualities of the old. Since the American has been taught that success belongs to push and youth, it is hard to revere those who no longer possess either. One can be fond of them, tolerate them, take reluctant care of them, speak whimsically of their crotchetiness and frailties, but these are far from the genuine homage of heart and mind. To build a code of conduct toward the old requires not only personal kindliness but generations of the practice of values from which the old are not excluded—of which indeed they are the summation.[37]

Thus, the culture which an American confronts as he turns 65—along with 4000 others on the same day—is a mixed bag of political freedoms, educational opportunities, religious choices, geographical availability, and mass media access. This American has by now, in almost every village, medium-sized city, metropolitan area or megalopolitan region, a new set of leisure tools that were, for the most part, not available a half century ago— from the public golf course to the Senior Center, to the use of the public shcool building for a wide variety of courses. He has professional persons, gerontologists, who are prepared to assist him and watch over legislation concerning his needs, including those that touch on his use of time. More effective are those associations that he has created to help him socially, medically, educationally, even politically. Yet, at the same time, it is a culture of crime that, in the big cities, often singles him out as an easy mark for medical rackets and con men.

Altogether, it is this massive configuration of plusses and minuses that decides, in an accidental or impersonal way, what will happen to this new 65-year-old during the next 10 to 30 years. Two anthropologists had this to say about personality:

---

[35]C. Kluckhohn, and Kelly in R. Linton, ed., *The Science of Man in the World Crisis.* New York: Columbia University Press, 1945.

[36]Max Lerner, *America as a Civilization.* New York: Simon and Schuster, 1961, Vol. 1, p. 59.

[37]Ibid. p. 615.

Every man is in certain respects
   a. like all other men
   b. like some other men
   c. like no other man.[38]

About the same can be said of cultures. Even a culture or civilization as open to observation as our own has provided the widest variety of interpretation, from de Tocqueville in 1840 to Green in 1977. The problem remains: how is the place of the elderly in our own culture similar to that of "all," "some," or "no other culture?" To this might be added two other types of questions, moving us from observations to social action:

1. In what respects *do we want every older American to be like all other Americans* (a sound economic base, a useful social role)?

—like *some other Americans* (living in Florida, taking education seminars, traveling)?

—like *no other Americans* (being close to his family, pursuing his own combination of leisure experiences)?

2. In what ways can the older generation of Americans modify the elements of their culture, massive as it is, so *that the goals and balances of conformity and individuality can more effectively be reached?*

Throughout this volume there have been bits and pieces in answer to the last question: what can we do? The last section of this volume takes us directly toward that path. If the culture as a whole cannot be quickly changed, nevertheless changes have occurred. That is the lesson of history and a charge for the gerontology of tomorrow: to contribute to those changes from the position of rationality and justice for the elderly's contribution and usefulness for society.

---

[38]C. Kluckhohn, and H. Murray, *Personality in Nature, Society and Culture.* New York: Alfred A. Knopf, 1948, p. 35.

CHAPTER 8

The Heterogeneous Community

When we leave our homes we encounter our "community," ranging from hamlet and village to New York City in population and diversity. Indeed, over a third of those over 65 live in rural areas of America. If it is a medium-sized or a large city, the chances are that the retired person was not born there, but will die there. Only five of every hundred among the elderly are in nursing homes and, even among most of these, the larger community still remains the immediate world in which they participate.

All studies of "community" performed by social scientists can be divided into BT and AT, Before and After Television. Classic examples of BT studies concerned entirely with leisure and recreation are: (1) the Lundberg study of Westchester County, near New York City, in the early 1920's;[1] (2) the 1929 and 1937 studies of Muncie, Indiana, carried out by Robert and Helen Lynd and their colleagues;[2] and (3) a WPA study of Chicago.[3] An example of an AT study is Herbert Gans' *The Levittowners: How People Live in Suburbia.*[4]

Television is the division to note because, with TV, residents of all ages are freed from their immediate surroundings without leaving the home, and they join what McLuhan has called the "global village." Furthermore, the "old old" among our retirees grew up or arrived as immigrants in the American community Before Television. In either case, they came to know their environment well before it joined the "world village."

Yet both types of studies, BT and AT, include convincing evidence of the physical and psychological impact of close environs. Here are the daily images that strongly influence our thinking and our moods—the streets, the build-

---

[1]G. Lundberg, M. Komarovsky, and M. McIllney, *Leisure: A Suburban Study.* New York: Columbia University Press, 1934.

[2]*Middletown.* New York: Harcourt Brace, 1929; *Middletown in Transition.* New York: Harcourt Brace, 1937.

[3]*The Chicago Recreation Survey.* Chicago: Recreation Commission, 5 Volumes, 1937–1940.

[4]New York, Pantheon, 1967.

ings, the traffic, the people, the stores, the open spaces, the colors and sounds . . . the variety of persons and facilities, the bridge to the outside world."[5]

Lewis Mumford has spoken of the city as a perpetual drama whose purpose should be to "unite the forces of life and give them a fresh expression."[6] The extent to which such expression is achieved in the community by the individual is, of course, a matter of personal taste, mood, and courage to explore. There was the woman in Los Angeles who, at the age of 87, still found her community fresh; her daily schedule included such items as attending court trials, improving her Polish accent in a missionary school, riding a bus to explore the city and the countryside, attending funerals of strangers (the younger the deceased, the more she cried), and climbing up the Hollywood Bowl for symphony concerts.[7] On the other hand, I met one native New Yorker, in her 30's, who had never visited the Statue of Liberty.

Boston, as Harvey Cox has reported, has managed to begin its "astonishing rebirth," largely through politically active neighborhood action groups in which many older residents have participated. We will see, in Chapter 14, how many elderly were organized by John Putnam, a leader with vision and initiative. As in few other cities in America, Boston's ethnic groups cling to the past and, with their strong religious background, exhibit what Cox has called an

unwillingness to accept the reality of the secular city. They still cling to town and even tribal styles of living. Within the city clan feuds between Irish, Italian and Yankee political war parties rage on, while in the suburbs harried escapees from the issues of the inner city deck out their modern homes with wagon wheels and fake colonial furniture.[8]

One result of these emphatic cultural and historical factors was seen in the strong resistance shown by various Boston areas to daily arrival of children being bussed by court order from "foreign" communities.

I am inclined to celebrate and want to affirm these distinctions, in contrast to Cox, who has called them a "disastrous self-delusion," and has argued that "Efforts to live in an eighteenth-century town or to maintain the purity and power of the tribe will eventually be exposed for the charades they are. . . ."[9]

For no reason that I can discern, Cox believes that "the actual interdependence and technological unity of the urban city will eventually require a political expression."[10] The more desirable condition, from the opposite view, is political expression, and commitment to cultural diversity between nations, regions, and cities. This diversity is being rapidly lost, and is one reason for the sense of loss within the community felt by the elderly—a loss, moreover, for residents of all ages. Children are being deprived of access to historical

---

[5]Max Kaplan, *Leisure: Theory and Policy*. New York, John Wiley & Sons, 1975, p. 243.
[6]Quoted in M. Kaplan, ibid., p. 255.
[7]My mother died chasing a bus in Los Angeles at the age of 87.
[8]Harvey Cox, *The Secular City: Secularization and Urbanization in Theological Perspective*. New York: Macmillan, 1965, p. 84.
[9]Ibid. p. 85.
[10]Ibid. p. 84.

continuity of the past, as their parents now park their cars in lots which formerly held buildings that were historical treasures, and might have been saved. Such European cities as Bucharest and Szombathely have had to create "village museums," so that the present generation may enter homes and streets of the type that constituted the Rumanian and Hungarian past.

In Tampa, old-timers recall the Spanish influences that once prevailed, as in the original section (Ybor City), and how these have been removed. In almost every city (Chicago provides unusual examples) such stories can be duplicated. In Cologne, one can stand in front of its magnificent medieval cathedral and see a contemporary art museum, which was built after an extended and futile debate in that old city.

The city in which older people presently live is, therefore, a testament of change, and often a regrettable symbol of "modernization." With recent recognition of the fact that in many cases old structures can be renovated more effectively than new construction, and with a rising respect for preserving the old, there is an opportunity to use older persons in the process of urban "renewal." This opportunity has yet to be realized, either by current sources of community power or by the elderly as their civic contribution. Such political, civic, cultural, and neighborhood participation to preserve the diversity and charm of the old is not a naive dream, but adds a needed dimension to the environmental movement for the twenty-first century.

For the older generation this form of urban environmentalism can be a particularly satisfying commitment. Of course, the movement must extend further than saving buildings and neighborhoods. When the Chinese community of Boston became threatened by the "bulldozer psychology," it set about to save its way of life. That is what a community is, and why it is the framework within which more specific environments (of the Senior Center, school, church, nursing home, or private residence) function and interact.

Implicit in such an avowedly old-fashioned goal is the use of such contemporary instruments as electronic police devices to detect the wave of crimes against the elderly. Yet, as the *New York Times* reported on July 3, 1977, the crime rate against the elderly in New York City was reduced by a third in one year not only by the deployment of more police effort, but by the mounting anger and organization of the elderly and the assistance of teenagers and other volunteers who served as escorts.

The function of the heterogeneous community for individuals has been admirably described by Paul and Percival Goodman in their small classic, *Communitas: Means of Livelihood and Ways of Life.*

Is the *function* good? Bona fide? Is it worthwhile? Is it worthy of a man to do that? What are its consequences? Is it compatible with other, basic, human functions? Is it a forthright or at least ingenious part of life? Does it make sense? Is it a beautiful function of a beautiful power? We have grown unused to asking such ethical questions of our machines, our streets, our cars, our towns. For nothing less will give us an esthetic for community planning, the proportioning of means and ends. For a community is not a construction, a bold Utopian model; its chief part is always people, busy or idle, en masse or a few at a time. And the problem of community planning is not like arranging people for a play or a ballet, for there are no outside spectators, there are only actions; nor are they actors of a scenario but agents of their own needs—though it's a grand thing for us to be not altogether unconscious of forming a beautiful and elaborate city, by how we look and move. That's a proud feeling.[11]

COMMUNITY: CONTEXT FOR LEISURE

The city as "means of livelihood and way of life" thus becomes both symbol and instrument for daily life. Leisure becomes increasingly one of its rationales; its major contemporary gadget, television, becomes the primary tool of simultaneous rootedness and vicarious mobility. The city had already been a bridge to the rest of the world, but now TV has brought other city characteristics to rural and semi-rural populations. Among these leisure elements have been traditionally the variety of persons and facilities as well as the association of city existence with "life" and "excitement." Der Kurfursten-damm and Champs Elysées are distinctly urban leisure romances, and the accessibility to persons of similar specialized tastes—whether for horse races or museums—has provided cities since early historic times with an attraction that was not merely supplementary to the advantages of work and trade, but often determined the choice of residence. And, indeed, the images and reputations of cities have derived from these elements of "living," as well as from their importance as production centers.

The city itself as a condition for leisure and work is both a physical and an organizational unit. All of us are familiar with the dominant elements that commonly identify cities as primarily serving business, industry, education, government, play, or, as in the case of many suburbs, family residence. One image or another comes to mind with the names of Oxford, Miami Beach, Bonn, or Essen. Each image has characteristic inhabitants, values, architecture, and general spirit. These are relatively small communities, and will remain what they were intended for. Future changes will more likely occur in larger communities and especially in the magnified community that Jean Gottman has called the Megalapolitan region.[12] As in the case he studied—the 30 million persons occupying an area from Boston south to Washington—such a super-community unifies many cities and semiurban and rural entities into a mass of man and nature in which there are common values and historical traditions.

Historically, the city has always been attractive for leisure purposes through its variety of inhabitants, its range of potential experiences, and its possibility for excitement. The variety of individuals naturally stems from variety of work, and from diversities of ages, museums, races, religions, tastes, educational backgrounds, and values. However, an interesting phenomenon of our times is the attraction of both urban and rural areas for the youth of many countries. I had occasion recently to be in the Rocky Mountain area of

---

[11]New York: Vintage Books, 1947, pp. 11–12. Copyright © 1947 by Random House, Inc. Reproduced by permission of the publisher.

[12]Jean Gottman, *Megalopolis,* New York, Twentieth Century Fund, 1961.

Colorado, where many young people can be found living, attracted by nature as a reality and as a symbolic rejection of urbanism, work, and materialist values. Yet, in cities such as Amsterdam, young people are attracted by peer support, "happenings," curiosity, and even by interspersings of prayer and music. Youth of our time seem to be seeking this convergence of playing and praying, of work and leisure values, of stability among themselves and of restlessness among the world of others.

Facilities for leisure, at least under private economies, will grow in the cities under public, semipublic, and commercial sponsorship, and my projection for the next several decades is for innovative syntheses and cross-fertilization of public and private facilities, and for the greater inclusion of leisure elements (such as libraries) within the work situation. An example of the latter is the symphony of workers of the Bayer Corporation, which I have heard in a Brussels concert.

RURAL-URBAN LIFESTYLES

The city will continue to grow in its services for all ages, especially as we encounter greater flexibility of work/nonwork patterns and less identity of age-oriented roles. But even this will not bring all older persons flocking to the cities. Recent studies in the United States have shown that in spite of what inflation-minded urban people may think, the traditional disparity of economic rewards between urban and rural workers continues. For example, a 1977 report (Table 8–1) noted that for all ages in urban, rural nonfarm, and rural farm areas, there was a substantial economic advantage for the urban dweller, with a difference in 1969 greater than in 1959 (a difference of $674 as compared to $544).[13]

---

[13]From U.S. Bureau of Census, 1960 and 1970, Tables 219 and 245; quoted in C. Grant Youmans, "The Rural Aged," *The Annals of the American Academy of Political and Social Science*, 429 (Jan. 1977).

Table 8–1   ANNUAL MEDIAN INCOME FOR MALES IN U.S., 1959 AND 1969*

	1959			1969		
	Urban	Rural Non-farm	Rural Farm	Urban	Rural Non-farm	Rural Farm
14 yrs. and over	$4,559	3,330	2,105	6,860	5,591	4,509
65 yrs. and over	1,961	1,351	1,417	3,188	2,205	2,514

*From U.S. Bureau of Census, 1960 and 1970, Tables 219 and 245; quoted in C. Grant Youmans, "The Rural Aged," *The Annals of the American Academy of Political and Social Science*, 429 (Jan. 1977).

Comparable differences exist among urban and rural women. Health is another basic factor in assessing the advantages of location and, contrary to popular opinion, in a 1971 study of self-reported ratings, "Rural older men consistently rated their health as poorer than did the older urban men;" the proportions of those who reported "good" health were 15% for rural, 47% for urban.[14] Among contributing factors may be better medical facilities in urban areas, as well as better transportation and higher income.

As to social life, a summary of various studies has noted that because of the greater distances between married children and parents in rural areas, visits between them were less common than in cities. More church activity was reported among the rural elderly, with more activity in various kinds of clubs among city residents. Differences between the groups were not dramatic concerning social visits with neighbors and friends. Youmans' study of over 1200 men and women, half from a metropolitan center and half from a rural area of Kentucky, revealed that:

> Older rural persons engaged in slightly fewer hobbies and pastimes than did the older urban persons. . . . A slightly larger proportion of rural older persons engaged in fishing and hunting, while a larger proportion of urban aged engaged in playing cards, woodworking and crafts, dancing, and collecting.[15]

Both groups were equally interested in having more leisure activities for themselves. More persons among the rural thought that time was a "burden," and that their lives could be more useful.

Similar comparisons between rural and urban as a whole, regardless of age, were reported in the 1970 *Survey of Outdoor Recreation Activities* by the U.S. Bureau of Outdoor Recreation (1972).[16] However, when these facts were placed within a more comprehensive consideration of "quality of life," two professors of Washington State University concluded that:

> Overall, satisfaction among all Americans is high. Even so, differences in generalized feeling of well-being do exist between rural and urban Americans and tend to favor living in rural areas. Rural people are well aware of the shortcomings of their communities, especially the inadequacy of important services. . . . However, these inadequacies are balanced by the more positive evaluations of other community qualities by rural people. . . .[17]

Among the "subjective" criteria that contribute to a greater preference of rural living (even by urban residents, who are readier to move to rural settings than vice versa) are air quality, safety, access to the outdoors, open spaces, and friendliness of people. Older persons, as well, were more satisfied to be where they were than their urban counterparts.

In recent decades there has been an increased possibility, in both urban and rural settings, for each to gain access to the advantages inherently offered by the other. The older person, more independent psychologically, has been

---

[14]Youmans, op. cit. p. 88.

[15]Youmans, op. cit. p. 87. Reproduced by permission of the publisher.

[16]This bureau is now known as the Heritage Conservation and Recreation Service.

[17]Don A. Dillman and K. R. Tremlay, "The Quality of Life in Rural America," *The Annals*, (Jan. 1977), p. 429.

freer to move his place of residence; transportation improvements have made it more possible (and comfortable) for the older urban dweller to visit the natural environment, or for rural inhabitants to visit the city. Certainly, the advent of television has brought the same images both to rural and urban areas, with undoubtedly an advantage of greater program choices for the city resident.

A philosophy of leisure for the elderly can combine these various values of small and large communities, from the farm to megalopolis, with medium-sized cities, suburbs, villages, and neighborhoods as various points within the total range. A successful "community center" or "senior center" in Chicago serves a comparable function, therefore, as a book review club in a rural or semirural area, which is to bring a balance to each setting—to diminish the "coldness" of the city and the "isolation" of the village.

THE PARK: A CONNECTING LINK

The city park remains a primary facility in which the advantages of rural and urban areas converge. Neighborhood parks have become increasingly valuable to the city, as a bit of nature, a refuge, a pause, a reminder of simple things, an outdoor meeting center, a play area for children, a drama in people-watching, and, especially for ethnic groups from warm climates, a necessity for day-by-day socializing and display. American cities, even in areas with long summers, have never widely adopted the European practice of sidewalk cafes. In midwestern towns there was a common pattern of a park in the center, with a bandstand, adjacent court house, and nearby stores and post office. Southwestern towns, such as Santa Fe, have their pattern of the central park, augmented by wide covered sidewalks with Indians selling their wares.

Such centers were not used by a particular group, as in the 1960's when young people took over some districts of San Francisco. They belonged to everyone. Jane Jacobs, in her classic polemic, *The Death and Life of Great American Cities,* has argued that neighborhood parks in large cities (and, I would add, these small-town squares) were typically used as "local public yards—whether the locality is predominantly a working place, predominantly a residential place or a thoroughgoing mixture."[18]

In some cases, as in Williams Park in the heart of St. Petersburg, Florida, there are enough persons there every day with little else to do except to keep this kind of park alive. Arthur Park in Los Angeles serves persons of all ages, with the elderly in the majority. Portions of Lake Park in Milwaukee were taken over on summer days by Jewish elderly in the 1940's and 1950's, for picnics, cards, and socializing.

To the extent that gerontologists have been involved in planning the park systems of their communities—and why shouldn't they?—their goal should not be special parks where only older persons sit but parks for all ages to use for different purposes at all times of the day and evening.

---

[18]New York: Vintage Books, 1961, p. 91.

Parks, for purposes of the elderly, could have interesting and changing pieces of sculpture, as well as workshops or sheds for arts and crafts. There should be a central area, where friends can meet. There should be open spaces where one can enjoy the sun. Even in small parks there could be a room of displays and sales of paintings. Just as the recreation profession has adopted a plan of "PTA's" for parks where children congregate, so regular attendees among the elderly can, together with younger residents of the area, form governing committees to develop procedures for the use and development of parks.

The next few years may see federal funds made available to local parks through The Heritage Conservation and Recreation Services. Innovative ideas by gerontologists and recreationalists will find fresh opportunities for expression. Above all, one impact of such decentralized control by the park's users may be to make them safer.

The park, which has existed for countless generations, has traditionally been an outdoor meeting place. Its rituals are at a minimum, for its human relationships are based only loosely on proximity, and hardly at all on organization. The common desire is for relative freedom from artificial enclosures, and for a celebration and participation in nature. The parade and outdoor pageant, or the *korso* of eastern Europe which still exists today, are examples of some degree of organization in the outdoors, but then the necessity is for ample space, as in the sports arena.

Thus, even today, the spontaneity of the park provides a nonrole experience that is creative and refreshing, comparable to the new American shopping mall. There, too, persons of all ages mingle, passing each other in a nonfunctional relationship, buying or not buying, moving at one moment and stopping at another.

The heterogeneous community, therefore, provides the possibility of this alternation between playing roles and relaxing from roles. It is roughly comparable to the psychological states of tension and relaxation or, on the sociopolitical level, the alternation between freedom and control.

We turn, finally, to a unique community in the United States, known for its high concentration of elderly. Here we can observe all the points raised in this chapter in microcosm.

ST. PETERSBURG

Next to Miami, which has almost 49% of its population over the age of 65, St. Petersburg ranks second in the nation with 30%. Most characteristic of its areas for our present purpose is the downtown section. In 1972, the *St. Petersburg Times* divided the city into five geographical areas and interviewed about 500 persons over the age of 18 in each area to find out what its residents "are thinking about, how they are living, their joys and their worries." Leisure satisfactions and actions played a major role in this study. The data below refers to an area that stretches about 35 square blocks from north to south and east to west. These downtown areas include the large public Williams Park (with concerts, shuffleboard, benches) in the heart of the section, and the attractive park area along Tampa Bay to the east. Free bus service carries retirees to the pier and its modern facility for browsing, shopping, and eating. At the entrance to the pier is a cooperative recreation club for its dues-paying members. Nearby is a small but interesting museum, the central post office, the Mirror Lake adult education center, and a shuffleboard club that claims to be the world's largest.

Mr. Ron Speer, of the *Times'* staff, has written of this area:

Here, more than anywhere else in St. Petersburg, the residents fit the image millions of Americans have about the city.

They are old, a great many of them, and it doesn't take a survey to find that out. Roam the parks, visit the library, check the shuffleboard courts, walk the streets, eat at the restaurants. . . . Retired folks. Living in tiny apartments, staying in boarding houses, permanent residents of hotels. . . . Others own small homes built years ago, especially to fit the needs of people without children. . . .

It's where dance studios and senior citizens' clubs and antique stores and junk shops and estate jewelry stores and blood pressure testers abound.[19]

The median age of those interviewed in this area was 69.1 years; their median income in 1972 was $4,900, with 8% earning over $15,000 but 25% earning under $3,000. Although the majority felt safe in the neighborhood, many did not go downtown at night. 36% of them had lived there for 10 years or more; 18% had arrived in the past year. There were few complaints about life in general; medical treatment in the area was generally considered adequate. The section closest to the water had the more expensive homes (median value, $23,400), more persons with college degrees (13%, compared to 7% of other portions of the "downtown" area), and more registered Republicans.

Although St. Petersburg is a major water sports capital, comparatively few of the elderly participated in swimming, boating, skiing, or fishing: on the weekends, 16%; during the week, 8%. Churchgoing was the most extensive weekend activity (20%), and television the most extensive during the week (31%). The full list and proportions of those who engaged in each activity is given as:[20]

	During Week	*On Weekends*
Watching TV	31%	19%
Housework, yardwork	22	10
Reading	19	14
Sewing, knitting	9	2
Water sports	8	16
Visiting, entertaining friends	7	14
Golf, tennis	6	6
Church activities	2	20
Going out to eat	2	9
Short trips, drives	1	8
All others	53	43

---

[19]*St. Petersburg Times,* November 2, 1972. Reproduced by permission.
[20]Ibid. November 2, 1972.

One shortcoming of the *Times* study was the failure to find out how much time was spent in each of these activities. We should also like to know something about individuals' tastes in TV and reading and, especially, to describe more fully some relationships—if they could be discerned—between the choice of activities and previous work lives and length of retirement.

The list of activities above provides some insight into persons who are relatively self-motivated. We may assume that if they used some of their time in club activity or senior centers, this proportion of time was small enough to be listed under the miscellaneous column of "all others."

I have at various times carried on explorations of the St. Petersburg region and submit here some observations to supplement the *Times* study. Not until the late 1960's did the municipal recreation department develop special programs for the elderly. For example, the major facility (Bartlett Center) was entirely youth-oriented until 1967. Now, space is provided for meetings of numerous special clubs such as state groups (New York, Massachusetts, Ohio, etc.) and the Scandinavian-American Society and Swedish Club. No attempt is made to cross generations, as in using younger people for volunteer purposes. Bus tours are arranged; one tour goes to the training camps of the major league baseball clubs during spring practice. According to the Center's director, all economic levels are served; however, no records are kept and no research is conducted to observe backgrounds or personal growth. At the time of our visit (1968) the department had no "out-reach" recreation programs to hospitals of the area. The rigidity of the center's program in 1967–1968, and, at the same time, its scope, is reflected in the following schedule:

Monday

Copper tooling	9:30–11:30 A.M.
Aluminum etching	12:30–2:30 P.M.
Basic sewing	9:00–12:00 Noon
Scrap craft	1:00–3:00 P.M.
Community singing	7:00–9:00 P.M.

Tuesday

Ladies exercise	9:30–11:00 A.M.
Ceramics and mosaics	9:00–11:00 A.M.
Modern contemporary art	9:30–11:30 A.M.
Scrap craft	1:00–3:00 P.M.
Modern contemporary art	7:00–9:00 P.M.

Wednesday

Bridge lessons	9:00–10:30 A.M.
Oil painting	9:30–11:30 A.M.
Oil painting	12:30–2:30 P.M.
Textile painting	9:30–11:30 A.M.
Scrap craft	1:00–3:00 P.M.
Card party	1:30–4:30 P.M.

Thursday

Ladies exercise	9:30–11:00 A.M.
Art workshop	9:00–11:00 A.M.
Art workshop	11:00–1:00 P.M.
Scrap craft	11:00–1:00 P.M.
Art workshop	1:30–3:30 P.M.

Friday

Pine needlework	9:30–11:30 A.M.
Portrait painting	9:30–11:30 A.M.
Ceramics and mosaics	1:00–3:00 P.M.
Dance instruction	1:00–4:00 P.M.
Bridge party	8:00–10:00 P.M.

Saturday

Variety show	7:00–9:00 P.M.

Other activities included checkers, social dance, swimming, music lessons, exhibits, picnics, horseshoes, badminton, canasta, lectures, and shuffleboard.

The St. Petersburg library has no records according to age of users or social background. Circulation of the 200,000 volumes in the whole system reaches over a million books annually. No Braille volumes are available in the three branches or two bookmobiles.

Many St. Petersburg churches have special educational and cultural programs for their older members, usually available to the general public. One example is Christ's Methodist Church, which has sponsored open concerts by the university musical groups (orchestra, chorus, chamber music). Held at 6:30 P.M., these attract large audiences; a string quartet I played with drew *1,500* elderly persons, most of whom were there long before the scheduled time. The First Congregational Church has both a band and orchestra for older persons.

The Mirror Lake Adult Center is widely known in St. Petersburg, running a column every Sunday in the *Times*. The Center is part of the Pinellas County Public School System, and has received special funds from the Older Americans Act. Courses include those in the categories of liberal education, citizenship and public affairs, and education for aging. Instruction is offered in piano, languages, and arts and crafts. Trial courses are announced to test the interest of the public. Fees are small and are waived, if necessary. Most students are between 55 and 60; however, anyone over 16 is eligible.

The cultural scene in this city is enriched by a series of concerts held in the Bayfront Center by the Gulf Coast Symphony Orchestra, the result of a union between the former symphony groups in Tampa and St. Petersburg; it is one of the few orchestras in the U.S. which operates in the black. Each concert is presented in both cities and is invariably sold out in St. Petersburg; the majority of the audience consists of elderly persons.

The Museum of Fine Arts is supported by the Steward Society, a private organization, and its members serve voluntarily as bookbinders, flower arrangers, gardeners, librarians, office workers, shop personnel, and hostesses. Art objects are created by the members for the Museum Mart and are sold to raise funds. Sunday afternoon lectures are held on such subjects as "Spanish Art" and "Indian Civilization in Mexico." The Museum's publication, *Mosaic* (February 1970), announced a special arts tour to Mexico and Guatemala for 46 of its members, a lecture on "Art and Television," a film on space exploration hosted by the member-parents of one of the astronauts, a series of five seminars on the history and appreciation of photography, and other miscellaneous art clinics, films, and social events.

Three communities lead the nation in their proportion of residents over 65—and all are in Florida. Miami has 48.8%, St. Petersburg, 30.7%, and Clearwater, 28.6%. They share a common image with the rest of the nation, suggested in two *New York Times* headlines: "Development Boom in Southeast Florida Megalopolis Creates a Host of Urban Ills" (April 22, 1973), and "The Florida Action: Fast Dogs; Frontons" (March 16, 1975). The data in this section, undoubtedly confirmed in other Florida communities, clearly indicate that for those older persons who want to enjoy the climate of a southern state and, simultaneously, to maintain contact with libraries, the arts, or other avenues of mental and cultural life, both can be found.

The challenge of this synthesis of promises extends beyond age groups or regions of the country. It is a problem confronting all communities everywhere, the resolution of two thrusts: the community as a place to live and to make a living, or the fusion of utility and amenity. The retiree is no longer concerned with his community as an environment for his working and his being. Yet, in many cases, he prefers to remain there because of the material base it provides. Why, otherwise, would older persons want to remain in New York City when they don't have to? But they *do* have to, for the atmosphere, the crowds, the "happenings" of people falling off buildings and climbing buildings, the afternoon in Central Park, their companions in the ethnic club, the varieties of shops, the *New York Times,* the good music on the radio at all times, the range of live theatre and concerts, a free afternoon at the Metropolitan Museum. All these, and a myriad of smells, sounds, sights, accidents, and human relationships make up the heterogeneous and unpredictable community. When the retiree finds himself without all these associations and images, as when he moves to Florida or Arizona, he can help to create at least some of the creative elements he desires. Among men and women of all ages, he will find a sympathetic ear.

CHAPTER 9

The Planned Community

Imagine a community center clubhouse second to none in the whole world. So spacious and so varied in the activities it offers, you'll need hours to discover all the delightful surprises within its walls. A magnificent private club you belong to the day you move in! And outside, there's water, water everywhere. The sparkling waters of King's Point Lake offer a picture perfect setting for shoreside picnics—boating on pedal and rowboats we provide—fishing off a private pier—strolling along our lake or waterways—and losing a golf ball in one of Florida's loveliest water hazards. Other waterways accent your community. And several swimming pools with spacious sun terraces all around.[1]

Thus begins the prospectus about one retirement community in Florida. Thousands have been lured to communities that have emerged for retirees by such appeals. California, Arizona, and Florida have, perhaps, the larger share. There are many types and legal arrangements. Rossmoor Leisure World of Laguna Hills, California, has described its two forms of ownership in its 1971 annual report—the cooperative and the condominium:

The cooperative mutual owns all the real property (dwelling units, carports, and laundries) and each member is entitled to occupy a specific dwelling unit under the terms of an occupancy agreement. Affairs of the cooperative mutual are governed by a board of directors elected by its members. The members pay monthly carrying charges which are based on their share of the corporation's mortgage payments, taxes, mainte-nance and other operating expenses as determined by the board of directors of the mutual.

The condominium mutual does not own any real property. Each member of the mutual owns a specific dwelling unit and an undivided interest in the common areas. The condominium mutual has certain responsibilities which include maintenance and management of the common areas. It is also governed by a board of directors elected by its members. Members pay a monthly carrying charge which is determined by the board of directors. Since the real property is owned by the individual member of the condominium mutual, any mortgage payments and taxes are the responsibilities of the individual and not of the mutual.

---

[1]King's Point advertising brochure.

In this Leisure World in California, the community consists of cooperatives and condominiums and is governed by the Golden Rain Foundation of Laguna Hills. This provides medical, recreational, education, security, and transportation services, and is directed by a professional administrator and a board of 14 resident members. The 1971 annual report noted a total of 350 individual garden plots in Leisure World, 55 classes with 1,200 enrolled students, more than 31,000 library books, an auditorium seating over 800, and a 27-hole golf course of 15,000 acres.

By the 1970's the retirement village concept had taken a strong hold in all parts of the country, including New England. As Lawrence E. Davies noted in a report to the *New York Times* (January 17, 1970), tens of thousands of elderly were leaving the clamor of large cities, looking "for people of similar ages and interests, for convenience, for peace and security and sometimes for a less expensive existence." As in the case of private nursing homes, abuses by community builders were publicized and by the mid-1970's more stringent state laws had been enacted that stipulated—especially in the recreational services—who owned and controlled what. With either the mutual or the cooperative arrangement, residents have a much greater involvement and power than in private nursing homes, with a high proportion of satisfaction in these communities.

Considerable disagreement has been encountered in the meaning of life in such communities, notably between those who choose to live there and outsiders. Dr. James Birren, director of the Andrus Gerontology Center at the University of Southern California, has emphasized the desire among many to "live with people like yourselves." Max Friedson, head of the Dade County Congress of Senior Citizens, argued that such communities "smell of death," and are a "poor substitute for living in a regular community with people of all ages." Dr. Maurice Hemovitch of the University of Southern California has concluded from his studies that the "guilt" of not going to work is eliminated here by the surroundings of ongoing play. Adjustment to the retirement community came rapidly, he found, without a need for retirees to live close to their families or to be prepared constantly (and with extra bedrooms) to entertain guests.

Several reports follow on activities in Leisure World, California and Sun City, Arizona with a more complete research excerpt from Sun City Center, Florida. These will suggest some potentialities for leisure that have not been realized.

LEISURE WORLD, CALIFORNIA

We will rely on one issue of the weekly newspaper *The Leisure World News* for August 24, 1972, for an account of leisure activities that covers both Laguna Hills and Leisure World.

Page 1: Announces a fashion speaker; three films in Clubhouse 3; a benefit concert by a chorus from Anaheim; a registration schedule for adult education.

Page 2: Attendance report on a theatrical production the previous week, with plans for booking more shows; an announcement of a piano concert by the Keyboard Concert Club; plans for a trip to the Queen Mary, in Long Beach, by the Naturalist Club.

Page 3: Announcement of a campaign speech by a Republican nominee for Congress; a buffet supper and entertainment at an "Evening on the Terrace" party by Opera 100, which also announces the Lyric Opera production soon to be in Laguna Beach.

Page 5: Photograph of a painting display by members of the Laguna Hills Art Association; announcement of a meeting of the Michigan Club.

Page 6: Picture of rehearsal of a Tyrolean waltz by members of Continental Singers Edelweiss; a lecture on drugs for Kiwanians; a meeting of the Illinois Club.

Page 13: All tickets are sold out for production of *Gems from Gilbert and Sullivan;* University of Santa Clara coach addresses Rotary Club.

Page 14: Bus trip announced to take 41 members of AEOLAC to Los Angeles; a meeting of Local Amateur Film Group; registration for Flea Market and Hobby Sales; a meeting of Ballroom Dance Club No. 1.

Page 16: Republican Campaign Headquarters to be opened; report of lecture to Leisure World Extension of Services to the Blind; lecture on his African trip by a member of the Rock and Gem Club.

Page 20: Cartoonist speaks to Lions Club.

Page 22: Fall course for transcribers in Braille; picture of bowling champions.

Page 28: Annual "Good Neighbor Picnic" planned for entire community; annual meeting of art club.

Page 41: Sea and Sage Audubon meeting.

Page 42: Meetings by Chi Omegas; Mason Auxiliary; Women's Club and Plymouth Circle.

Page 45: Art Association TV program; table tennis tournament for septuagenarians.

Pages 46–48: Announcements of various church services for Sunday.

Pages 50–51: Tennis Club and other sports reports.

Other pages listed numerous sport events, store advertisements, and classified ads. The number and variety of these activities, covered in one newspaper, speak for themselves.

There is no need to report on the range of activities in other retirement communities; in every case we may expect a similarly extensive list. One characteristic to be found everywhere is the involvement by the residents. It is *their* community—a real community minus younger persons, and missing only those ingredients that exist where young people are found, such as Boy Scouts and playground activity. Endless debates can be held as to whether such retirement communities, as mirrored in the activities above, are overorganized. However, missing from the newspaper are images of home life, for we may assume that not everyone is busy, busy, busy, going to all of those meetings, concerts, lectures, and socials. Leisure World, at the end of 1971, had 13,778 residents in over 8,300 living units in a total area of 918 acres.

SUN CITY, ARIZONA

An example of creative activity on a community level is the monthly journal issued by residents of Sun City, Arizona, called *Here*. A random issue, that of Volume 1, No. 6, March 1976, is an attractive, well-written 32 pages. For the April 1976 issue book reviews, some by residents about books written by other residents, were to be added. The March copy carried five "columns," with reports of golf, crafts and hobbies, finances, and anecdotes about residents; one article, covering a forthcoming rock and gem show; two "recollections"—one recollection of World War II by a resident, the other about her mother—plus poetry, humor, fiction, and a "chronology" of the automobile in American history.

SUN CITY CENTER, FLORIDA

In 1972 a team from the University of South Florida proposed a leisure program (in addition to golf) for the expansion of Sun City Center (SCC) by the developers, Walters-Gould Corporation.[2] The present writer served as chairman and major writer of the report, portions of which follow.[3] The report will serve as one method for the study of a retirement community, a report of activities by residents, and examples of innovations that the team felt were feasible. Only portions are presented below.

Cable Service

Today's citizens are bombarded by a plethora of messages. The bulk of them are manufactured with the basic intent to persuade. These messages represent substantial investments and are professionally produced by experts in the field of advertising. Accompanying these messages are well made entertainment products also disseminated by the mass media. They contain primarily the ingredients of escapism.

On the periphery of these heavily consumed products are informational and educational materials. These are less attractive for mass audiences, principally because they do not serve a felt need. However, with the rise of cable TV, a range of previously unavailable services can be offered to the public. The costs of over-the-air programs have been prohibitive due to the shortage

---

[2]Others on the team in addition to myself included Professors Emanuel Lucoff, Richard Brightwell, Richard Bowers, and Nelson Butler.
[3]University of South Florida, 1972. Unpublished report.

of spectrum space. The premium on spectrum has been shattered with the introduction of multichannel capacity. The ready availability of channel space has dramatically encouraged the development of software by a wide range of persons.

Consumers of the mass media, weaned on entertainment almost since birth, can be lured toward nonentertainment services if and when such products are not only easily accessible but also have a high personal priority. Many of these priorities have been identified at Sun City.

One area of great concern to senior citizens is medical information. Advisory and/or preventative data would be, in all likelihood, favorably received by SCC citizens. The development of a health-related services package is the primary focus of the cable TV proposal.

Recommendations

1. That a grant be sought to underwrite the costs of the project. Participants in the project could include the Walters-Gould Development Corporation, Teleprompter Corporation, the University of South Florida (USF) Medical School, and both federal and state governments. The modules of information would be recorded in the USF studios in color on video cassettes. These cassettes could be either aired on Channel 16 or plugged into Teleprompter's Sun City Center Cable Service on an appropriate channel, or the program could be recorded on cassettes at SCC and replayed at times most convenient to residents.

2. That program formats would feature university medical professors, area practitioners, nutritionists, and recreational experts, community residents, and outside consultants as needed.

3. That program content would be aimed toward answering questions about health costs, preventative medicine, available facilities and services, and special interest areas of senior citizens.

4. That the series would have a continuing moderator, a rotating panel of experts, and a budget for on-site filming for integration within the program.

5. That the success of such a series would be validated by staging a heavy publicity campaign in SCC before program plays. After playback, inquiries would be made to determine exposure rate, and information retained. Future program interests would also be elicited.

6. That the TV series would be accompanied by associated materials processed for dissemination through SCC's newspaper. Lengthier articles would be developed for expansion of particular questions raised during the program, but at which time did not permit in-depth clarification. Letters and other feedback devices would be employed (e.g., answering service) to involve citizens further.

7. That guest speakers would be invited to SCC to expand further on the outline presented through the TV programming. Thus, SCC would become the testing ground for a joint effort by concerned professionals aimed at upgrading the level of understanding of contemporary health care. The success of such a project is intimately tied to the cooperation of a broad range

of special interests: the private sector, the university, and the federal government. The combined energies and resources of these various agencies suggest a new approach in the utilization of new technology. The syndication of such a package of material also represents a new thrust for the Walters-Gould Development Corporation.

8. That the series would use SCC as the backdrop for the programming through national syndication and distribution. The programs would feature the imaginativeness of Walters-Gould as the innovators of a particularly high quality brand of service to its residents. SCC (Walters-Gould) would be credited by the viewing audience as a "corporation that cares." Program possibilities might include some of the following titles: *Stroke Management, Diabetes, Cancer Detection, Headaches, Malnutrition,* and *Anemic Patient.* In addition to making the series available to other cable companies, over-the-air TV plays should also be encouraged.

9. That the support of area congressmen should be sought for such a grant. A large segment of their constituencies are senior citizens. The series, if carefully produced and nurtured, could bring substantial publicity and visibility to SCC. The project, however, should be sold as a pilot demonstration project aimed at utilizing the new technology for specialized audiences when it is presented for funding in areas previously untapped.

The next step is to secure a financial and/or hard commitment from the private sector, together with the cooperation of the university, and present such a package to a funding agency.

Educational Program

The educational program in a Cultural Center for a community of retired persons should be developed gradually and in stages, utilizing specialized leadership which would draw upon all available resources.

The purposes of an educational program should be several:

1. To provide opportunity for those adults who indicate an interest in continuing their education.

2. To provide a general and interdisciplinary education for intellectual attainment, for personal and avocational interests for those interested.

3. To provide learning experiences for those persons over 50 years of age.

4. To develop interest in goals, and thus purposeful objectivity toward oneself, for the further pursuit of life and happiness.

5. To provide opportunity for older citizens to complete an unfulfilled educational objective, at whatever level.

6. To enable older citizens to develop abilities and skills to merge gracefully into a retired community.

The philosophy of building an educational component in a Cultural Center should include the following criteria:

1. Scheduling should be flexible and convenient to normal daily activities of older citizens.

2. Lengths of classes and terms should be relatively short.

3. Admission should be nonrestrictive.

4. A variety of courses should be programmed as the size of the community warrants, emphasizing those classes which help bridge the change of lifestyle from work to retirement.

5. Community leaders should be involved in program planning.

6. Since the work ethic is part of our culture, retirees should be encouraged to volunteer for duties relating to classes.

7. Education should be included as a way of life at Sun City.

8. Educational programs should be geared to some kind of physical action or skill when possible.

Some educational resources are as follows:

1. Institute of Lifetime Learning. The AARP has much experience to offer a community of retired persons, and indicates those programs and courses (activities) which are of the most interest to older citizens.

2. Hillsborough County Public School Adult Education Division. Classes offered by the public school adult education department are subsidized by state appropriations. It will be feasible for the county to staff and offer courses in Sun City as the community increases in population.

3. Courses taught by retired citizens.

4. Graduate students and faculty from various colleges and universities are available to teach a variety of courses. Manatee Junior College, Hillsborough Community College, and the University of South Florida do provide resources to be tapped.

5. Retired citizens can always commute to nearby higher education institutions, should they have the interest and desire for further education.

Recommendations

1. That an education counselor be included in the permanent staff of the Sun City Cultural Center. The role of this person would be as follows: (a) determine first-hand needs and educational desires of adults in the community; (b) determine those activities which would add to a fuller life for adults in the community, and survey all potential educational offerings available in the geographical area; (c) seek instructional staff from qualified adults in the community; (d) obtain instructors from outside the community; (e) obtain classes and instructional assistance from other educational institutions; (f) arrange for facilities and equipment for classes; (g) promote the educational program; and (h) consult daily with adults in the community.

2. That leaflets and informative bulletins be published regularly to emphasize (a) aids to a better life; and (b) potential educational aids.

3. That there be established an exchange program of citizens and students to develop further their interest in educational and vocational subjects.

4. That among possible classes the following be considered:

Orientation to retirement
Personal finance
Investments
Budgeting on a fixed income

Psychology of change

Public speaking

Lip reading

Recreational education

Reading for enjoyment

The senior citizen and the urban environment

Organizing for power

Consumer education

Vigor in maturity

Florida gardening

Marriage in later years

Art appreciation

Painting, sculpture, drawing

Workshop

Study/discussion groups

Independent study (painting, literature, etc.)

Correspondence study

Educational television courses

Foreign language courses

Politics and foreign affairs

Languages

Social sciences

Interdisciplinary liberal arts

Urban affairs

Socioeconomic affairs

World affairs—foreign policy

Specializing in the arts

Literature

5. That there be a flexibility in the way in which educational services are delivered, including classes, private study, correspondence courses, independent study, educational TV courses, CLEP examinations, GED, study/discussion groups.

Film and Tape Production and Use

There are unusual opportunities in regard to films, based on the internal characteristics of SCC and its distance from Tampa. As to the first, there must be a multitude of life stories among the residents worth taping and filming, in addition to ongoing activities in the community. There are filmmaking groups in the region, both professional and student. Further, one of the consultants has recently been active in establishing an international group for making and encouraging TV films on all aspects of leisure; the issue of retirement was placed on the agenda of major topics. SCC could become known as a major setting which carries on an active film and taping program related to retirement issues.

Recommendations

1. That steps be taken to develop a joint project with such regional, state, or national agencies that show interest, to initiate a joint project of extensive tape interviews with residents of SCC, as an ongoing American "living history" of older persons. Grants might be sought.

2. That the contacts with CBS, already begun, be pursued, as well as the proposal for a series of TV dramas.

3. That funds be sought, in connection with the international film program mentioned above, to produce one or more half-hour films, either

with regional production, the help of funds from Public Broadcast Corporation, or the cooperation of the National Film Board of Canada.

4. That consideration be given toward the establishment of a film production unit among residents of SCC. Groups of four are ideal for such purposes.

Recreational-Social Program

Most all retirement communities emphasize recreation programs. In Florida these include water and beach use, golf, tennis, shuffleboard, lawn bowling, indoor games, etc. The consultants recognize the validity of offering such activities but propose that SCC go beyond the traditional practices by providing a balanced approach that includes an interrelated educational, cultural, and recreational program.

The overall purpose, made known to present and potential residents, would be to relate the program to special needs of persons and/or groups, as we have incorporated in the recommendations below.

Recommendations

1. That there be established a counseling service, possibly funded and in cooperation with county, state, or university programs. Care would need to be taken to dissociate this from emotional or mental illness, but it should be tied in with the medical program. This could affect personal activities of a physical nature; psychological techniques, combined with good personal counseling, could be established experimentally. This type of program has been tested informally among retirees in Tampa, with sufficient interest to warrant such a program.

Included in the counseling program would be a leisure interest profile (Lip). The "Lip" service would be to identify the particular interest of each SCC citizen and assist them in contacting similar interest groups for their specific purposes.

2. That in conjunction with an expanded health service, a physical condition and medical inventory be taken of every SCC citizen. This inventory would provide the basis for individual programming of particular exercises and/or related sports activities for each person in SCC regardless of his general health. Such an approach could provide assistance to a sound preventative health maintenance program. In order to achieve this it will be necessary to develop an exercise facility with appropriate equipment. Possible staffing relationships may be available on an internship basis from the university's physical education department.

3. That for the enjoyment, relaxation, and learning capacities of SCC residents, as well as immensely exploitable promotional benefits, a series of workshops and/or clinics in the areas popular to leisure interests, such as sports (golf, tennis, shuffleboard, fishing), handicrafts, woodworking, etc., be conducted periodically. These activities should serve to give maximum exposure not only locally but on a much broader scale as well. For example, the proposed Sportfishing Clinic can be promoted regionally and nationally and

will draw attention to SCC from anglers, environmentalists, and naturalists from all over the U.S. Additional benefits to Walters-Gould and SCC would be derived by attracting potential residents to these events.

4. That as a result of comments which appear in the questionnaire returns plus consultant observations, further efforts and/or funds be expended to alleviate immediate concerns as follows: (a) additional golfing facilities; (b) lighting of shuffleboard courts; (c) construction of tennis courts; and (d) development of an exercise facility (health studio type).

5. That a full social program, presently so popular in SCC, be assessed in terms of additional rooms, equipment, and leadership. But in addition, based upon personal observation, we recommend that space provision also be made for small groups to meet for social exchange in rooms which are not duplications of home living rooms, but are more intimate and comfortable than present facilities in the SCC recreational areas. These might also be flexible, and useful for the showing of slides and films, or for committee meetings.

Aesthetic Experiences

Among residents of SCC are many who came from communities which had provided them with a rich cultural life in terms of lectures, concerts, museums, etc. The surrounding area has numerous events, provided by the several colleges, the Tampa Community Theatre, the Florida Gulf Coast Symphony, etc. In SCC itself, visiting groups are brought for performances. Just as music festivals and live theater in Sarasota now attract audiences from the region, first-rate artistic events in Sun City Center can equally attract visitors and potential residents who will look upon this as a major factor in choice of location.

There is presently in SCC a small but dedicated group of music-makers who have expressed an interest in sharing and expanding their activities. There is presently no center in the U.S.A. which has an ongoing program for all the arts directed at older persons.

Recommendations

1. That in close cooperation with present SCC residents there be planned a week-long "chamber music festival" at SCC, open to retired persons from all parts of the country, for which visitors would pay a fee. The festival might include at least one concert by a professional group, but would otherwise provide an opportunity to play in a variety of musical groups, including recorders and string ensembles. This could become an annual event; schedules could be coordinated with concerts by the Florida Gulf Coast Symphony (which has a number of retirees) and the Orlando Philharmonic (almost all retirees).

2. That the Cultural Center include plans for an indoor-outdoor theater, for films, live performances, lectures, etc. The new USF theatre chairman, Professor Herbert Shore, is very much interested in having faculty and students involved with community and older persons, and has expressed particu-

lar interest in SCC. Important spin-offs might develop; the USF group might be brought into the planning for both physical facilities and programs.

3. That the presently successful painting-sculpture group in SCC be consulted as to the need for new programs and facilities, both for classes and exhibitions, and that plans be made accordingly for the Cultural Center. As with theatre, there are USF faculty and students who have already expressed interest in participation in SCC. Among these is Professor Richard Loveless, founder and director of The New Place—a highly successful settlement-type of art program for children.

Displays, Exhibits, Museum

Flexible space in the Center should provide for several uses—as open lobby space for art displays, special exhibits, and so on. Particularly since there is no museum of significance in Tampa, one might be conceived for SCC, with a focus to be determined by a committee of residents. One example of a theme is a history of Florida. It is possible to plan for outdoor as well as indoor exhibit space. There are in the U.S.A. no miniature projects equal to Madurodam in The Hague, or Legoland in Denmark. We have direct contact with the Legos firm in Billund, which has created a village of miniature buildings from their famous construction toys that attracts visitors from many countries; they are presently constructing a similar village in Lübeck, Germany, and might consider a project in the U.S.A.

Recommendations
1. That the SCC staff pursue this matter with interested persons in the community, and if the discussions are promising, enter into negotiation for outdoor space needs with the Walters-Gould Corporation.

2. That if interest in a museum is found among residents, a committee be established to undertake preliminary inquiries on types of themes, sources of materials, costs, etc.

3. That the national celebrations of 1976 be kept in mind, marking a dramatic year for formal ceremonies related to the launching of a museum based on the history of this region.

Publications, Library, Bookstore

Some replies to the survey above indicate a need for library expansion. This may be difficult in its present location. Expansion should be considered not only for reading materials, but in all types of services. For this community of persons with varied backgrounds and time for extended activity, the library should be conceived as one part of a larger program, including education, cable TV, films, music listening rooms, etc. Among such components might be a publications program which goes beyond a community newspaper or bulletin. For example, we can conceive of Sun City Center Publications, Inc., to include a magazine and booklets for sales on a national level. With a growing population of elderly (presently, 27 million over the age of 60, one million in

Florida alone), there is a market for such materials. Contributors need not be limited to residents of SCC.

Recommendations

1. That meetings be held with the librarian and other persons in SCC to study the present library, its policies, degree of use, types of holdings, and so on.

2. That based upon the findings, plans be made in respect to expansion, relationships with other libraries and the USF School of Library Science, the Florida State extension system, the state extension library, and similar resources.

3. That meetings be arranged with interested residents to explore the need for and the nature of a publications program, with attention to such factors as potential markets, staff, sources of investment funds, printing facilities, etc.

4. That a bookstore be considered as an integral part of the Cultural Center, to sell reading materials of a general nature, with special concern for literature of potential interest to older persons.

Research

There are about thirty university programs for the training of leaders in gerontology, such as the Aging Studies Program of the University of South Florida, the Ethel Andrus Gerontology Center of the University of Southern California, and the oldest and best known, the Institute of Gerontology of the University of Michigan. Many of these centers, of course, carry on significant research, hold conferences, publish, and in general have various foundation or federal funds as well as the resources of major universities behind them. In addition, each state has a Commission on Aging, which works with state and federal funds from the Office of Aging, HEW.

It might seem presumptuous to think that a research program in SCC could reach the level of such professional agencies or institutions. Yet a closer look suggests several important and positive reasons for believing that a research program at SCC is both necessary and potentially of the greatest importance.

First and most simply, here is where older persons are—not in textbooks nor in classroom illustrations. What can be more rational than research about the lifestyles of older persons taking place where they live, moment by moment, week by week?

Second, SCC is itself in the midst of one of the nation's highest concentrations of the elderly; the possibilities of research on a regional level are unending. Further, within this region there are experts in the universities and in public agencies who can be called upon, as well as graduate students.

An additional advantage is that studies can be made of older persons from other parts of the U.S.A. who come to Florida for explorations of potential retirement sites. Along these lines, USF has been host to Dr. Francois

Cribier, member of the French Academy of Science, to study this specific problem of "migration" in retirement.

Brandeis University's Heller School for Advanced Studies of Social Welfare has demonstrated, in a study of the health needs of older persons, that older lay persons themselves can be highly effective research aides in such community studies.

Also, a research unit could be closely integrated with all other activities or programs outlined above, providing an ongoing series of observations about a community in action and in the process of formation and transformation.

If these advantages are built upon with skill and imagination, a research program of national and international importance could be developed.

Recommendations

1. That the Walters-Gould Development Corporation examine the possibilities of a research unit within the Cultural Center context, in respect to functions, staff, and needed funding.

2. That explorations be started, after appropriate preparations, to invite the cooperation of institutions or agencies for the consideration of specific projects, the integration of SCC into regional studies, and the development of residential internship programs.

For more recent studies of retirement communities, Frances Carp has reviewed mobility patterns in Houston, Thomas Meehan in Heritage Village of central Connecticut, and Jerry Jacobs in "Fun City,"[4] located 90 miles from an unnamed metropolitan area. In his conclusion on the lifestyles of his subjects in respect to the "disengagement theory" of Cumming and Henry (Chapter 1), Jacobs observed that "there is no proof for or against the contention that their disengagement is beneficial, either for them or society. . . ." The findings reveal that the older person's search for heaven on earth in the form of a retirement setting of his choosing frequently leads him to a "false paradise." Our own survey of Sun City Center indicated, however, that many find their needs met in such a residential situation. Perhaps someday a gerontology center will be established within such a community, with the residents as ongoing observers; only then will we have the longitudinal research over at least a half dozen years that is essential for an assessment.

---

[4]Frances M. Carp, "Mobility Among Members of an Established Retirement Community." *The Gerontologist,* 12 (Spring, 1972), pp. 48–56. Thomas Meehan, "Letting the Rest of the World Go By at Heritage Village." *Horizon,* 15 (Autumn, 1973), pp. 16–25. Jerry Jacobs, "An Ethnographic Study of a Retirement Setting," *The Gerontologist,* 14 (December, 1974), pp. 483–487.

CHAPTER **10**

The Senior Center

If parks bring a rural element into the city, then the Senior Center and Club are unique integrations of the sociable element of the *gemeinschafft* and the intellectual and cultural elements of the urban tradition at its best. We will present first a national summary, and then give brief reports on numerous centers in various parts of the country. For a general summary we will depend on a 1975 report of the National Institute of Senior Centers (NISC), an integral part of the National Council on Aging (NCOA).[1]

Questionnaires were sent to a 25% sample of the 4,870 organizations that were eligible for study on the basis of three factors: the center or club had to have a program directed to older adults that functioned at least once per week on a regular basis and provided some form of educational, recreational, or social activity. Although the summary below will concentrate on recreational programs and services, the study itself covered many issues pertaining to administration, staff, facilities, budgets, and programs. The final report provided data on 832 programs, of which 472 called themselves "Senior Centers," 233 were clubs which were parts of larger organizations, and 127 were independent clubs. Furthermore, 30 Senior Centers were visited.

SURVEY FINDINGS

Broad generalizations are summarized below from the final chapter (VI), "Implications for Policy, Practice and Research." The findings that are most relevant for our purpose are that: older persons increasingly accept Senior Centers as appropriate and accessible resources and facilities to meet "needs of older persons"; a growing number are "multiservice"; they serve a broad cross section of older persons; they provide an important "opportunity structure" for continuing self-realization; inadequate facilities can severely restrict the program of service; and considerable variation exists with regard to the

[1]*Senior Centers: Report of Senior Group Programs in America, 1975.* Washington, D.C.: National Institute of Senior Centers. HEW Grant, 93–P–57544/3–03; Joyce Leanse, Project Director, Sara B. Wagner, Principal Investigator. For a summary of this report, see Appendix 1, "Background Information on Senior Centers," pp. 41–53, Hearing before Special Committee on Aging, U.S. Senate, 95th Congress, First Session, U.S. Government Printing Office, October 20, 1977.

perception of senior centers as meeting places and community focal points. On the last point, the report concluded that:

> Area agencies on aging, local councils on aging and boards of voluntary agencies in many communities have not fully exploited the potentiality of Senior Centers as a place where persons needing or wanting services or activities find them available without any stigma attached. They also have not recognized the potential of Senior Centers and clubs to expand their function and to become multi-service facilities and multipurpose Senior Centers.[2]

The number of Senior Centers which offered various types of leisure activities is shown in Table 10–1, together with numbers of participants.

Table 10–1 PARTICIPATION IN ACTIVITIES (CENTERS ONLY)*

	PER- CENTAGE OFFER- ING	AVERAGE NUMBER OF OLDER PARTICIPANTS	AVERAGE NUMBER OF REGULAR OLDER PARTICIPANTS
Active recreation (hiking, dancing, sports, exercise class)	55	170	98
Creative activities (arts and crafts, drama, music, preparing bulletin/newsletter)	86	150	105
Sedentary recreation (cards, bingo, movies, spectator sports, parties)	87	249	180
Classes, lectures (discussion groups)	63	154	93

*Senior Centers: Report of Senior Group Programs in America, 1975. Washington, D.C.: National Institute of Senior Centers, p. 29.

As might be expected, there were considerably fewer participants in "active" programs and in "classes and lectures," as well as in the proportions of those who could be counted on from session to session.

	PERCENTAGE OF REGULAR PARTICIPANTS AMONG THOSE WHO COME OCCASIONALLY[3]
"Active" activities	36
"Creative" activities	41
"Sedentary" activities	41
Classes, lectures	37

This suggests that of every ten participants in one week, the recreation leader in the Senior Center could expect between three and four persons to return the following week.

Of the total time spent in the Centers, sedentary activities and meals were the most extended (Table 10–2).

---

[2]Ibid. p. 180.
[3]Ibid. p. 29.

Table 10–2 AVERAGE HOURS PER MONTH EACH ACTIVITY OFFERED*

	HOURS PER MONTH	PERCENTAGE OF TOTAL
Active recreation	22	.05
Creative activities	58	.14
Sedentary recreation	61	.15
Nutrition counseling	15	.038
Education	22	.05
Counseling	34	.08
Information and referral	50	.12
Other services (employment, health)	40	.10
Meals on premises	64	.16
Governing activities	10	.02
Leadership development	11	.02

*Senior Centers: Report of Senior Group Programs in America, 1975. Washington, D.C.: National Institute of Senior Centers, p. 30.

Table 10–2 indicates that in these "multipurpose" centers as much as 39% of the total hours were devoted to leisure programs of one kind or another. In justification of this much time, the investigators noted that such activities as crafts and trips "can have a meaning beyond their apparent frivolity. . . . They can represent learning opportunities for those who had little or no previous opportunity to travel or to develop hand skills."[4] Perhaps the writers of this report were unnecessarily on the defensive; these activities, or others, stand on their own, for all ages and under any conditions.

Who were these participants? Indeed, a prior issue is the *target* that is sought, for a constant question in all public services is whether all those who should be reached do know what is available and can get to it. Two thirds of the Centers reported having a "target" population (usually those who are over 60 years of age and live in a fixed geographic area), and estimated they were reaching 28%. Clubs generally had no target but, of those that did, 22% were being reached. (The average population of the city, town, or county of the Centers was over 350,000.) About half of all Center participants were in the 65 to 74 age bracket; nearly one quarter were between 75 and 84 years of age; 85% were whites and 10% blacks; three of every Center participants were women; relatively few Center users came from professional and managerial work backgrounds (16%), while former blue-collar workers made up 47%; one third of Senior Center participants were so poor that they had difficulty with dues; almost 60% of those who came to Centers lived alone (for clubs, between 48 and 52%); about 10% in Centers were physically disabled; and about the same proportion were deaf. Among 574 organizations, "the senior program is the major outlet."[5]

Tours and trips were among the most popular reasons for coming to Centers, especially for women and blacks. Table games were highly popular. Musical activity was provided more often than were other arts. The more

[4]Ibid. p. 30.
[5]Ibid. p. 44.

popular educational courses were those that prepared members for coping with daily problems, such as Social Security. Less than 15% took educational courses in the academic sense, usually high school graduates with higher incomes than the average.

"Opportunities that give recognition and status to participants are considered a major potential function of Senior Centers and clubs,"[6] as in self-governing bodies, with educational background a major determinant of success in attaining office. More would have liked such responsibilities (about one third).

Loneliness and the desire to meet others was a prominent reason given for attendance at Centers; others came because of services and meals. Half saw the Center as a place for leisure activities. Various researchers disagreed as to the effectiveness of Centers in establishing "meaningful relationships."[7] However, strong attachments developed among members toward "their" Center, especially among black members. "Participants' loyalty to the director was pronounced. Even at inactive Centers whose members appeared apathetic, the participants expressed praise for the director and other staff members."[8]

Barriers to attendance, as might be expected, included such factors as health, inadequate facilities, lack of "interest," poor transportation, family problems, and hours of operation. Among the major differences between users and nonusers of Centers were education (less income = more attendance), status as widows (more attended), perceptions of safety in getting there, and past record as "joiners." Center users had more likely belonged to other groups.[9]

Both the NISC and the NCOA-Harris studies inquired about the total leisure patterns of older persons who used Centers. A "lot of time" was spent in "participating in recreational activities and hobbies, socializing, walking, volunteering and attending fraternal or community organizations. Non-users spend much time with family, working, or "just doing nothing."[10]

A large majority of Center users reported that they had at least five "close friends." Whether or not Center attendance was responsible in whole or part, users were more likely to be "satisfied" with their present lives.

This report of NISC was supplemented by detailed reports of 30 Centers, totaling 85 pages. What is presented below is merely a brief summary of the type of community and the leisure program provided in each. The sole purpose is to exhibit the wide variety of Centers, a variety that needs to be stressed after an extensive review of averages and generalizations. The student is urged to go to the original source, and to consider a similar outline used by the NISC investigators for his/her own observations (community, facility, staffing, governance, program, community relations, problems) and comments.

---

[6]Ibid. p. 49.
[7]Ibid. pp. 52–53.
[8]Ibid. p. 55.
[9]Ibid. pp. 66–67.
[10]Ibid. p. 69.

CASE REPORTS*

CASE–1

A small northern city; large corporations; diversified industry; liberal pension plans; many single home units; few apartments.

Leisure program: Music and sedentary games predominate; members provide programs for schools and community groups.

CASE–2

Inner city of northeastern manufacturing area; Center provides administrative support to clubs that meet in churches.

Leisure program: Secondary to "services" such as counseling and referrals. Many lectures. Members serve as volunteer club to help other older groups in community.

CASE–3

Multipurpose center, small city in Midwest, farming and natural gas area.

Leisure program: Uses public funds, administered by city recreation department. Emphasizes creative activities and sedentary activities; many trips; few "active" programs.

CASE–4

Small midwestern town, a "wheat capital;" much diversified industry, low-cost housing, and liberal pensions; little public transportation.

Leisure program: One staff person; creative and sedentary activities; coffee at 8:45 A.M. daily; a public library service.

---

*Excerpted from *A Report of Senior Group Programs in America,* 1975, copyright © 1975 by the National Council on the Aging, Inc., 1828 L Street N.W., Washington D.C. 20036.

CASE–5

Sponsored by recreation department; small western city, five miles from a large retirement community; in a small part, surrounded by commercial property and apartment complexes.
Leisure program: Much sedentary activity—sewing, knitting, pool, and cards; stages a biweekly TV show aimed at older persons.

CASE–6

Small northeastern industrial city, near shops and restaurants; Center emerged from a club going back 25 years ago; five blocks from public transportation; Lithuanian, Ukranian, Italian, Polish, Scottish residents mingle well in Center; 99% white, blue-collar.
Leisure program: Run by city recreation department; activities segregated (by sex) except tours. Activities organized by small clubs within space limitations.

CASE–7

Remote section of industrial park in large northern city; a basement, formerly a storage room; nearby, high-rise apartment buildings, public housing and run-down single homes.
Leisure program: Arts and crafts, and sedentary program. Entertainment taken to shut-ins.

CASE–8

Small city; West Coast; favorable weather; many recreational sites; low crime; residential area; renovated warehouse; new floor for dancing; frequented by one third of area's elderly; little poverty.
Leisure program: Designed after a questionnaire study, and modified as requested by members. Much active recreation, social events, classes, lecture groups; popular education program offered

by local college; "eminent speakers series" offered free, with good publicity.

CASE–9

Urban renewal area, western city in agricultural county; ground level of high-rise for elderly; shares space with AARP-RSVP, and other agencies.

Leisure program: Emphasis on creative activities: classes, lectures, discussions; developed their own instructors to teach themselves and emphasize "learning."

CASE–10

Renovated factory, low-income area, large southern city; a satellite of a network of multipurpose Centers; part of public housing project.

Leisure program: "Wide range of social and recreational services," not specified.

CASE–11

Southwestern urban area; low income level; evident pride by members; small homes; good transportation.

Leisure program: Sponsored by city/county community services agency, serving public housing residents: "Social and recreational activities were most frequently offered and best attended," but not specified.

CASE–12

Pacific Northwest, 14% over 65, no public transportation; one room in a city building—combination office, meeting, and activity room.

Leisure program: Uses 12-passenger bus for shopping and trips (private donations); daily physical therapy class; potluck dinners, cards, quilting (for nursing homes), group singing, films, orchestra to entertain nursing homes; bingo, lectures, and discussions linked to meals.

CASE–13

In a beautiful city park, small city in Pacific Northwest. Many former lumber workers; large facility serves 4,000 per month; funded by bequests; housing authority, recreation department; good transportation; reaches 60% of area.

Leisure program: Professional "artist-in-residence" serves a broad cultural program; volunteer instructors; woodshop activities for men.

CASE–14

Northeastern city; private, nonprofit, social service agency; corporation also directs senior citizens' clubs and services in seven areas of community (Jewish and Salvation Army centers, churches and public housing projects.)

Leisure program: Educational programs through cooperation with local university. Emphasis on services; specific activities not mentioned.

CASE–15

Large colonial house, old section of old southeastern city; sponsored by recreation department. 75% of participants over 75 years old; many from professional and managerial backgrounds.

Leisure program: Creative and sedentary activities; music classes and a band (community performances, as in nursing homes); classes, lectures, discussion groups. "Scholar's program" by local university.

CASE-16

Small city, northeastern agricultural state; created in 1970 to serve former mental patients and persons over 60. Former construction or factory workers; poverty, poor housing; Center surrounded by industrial zone. Advanced infirmities; transportation needed for most members.

Leisure program: Dependent on federal funding. Emphasis on crafts; rigid program. Many men; daily attendance. Lack of professional leadership. Closes at 2 P.M.; reopens evenings.

CASE-17

Small, industrial northeastern city; economy based on making cars, metal products, textiles. Older persons 22% of the total city. Shopping and community facilities 2 to 3 miles away. Adequate transportation. Center in a single-family dwelling; limited space; no room for wheelchairs; poor physical facilities; 95% of members live alone.

Leisure program: Concentration on crafts and sedentary activities; classes and discussion groups. Members encouraged to volunteer and teach classes in four other programs.

CASE-18

Southern university community; multipurpose Center; old, renovated church in middle-class residential section; near many facilities. 60% of county's elderly live alone, 35% minority members. Serves 1,000 persons. Politically active group. New Center to be constructed with revenue-sharing funds.

Leisure program: Some placed as volunteers for young and the very old; preretirement classes for persons over 45; a Center garden is maintained.

CASE–19

Southern county, network of seven locations, six in public housing projects (activities on first floor). Recent high unemployment; good homes vacated in recession, bought up by elderly.

Leisure program: Recreation supplemented by education programs; activities not otherwise specified.

CASE–20

Jewish center, midwestern community of 300,000. At a busy interchange, no public transportation. Middle-class neighborhood. Many nonsectarian activities.

Leisure program: Recreation is center's major focus. Weekly general club meeting; choir, dancing, reading, and drama groups; intercity meetings; annual awards dinner; birthday parties; holiday celebrations. "Friendship" groups; groups developed by participants as they "discovered" their own interests.

CASE–21

City of 10,000. Many railway workers. Near mountain ranges. Two four-year and one community college in valley near city; seven four-year colleges within 60 miles. Modest, individual homes. Run by parks and recreation department; recently begun; open to those outside of city.

Leisure program: Monthly potluck luncheons. Craft programs and classes in sewing, quilting, guitar, knitting, cake decorating, ceramics, often taught by members. Monthly bus trips in groups of 10 or 11, to resort areas of Virginia, Florida, Tennessee (Grand Ole Opry). "Minibreak" on Wednesday afternoons: refreshments, games, cards, bingo.

CASE–22

Multipurpose Center in rural midwest; area once served as resort area for metropolis; during post-war housing shortage became permanent residential area. Limited medical services; all socioeconomic levels. Formerly a car agency showroom; minimal renovation. Five-member office force worked in a wide corridor. Substandard recreational facilities on and around furnishings used for dining.

Leisure program: Interested to serve all generations; now a de facto Senior Center. Recreation subordinate to service program (fund drives, repair toys, etc.) Arts, crafts, social affairs, bingo, cards.

CASE–23

Affluent suburban area near large midwestern city. Center began 20 years ago; near businesses and shopping, excellent homes nearby. Minimum age served, 50. Males, 42% of membership; 97% former professional and managerial positions; 16% over 85; annual dues, $15 for one, $25 for couple (scholarships available.)

Leisure program: The 50 or more weekly scheduled events include recreation and education, current affairs, bridge, and socializing. Numerous tours and trips, including persons in their 90s; "protected" by matched individuals to assist each other. Programs segregated by sex, with following rationale:

The men's program was originated by a small group of men who felt a need to discuss business, the economy and other common interests with other men. . . . This program includes a weekly speaker and discussion on current affairs, investment club, weekly breakfast and lunch, sports, cards, etc. . . . While the club did provide an atmosphere for socializing and an outlet for recreation, an underlying objective was to provide leadership roles for those who may have relinquished management roles through retirement."

CASE–24

Multiethnic state-supported Center, serving Japanese, Chinese, Hawaiian, Filipino, English-speaking persons; planned target: 24 inner-city census tracts. Majority users, 65 to 74, mostly farm labor backgrounds, education of five to eight years, annual income less than $3,000. Came by foot or public bus. From community, 100 instructional volunteers. Federal demonstration project originally; now, state funded.

Leisure program: Each week 57 activities offered; include recreational activities geared to ethnic interests (such as crafts and classes). No segregation required within activities. Department of education offers sewing, basic English, foreign languages, citizenship, flower arrangement, ethnic traditions. Classes in folk and ballroom dancing, crafts, music, swimming, religion, trips, etc.

CASE–25

Storefront Senior Center, small midwestern city, agricultural county. Over 85% of members live outside the town; heavily blue-collar and farm backgrounds; some blacks and Spanish. Title III funds began the program. Local support not provided; financed by United Fund.

Leisure program: Potluck meals, sedentary activities, education; craft activities, bingo and pool used to raise funds.

CASE–26

In suburb of large midwestern manufacturing city. Diverse industry, general economic security, favorable pension plans. Somewhat inadequate transportation.

Leisure program: Both sedentary and active programs: exercise classes, pool, cards, arts and crafts, bowling, swimming, lectures, and discussions. Youth volunteers visit and escort. A satellite storefront Center opened in 1974, serving drop-ins for coffee and company; attempts to intermingle storefront and suburban groups have failed.

CASE–27

Small, midwestern town; 20% elderly in county area of 50,000. Originally mining community with many immigrants; now primarily industrial. Modest housing, nearby high-rise for retirees, nearby hospital and library. Merger of federal and state funds.

Leisure program: Events scheduled: ceramics, cards, art classes, quilting. Sufficient room for simultaneous activity (cards not acceptable to some.) Staff contributions to musical activity: housekeeper also a guitarist; secretary plays piano for "kitchen band."

CASE–28

Center known as a national model, with numerous visitors. New building, unusual variety of activities. Many volunteers. Opened in mid-1950's. Present membership 3,500. Basic dues, 3 to 5 dollars per year.

Leisure program: Original activities: classes for sewing, millinery, oil painting, woodwork. Later: basic education for blind, training center for adult leaders, etc. Now, largely a mental health and adult education program.

CASE–29

Eastern city, network of central Jewish "Y" and 24 senior adult organizations, ranging from 40 to 400 members. Serves 2,500 persons. Main building in center of large metropolitan area; two large satellite centers. Most groups meet weekly in branch buildings, synagogues, housing developments, and public libraries. All represented on JYC Senior Adult Council.

Leisure program: "The Center was a beehive of activity. Classrooms were filled; a holiday program was underway in the auditorium, and a men's club was meeting on the lower level."

CASE–30

Inner core of old industrial northern city. Nearby high-rise apartments, commercial and public buildings. Other public facilities close by.

> **_Leisure program:_** Much sedentary recreation, with mixed ethnic participation, also ethnic clubs. Movies in native languages (Polish, Portuguese, etc.); coffees, potluck dinners, trips. Many club meetings.

The variety of conditions and programs among these 30 Senior Centers is apparent. While an explanation of some "principles" for conducting leisure programs will be attempted later, a few observations can be made in closing.

The one theme that runs through these summaries of Senior Centers and that holds true for the almost 3,000 in the nation is that they provide some form of human companionship. This should not be taken lightly when one of the important characteristics of industrial society is the development of characteristic places and patterns whereby relative strangers can meet on various levels of activity, whether through drink, conversation, games, dance, or the outdoor "social." There are many factors that propel us toward a growing anonymity and removal from both neighbors and friends: the smaller family, the larger urban center, the impersonality of work, the withdrawal from others through television. The elderly, especially in this country, have never been attracted to the lounge, an upholstered version of the old saloon. Nor, conversely, do other countries have quite what we call the "multipurpose" community center. The _Verein_ of central Europe is specialized even within the recreational sphere. Perhaps the Center, like the supermarket pioneered in this country, is typical of our efficiency.

CHAPTER **11**

The Nursing Home

About 79% of all the institutionalized elderly, or over 754,000 persons, are in private or commercial nursing homes. The remainder are divided into:[1]

	Number		Persons
Religious homes	1,500	@	117,000
Fraternal, trust	1,225	@	66,000
Governmental	670	@	63,000
Total		@	246,000

Altogether, it can be assumed in the U.S. that about 5 of every 100 persons over 65 live in some form of institutionalized environment. The presence of medical care is one reason for such a living preference. Other reasons may be that: (1) there is no other family to care for them (or the family will not); (2) there are insufficient funds; (3) such agencies as VA facilities provide better all-round care (including recreational) than is otherwise available; and (4) the individual can be with peers, friends, or professional colleagues.

Who are these people? Of every 100 residents, 96 are white, 50 have no living relatives, 78 is the average age, 70 are women, 60 to 80 are poor, 85 will die there, 16 have serious hearing defects, and 87% have some degree of "mental illness." A 1973–74 survey showed that of the over 960,000 older persons in nursing homes, 40% were 75 to 84 years old, 72% were women, 69% were widowed, and 40% of admissions came from private homes, 36% from general hospitals, and 14% from other nursing homes.[2]

After 1965 Medicare and Medicaid became available as federal funds, providing a bonanza for the establishment of commercial nursing homes. Stories began to circulate nationwide about the slipshod care being provided in some homes. For examples, scandalous conditions were uncovered in New York City alone in 1958 to 1960 and in 1974 to 1976. According to a *New York Times* report (May 7, 1976), a 1958 team of investigators "went on a series of night raids on the city's welfare nursing homes. They found horror scenes, with

---

[1]Robert Butler, *Why Survive? Being Old in America.* New York: Harper and Row, 1975, p. 262.

[2]Ibid. p. 267 and Senate Sub-Committee, op. cit. 1977.

patients famished and untended. . . ." Similarly, a state survey in 1974 found serious deficiencies in two thirds of the city's nursing homes, largely operated by one "cartel," with the amount of fraud estimated at over $70 million. One official called the nursing home industry a "racket;" the investigating commission, asserting that many proprietary nursing homes give good care, described the industry as riddled "with real estate operators seeking the fast buck."

Dr. Robert Butler, speaking as both a general observer and a psychoanalyst, had this to say of the rights of persons in many private nursing homes:

> These institutions are set up more for their own convenience than for the persons they serve. Institutional programs are controlled, regimented and often intimidated. . . . They resist change. They are impersonal. They lack the most ordinary pleasantries of life. . . . What about keeping a small pet? Why not one's own furniture? . . . What about privacy for sexual activities? . . . The poor have been pushed and crowded all their lives; but the middle-class patients are likely to be shocked by the loss of both choice and privacy that occurs in nursing homes, sectarian homes for the aged and related facilities.[3]

It would, on the one hand, be presumptuous to condemn all private homes, and on the other, to assume that all nonprofit homes are ipso facto providing a better level of service. The fact is that across the country, in whatever the nursing home type of sponsorship, a wide variety and level of services are provided, from the flagrant "racket" to the most exemplary.

Our interest here, however, is "lifestyle"—the quality of life for the elderly that goes beyond physical survival or comfort. As we have noted in previous chapters, governmental programs in recreation, for all ages, are often central concerns, with job specifications for professional persons. The profit situation described by Butler is hardly calculated toward a concern with such matters. The presence of a television set and the daily newspaper often suffices. Funds to engage a "social director" are present in the budget in some cases, but minimal duties are expected from the person who often doubles in other capacities. Even the possibilities of involving volunteers from the community are ignored, for the management would rather keep outsiders away, whatever their purpose. The proposal has even been made that retirees might themselves act as "volunteer inspectors" to rate nursing homes; with or without official sanction, such bodies could have immense influence.

With all this said, the remainder of this chapter will continue on a positive note to report some situations in both profit and nonprofit homes. The realities of every situation confront the recreational leader, and require adjustment based on perceptions of the actual situation.

DYNAMICS OF THE ENVIRONMENT

From the "quality of life" level, nursing homes primarily provide a place of ongoing sociability with one's own age level. As the columnist Robert Peterson has written (syndicated column, *Life Begins at 40,* March 2, 1973):

---

[3]Butler, op. cit. pp. 266–267.

Gone are the sad-faced patients who have nothing better to do than rock and rust. Their counterparts today are much too busy to rest, thanks to stimulating handicrafts and social activities. . . .

Thus the central dynamic factor of the nursing home is its actual or potential self-sufficiency—a place to sleep, eat, obtain medical care, feel secure, and have companions and things to do. A sense of *community* is possible. From a programmatic view, "extrinsic" and "intrinsic" strategies are available to the recreation director. The first develops a sense of community by relating the institution literally to the external community. *Nursing Homes* of December 1972 described one such experiment in the Evangelical Home for the Aged, Brooklyn, New York. Children living nearby were invited to use the Home's large parking area as a play space. An "Evan Youth Center" was created for the period from July 10th to August 25th, with supervised games and organized trips. The director of the Home began the project by placing invitations in all mailboxes in the four surrounding blocks. Seventy-five children, ranging from 8 to 13, enrolled and, with the help of the Home's residents, were exposed to athletics, puppet shows, a ride on the Staten Island Ferry and other activities—all free to the children and funded by the Home through antipoverty funds allotted to the Community Corporation of Bushwick and the use of personnel from the Neighborhood Youth Corps. As Janet Perry Farhurst wrote:

There was great excitement, one Tuesday, when ABC-TV came to televise the activities that were taking place. . . . The residents of the home, although white-haired and not so spry, were found in the garden, playing games with the boys and girls—dominoes, bingo, scrabble, and the checker games that some called "our own Fischer-Spassky match."[4]

Most of the recreational activity of the nursing home is what David Riesman might have called "inner-directed," as distinct from the other-directedness in the Brooklyn example. The sense of community then emerges—to the degree that it does—from social affairs, the informal chitchat, the shows, the religious activity or, simply, from being thrown together. As we will see later, the issues arise specifically in seeking to define the "religious" home, for the sense of being with "one's own" becomes basic.

The easiest sense of "community" emerges when the residents of a nursing home share a common background. Two case studies will be used here. One is based on a previous occupational homogeneity, in this case past members of the motion-picture industry. The other, an experiment in communal living, is the Weinfield Group Living Residence, near Chicago, which capitalizes on the best aspects of the traditional nursing home.

A TRADITIONAL NURSING HOME

The nursing home to be discussed below is located in Hollywood and combines the Hospital, the Lodge, and the "Country House." Lodge residents were relatively independent of supervision or care. Residents of the cottages

---

[4]*Nursing Homes* (Dec. 1972).

that made up the Country House lived independently, with maid services and two daily meals in the central dining room. Eligibility for residence was open to former members of the motion picture or TV industry who had been Guild members for 15 years or more. The majority of residents—who turned over all their assets upon admission—were former directors, writers, and grips; there were also a few actors at the time of the visits.[5]

The occupational therapy room of the hospital had equipment for pottery, ceramics, beadwork, and needlework. The lodge was inhabited mostly by residents in wheelchairs; their lounging areas had tables for four, easy chairs, a piano, and magazines. Most of the 54 units in the cottages were for single persons. There were small spaces in front of each cottage for gardens. The library for cottage residents was well equipped; materials could not be taken to the rooms. A bar was maintained, but liquor was not permitted in rooms. A modern theater was maintained for first-run movies and concerts.

An arts and crafts room in the Lodge was available for use by the residents whenever they chose, with instruction in various crafts provided once a week. Sewing seemed to predominate. An occupational therapy room was staffed by an OTR.

Recreation programs for others were planned and supervised by volunteers and an occupational therapy aide. Tripoly, travelogs, and bingo were each held one evening a week, sometimes in the occupational therapy room, at other times in the employees' cafeteria.

A special musical program was conducted by a volunteer for the wheelchair patients every Saturday morning from 10:00 to 11:00. This group, called the "Dingalings," participate in an annual extravaganza, complete with costumes. All organization, planning, and costuming were done by the volunteers. The other annual special event was a wheelchair parade for which the volunteers spent many long hours in decorating the chairs. Prizes were awarded. Birthdays were acknowledged with gifts from the volunteer guild. Barbecues were held on the patios once or twice a year.

There was a great deal of community involvement through entertainment groups which came to the theater to present a variety of programs.

There appeared to be no involvement of the residents in program planning, decision making, or other input. The direction of all programs came from the volunteer staff. All programs appeared to be routine with little flexibility and variety. The philosophy was one of catering to the wishes of individuals because of "their contribution to the industry." "We take care of our own." Apparently, friendships were renewed upon entering the facility. The level of activities was minimal and simple in nature, and organized primarily for groups. The philosophy appeared to be laissez faire: "There is no need for togetherness—they would rather be by themselves." Children over 16 years of age could visit but intergenerational activities were frowned upon.

---

[5]The following account is based on composite reports by several graduate students, Lu Charlotte, Sue Schock, Barbara van Putten, and Lynn D. Warner, from the Andrus Gerontology Center, University of Southern California, following visits made in the summer of 1973.

Meanings and impressions were assessed by graduate students in my seminar at the Andrus Center of Gerontology of the University of Southern California, all professional workers in recreation:

The prevalent tone is a mixture of both warmth and patronage. The milieu seemed secure, comfortable, adequate in terms of basic services but mostly sterile and non-stimulating. By virtue of presumed past life styles of residents, we expected a far more creative atmosphere than would be found in most other such facilities. Rather, there appeared to be far less than most. Although a tri-level facility, the hospital influence dominated. There is no basic recreation philosophy, plan or program as such. Although there are opportunities for volunteer staff to become involved in more complex responsibilities, they appear to prefer the role of handmaidens; i.e., our guide stated her preference for making beds in the acute ward.

Latent needs of the residents were not developed. As one volunteer said, "What you see is what you get." This was unexpected, in view of the talents which residents of such a facility possess—talent that is being neither displayed nor developed. If we regard aging as the continuing of one's lifestyle with dignity, what a dilemma for those who were the image makers now to be the victims of that very image.

In respect to the "balances" that are useful for assessing recreational programs, the evaluation by the same observers, van Putten and Warner, were:

1. Between involvement in selectivity and in activity: it appears that the residents are not involved in the decision-making process; activities are offered to them without choice or many options.

2. Between flexibility and routine: most activities are the same—offered at the same time, week in and week out; new "challenges" appear in the form of large, planned concerts brought in to residents.

3. Between familiarity and variety: activities are well known; new experiences are not generally thought of.

4. Between simplicity and complexity: the only activity which is of a complex nature is the once-a-year show that is put on by a small group of residents.

5. Between individual and group activity: most are solitary activities; however, the innate homogeneity of the group creates a "feeling" of closeness.

6. Between peer orientation and intergenerational orientation: activities are provided only for peers; families may visit, but no planned program for such visits or visitors is provided.

7. Between ambulatory and non-ambulatory: this is manifested in a positive way in facilities and programming.

WEINFIELD GROUP LIVING RESIDENCE

Quite contrary to the situation in the Hollywood home is an experiment just north of Chicago where a "communal" situation has been in progress for four years. The following is based on Judith Wex's report in the *New York Times* of November 21, 1976. The location is a renovated townhouse complex in Evanston, Illinois. Eleven women and one man who live there are all Jewish and average 82 years in age. Few can afford the $500 monthly fee;

Jewish Federation funds pay some of the cost. Similar innovations exist in Philadelphia and Bethesda, Maryland, adapted from comparable programs in Sweden and England. The overall purpose is to encourage each resident's independence by maintaining community and family ties while providing only as much help—counseling, homemaking, health care—as is needed, no more, no less. Aside from a cook, a parttime therapist and nurse, social workers, and psychiatrists are on call.

"Programming" in the recreational sense is not highly organized, but is built into the situation. Privacy can be achieved in each of the six units that houses two residents and includes a private kitchen, two bedrooms, a shared bathroom, and a livingroom. Private possessions and individual colors are encouraged. One woman sews children's clothes to be sent to Israel; others take trips on the minibus; some read; everyone is "busy and buzzy"; cooking is shared and takes up someone's time during the day; a volunteer male comes in weekly to read from the Yiddish Press; the residents play bingo and go shopping.

Three of the original four male residents have died. One of the consulting psychiatrists, speaking of such losses, emphasized the family atmosphere, "so intense emotion becomes involved" and feeling proves you're "alive."

Political discussions pervade much of the conversations: "philosophies and theories heat up the roast-chicken-scented air"; everyone is waiting to see the next installment of "90 Minutes at Entebbe."

Dan Silverstein, the council's program director, confessed that he didn't know how to evaluate this communal experiment. "Are we improving 'the quality of life,' and if so—by whose definition? Does this program help them live longer and is that our ultimate goal? Do we still foster too much dependency? And what is too much?"

The next Weinfield experiment, planned for 24 persons, will promote not only more family ties but also "more outside contacts," to keep the residents from retreating.

An outsider might contrast the greater *formality* of the larger movie- and TV-industry home with the obvious *informality* of the second group. The ultimate question in all group living situations, from the view of the leisure observer, is whether the intrinsic or built-in companionship and alternatives in activity are obtained at a price of loss of independence from persons who are *too* close, physically and psychologically. In reverse the question is whether the emotional price of living privately is that of potential loneliness.

Two alternatives present themselves in approaching the problem. One is the model whereby the colleagues in leisure do not live together, but congregate for the evening, or for the special activity—the bridge game, the social dance, the shuffleboard. This is the scenario known as the *Senior Center*. A second alternative model is the retirement community, in which residents live near each other, yet privately, sharing a program of activities that are community, but not communal, in their orientation—the common lapidary, but not the round table found among the Weinfield residents.

DALLAS HOME FOR AGED JEWS

This institution, headed for over 20 years by Dr. Herbert Shore, is located in the Rock Lake district, east of central Dallas. One hundred forty-eight residents live in the Home or central facility, with its living-bedroom, eating and medical facilities, several library areas, numerous meeting rooms, a Synagogue and stores, OT department, recreational areas, and offices. Near the main building are several one-story apartments for 46 persons. In between, in a pleasant campus atmosphere, is an Activity Center. The total of 176 persons, mostly Jewish, come from many parts of the country; several are recent immigrants to the U.S.A. (such as from the U.S.S.R.). The average age is 84 years, and the residents are served by 170 staff members. All pay a monthly rental, with no other financial commitments.

Residents in the Home proper consist mainly of the bedridden or chair occupants, whose major concern in coming here is their health. Apartment residents pay less than Home residents, since medical care and food are not provided for the first group. A full recreational program is carried on in the Home, whereas the Center, built in 1975 with a private gift, is largely designed for use by apartment residents, and invites older persons from the surrounding community (within 10 miles) to use its facilities for a $10 annual fee. Average stay is 23 years, with a trend for residency to begin at a later age than in former years.

Dr. Shore's views below are derived from both written articles by him (see Bibliography) and from an interview held in Dallas on September 7, 1976.

Dr. Shore noted a tendency for such institutions as this to become more flexible in their services and types of clientele. For instance, he was developing plans to enlarge "drop-in" and "day-care center" services, thereby enlarging options for those in the community who could live alone outside but were "afraid," and needed occasional or ongoing partial services, such as in the recreational area. For the recently widowed the transition to independence is often difficult.

His response to my question "What is Jewish about such a place as this?" began by noting that there were 105 nonprofit Jewish nursing homes, 20 in New York City alone. This question has been debated, with Workman's Circle homes arguing for a stress on "culture" rather than on theology.[6] Dr. Shore's own summary, applicable to the Dallas institution, included the following characteristics: observance of the dietary laws (which serves the Orthodox residents and does not interfere with the Conservative and Reform); religious services; an active unified interest in Israel, as in fund-raising and discussions and programs; a library of books in Yiddish, used, however, by only a few residents; and a Saturday afternoon Shabat, or traditional social affair

---

[6]The Workman's Circle is an established, fraternal, originally Socalist oriented, educational organization for Jewish persons that was influential in the early immigrant decades. See Irving Howe, *World of Our Fathers,* New York, Harcourt Brace Jovanovich, 1976.

with religious overtones, generally with a reading on Jewish matters, accompanied by discussion. In general, the common "Jewish" component was "more cultural than religious," a sense of being with others of a common background. However, aside from the services, such holidays as Passover have a special meaning, giving an opportunity for women among the residents to cook symbolic foods and for others to prepare special services.

An interesting sidelight of the cultural-historical atmosphere was the presence among the staff of many black persons, who were often well versed in the Old Testament and exchanged such knowledge with the residents.

The Activity Center, directed by Mr. John Fletcher, is a handsome structure with adequate space for a flexible range of leisure activities, high-beamed wooden ceilings, cafeteria, and library, lounge spaces, offices, and meeting rooms. Of the 39 apartment residents, Mr. Fletcher reported that 75% used the Center three or more times per week, augmented by about nine residents from the Home. A small gift shop sold objects made by residents as well as some donated by businesses of Dallas; all profits were used by Center activities. Ceramics classes on the intermediate level were held, with members of this group teaching beginners. An outside musician came in weekly for community singing. Motion pictures were shown; occasional trips were arranged for entertainments in the area; a Rabbi came in weekly for discussions that usually attracted 10 to 15 persons; monthly bingo games occurred in the Center (more often in the Home). Yoga classes were popular.

Mr. Fletcher noted the problem, familiar to all conscientious leaders, of finding a balance between leadership on his part and autonomy by the residents. His major training was in the social sciences and general gerontology; indeed, he found that tending to human relationships (conflicts in helping residents to find their functions in the group, etc.) took more of his time than activity leadership or organization. Not Jewish himself, he had learned enough about the tradition to evoke Jewish values in settling disputes. Asked about a "scenario" of an ideal situation at the Center in the next three-year period, Mr. Fletcher listed: (1) a feeling on the part of every resident that he/she has a role to fulfill through the Center and, therefore, feels needed; (2) a substantive contribution by the Center to the growth of each participant; (3) a closer relationship to community colleges of the area, beyond the present level of introductory courses in various crafts, so that residents would take general liberal arts courses and, in exchange, college students would intern in the Center. Residents paid a $5.00 annual fee for access to all Center activities.

An intriguing part of the total structure is the Dallas Geriatric Research Institute, located in the central Home building, serving the institution as a bridge from theory to social gerontology, but free of any research functions. Its director is Dr. Marvin Ernst, a sociologist. This Institute was incorporated as a nonprofit corporation in 1972 with a sizeable gift from Mrs. Edward Byer of Dallas. Its publication of December 1975 stated its purpose:

DRGI was established to further knowledge concerning the social, psychological, physical and environmental aspects of the aging process in general and of the aging individual in particular through scientific study and investigation. While concentrating its efforts on long term health care and services, the Institute recognizes that aging patterns cannot be understood without adequate information concerning *all* aspects of the aging process. The research program, therefore, is conceived of as a broad and diverse investigation of the total aging phenomenon.

Research completed thus far has not centered on leisure-oriented topics except for a study of "art preferences among nursing home residents."

CHAPTER **12**

The Library

In her paper "Reading Interests and Needs of Older People," Dorothy Romani of the Detroit library system wrote that more of the leisure time of retirees was spent in reading than during their work years.[1] A survey of 5,000 noninstitutionalized adults by Matilda W. Riley and Anne Foner (1968) revealed that those over 60 read more books and magazines than the 40 to 60 group.[2] However, 7% of the elderly studied had no schooling, 20% had four years or less, and 70% had eight years or less of formal education. Differences between the "old" and the "new" elderly were drawn earlier in this volume and, for libraries, the difference in education is crucial. Furthermore, over 5% of the "old" generation of the elderly were born abroad, and only a foreign language was read by many of them. In cities under 50,000 population, a survey for *Library Trends* showed that a major problem was that of supplying books for such persons. Only 27 of the 75 libraries surveyed carried such special collections.

Romani summarized the reading interests of the elderly as a whole from a variety of sources: "light romances with no sex, biographies, books in large print, westerns, mysteries, and no science fiction and no books containing violence."[3] This general summary was borne out by the Rhode Island Department of State Library Services when it had 53 persons over 65 read and review books over a 4-month period. Differences from the reading habits of younger adults were not marked, according to a 1969 study by Nelson Associates of 120,000 users of services to the blind and physically handicapped. Romani also summarized various techniques used by libraries in St. Louis, Milwaukee, Detroit, Boston and Cleveland to encourage more reading among the elderly: mobile units with hydraulic lifts, preselection for shut-ins, speakers, and films. Dallas started an Independent Study Project in 1971 which assisted older persons in studying independently for credit-by-examination at Southern Methodist University.

---

[1] *Library Trends,* vol. 21, no. 3 (Jan. 1973), p. 391.
[2] Ibid. p. 391.
[3] Ibid. p. 400.

Over 2½ million older persons are qualified for special help by the Division for the Blind and Physically Handicapped of the Library of Congress. The largest number of these, over a million, suffer from severe visual impairment. The American Library Association issued a special list of large print materials in 1959. The New York Public Library, with federal help, started its Large Print Book Project in 1966. By 1968 the number of publishers issuing books in 18-point type had grown from two to nine. For example, G. K. Hall issues popular titles; the Franklin Watts Company issues older classics; Ulvercroft, one of the pioneers, with 500 titles, has the largest lightweight collection in large print. Talking books, braille, cassette tapes, and illuminated magnifiers are available from the Library of Congress.

All told, this proliferation of special services for the elderly is impressive. Its gaps were studied in 1971 by 11 graduate students of Wayne State University's Department of Library Science in ten cities. They concluded that only a small proportion of the elderly are being serviced by libraries, and that "more and better training is needed for librarians in the field; more useful information is required on the reading needs of the aged; and governments must supply more money to provide better and more complete service."[4]

Research. Emily W. Reed noted that less than 20% of American libraries offer specific services for the elderly, perhaps because most older persons who appeared showed little extra need.[5] However, she noted further that there were almost 4 million elderly whose special needs were not met, more than 2 million who could use group services, and 2 million who could use special materials.

THE HISTORY OF LIBRARY INTEREST

Libraries, like other types of community services, have reflected society's general attitude toward the elderly. Historically, therefore, libraries did not become aware of the special needs of this generation until the late 1950's and early 1960's. Yet, in little more than 15 years, the professional library literature and the services offered by these important institutions have grown significantly.

To examine the degree of awareness among librarians, Elliott E. Kanner reviewed their professional literature from 1876 onwards in a dissertation that has had a wide impact.[6] The American Library Association, in 1915, had listed the three categories of "special services" as prisons, hospitals, and institutions for children. This neglect of older persons continued into the 1920's under the influence of E. L. Thorndike's theory that only up to the age

[4]Melody Kuhlen, "Minot Serves Aged," *American Libraries*, 2:1198 (Dec. 1971), quoted in Romani, *Library Trends*, ibid., p. 400.
[5]Emily W. Reed, *Library Trends*, vol. 21, no. 3 (Jan. 1973), p. 404.
[6]*The Impact of Gerontological Concepts on Principles of Librarianship.* Madison: University of Wisconsin, 1972.

of 45 could learning occur. Until 1941 education for the elderly was overlooked, even in discussions of "adult education."

During the war years and later, librarians were influenced by research in public policy and the emergence of such policy as it affected the segment of older persons. Research came from the fields of physiology, psychology and other social sciences, medicine, public health, social welfare, and law. Especially important was the Kansas City study of adult life, under the leadership of Professor Robert Havighurst and the University of Chicago's Committee on Human Development (1957). The *Gerontologist* began publication in 1961. Libraries and research centers that attained leadership in this field were at the Universities of Michigan, Connecticut, Iowa, Florida, Washington (in St. Louis), Miami, and the National Institute of Mental Health.

A major step in developments in public policy that were to affect libraries was the first White House Conference on Aging in 1961. Two areas among the eleven treated in this conference (population change, employment, income, etc.) dealt with subjects concerning leisure: education and creative and recreational activities. Within five years, in part due to this conference, 25 states formed commissions on the aging. Activities of the 1950's could not fail to attract the attention of librarians: formation of the National Council on Aging (1950), the new Federal Council on Aging (1956), and creation of a Senate Subcommittee on Aging (1959).

The 1961 Conference on Aging led not only to Medicare, but to the establishment of the Administration on Aging in 1956. As was to be the case with the 1971 White House Conference on Aging, a vast educational and research effort in all the states preceded the actual conference, with a substantial reference to leisure and recreation.

Kanner's careful content analysis of the literature among librarians concerning their own field indicated that "Gerontological concepts did not become widely known in the library profession until nearly a decade after the formal establishment of gerontology as a field of research and practice."[7]

The special services reviewed above testify to the fact that if a library does not now provide special services, it is not for lack of professional attention. Local circumstances may put pressure upon the library for special services in other areas, or there may already be provisions for the elderly in other neighborhood resources, or the educational and health level of the elderly who are presently served does not distinguish them dramatically from other populations.

Perhaps the central question that will confront the libraries of the next decade—especially the public or municipal institution—will be its relationship to a network of both private and public services and facilities. Librarians have moved far indeed from the stereotype of being a "keeper of the books," occasionally letting them out amidst an appropriate atmosphere of quiet and respect. It must be remembered, in reviewing the relatively new services for the elderly, that there have been many other community needs and special

---

[7] Ibid. pp. 89–90.

populations that also have needed rethinking, retraining of staff, enlarged funding, and innovative services. The full picture represents a veritable revolution in the functions of libraries.

Even a brief review of the services in this one area alone—serving the elderly—already suggests that the relationship to other types of community service has developed. The modest library in Sun City Center, near Tampa, Florida, is a branch of the Hillsborough County Library system. Perhaps hundreds of nursing homes are serviced regularly by bookmobiles or collections deposited in the homes. Libraries respond to requests from government agencies which work with the elderly. Church groups make known their needs for materials for special programs. And, in countless other ways, either regularly or on occasion, libraries find their staffs purchasing materials, arranging displays, developing bibliographies, arranging public lectures in library quarters, and answering telephone questions, all in response to the needs of older persons.

However, the "network" concept, on an organized rather than an ad hoc level, is bound to expand far beyond present practices. This concept should not begin with libraries, merely to augment the services that already often tend to drain their funds and staffs. The place to begin is at the widest level—a rich life in every community for the older person—and then to call upon the services of *whatever* institutions or sets of services are needed. We have already noted the network implementation in England (Chapter 7).

Summary: Social Roles Within Environments

In Chapter 1 the "social role" concept was described in terms of four components: social circle, function, status, and self. According to Znaniecki, who developed this construct at great length, each situation emphasizes one or the other. Furthermore, each of our roles (mother, sister, citizen) constitutes a synthesis of these components. Our task now will be to note the nature of role components in Chapters 7 to 12.

NATIONAL CULTURES

This is the broadest context, providing the widest range of role possibilities. In Chapter 7 we noted some major distinctions: in Japan, for example, the nation puts aside one day per year as a tribute to the elderly. In the U.S.A. we do not honor the elderly, but reject them from productive possibilities. In respect to social circles, the retirement from the work place may or may not affect the access which this segment subsequently has to other persons. Crucial issues, perhaps, are the relation of work friends and associates to one's lifestyle, and the relation of income to lifestyle. The argument of Chapter 1 was that leisure roles are responsive to their own social circles—the club, one's fellow tourists, one's neighbors.

The national culture contains specific clues to the functions of the elderly. The "disengagement" theory of Cumming and Henry, unfortunately, was interpreted by some as a prescription: the elderly *should* let go of commitments. It may be predicted that in the coming years, as mandatory retirement is eliminated or pushed upward in numbers of years, there will at first be a considerable number of workers who will continue to work beyond the age of 65. This proportion will slacken within a decade, during the 1980's, as the *alternative* will become important to human dignity. The very possibility of such alternatives will bring a different image to retirement, not of rejection but of choice.

Loss of status among the elderly is similarly apparent in our culture. Often, the "reputation" that a person has among his professional or work peers is unknown or underestimated by his nonwork community. The occupation itself—physician, teacher, mechanic—carries a characteristic weight across the board, so that even a bad or mediocre physician gains from the high status accorded his group. Once retired the "external" reputation may be preserved, but the standing within the profession is lost, with rare exceptions. Further, one's "status" as a retiree who becomes an expert philatelist does not carry the weight of the former occupational role.

Consequently, the *self* image becomes tarnished in our culture. Rejection by others often becomes rejection by oneself. If someone brings up the past, he is accused of "living in the past." To those who start new activities—especially those that are unconnected in the public image with aging, such as learning how to dance, or remarrying—we say, "Act your age." The ego can thus be seriously weakened. The economic and social adjustments of retirement are difficult enough without the psychological task of reconstituting one's confidence and affirmation as a person.

Finally, the losses in each of these components reinforce each other. To lose status because one is nonproductive makes one even less capable of undertaking a new career or a challenging leisure activity. Of all the environments discussed in Section 3, the national culture is the most pervasive and potentially damaging or reinforcing to the person. On the negative score, "ageism" is the core of the issue in the United States. The position taken in Chapter 7 was that a radical change in the culture is too much to wait for; the elderly, who will amount to 40% of the population by 2000, must be their own leaders in effecting change.

THE HETEROGENEOUS COMMUNITY

The community is, in one sense, the nation "writ small." Yet, even a city as large as New York is only one small portion of the national map. Its evident variety of people and activities does not subsume all the interests and shades of our national life. Thus, even assuming the attitude "You can't fight City Hall"—a manifestation of the big city's (or big apple's) impersonality—the individual does have some control over his lifestyle. On the one hand he can, under some conditions, move to another city as a last resort, but wherever he lives he can have some knowledge of the community's resources: its parks, its theaters, its sports facilities. He has accessibility to many social circles and varieties of persons. "Just the presence of this variety is in itself an element of high importance. It obviously means that we can expect to find here a wide variety of interests, audiences, listeners, and participants."[1]

Assuming, as this volume does, that leisure participation can be considered a valid social role, the social circles are the members of chess or bridge clubs, baseball teams, or library or educational groups to which one belongs. Different elements are to be found in each situation, as we will see in Section 4, and thus there is a comparable variety of functions, statuses, and "self" attitudes.

---

[1]Max Kaplan, *Leisure: Theory and Policy.* New York: John Wiley & Sons, 1975, p. 242.

THE PLANNED COMMUNITY

The intention of the planned community for the elderly is close interaction. All the recreational circles are right there, in constant sight and mind. A minimum effort is required to be on the golf course, in the lapidary shop, over the bridge table. In Sun City Center, Florida, the list of organized activities numbers almost 100. Those residents who are not active are the deviants. The rewards of participation are immediate. There can be no problem of exclusion because of ageism; just as in Israel there is no need to assert one's Judaism, so here there is a naturalness in acceptance that contributes to the satisfaction of living in the homogeneous community.

And, all the components of social role in the planned community reinforce each other; all are positive. This does not mean that such a life is suited for everyone; it is there for those who need and choose its psychological security and its confirmation of an ongoing leisure role.

SENIOR CENTER

Social roles in the Senior Center are those of transient participants as well as of more or less stable members or repeaters. Much depends on the size and nature of the center as to which predominates. Where centers are in ethnic sections of the community, a large degree of homogeneity may be expected, as among the center for Indians in Tucson, Arizona.

Social circles within the centers are specialized, constituting a set of subfunctions based on activities. Loneliness is counteracted, helping the "self" to find support through the elements of "pleasant anticipation and recollection" that is an integral part of leisure.

THE NURSING HOME

So closely linked are the lives of residents in a nursing home that emotional security predominates. Merely *being* there is the major reason for being there, assuming that the residency results from deliberate choice rather than from reasons of health or economic want. However, even where choice does not prevail, closeness of living is confused by some managers with sociability, and a TV set is all that is felt to be necessary. In such a situation the "self" is defeated as inactivity takes over; leisure functions and statuses are minimal.

Where there is an active program of activities in a nursing home, the sociopsychological milieu can approximate that of the Senior Center.

THE LIBRARY

Individualism is the hallmark of the library for persons of all ages in spite of special programs for older clientele, such as film shows, story hours, or discussion groups. These, no matter how effective, are supplemental to the primary reason for the library's existence, which is to provide materials for reading. It is possible to have a library within a center, or a nursing home. It is possible, also, for rooms to be constructed within a library complex for lectures or other gatherings. The library as library is based on a minimum of social circles, a highly personalized leisure function, an amorphous status for its users, and (to the reader in the library or the book borrower) a high level of selfhood.

SECTION 4

Activity Experiences

INTRODUCTION

There are no "official" sets of categories for leisure or recreation activities, for all such lists are constructs created for a specific purpose. Tools must never be confused with ends. Dumazedier has used these categories in the international projects he has headed: physical, intellectual, social, aesthetic, and semileisure. I have used this list, with some modifications, in my 1975 volume.[1] The present section enlarges the list.

Chapters 13 to 20 are each fragmentary in that they extract from a variety of many other examples that could be given. Yet, the selection is sufficient to understand something of the dynamics of roles, motivations, and time factors in various environments. It is hoped that we may also obtain a glimpse of how the uniqueness of the elderly applies to a given category.

One immediate problem is that some leisure activities, such as watching television, cut across several or all categories, even the physical (like sitting up into the late hours). Just as anything can be leisure, so there are no a priori limits as to those situations in which "social" types of leisure can be found: within watching TV, conversation, games, travel experience, or adult education.

A second issue of some concern to statisticians is the fact that we often do several things at the same time. Research has shown that more educated persons tend to engage in simultaneous activities; for instance, teen-agers may "study" as they listen to music, answer phone calls, and eat. A 12-nation team

---

[1]Max Kaplan, *Leisure: Theory and Policy*. New York: John Wiley & Sons, 1975.

finally settled on tabulating no more than two activities, listing as the primary one that which was mentioned first by the subject.

A relatively new issue that has arisen in research is the *timing* and *sequence* of leisure activities. This has special relevance to studies of the elderly. As Szalai noted:

> While timing refers to the point in time at which some activity is undertaken, sequential order refers to the position such an activity has in relation to those preceding and following it. We know from everyday experience that there is some "logic" in the way people carry out their activities. . . . Little do we know, however, about internal motivations and external restraints or contingencies governing sequential behavior of this kind.[2]

Again, what Szalai called the "spatial" or "locational aspect" is relevant to our understanding of the day-by-day life and leisure of all age groups. "To meet friends at home is not the same as to meet them in a club or in a restaurant." As he stated, "Even the mere proportion of time spent during the day in various locations—indoors and outdoors, at home and around home, in streets and public places . . . is highly characteristic of people's way of life."[3]

No description of contemporary Greek life, for example, is complete without noting the men sitting in the taverns all day and evening, playing a game. Or, one may see older men, former cigar makers, playing checkers or cards throughout the day in the Cuban Club of Ybor City, the original Latin section of Tampa.

An additional question has been raised by Eleanor Nystrom, an occupational therapist:

> Does participation in activity decrease with age. . . ? Are age-related changes responsible for passive rather than active forms of activity? Does a preference for various kinds of activity found among a group of the elderly reinforce the activity orientation assumed by gerontologic practitioners?[4]

Of course, this is a major issue—the differences, if any, in the leisure patterns of different ages, and what contributes to those differences. The greater amount of time among retirees would seem to be the considerable objective factor. Yet a recent Harris poll (1977) noted that activities of different age groups are quite similar:

> Comparable numbers of the young and old, for example, spend a lot of time sleeping, reading, sitting, and thinking, participating in fraternal or community organizations or going for walks. The only areas where the two groups part are (that) older people spend more time watching televi-

---

[2]Alexander Szalai, ed. *The Use of Time: Daily Activities of Urban and Suburban Populations in Twelve Countries.* The Hague: Mouton, 1971, p. 4.

[3]Ibid. p. 5.

[4]"Activity Patterns and Leisure Concepts Among the Elderly," *The American Journal of Occupational Therapy* (July 1974).

sion than the young, while the younger group spends more time in child care, at a job, or engaged in sports.

Under the consultantship of four authorities (Abbott L. Ferriss, Rolf Meyersohn, Wilbur Schramm, and Clark Tibbitts), a comprehensive research summary of some major differences and similarities between the leisure of older and younger persons was compiled.[5] A general observation introduced the 15 tables of data:

> Older people appear to use their leisure for many of the same activities as younger people, but with varied age patterns for different activities. One set of activities (fishing, hunting, or moviegoing) appears characteristic of the young. Another set (gardening or walking) seems characteristic of older people. Still another set (swimming, museum attendance, or playing a musical instrument) is widespread among the young, but largely unfamiliar to today's older generation—a possible portent of social changes to come. Thus a "mass" culture may exist at the younger age levels that will permeate society only as these cohorts (generations) reach maturity.[6]

The consultants correctly noted the difficulties in compiling data for the elderly ("confused definitions and connotations of leisure") and the lack of accurate data for the different activities.

Since the volume appeared in 1968, none of the 15 tables present data later than 1966 (on radio listening). A rough digest of the summaries is presented below. (The reader is urged to consult the original volume for sources of data.)

Older persons (those over 65) had more free time than middle-aged, i.e. about five hours on weekdays. Older women remained more occupied because of housework. Older persons reported most frequently the activities of visiting, reading, and gardening. Idleness ("*no* activity") was conspicuous for older persons. There was little evidence for adoption of new avocations.

About two thirds of older persons averaged two hours daily visiting with others, but less for those who lived alone. Visiting declined from the teens to the 50s, rising over the age of 60. There was much TV watching among older persons, little radio listening, and more interest in "serious subject matter" than among younger people. About one hour per day was given to reading, the amount of time rising with education; book reading was not much different than among younger persons. Movie attendance was markedly less for older persons, and also for theater, concerts, and outdoor sports.

---

[5]C. Gordon, C. M. Gaitz, and J. Scott, "Leisure and Lives: Personality Expressivity Across the Life Span," in *Handbook of Aging and the Social Sciences,* R. Binstock and E. Shanas, editors. New York: Van Nostrand Reinhold Co., 1976, p. 333.

[6]Ibid. p. 511.

As to hobbies (woodworking, photography, etc.), little variation was seen among age groups.

Most outdoor activities declined with age, except for walking. Gardening activity increased.

As to vacation and outings, older persons over 65 took fewer, shorter trips.

Many of these and other activities will be discussed in the eight chapters of this section. I would note that, valuable as the data above remains for the purposes of leadership and public policy, such studies tell us about *what is;* they provide us with some sense of reality about what is expected or achieved by the leadership. I remind the reader of Chapter 4—the need to become concerned with potentiality as another form of reality. Hence, we need to start with such generalizations as those given above, and then move on to innovative possibilities that do not fall into the purview of either scientists or pollsters.

Each of the chapters in Section 4 will provide illustrations of activities; more, they at times point to new directions. Research studies will not be ignored, yet such reports are not the primary purpose of this section.

CHAPTER **13**

Aesthetic Activity Experiences

With the aesthetic way of approaching life, we turn directly to matters of personal growth, internal security, and potentials of self-realization. As I have noted, it is a focus that

is based on the essence of originality in putting together things, objects, ideas, forms, and time and space relations in ways that have not been done before, but on the principle of beauty. . . . Analysis and assumption of many kinds enter into the aesthetic or creative process. But it has added a third element—subjectivity—whose essence, by definition, is that it cannot lend itself to generalization or objective verification. . . . This is its strength and reason for being. . . .[1]

The aesthetic, thus viewed, reaches far beyond the arts. There can be creative, transformative, and subjective elements in travel, games, educational experience, conversation, love, and family relationships. It cannot be assumed that the uniqueness of the aesthetic as a whole or of the arts as one of its manifestations is more valid than other forms of experience that are available to the elderly. We can say that, in some situations, the uniqueness of the arts is as relevant to some as the essence of the analytic experience in the sciences, or the nature of the assumptive experience in religion, is meaningful to others. What we have in the arts are such elements as a continuity with the past of civilization or of one's own existence, an ongoing alternation of tension and relaxation, a range of participation from that of the novice to that of the artist, access to a magnificent array of masterpieces in such varying genres as music, theater, painting, sculpture, dance, architecture, and literature and, finally, a common social value that serves to create friendships across lines of faith, creed, origin, skin color, material possessions, or educational background. There are, within this range of specific characteristics, the possibilities for experience in the arts that concentrate on such internal elements as line, form, color, thematic development, climax, and imagination or, on the other hand, such external factors as an evening away from home or the stimulation of memory.

---

[1] *Foundations and Frontiers of Music Education.* New York: Holt, Rinehart and Winston, 1966, p. 20.

137

AESTHETIC AND SOCIAL FUNCTIONS

We would ourselves sell the elderly short and fall victim to "ageism" if our whole approach to the arts were to emphasize their social functions. At age 66 one does not have diminished feeling for pure color on a canvas or the shape of a sculpted piece. If anything, the transition from 26 and 36 to 66 is towards sensitivity of the nonsocial experience, increasingly supplemented and enriched by the accumulated emotional experience that comes with maturity and years.

The social and aesthetic are not necessarily antagonistic, as may be shown by an example from Boston University in the early 1960's, when we brought 45 persons, all over 65, into the arts for the first time as active participants. Twelve of them became students of painting in the School of Fine and Applied Arts, under the instruction of a young lady who was thereby earning her Master's degree in Art Education. The others were taught piano or organ by university students who earned credits toward their own degrees. Professor Louis Lowy of the School of Social Work and I met with the young teachers and, while freeing them of fears about relating to persons old enough to be their grandparents, discussed with them the careful records we wanted after every lesson. These records covered the content of conversation, observable changes in aesthetic growth, relationships with family or friends resulting from this experience, and technical progress with the instrument or the paintbrush. We were also concerned with evidences of a growth *future orientation*, in such ways as planning for the trip to the University and anticipation of their miniconcerts and exhibitions for friends. The experiment grew out of a panel discussion several years previously, when Robert Kastenbaum and other psychologically oriented gerontologists were beginning their research into death. I had maintained that one way to do this was to explore death as antithetical to birth, rebirth, replenishment, and exploration—in short, through the arts.

As expected, from our close observations and many interviews with both generation groups, we found a growing bond and even a love between older student and younger teacher in almost every case. The "future orientation" amounted, indeed, to new purposes for living. New relationships could be observed between our students and their children, based on respect for their accomplishments. A new communication arose between our students and their grandchildren, especially in those cases where both came to the Commonwealth Avenue building together, each to take instruction in one of the arts with his own peer group. Where, in such a program, do the social and aesthetic components diverge?[2]

The second illustration of pure and social functions existing within each other is the current Chicago project known as Free Theater Too, begun in 1975 as an outgrowth of the Free Street Theater (organized in 1969). According to Richard Driscoll, technical director of the parent group, the project

---

[2]Ibid. pp. 155–158.

with older persons grew from an interest in breaking down barriers—racial, economic, or age-related. "I am concerned that it not become a project for aging Americans only. Our whole purpose is to continue an ongoing intergenerational communication."[3]

In the beginning 20 members of the company worked with about 20 volunteer seniors. Long informal conversations were held so they could get well acquainted. No technical training in theatre was given at first, but came along later as needed. Extensive information about the lives of the older persons was gathered, and fed back by the younger people to interpret attitudes and feelings. Out of all this came a set of life stories, which were then tied together with narrations by the actors about their lives and aspirations in a form that appears to be an ongoing improvisation to the audience.

In their beginning explorations with institutions that serve the elderly, the organizers were told again and again, "This is not for our people. Their lives are programmed. They don't have the energy." The problem was to go beyond the administrators, who were in a direct sense practising "ageism." By now the group has traveled to 20 or more states in a van, and has performed in shopping plazas, for conventions, schools, and on street corners.

The comments of one participant, Ed Rawson, illustrate the meaning of this experience:

I really didn't join Free Street; I was dragged into it. I am a 77-year old mechanical engineer with a background of orderly thinking, planning, developing, reaching an objective at low cost in a hurry. When I retired last year, our daughter heard about Free Street and insisted we join. We said absolutely not. Mother had played piano professionally but I had never done anything like this. She persisted and we were dragged down there.

My interview consisted mainly of my alibis. I said if it were for children, I'd be great. I've always been good with kids, telling stories, improvising. But I couldn't do it with adults.

We reluctantly went back. I'd seen the junior company eight or ten times and was impressed with what they did but didn't have the slightest idea what this thing was going to be all about for us. We met every day for a month and it looked like a mixed-up mess to me, like a joke.

But we started falling in love with the young people we were working with and I found out they were falling in love with us. If it had been all seniors I don't think I would have ever made it. I had a wall built up in front of me about seniors, even though I am a senior. I had seen my father in a home for 10 years and had seen what the seniors do in Florida with the usual play acting. I said I would never be a part of that.

After a couple of weeks, though, I was kind of anxious to go down there every day and pretty soon I saw something jelling. I saw some scripts developing. The third week I began to see what was formulating. I began to see this thing developing as if I were developing a piece of equipment. I got very much interested and got over being scared. When the final script developed, I was absolutely amazed; it was just fabulous. I look back in wonderment at what happened. I've learned some very profound things about myself. The creative ability I had with kids and in my engineering work apply to what I'm doing now. It's changing my lifestyle and I have a whole new career at 77.[4]

---

[3]Personal communication.

[4]Ed Rawson, *Arts and the Aging, An Agenda for Action.* Washington, D.C., The National Council on the Aging. Jacqueline Sunderland, editor, 1977, p. 38. Proceedings of Minneapolis Conference, Oct. 17–19, 1976, convened by the National Center on the Arts (NCOA) and Minnesota Arts Board, and the Minnesota Governor's Citizens Council.

Portions of the script to which the remarks above refer are given in Appendix A.[5] It indicates the technique of building a dramatic interplay by the use of material from oral histories.

WAYS OF BECOMING INVOLVED IN THE ARTS

Aesthetic activity experience in relation to social organization includes four elements:

Creativity—writing, composing, painting, etc., as well as performing;

Distribution—library, church, government, etc., to provide a bridge from creators to public;

Consumption—public to both live and recorded or reproduced art;

Education—preparation for the three above, whether or not in formal school situations.

Each of these opens a wide range of leisure opportunities for older persons. Amateur creators, for example, are found in all the arts—as painters, composers, writers, filmmakers, and so on—and in even larger numbers are re-creators on the stage, dance floor, or in the home. The 1500 or more symphony orchestras in the United States are, for the most part, "community" groups, often composed of persons from high school age to retirees. Many thousands across the country are to be found in tasks that make the arts viable, from raising money for a local museum to making costumes for the local theatre.

The elderly, as well as all age groups, participate in the arts as consumers, either as formal members of audiences in theaters, concert halls, and galleries, or as an informal public that is served by architecture, radio and TV, and industrial design in the home.

Most of us, no matter what our age, enter into the aesthetic scene as consumers or public. National figures on the degree of interest are impressive. A significant report was issued in 1977 which concluded that 89% of American adults (almost 130 million) consider the arts as important to the quality of life; 64% (over 93 million) were willing to pay an additional $5.00 in annual taxes for support of the arts. The need for developing arts interest among the elderly is clear from a Ford Foundation study as well as from this data. The former noted the decreasing number of elderly in audiences at professional performances; for example, in the year preceding the study, 7% of those over 50 had attended a symphony concert, compared to 9% of those in their 40s, 10% in their 30s, 11% in the 20s, and 13% of younger persons.[6] The Harris study noted a comparable result: "People 16 to 20 and those 21 to 34 attended museums an average of 4.4 and 4.7 times, respectively, during the year prior

---

[5]Reproduced with the kind permission of Mr. Driscoll and Free Theater Too.

[6]"A Survey of the Characteristics and Attitudes of Audiences for Theatre, Opera, Symphony, and Ballet in 12 U.S. Cities," *The Finances of the Performing Arts,* New York: Ford Foundation, 1974, Part II, p. 16.

to the survey, compared with 1.9 times by those 65 and over. Sixty percent of the elderly never attend any of the performing arts."[7]

The most intensive study of the elderly as public for the arts has come from the Arts Management Program of the University of Wisconsin. Professors A. C. Johnson and E. A. Prieve recognized that many older persons simply cannot afford concerts, or lack transportation, or prefer to stay home at night. Yet, in their report, *Older Americans: The Unrealized Audience for the Arts,* they insisted that "Rich in life experience and often possessing substantial leisure time, the older Americans would seem a natural addition to an arts audience."[8] Their survey indicated that older persons constituted less than 10% of the audience in nearly 80% of all the arts organizations they surveyed. Perhaps as regretful was the fact that among arts administrators less than 8% were interested in the elderly. While 60% of organizations agreed with the difficulty of attracting the elderly, less than half (43%) offered discounts on tickets, as the majority do for the young.

As shown above, many older persons are students of the arts. This section will turn to the first and third of the schematic elements already noted, creativity and consumption. The theater, as we have noted, offers particular advantages for our purpose. Current efforts of the American Theater Association underscore the possibilities. The ATA numbers over 6000 members who represent all theater except Broadway (professional, community, children's, etc.). Several years ago the ATA appointed a committee of its former presidents to recommend a program by which theater experiences could be developed with elderly persons. A tentative outline of "types of participating experiences" was drawn up as a guide, while a series of regional meetings were being considered to lead to specific programs throughout the country.[9] This guide is reproduced below.[10]

Theater of Creative Experiences

1. Performances of short and long plays, and cuttings from long plays, in the traditional style (lines memorized, business, movement, simple or elaborate productions).

2. Performances of short or long plays or cuttings in the script-in-hand or Readers Theater style.

3. Improvisational theater (creative dramatics). Many forms. Very acceptable and used very successfully under skilled leadership and direction.

4. Participation in the production of college, community, school, Children's Theater and other theaters in appropriate acting roles and suitable production and

---

[7]Louis Harris Inc., *Americans and the Arts, a Survey of Public Opinion.* New York, 1977, p. 31.

[8]Madison: University of Wisconsin, Graduate School of Business, 1976.

[9]The chairman of the ATA committee is Dr. Robert Kase, The Canterbury Tower, 3501 Bayshore Blvd., Tampa, Florida, 33609, former Director of Theater at the University of Delaware. Other members are: James Butler, Roger Cornish, Marjorie Dyke, Kenneth Graham, Paul Kozelka, Vera M. Roberts, Horace Robinson, Dina Rees Evans Shaw, Loren Winship, and Brian Hansen. According to a letter of February 23, 1978, the Senior Adult Theater Project of ATA had received a grant from the Alliance for Arts Education "to conduct a status study of the varieties of theater opportunities and activities for Senior Adults, as well as of the literature in the field."

[10]From an informal memo drawn up by Kase and his committee.

management positions (especially backstage, shop, publicity, house management, box office, etc.). Not to replace students or other regular members of the theater, but to release them for other positions. This contributes to bridging the generation gap and provides opportunity for cooperation with the NARP Generation Alliance Program and similar programs.

Theater of Audience Experiences

1. Reduced rate or free tickets to encourage attendance at regularly scheduled performances. (Unlimited or restricted but aimed at securing capacity audiences.) Almost every theater can at least fill its unused seats in this way. Consider also special daytime performances.

2. Invite Senior Adults to attend class and lab performances. More varied audience reactions would be helpful to the production.

3. Tour productions of all kinds, especially Senior Adult production to other Senior Centers or organizations.

Some Suggestions

1. *Contacts.* In every community there are Senior Adult clubs, organizations, retirement centers, etc. Consult local governmental agency on aging.

2. *Approach.* The Senior Adults may be small on theater experience, but they will be large on life experience. Keep this in mind in determining your attitude toward the group with which you are working.

3. *Cooperative effort.* From the beginning the program should be a cooperative effort of ATA members and the Senior Adult group. It should be their project as well as yours. You are working with them, not for them. They should share problems of rehearsal space, production facility, transportation, expense (even minimal items like scripts, royalty if any, etc.). The project should involve not only cast, but prompter, understudies, assistant directors, stage managers, property and costume people, etc.

4. *Simple productions.* Keep productions simple in the beginning. In curtain speech ask audiences to use their imaginations as they do for movies or television, but in a different way.

5. *Script-in-hand performances.* Script-in-hand or Readers Theater type performances are often good to start with, as they overcome the initial imagined fear of memorization. According to many, memorization is not the obstacle it appears to be at first.

6. *Play selection.* It is probably best to start with plays easy to cast and with subject matter of special interest to Senior Adults. The cast for *I'm Herbert* by Robert Anderson (Dramatists Play Service) requires only an elderly couple and is very funny. Two collections of short plays written especially for Senior Adults are *Short Plays for the Long Living* by Cornish and Orlock (Bakers Plays) and *An Evening of One-Act Stagers for Golden Agers* by Brown (Bakers Plays). A list of plays which have been used successfully is being compiled by the Committee. Remember, however, that the real value of the program will be realized by the quality of theater which is experienced.

7. *No staff members available.* Here is a real opportunity for your best-trained upper-class and graduate students to get valuable experience.

8. *Expenses.* Financial support of programs for the elderly is usually available in every community through government agencies, local business and service clubs, etc. Even the productions will have some expenses, as for scripts and royalties. Royalty fees are often reduced or remitted on plays given by a group before its own members, provided the request is submitted well in advance to a play publisher. Senior adult organizations often have some funds of their own for expenses.

INTEGRATION OF TYPES OF PARTICIPATION

There is no need for an arts policy for older persons to differentiate between creating, assisting in the promotion, or serving as public to the arts. Examples of their overlapping are seen on the neighborhood level, and have recently been encouraged by federal funding. Virginia Cassiano, Project Director for the Neighborhood Arts Project of the National Endowment for the Arts, has reported on urban developments:[11]

Many of the neighborhood groups are trying to draw on the rich cultural backgrounds of now-aging immigrants or first-generation Americans. The aging in these urban centers are the vital link that transmits culture, values, and heritage. One of the ways that this takes place is through the arts. Creative expression has been for many an informal activity throughout their lives—embroidery, weaving, and ceremonial decorating, for example, with the products a creative expression of their particular culture. Many older Americans who were immigrants brought with them a lifestyle rich in tradition of caring about the esthetics of everyday life. Those same individuals are still stimulated by the need to create and can arouse others with their unique perceptions of the environment. . .

A few neighborhoods have sought to develop programs which serve these creative needs of the older residents. A neighborhood in Baltimore, Md., is involved in an operation called Southeast Arts and Crafts. It is a design, marketing, and production operation established to meet needs of the Southeast Community Organization, a nonprofit organization of more than 50 local neighborhood groups. Southeast Baltimore is a unique community with a large proportion of the population being first- and second-generation immigrants from the Ukraine, Poland, Greece, Italy, and Finland. Also, the elderly population in the community comprises twice the national average of elderly. Implicit in this population mix is the need to supplement the fixed incomes of senior citizen residents and to find ways of preserving and transmitting their cultural heritage.

One year ago Southeast Arts and Crafts expanded its production capacity, and therefore its income to local senior citizens, by establishing its own marketing and designing operation, called Ethnically Yours. Ethnically Yours is a line of clothes which exhibits ethnically inspired designs. Recently, Ethnically Yours has moved into more contemporary styles and will market a higher quality of items.

In Cleveland the organization Peoples and Cultures supported workshops on folk arts and crafts to reacquaint the participants with their heritage. Started with very small seed grants, Peoples and Cultures is showing what the aging through their experience and through their heritage can do in the arts for the city of Cleveland.

The UAW retired workers' centers in Detroit, dissatisfied with the usual kinds of creative expressions given to older individuals, have introduced workshops under a grant of the Michigan State Arts Council, emphasizing colonial crafts, especially those of dyeing, spinning, and weaving. Classes include historic background, methods used, demonstrations, and participation in all phases of the process. The revival of the craft of weaving provides another form of productive creative expression for those retired workers, many of whom have previously worked with their hands for a living and now can use these skills to create for themselves.

The Museums of Lithuanian Culture in Chicago organized a program for crafts workshops in which the seniors act as consultants to the professional teacher. Jobs through the Comprehensive Employment and Training Act were given to seniors in the neighborhood to work in the gallery and archives because of their knowledge of the culture and the fact that they are bilingual.

Arts programs must grow out of an environment which views the elderly not as clients or problems but as fellow members of the community, who can and should contribute ideas and energies toward the planning and realization of the programs.[12]

Other directions were summarized in the Senate Subcommittee hearings of December 15th, 1976. Below are listed examples of grants provided to

---

[11]Senate Subcommittee Hearings, December 13, 1976. The report comes from the National Center for Urban Ethnic Affairs, Washington, D.C.
[12]Ibid.

facilitate exposure to professional exhibitions and performances, as in the provision of transportation.

—The Old Creamery Theater Co., Garrison, Iowa, provides ticket discounts for the elderly to attend its dramatic performances;

—The Dubuque, Iowa, department of recreation provides persons 60 years and older with tickets and transportation to plays, concerts, historical tours, and art exhibitions;

—The Hispanic American Dance Co., New York City, devotes 1 week of its annual season exclusively to performances for senior citizens;

—The Opera Guild of Greater Miami brings opera concerts and staged performances of opera and piano to an estimated 30,000 older persons of Dade County at an average admission price of $2 per ticket;

—The Cincinnati Ballet Co. programs weekend concerts for the elderly which include free tickets and transportation;

—The Circle in the Square, New York City, is continuing its program of distributing free tickets to the elderly and economically disadvantaged to its four major theatrical productions each season;

—The Chinese Cultural Foundation of San Francisco maintains a strong, multiarts community program for older persons, including touring performances and festivals;

—The Maryland Arts Council is expanding its 10-year-old program of art exhibitions from the Baltimore Museum of Art to facilities serving the elderly;

—The Durham, N.C., Arts Council sponsors twice-monthly professional arts programs in senior residential communities;

—The New Stage Theater, Jackson, Miss., is offering a series of free tickets for plays and transportation to 3,000 low-income elderly citizens, which includes after-performance seminars led by directors and actors; and

—Hospital Audiences, Inc., and its affiliate chapters across the country are continuing their successful programs of free and discount tickets to older persons, as well as bringing professional artists into hospital wards and nursing homes to give performances.

Among the federal programs funded in 1976 to provide direct experiences for the elderly in "hand-on" creative experiences were:

—Artkare, Inc., Dayton, Ohio, sponsors artists who give weekly workshops and demonstrations in area nursing homes;

—The West Nebraska League of Arts has developed an "artists outreach program of professional artists in several disciplines who give workshops and instruction in senior citizens centers and nursing homes;

—The Theater Project of Antioch College, Baltimore, Md., is developing a personal oral history and performance project with older Americans based on its successful arts exposure program with the International Ladies Garment Workers Union;

—The Madison Civic Repertory Theater, Madison, Wis., is involving the elderly in a variety of activities at the theater, including workshops in playreading, costume and set design, acting and directing classes, and play discussion groups;

—Akron Rehabilitators of Community Houses is providing a ceramic art training program for senior citizens under the direction of a master craftsman;

—Free Street Theater, Chicago, Ill., gives instruction and training in the theater arts to older individuals who, in turn, have formed their own repertory company (Free Street Too) and perform for audiences of older persons around the country. Presently, the two companies are developing ways of integrating their casts and activities to promote intergeneration programs for individuals of all ages. . .

In 1976 the National Endowment for the Arts supported several special projects to serve as models for the nation:

The Minneapolis State Arts Board and the Community Arts Agency of St. Paul-Ramsey Arts and Science Council (COMPAS) is providing opportunities for older persons to become involved in many art forms. Workshops conducted by professional artists are offered in music, painting, pottery, dance, theater and writing. A senior chorus and theater group give performances by seniors themselves. During the year these workshop activities were integrated into another COMPAS arts project for seniors funded by the Administration on Aging. This successful 2-year demonstration project placed artists in long-term residencies with older persons in housing sites, nutritional sites, and senior citizen centers.

An Endowment grant to the Iowa Arts Council is permitting the continuation of a music, poetry and visual arts program for older Iowans. "The living arts program" involves professional artists who work with 300 older persons at 13 sites throughout the State in developing skills and exploring dormant talents. The program is being expanded to include 20 artists at 40 sites during 1976–77. The poetry component of this program recently published a book containing the poems of senior poets entitled "Speak Easy."

The Endowment's folk arts program has funded a significant number of older folk artists and projects by and for older Americans. Approximately two-thirds of the folk arts program's $1.6 million budget for fiscal year 1976 was devoted to preserving our Nation's cultural heritage by providing opportunities for older artisans to perform, teach, and exhibit their crafts and by recording these contributions to our cultural legacy. Included among the many grants of the folk arts program which utilized older Americans as the transmitters of a culture from one generation to the next are:

—Support to make videotapes of the stories and life-styles of storytellers in the upper east Tennessee region;

—Support of a project to document black Mississippi folk arts for an exhibition within the State and for archival uses;

—Support to document the Indian tribal traditions through and by elderly tribal members of tribes in the upper Northwest;

—Support of a team of trained field collectors, all of whom are older Americans, to work with the Oklahoma Indian tribes in recording and photographing their cultural traditions;

—Support of a project to strengthen the tradition of sacred harp singing through a program of demonstrations conducted by experienced older teachers; and

—Support of a festival in Los Angeles presenting American folk music and dance in concerts and workshops involving older artisans as performers and instructors.

The Endowment's Bicentennial program, "City Spirit," assists planning activities for a variety of cultural efforts which seek to broaden the role of the arts in a neighborhood, town, city, country, state, or region. The program is based on the concept that the interaction of a community's diverse interests—business, labor, government, religious groups, educational institutions, civic organizations—can provide new cultural programs for the community. The inclusion of organizations and institutions serving older Americans has been well represented in "City Spirit" grants.

These federal programs in the arts, in addition to their inherent value, have thereby helped to keep the elderly in touch with the mainstream of American social, educational and creative life.

Further initiatives and innovative demonstrations may be anticipated in the future. However, the impetus will eventually have to come from new patterns of cooperation between professional and community artistic components on the one hand and the elderly themselves on the other. These trends and needs must, of course, be viewed in the large context of images that the elderly and the artistic community have traditionally held about the other.

TRADITIONAL TENSIONS AND CHANGES

The arts, say the purists from the arts community, take long preparation and sustained commitment; it must at all costs avoid dilettantism, Sunday painters, Lawrence Welkians, and the community songs of Keen-Agers, Golden-Agers, or Senior Citizens. Mid-cult and Mass-cult are bad enough without Medicaid culture! An association of art with the elderly flirts with the bad word "recreation" and the suspect phrase "art education." These deal with social or human values, and are therefore akin to the lower level aesthetics inherent in program music, opera, and the Tschaikowsky-Menotti-Bernstein syndrome. Furthermore, there is a strain of "therapy" here that lends extra impurities to a situation which, like the "Legionnaires" disease of Philadelphia, evades accurate analysis but strongly suggests avoidance. Such is the "purist" art attitude.

The elderly, for their part, also have characteristic traditions to protect and stereotypes to enjoy. Six or seven decades of living have included, in all cases, some contact with the arts; everyone has been affected, from all sides, by architectural shapes, fashions, and symbols, music, from TV commercials upwards, pictures, product design, and posters, and motion pictures, church rituals, and pageantry. How deeply, how purposefully, and on what level of creativity or consumption is an individual matter for all age groups. Yet our elderly have grown up with the fashionable stereotypes of a half century ago: first things first, such as hard work and practical matters; talent is something one is born with; my son, the successful doctor, and not (heaven forbid) the starving actor; the arts are nice, but not with my taxes. In this situation the elderly are avidly assisted by those within the settings of community centers and nursing homes who are responsible for stimulating the "client" or "resident." Their training is to comfort, soothe, and schedule, rather than to challenge, stimulate, or innovate. Social gerontology as a whole divides itself into those who stress "disengagement" or "activism," but in general those older persons who lean toward the simple games and socials—disengaged, in a sense—have had considerable help from recreational leaders in their midst. And, only 5% of our elderly live in nursing homes where there might be an organized program for creative activity; the majority of these are in homes where the TV set is often the basic recreational equipment in what has been called the "half-way house between society and the cemetery."

Thus, in general, there has been a marked indifference between the arts and the elderly. For the arts, social or personal functions have seemed to be on a lower order, remindful of therapy at best, propaganda at worst. For most elderly, active participation in the bulk time of retirement has gone toward activities in which they feel secure, that take little fresh learning, and that are free of elitist taint.

New factors are developing on both sides. The professional art community has found its destiny intertwined with the general social, political, economic, and technological scene. Revolutions that emerged from the stirrings of women, blacks, and youth have had deep impact, as in the arts of the "inner city" and the schools. Television has enlarged audiences and affected taste. On the international level as well the new intent to "democratize the arts" was clear in 1970, when I sat with the ministers of culture of the Western countries, called together by the Council of Europe, to ponder their responsibilities to the larger community as well as to the concert hall and museum. On several recent trips to Iran, I have observed their social planners wrestling with ways of maintaining Islamic traditions in the midst of dramatic industrialization. One example was the creation of national workshops; a more recent example is the forthcoming Farabi University, to be entirely devoted to three curricula in the arts—creativity, national cultural policy, and scientific analysis of the arts as social process.

In our own country, Bicentennial year assessments of our national trends and values merely climaxed serious discussions that were already underway concerning the place of the arts in a democratic society. Inflation, recession, energy shortages, Vietnam, and Watergate, together with the revolts of minority groups, combined to raise questions about the quality of life. It was clear that material goods alone, even the high level for many of us, had raised the question not only of equity but of anxieties, goals of life, and the issues of technology vs. humanism—issues raised by Jacques Ellul, Lewis Mumford, Alvin Toffler, Eric Fromm, and others. The arts, aside from the bread and butter issues of their survival, as studied by the Rockefeller and Ford reports, became a central issue in discussions of national purposes. The familiar issue of "mass" vs. "popular" culture, although still occasionally revived in the *New York Times,* is fundamentally a dead issue: the arts *are* now accessible to the masses; social class is *no longer* the determinant of taste; government *has* a responsibility; the amateur is *no threat* to the welfare of the professional; the culture complex is an integral part of the *community and region;* and, even in a free capitalist society, the ultimate commitment of the artist to his subjective ideals *is* affected by and *responds to* social trends as, indeed, it also articulates new social directions.

If the arts community moves towards a closer relationship to society as a whole, the segment of the elderly has emerged as a unique one for attention as both a public and a creative force.

The danger, however, is that too much attention is given to this one datum of age as the factor of retirement. Age is only one condition, along with health, income, family, place of residence, education, amount and structure of time, values, and aspirations. We must be wary of trapping ourselves in a theoretical box, as the recreation profession has generally done, by counting individual activities. The need is for a holistic approach, not only to the arts, but to all leisure experiences and, indeed, for a perspective on aging as part of the full life process. Older persons with creative propensities—a minority, no doubt, but so it is among all age groups—do not wish special treatment through special bureaucratized projects, with earmarked funding and patronization. There are among the 23 million over 65 as large a proportion of experienced or potential writers, filmmakers, actors, directors, composers, painters, sculptors, ceramicists, and printmakers as in any other segment.

Favoritism is as futile as ageism. However, as with the black and women, the elderly want equal opportunity and access; their availability of bulk free time in retirement is surely an advantage, and more so is their accumulated insight.

RESOURCES FOR FURTHER INSIGHTS

Two important general resources to arts for the elderly are a booklet prepared by Jacqueline T. Sunderland and a national conference which she arranged in Minneapolis in 1976. The 64-page booklet, *Older Americans and the Arts*[13] provided for the first time a formulation of social values of the arts, examples of present programs, and approaches to programming. As examples of current programs in senior centers she described such activities as those in Menlo Park, California, the Creative Drama Workshop in Atlanta, Hospital Audiences of New York City, the New Jersey Institute for Film Art, and the Appalachian Craftsmen, Inc., West Virginia. Ms. Sunderland's bibliography and directories of state offices of aging, state arts councils, and national arts organizations are a valuable resource. In October 1976 she arranged in Minneapolis the first conference on arts and the elderly, followed some months later by a similar conference in San Antonio sponsored by the Associated Councils of the Arts.

In Minneapolis, Arthur Fleming, Commissioner of the Administration on Aging, identified the "national aging network" and the "point of entry" through which partnerships could be created with the arts. Michael Straight, then Deputy Chairman of the National Endowment for the Arts, sketched the points at which art comes into the lives of the elderly as entertainment wears thin:

> Heightened perception of the world around us, . . . clarification, the inward perception of ourselves, . . . identification through the traditional arts, . . . [to] know where we have come from, where we are going, where we stand at this point, what we want out of life, . . . to participate in the act of joining together, . . . art offers the concept of reconciliation by the living that we are not alive for long.[14]

There followed in the Minneapolis conference a fruitful discussion in workshops that dealt with specific areas of theater, music, visual arts, and museums, as well as the four issues of building the arts/aging alliance, expanding cultural services, intergenerational programming, and reaching the "vulnerable and institutionalized" aged. The more than 200 participants from 31 states represented a total of 135 public and private agencies—51 from the arts, 84 from government, recreational, educational, religious, and other groups. Heard in the various discussions were such questions and comments as:

---

[13]Washington, D.C.: National Council on Aging, 1973.
[14]*Arts and the Aging, An Agenda for Action.* Washington, D.C., The National Council on the Aging. Jacqueline Sunderland, editor, 1977, pp. 4–6. Proceedings of Minneapolis Conference, Oct. 17–19, 1977, convened by National Center on the Arts (NCOA) and Minnesota Arts Board, and the Minnesota Governor's Citizens Council.

So far, most of our energy has gone into the hard services—health care, transportation, legal aid, counseling.

I'm staggered by how many arts programs there are.

Where are the older people on these panels?

If people are concerned about survival, they can't be concerned about the arts.

—Arts and Older Americans, not Arts for Older Americans.

They need to break down their fear of creating.

We started falling in love with the young people we were working with.

Working with the seniors has profoundly influenced my own career.

Finding the right teacher is the key. . .

I didn't realize that he had cataracts.

It was easier to obtain an audience from the elderly community than from schools or community centers.

But they couldn't provide the transportation.

The institutionalized elderly . . . live in a closed system. The arts can help chink away at that closed system.[15]

Finally, in relation to the elderly, as noted above, there runs through discussions of the arts the suspicion among artists of amateurism, or art as "fun," or therapy. The poet Kenneth Koch has made a contribution to this issue in *I Never Told Any Body: Teaching People in a Nursing Home to Write Poetry.*[16] His demonstration took place with about 25 men and women on the lower east side of Manhattan, most of whom had previously worked as messengers, short-order cooks, and domestic help. Most had "given up on life." In this atmosphere, common to many nursing homes, Koch and Kate Farrell appeared to talk about poetry. (His $600 grant, by the way, was not renewed.) He had them think out a sentence, something about a color, and then of some associations of this color to their lives. Here was an early attempt: "I like green/I used to see so many greens on the farm/I used to wear green, and sometimes my mother couldn't find me/Because I was green in the green."[17]

More boldness and imagination developed, as Koch read from Walt Whitman and other poets. The class spoke and wrote their poems, "unrhymed, nonmetrical, fairly unliterary." But note Koch's objective throughout:

I don't think I would like to adjust to a life without imagination or accomplishment, and I don't believe my students wanted it either. It is in this sense, perhaps, that it can best be understood why it is better to teach poetry writing as an art than to teach it—well, not really teach it but use it—as some form of distracting or consoling therapy.[18]

---

[15]Ibid.
[16]New York: Random House, 1966.
[17]Ibid.
[18]Ibid.

Perhaps, with the help of the Kochs and Farrells in the country, we can restore a child-like sense of wonder to the elderly, for their creativity has been stifled over many decades in school and work. Perhaps, on these levels, we can cut across ages and backgrounds, so that short-order cooks and messenger boys and young people can meet in nursing homes, playgrounds, and ordinary homes to write, act, paint, and make music together. Creation does not rely on age, but on insights, wholesome naiveté, inner courage, and the desire to see and hear and say and sing.

When Mr. Koch discussed his effective but short-lived program at a San Antonio conference (April 1977) sponsored by the Associated Councils of the Arts, I checked him on his philosophy and motives. I noted that he could more easily obtain a further grant if he continued to teach as he did, while justifying his results in the usual quantitative, pseudopsychological lingo that the granting bureaucracy prefers. But Koch stuck to his point, and I go along with him entirely, no matter what the by-products might be to his students as people. He approached the elderly as if they were young, formative poets, so that they could look at their "unusual lives," in the present "unusual time," bringing out now a "fine and delicate sensibility" that could be "expressed with eloquence in words."

We need to be reminded that children as well can learn to create poetry as an "art." The following fantasy was written by a fifth grader, officially classified as an "underachiever":

I see dogs and birds the dogs are flying around and the birds are running but they can't seem to get off the ground. The dogs are flying fast. There are monkeys and shirts. The shirts are going from tree to tree. And we are wearing monkeys. And I see ships and clocks. And the clocks are floating in the water and we are telling time from the ships. And I see a pencil sharpener and a sink. And we are sharpening our pencils in the sink. And we are washing our hands in the pencil sharpener. And I see a TV and a blackboard. And we are writing on the TV. And we are watching the blackboard.[19]

Perhaps there *is* a new frontier based on literary expression, for intergenerational communications.

---

[19]Julie Cassidy in *Python* (1976). Federal Project, Poetry in the Schools, School Board, City of Tampa. Reproduced by permission of Professor Hans Juergensen, editor.

CHAPTER 14

Civic Activity Experiences

In his Inaugural Address of January 20, 1969, President Nixon called on Americans to volunteer in their communities to help solve our mounting problems. In the next few weeks some 300 cities were put to the test when the Gallup poll asked the question: Suppose you were asked to serve on a committee which would deal with some local problem, such as housing, recreation, traffic, health, and the like—would you serve? Six persons of every ten, 69 million, said they would; their ages ranged from 21 up.

The criteria found to affect the degree of participation were: (1) a genuine interest by the person in the project; (2) a feeling that one's efforts would be meaningful toward achieving some result; and (3) some recognition for the participant. A detailed breakdown in age groups showed that the elderly would volunteer in the same proportion. Research in Buffalo was carried out to explore those social and individual attributes of older persons in a white, ethnic, working class neighborhood with an interest in participating in volunteer programs.[1]

A more detailed study of potential volunteers among the elderly was carried on in a Boston suburb five years before the Gallup poll.[2] About 25% of those interviewed said they would volunteer; another 15% felt they should be paid. A commonly expressed feeling was that their services would not generally be wanted. Older volunteers would prefer jobs that brought them into contact with other people; the Brandeis University investigators found that the volunteer openings were usually those with a minimal responsibility, and that among social agencies the typical attitudes of "ageism" prevailed.

My own impression is that the number of retired volunteers across the country would range somewhere between those figures of the Brandeis group

---

[1]A. Monk and A. C. Cryns, "Predictors of Voluntaristic Intent Among the Aged," *The Gerontologist,* 14, No. 5 (Oct. 1974), pp. 425–429.

[2]C. Lambert, M. Goberman, and R. Morris, "Reopening Doors to Community Participation for Older Persons: How Realistic?" *Social Services Review,* 38 (July 1964), pp. 42–50.

and Gallup—neither 25% nor 60%, but perhaps four persons of every ten who are physically qualified to do whatever is needed.

Times have changed. Perhaps the urban, middle-class American is less committed to his community, neighborhood, or ethnic group. Yet a 40% estimate of volunteers among retirees comes to 6 million persons, serving four hours per week—24 million hours weekly, or (over a 40-week year) 960 million hours annually!

Yet a hypothetical figure is quite useless, for volunteerism increases in times of crises—wars, earthquakes, floods, fires. It varies among communities, ethnic groups, and social classes. Certainly, in the U.S.A. as a whole, we are a generous people, and the stories of persons who don't want to "get involved" when they see a crime committed is more than offset by a tradition of helping each other that goes far back in our history.

THE TRADITION OF VOLUNTEERISM

The "old old" or immigrant generation had long ago developed a tradition of volunteerism to serve itself; these pockets of Irish, Cubans, Jews, and others became adept at money raising, hospital organization, self-education, and political action. It was among immigrant groups that Jane Addams established Hull House in Chicago. Writing of the Jews in *World of Our Fathers,* Irving Howe noted that this setting for built-in volunteerism was the *landsman-shaft,* a lodge or club of persons who had migrated from the same eastern European town. "Immigrants, feeling themselves lost in American cities, would seek out old-country neighbors . . . they found modest little organizations that kept alive memories and helped them fit into the new world."[3]

Later these groups gathered funds for the victims of Naziism. By pooling funds, cooperating groups of Jews were able to establish hospitals, convalescent centers, and homes for the elderly. We may find a miniature reconstruction of the *landsmanshaft* in the contemporary associations of retiree associations from various states, or even from cities in the U.S.A. and Canada. Among the retiree clubs listed in St. Petersburg, Florida, are those named after every state in the union. These, however, fall far short of the elderly immigrant associations which, to be sure, provided a fixed time with close friends for a meeting at which "you could relax over a game of pinochle, get caught up in an intrigue over who the next president would be, enjoy the solemnities of parliamentary ritual, and once in a while share the excitement following a treasurer's departure with the funds. . . ."[4] But more, the goal of Americanization was implemented with insurance schemes, medical benefits, and assurance of burial expenses.

The rural tradition is usually called upon as the model for cooperation among persons beyond the family circle. We are reminded that farmers

---

[3]*World of Our Fathers.* New York, Harcourt, Brace, Jovanovich, 1976, p. 184.
[4]Ibid. p. 189.

helped each other in times of need, teaming up for special tasks in repairing and building homes, tending the sick, and so on. In contrast, the urban tradition, particularly as seen by outsiders after the turn of the century, was one of "anonymity," comparative coldness, and disinterest. These were more than stereotypes, and the "lonely crowd" had some basis in fact. Much of the early sociology of the city was devoted to the general distinction of *Gemeinschaft* and *Gesellschaft,* and upon this distinction there was built up a literature in the vein of *The American Tragedy.*

A second tradition, which grew along with the emergence of large cities and the arrival of masses of immigrants up to World War I, was the service motif found among the wealthier women of the community, extending into money raising for a variety of purposes, hospital work, many forms of "social work," the arts, education, and politics. As far back as 1752, a group of "rich widows and other single women of the town" provided funds in Philadelphia to pay for drugs being shipped from London for charity patients. (Hospitals have relied heavily on volunteers for both funding and services ever since.) Meanwhile, the immigrant communities often established clubs which, in addition to maintaining a certain *gemütlichkeit* and attempting to preserve the heritage, established such services as insurance, burial arrangements, hospital plans, and visitations. For many years my father served his Workman's Circle lodge in Milwaukee as "Hospitaler," visiting sick members, and reporting their condition to the next lodge meeting. Many larger cities, beginning in Chicago with Hull House, developed what are today called "multipurpose" community centers, but which we knew in our youth as settlement houses.

Thus there grew up an enormous community apparatus of services, centers, and agencies in American life through which, especially after the depression, a professional corps began to dominate the welfare scene. This was accompanied by and to some extent due to the flowering of social services and the expansion of governmental functions. Yet so large has the dimension of services for welfare and recreation grown that volunteerism, while changing its role, has continued to expand. Changes have occurred, so that a revolution is taking place in the conception, quality, composition, and power of the volunteer.

1. The *conception* of volunteerism has changed. The professionalization of social work, together with the expansion of public and private agency services, calls for volunteers who are more than persons of good will who have the time to give; they are also literate and knowledgeable in special fields. The volunteers, for the same reasons, respond with demands for more significant assignments, and even for a hand in policy making.

2. The *quality* of volunteerism is a reflection of the greater literacy within the field of service, generally higher levels of welfare than a half century ago, and the larger number of volunteers who come from among retirees with a lifetime of experience. In such programs as the Peace Corps and VISTA latent idealism has been encouraged rather than squelched by tough selection, training, and type of assignment.

3. The *composition* of volunteerism in one sense has increasingly moved

"down" into the social class scale, since more middle-class men and women have the time, or see fit to use their free time, for service to others. In another sense the movement has been "upward," for many of those who as first generation immigrants were of the working class are by now well settled in the middle class. Over 20 million of us, with both parents born abroad, are still alive. The American black community will be the next major segment to observe. Its efforts to achieve rights and identity will turn increasingly toward inner resources to accompany governmental policies, and the hoped for rise in affluence, self-education, and family stability will probably see some repetition of community service patterns as with prior ethnic groups.

4. The *power* of volunteerism is a direct outgrowth of the policies of involving the poor in such Great Society legislation as HUD and the OEO. Even before these acts were passed there had been a growing resolve by many to take more direct action in their own destiny. Indeed, some observers feel that this aspect of federal programs—equal power in the planning of local programs—may in the long run overshadow the actual program itself. The fact that in many cases the democratization of planning power has not worked well does not diminish the long-range consequences for both social class power and the future of volunteerism. Obviously, a second cause for the new power of the volunteer, especially in the ghettoes of this country, is the civil rights movement. Organizations such as the NAACP and SNCC have their administrative base in a professional body of workers, but the most effort on behalf of their movements is by volunteer workers and by larger groups in their "leisure" time.

Aside from all these social movements, changes, and revolutions in the nature of governmental or community responsibility, the major issue which comes through is best put in question form: Are we here developing a series of "models" and experiences for many more Americans of all backgrounds and social positions who may have large amounts of free time in the future? Does the Peace Corps point the way for cooperation with peoples of other nations and cultures? Will the future bring other crises and causes which will call upon the dedication of large numbers, especially those who are basically content with the political and social status quo? We can say with some security that "service" remains a significant, and perhaps a growing, area for leisure purposes and concepts. With this category we stake a position for the realities and potentials of leisure as both a revolutionary factor and a stabilizing factor—to maintain present social order on the one hand and to transform it on the other.

JOHN PUTNAM OF BOSTON

As so often happens, contributions stem from one individual with an idea, initiative to implement it, and persistence in confronting the odds. John Putnam is a Bostonian from a well known family, but with little financial resources. Without the "proper" academic credentials he has worked since the early 1960's to establish a self-help agency that came to be known as the Civic Center and Clearing House. To determine the dynamics of such a project we need to examine origins and motivations. Here is his account, written in 1965:

The Center originated in a meeting held in May, 1961 of a number of professional educators, social workers, public health leaders, civic leaders and others. At this meeting it was decided that some form of independent agency was needed to focus the community's different resources that were concerned with the basic problem of retirement and leisure time. No particular program was established. A small foundation grant was secured, and the Boston Center for Adult Education provided space and temporary sponsorship.

The first year was exploratory. The Executive Director sampled community opinion and tested out various ideas relative to the constructive use of leisure, particularly, but not exclusively, by retired persons. After a year the name, "Center for Applied Studies in Aging and Citizenship" was adopted and the operation was moved to 3 Joy Street under the sponsorship of the Twentieth Century Association.

During the next 15 months the operation developed further ideas, held major institutes on the civic role of the older person, attracted and placed a number of older volunteers. At the beginning of 1964 it was decided to change the name to Civic Center and Clearing House, among the reasons being the self-defeating use of the word "Aging" in the title of an operation aimed primarily at maintaining the independence, usefulness and self-respect of the older person. Shortly afterward the first major foundation grant was received from the Charles E. Merrill Trust which virtually secured the operation through 1964. At about the same time the sponsorship of the Old Colony Charitable Foundation was substituted for that of the Twentieth Century Association and the Civic Center and Clearing House Trust was established.[5]

In a few years the Center obtained other grants and Mr. Putnam, deciding that its direct operation "needed more professional hands than mine," turned the project over to professional persons.

Several programs carried out under the Center's sponsorship in its early years may be noted.

1. A group of 15 older people began in May 1962 to gather information regarding the origin and historical development of a number of buildings and blocks in the South End of Boston at the request of the South End Urban Renewal Committee. This project was successfully completed by February 1, 1963.

2. New projects were then assigned to the group, which adopted the informal name "Boston Volunteers for Civic Studies." One project called for the location, identification, and recording of historic site markers in downtown Boston for the Historical Division of the Boston Redevelopment Authority. This was completed and the workers extended the coverage to other sections of the city. Another project was the revival of an early century effort to compile a registry of all public and semipublic art in the city.

3. The Civic Center and Clearing House persuaded the State Department of Education to include a course on metropolitan conservation in the Division of University Extension to bring the facts, needs, and opportunities for action in the field of conservation to the public, particularly to urban

---

[5] "The Civic Center and Clearing House," *Memorandum* (1965), mimeographed. Reproduced by permission of the author.

residents. This course proved successful, with approximately 50 enrolled. A series of action projects followed the course, one of them a shade tree inventory in Boston.

The Center received an award for pioneering from the Adult Education Association in Massachusetts in November 1964. Putnam also organized the Center for Applied Studies in Aging and Citizenship and the Boston Center for Adult Education. In these efforts he was able to muster the cooperation of educational and welfare agencies, including Brandeis, Tufts, and Boston University.

Mr. Putnam evaluated what these and other volunteer projects can accomplish:

a. That the person of average competence and no background of volunteering can make an important contribution to civic affairs to his own satisfaction and enrichment.

b. That many people with new leisure time are waiting to be called to new and challenging types of volunteer work.

c. That the opportunities for creative "Second Careers" in citizenship are unlimited provided imaginative civic leadership is enlisted in their development.

d. That in order to accomplish a major change in the concept of volunteering and in attitudes towards civic affairs, improved means of reaching people before they retire must be devised, else too many people will settle into new leisure inertly or inconsequentially.[6]

Another person of initiative is Mrs. Donald Cooley of Old Greenwich, Connecticut, who formed a community group known as SPRUCE (Small Projects to Reduce Ugly Conditions Everywhere). She was quoted in Robert Peterson's syndicated column, "Life Begins at 40" (November 10, 1973):

Our members keep their eyes out for ugly unattractive situations, and then we sit down and figure out the best way to effect improvements.

Sometimes it means writing a letter on our stationery to the owner of an ugly lot or building, and in a warm, friendly manner tell him how much we'd appreciate his cooperation in sprucing up his property.

Sometimes we take direct steps to beautify conditions. Where there are patches of town-owned property which need ground cover, we may get a local resident or firm to contribute some plants such as pachysandra or myrtle, or some shrubs which will add to its beauty. Or we may get local merchants to fix sidewalks, or work toward more uniform store-front designs.

We operate very informally. Many of our members are retired folks who, through us, have a medium for helping their community stay beautiful.

In circles of American big business there have been efforts to release employees for community service during their years of active service. For example, the Xerox plan is impressive because it includes all age groups, with the only proviso being that applicants must have been with the company for at least three years. As reported by Carol Offen, 24 workers were selected in 1972 for a full pay leave to work on a community project of their choice. Participants, selected by a seven-member panel representing all employees, ranged in age from 29 to 60. "They are not going to have to wait until they

---

[6]Ibid.

retire," according to C. Peter McColough, Xerox President. "Participants have worked with a wide range of problems and agencies: mentally-retarded pre-schoolers, minority-group businessmen, environmental planners, drug addicts, the aged, hard core youth in an inner-city area, and school children on an Indian reservation in South Dakota."[7] One employee, a Xerox staff nurse nearing retirement, served in 1972 as director of nursing at an inter-denominational crippled children's hospital in Bethlehem.

Among federal programs the National Center for Voluntary Action is the network of local efforts throughout the country, and now includes the Peace Corps.

---

[7]*Hy/Retirement Living* (April 1972).

CHAPTER 15

Intellectual Activity Experiences

Intellectual activity is that in which the mind is used as the major element. Intellectual "study" and "production" are two major forms of such activity, one motivated by the desire to understand, the other by a need to create.

As to the first, attaching of leisure to intellectual understanding presumes that one is in the role of student or amateur. As such, the adult "starts with a strange motivation to learn; he proceeds at his own pace; he may join with others interested in similar subject matter; he brings to his new action a lifetime of experience; his approach to his teacher, if there is one, is not of a captive student but of a voluntary devotee."[1]

On the other hand, intellectual production by the amateur closely approaches that of the professional; the serious amateur who writes his first novel goes through substantially the same process as a craftsman. But, not being responsible to a public to cultivate its financial support, the amateur benefits from a freedom to move in his own directions.[2] The American composer Charles Ives comes to mind as a remarkable example. The norms that direct serious leisure intellectual activity are precisely those that dominate the professional scholar in the university—the search for truth, the canons of rational thought, a knowledge of what others in the field are doing, and so forth—but what distinguishes the amateur philosopher, novelist, poet, or scientist is that his preoccupation may persist over time and end in a contribution but it *need* not.

There is no serious journal in the U.S. devoted primarily to issues of concern to the elderly. This lack corresponds to a general ignorance of the fact that there is an audience for far more substantive materials than those provided in the journals *Modern Maturity* and *Retirement Living*. Indeed, there is no reason to believe that the 23 million persons over 65 are less intelligent than those of any other segment of that size.

---

[1]Max Kaplan, *Leisure: Theory and Policy.* New York: John Wiley & Sons, 1975, p. 302.
[2]Ibid. p. 303.

Enormous damage was perpetuated by the message that came from the quarters of educational psychology in teachers' colleges for many years; this was the data purporting to show that ability to learn decreased rapidly after adolescence. Even today most graduates of university education departments have had little or no instruction about adult education, and less about the elderly.

Nevertheless, as reports of the Adult Education Association of the U.S.A. have indicated, there has been a proliferation of programs under the auspices of universities, high schools, churches, labor unions, and private or proprietary bodies. It is estimated that about 20 million Americans are presently enrolled on a regular basis in one or more courses.

The needs of retired persons can usually be met by such agencies; for example, the junior and community colleges are settings in which persons in their 20s and 60s may be seen together in a natural relationship. As the Bicentennial Year in 1976 approached, some colleges introduced courses in "history" built around the lives of its students, and older students found themselves becoming "teachers." The federal RSVP (Retired Senior Volunteer Program) provided many such teachers for elementary and secondary schools through its Living History Program.

Before turning to specific examples of education in which the elderly participate or, indeed, play a leading role in organization or instruction, we may consider the matter of mixing generations vis-à-vis special educational opportunities for retirees. In some ways the issue of mingling or separating the elderly in education is comparable to the field of housing. Some authorities, not to mention the elderly themselves, are dubious about segregating the elderly from the natural diversity that exists in the usual neighborhood. However, the residents of retirement communities emphasize the freedom from children, noise, and physical danger. What happens in a classroom when 20- and 50- or 60-year-olds are together? Does each stimulate the other, for different reasons? Can the instructor deal with this age diversity in a comfortable or productive way?

The element of fear generally marks the older student who undertakes to return to education after a lapse of decades, while awkwardness seems to overtake many younger persons in a learning situation with older persons. A common experience among those of us who have instructed in such a situation is that the tensions and fears do not last long. In the musical instruction at Boston University previously described (Chapter 13), a close personal relationship developed between two people often 50 years apart. Several years ago the gerontology department of the University of Michigan invited a group of disparate ages to spend a weekend together in a motel conference situation, and tapes were made of the freewheeling conversations. The result was a greater degree of understanding, even on such matters as drug use, dress, and attitudes toward the "establishment." In short, it is conceivable that in a college or other learning situation adults of all ages can study and interrelate socially.

The primary value for classes or programs predominated or maintained exclusively for retirees exists when: (1) funds are available exclusively for such a program; (2) the educational program is locked in with such supplementary experiences as travel; (3) the existing secondary or college facilities are already so crowded that the presence of older persons raises serious objections; (4) a primary intent is the study of problems unique to the elderly; or (5) the educational component, as in the Institute of Lifelong Learning (AARP), is a natural outgrowth of previous friendships and activities by the same circles.

In 1972 the American Association of Community and Junior Colleges (AACJC) conducted a survey on the number of academic programs that "prepare manpower for the field of aging." Of over 1000 colleges, 58 had such programs, and over 100 more were planning them in the next two years. We may assume that among the 200 or more programs that exist by now general courses in some of these curricula are open to the elderly themselves. Two examples where this is so are junior colleges in St. Petersburg and Minneapolis (St. Mary's).

Many such colleges also absorb older persons from the community to teach courses in their former fields. Special educational programs designed for retirees are to be increasingly found throughout the U.S. The Kirkwood Community College in Cedar Rapids, Iowa, provides an illustration.[3] Its program followed a community survey to verify an interest; funding came from the Iowa Commission on Aging. Comparable educational programs for retirees exist at the Edmunds Community College (Lynwood, Washington), Catonsville Community College (Catonsville, Maryland), New York City Community College (Brooklyn), and Florida Junior College (Jacksonville).[4]

We may anticipate an expansion of federal programs, either for an age integrated student body or for retirees. Their many functions will include general information about what it is to be an older person in our society, services available to older persons in that community, concrete assistance on financial, health, or family problems, counseling on leisure opportunities, and second career prospects for those who wish to work.

Other agencies may increase their educational services to the elderly, including churches, libraries, labor unions, and community centers. Networks between such diverse services may be in the offing.

We turn now to several important college programs designed for the elderly, each of which has attracted national attention.

INSTITUTE FOR RETIRED PERSONS (IRP): NEW YORK

This pioneering effort in education was specifically designed for retirees *by* retirees; it was established in 1962 in the New School for Social Research. According to the Director, Dr. Hyman Hirsch, its basic philosophy rejected

---

[3]R. A. Feller, "Community College Approach to Aging," *Community and Junior College Journal* (Aug./Sept. 1973).

[4]Ann Maust, "The New Frontier," *Community and Junior College Journal* (Aug./Sept. 1973).

the idea that universities should provide programs for retirees and assumed that universities should give the encouragement and framework for programs by retirees. The students number more than 650 men and women, ranging in age from 55 to 90, with a long waiting list. Over 70 courses and seminars are initiated and taught by members. Access to all Institute activities is obtained by an annual membership fee, providing all funding needs. A workshop for other universities was sponsored by IRP in November, 1976, with proceedings to be published.

INSTITUTE FOR POST-RETIREMENT STUDIES: CLEVELAND

The following account, titled "Progress Report," was provided by Dr. Ruth Glick, director of the Institute at Case Western Reserve University.[5]

Two lines of thought converged to provide the basis for the establishment of a University based graduate study program for retired and semi-retired persons age 55 and over. The first of these was the sorrowful condition of the older person in our society related to the loss of his traditional role, the weakening of institutionalized support (i.e., kinship, church and synagogue, the neighborhood, the family doctor), the shrinkage of choice, freedom and dignity, and generalized indifference to his plight and the neglect, devaluation and exclusion which are the lot of the many.

For the more fortunate minority who are still independent, healthy and relatively secure economically, the later years of life may not be a catastrophe or may even be good. Nevertheless, even for this group as for the majority, rewards dwindle, and loneliness and isolation increase in the wake of compulsory retirement, the death of contemporaries, the specter of abandonment as children live their lives and grandchildren move away. One need not be poor to be needy. Worst of all for older people is the threat of the loss of their intellectual competencies in the face of diminishing opportunities to pursue those interests and activities which gave their earlier existence its meaning. To those individuals whose careers challenged them to continue to learn, to study, to solve problems, the greatest fear may be not only the erosion through disuse of their talents, abilities and skills, but also the loss of a sense of purpose in life.

The second line of thought centered around our interest in leisure and its natural tie to continuing education. In a work-oriented society where work and life are frequently coterminous (Time is Money, says the adage) the concept of leisure is mistaken for free time as Sebastian de Grazia says, and is so thought to be the opposite of work and therefore, unproductive. He further states: "But leisure as an ideal is not hours free from work but rather a state of being free from everyday necessity so that one can undertake activities desirable for their own sake. The ideal of leisure offers the chance of discovery, creation, exercise of the mind and contemplation."

It seemed then that continued learning and the further pursuit of knowledge provided a route to these destinations.

Background

In consideration of these needs, early in 1970, two psychologists, Dr. Raymond Balester and Dr. Ruth Glick, began to explore with University personnel the feasibility of organizing a program to implement the concept of life-time learning. There was no educational facility in Cleveland which was reaching out to serve retired persons whose past careers demanded intellectual achievement associated with higher education, not alone for their benefit, but also because it placed a high value on the continuity of

---

[5]1977, unpublished report. Reproduced with the kind permission of Dr. Glick.

intellectual and cultural experience and saw these people as the historians of their time in their places.

Our goals were implicit in our belief that intellectual stability is the key to a decent old age and that mental stimulation and the challenge of learning are powerful forces against the phenomena of disengagement, boredom, senility and despair. The intention was to demonstrate the strong influence of education in the promotion of effective performance, growth, renewal and hope. It was time also to work toward a model with utility for a future society not far ahead in which more of its members reaching retirement age would have had a college education. The first group of men and women who attended college under the G. I. Bill will begin to retire from their work lives during this decade. Many still in their fifties will be ill prepared for the long years of "leisure" ahead. Finally, we hoped that the exploration of a serious educational effort with an already educated group would yield information and insights to permit the development of appropriate models to older individuals who had not been college educated.

The outgrowth of these convictions and objectives was the establishment at CWRU of the Institute for Post-Retirement Studies which opened its doors on February 1, 1972 on a very low privately funded budget.

The Program

1) The Institute is part of the University and as such its members must register for a minimum of one University course per year. The rationale is to integrate older students into classes with "regular" students and to engender an attitude of belonging to the University and its affairs. Courses may be taken for credit, for audit or toward fulfilling a degree requirement.

Members have registered in courses at every level from freshman undergraduate to post-graduate in Art, History, Sociology, Philosophy, Religion, English, Literature, French and Accounting. A librarian was enrolled in Economics, a businessman in Religion and a health planner in Organizational Theory. One member is beginning Classical Greek in the Fall. Several who have already fulfilled their one course per year requirement are registering again and going on in the same field of concentration. Others have become more confident and are taking off in new directions.

2) The Institute also offers its own classes. These are organized by the members themselves in accordance with their expressed interests and taught by leaders with expertise drawn from within the group. During its first semester, the participants developed five courses and many members were enrolled in two or three. These were 1) Social Problems, 2) Music, 3) Psychology, 4) Writer's Workshop, and 5) French Literature in the French language. With increasing enrollment, a broader choice will be available. A minimum of one Institute course per semester is required.

Toward the end of Spring semester, the members made their own critical evaluations of these Institute courses. One result was an immediate demand for a course in Library Orientation so that they could prepare more scholarly bibliographies and learn how to zero in with greater precision on the kinds of data they seek. They imposed on themselves more rigor and discipline. One member said "We need to shake ourselves out of old ruts and routines and habitual ways of looking at things. I discovered that I was carrying around a big bundle of opinions I didn't believe any more."

Present Status

At the conclusion of our first semester we have developed a structure for a model that was virtually nonexistent and have enrolled 38 members. The age range is 49–84. Forty percent are under age 60. Twenty percent are in their seventies. The median age is 64. The members represent a wide range of interests and backgrounds including teaching, social work, law, business, religion, library science and public service. Many are alumni of Western Reserve University but at least 20 other alma maters are represented, among them Yale, Oberlin, Northwestern, Morehouse, Smith, Columbia and Wayne State.

Fifty-seven percent hold master's or other advanced degrees. Five percent have no undergraduate degree. The latter were accepted on the basis of their life style and/or intellectual interests, ability and high degree of motivation to study. Six percent are still fully employed or only semi-retired. We encourage older persons facing retirement to join the Institute while they are still working if possible. The return to academic life, a new alternative to the traditional post-retirement options, makes the transition into retirement easier for those who approach it with dread, as well as for those who welcome it but wonder what they will do next.

A nun has been appointed Director of Retirement for her community as a direct result of this program. A fifty-seven-year-old man who was forced into early retirement is planning to take a bachelor's degree. A fully employed health planner is back to sharpen her skills. One member is writing a biography of her father, an inventor who developed an early model of the helicopter.

The most frequent reason given for joining the Institute in a just completed questionnaire is "for intellectual stimulation" and "to give more purpose to living." Members repeatedly referred to a new sense of achievement, greater self-esteem and improved feeling of well being. One man wrote to President Toepfer, "There was no other place to which I could turn." Another said, "One can build a whole life around this." A widow wrote, "I have protected others all my life, now I want something for myself." A patent attitude of belonging to the group has emerged. The overall atmosphere here is charged with excitement, pleasure and planning.

Perspective

This program is fully consistent with the recommendations of the Continuing Education Committee of the Cleveland Commission on Higher Education. Of all aspects of continuing education for persons other than "regular" students, those concerned with the older person have been considered most difficult to implement. This pilot program has demonstrated that older persons can reengage in academic life benefiting not only themselves but the University community as well. An unexpected spillover has been the stimulation of interest in the area of aging and older persons in the young students and members of the faculty. For example:

1) A historian explored with us the idea of a History of Aging. No such work is to be found either in the social history or in gerontological literature.

2) A participating psychologist in the Institute's Group Dynamics course has shifted her previous interest in the group process of younger individuals to that of older persons.

3) A professor of philosophy held one session of his course at the Institute after which the younger students expressed a high degree of interest in the philosophical implications of aging and proposed a collaboration with Institute members in a joint seminar.

4) A 54-year-old full professor in one of the professional schools has formally joined the group.

5) Several members of the faculty have openly expressed their pleasure in having older persons in their classes because of the dimension added.

The relatively small cost involved in this project should be seen as an investment in the mental health of the older population and weighed against the social cost of maintaining individuals who have been wasted as a consequence of having no purpose in life. Further it should be seen as contributing to the quality of life itself through encouragement of concern of human beings for each other throughout the life span. Finally, and more importantly, this project must be regarded as emphasizing the centrality of the university as the ultimate resource of intellectual life in the society.

INSTITUTE FOR CONTINUED LEARNING: SAN DIEGO

The following report consists of materials that were gathered during a visit to a meeting of the ICL Board of Directors in early September, 1976. I am especially indebted to Ms. Doris R. Brosnan, coordinator of the program.[6]

The ICL (Institute for Continued Learning) was conceived by retired persons and is directed by its members in an affiliation with the University of California Extension, San Diego. For an annual individual membership of $75 ($120 with a spouse), the program includes:

1. *Study groups:* discussion sessions led by other members. Examples: Mexico, Brazil, English History Through Biography, and USSR-USA Relations.

2. *Courses:* taught by members.

3. *Activities:* bus trips based on special interests (music, theater, etc.), as well as occasional chartered flights to New York and elsewhere; social affairs; development of a "resources bank" to acquaint educational and community institutions of the skills and availability of members.

4. *Forum lectures:* on alternate Fridays, 10 A.M. to noon.

In addition to their own programs, ICL members have full privileges at the various University libraries, a language laboratory of 6000 volumes and 50 languages on tape, and a craft center with facilities for ceramics, photography, jewelry making, stained glass, and enameling.

Members must enroll in at least one University of California at San Diego (UCSD) extension course and one ICL study group led by another member.

The personal data sheet submitted by new members requests information on education, work career, honors and publications, past and present community activities (local, state, national levels), and hobbies or special interests. Questions asked in the last category were:

Music: Is music a regular part of your life? . . . As a listener? . . . As a music-maker? . . . If the latter, what instrument, choir, orchestra, chorus, ballet, etc.?

Forensics and drama: Ever belong to a debating society, Toastmasters, or the like? . . . Can you make a pretty good speech? . . . Little theater work?

Fine arts: Professional . . . Amateur . . . Media and style.

Other favorite leisure time activities: such as reading, travel, photography, theater-going, handicrafts, sports; and if you've had exhibits, won prizes, or any other honors, tell us about them. . . .

Finally, the application form asks the applicant "What learning areas are you most interested in pursuing now?" and "In which specific areas are you willing to be a resource person for UCSD and/or the community?"

ICL lectures and speakers for the Fall Quarter of 1976, between October 8th and December 3rd, were:

"Cultures of the Third World," Professor Sylvia Wynter, Department of Literature, UCSD, formerly with the BBC.

"Making it in the Sixties," Morton H. Shaevitz, Dean and Director of UCSD Counseling Services.

"Roles of Editorials in TV Broadcasting," Clayton Brace, Vice-President, McGraw-Hill Broadcasting Corporation.

---

[6]Also see Appendix B for a more detailed description of some of the courses offered by the ICL in the fall of 1976.

"A Man Novelist Looks at Three Women's Works," Walter S. J. Swanson, La Jolla author.

"San Diego: Yesterday, Today and Tomorrow," Paul McKim, architect (followed by a walking tour of the area to be discussed).

An example of a "special program" is the tour made at the close of each quarter to the Scripps Institute of Oceanography, providing a closer view than the general public receives of the Marine Museum, aquarium tanks, and the fleet of six vessels. Among other activities scheduled for the Fall 1976 period were: annual meeting and luncheon for ICL members, a field trip to the Mount Palomar Observatory by members of the Bio-Med-Science study group, overnight birdwatching hike, a bus trip to the Los Angeles County Museum for the exhibition on Franklin and Jefferson, and a bus field trip of North County by the California History Study Group to visit missions and other places of interest.

ELDERHOSTELS: THE NEW ENGLAND CENTER

America has recently witnessed the birth of a new idea in education for retirees, the "Elderhostel." Below is reproduced an announcement of the plan for courses in the summer of 1976, based on the experience of the year before.

For many of the 20 million American citizens over the age of 65, retirement and high age brings financial, physical, and social problems. Pervading and transcending these concrete issues is an intangible which afflicts the consciousness of everyone, young and old, in this industrial society. The concept of the used-up elderly is so much a part of modern America that even those dynamic elders, whose creative, service-oriented lives belie the myth, feel themselves a burden. For them, high age is a time to be endured with dignified sadness and resignation; for less fortunate elders, serious psychological problems develop. This state represents approximately ¼ of the average life, an unconscionable amount of human time and resource to be wasted.

Elderhostel, a low-cost program of educational hosteling, was organized at the University of New Hampshire in direct attack on this concept. Recognizing that a college community is a self-contained world of intense intellectual and social stimulus, the Elderhostel staff planned a program which would offer these resources, at true costs, to people of retirement age. The Elderhostel program, in week-long units, includes study in non-credit courses, hostel-style accommodations in dormitories, meals in college dining halls, and participation in ongoing campus life. Tuition costs are paid for by state and federal grants; hostelers pay the actual room and board costs. Hostelships are available for those who could not otherwise participate. Following the 5-campus, New Hampshire pilot project of 1975, 21 New England colleges successfully hosted the program in the summer of 1976.

Of the immediate impact of Elderhostel, there can be no question. Hostelers are personally revitalized by the experience, reporting new energy levels and increased self-esteem. Faculty members are overwhelmingly enthusiastic about the program, often realizing new dimensions and possibilities in their teaching. While no monetary profits are realized, colleges gain public relations benefits that literally could not be purchased. Many administrators are beginning to sense a lessening of the mistrust and resentment traditionally felt by elders towards institutions of higher education, and intend to use the Elderhostel program as a springboard towards further total community involvement.

A total of more than 100 informal courses were taught with dormitory accommodations and the use of campus dining halls. The full cost of accommodations was $60 per week, with no costs for instruction to those 65 years of age or on Social Security. Sponsors and planners have been the Office of Residential Life of the University of New Hampshire, the New England Gerontology Center, the UNH Division of Continuing Education and the UNH Resource Development Center. Funds for developing Elderhostel, including the cost of courses, came from the Spaulding Potter Community Fund (N.H.), Title I (N.H.), Title I (Vt.), Title I (Ct.), and the Administration on Aging through the Massachusetts Department of Elder Affairs.[7]

In 1977 Elderhostel operated in the six New England states and Iowa, with new programs in New York, Del-Mar-Va, Pennsylvania, and North Carolina. By 1978, the program was to be found in over 100 colleges and universities. After a grant was received in 1978 to engage a full-time staff of three persons, Martin Knowlton, founder of Elderhostel, resigned to undertake new programs.

Courses have ranged widely:
"Life in 18th Century America"
"Our Changing Society"
"Role of Philosophy and Religion in Our Lives"
"Your Physical Health"
"Seniors in Today's Society"
"What's Happening to the American Family?"
"Plant Growth and Propagation"
"Contemporary Art and Its Sources"
"Oral History Course"
"Is Shakespeare Still With Us?"
"Music in Early America"
"Great Books"
"Reader's Theater"
"The Appalachian Dulcimer"
"Current Affairs"
"American Politics and Literature"
"Photography"
"Poetry of Robert Frost"
"Writing Workshop: Science Fiction"

Finally, one example of a personal experience in adult education will be presented.

"AT 85, GEORGE GETS IN THE THICK OF THINGS"[8]

Return to school in September—the traditional image conjures fresh blooming youth entering new classrooms with a mixture of fear and intense anticipation.

But in this age, the image must change to include such people as 85-year-old George Pray returning with the same feelings to his classes at Catonsville Community College.

"It's been one of the best things I've ever done," he said about his initial return to school last year. "It's helped me greatly, both mentally and physically. I enjoy the fellowship of the students. At my age, I have friends who are becoming senile. I'm fighting that. I want to keep my mind active."

[7]Martin P. Knowlton, "Liberal Arts: the Elderhostel Plan for Survival," *Educational Gerontology*, 2 (1977), pp. 87–93. Reproduced by permission.
[8]Reprinted from the *Baltimore Sun*, September 10, 1975.

"It's a challenge. I don't get the high marks in book learning, you might say. A written test is very difficult for me; senior adults don't think as quick. But anything to do with the hands, like painting, I get A's and A-pluses."

It's obvious this member of the 1908 class of City College and 1913 graduate of the Maryland Institute of Art needn't worry much about senility. Friends say that supporting his slight physical frame is a mind always quick to grasp the nuance and humor of life. His late wife, Margaret, always told him he never grew up.

Mr. Pray was devoted to his wife, a long-time Catonsville school teacher who died in 1972. After 19 different jobs as a commercial artist, Mr. Pray had settled at the age of 51 into the security of work as a technical illustrator with the Bendix Corporation.

He retired 18 years ago at the age of 67 and he and his wife settled into a comfortable routine, centered around their domestic life, which included visits with their one daughter and grandchild. Then he was suddenly alone.

"When I became a widower, there was nobody to talk to," he said, "nobody to share experiences with, to help make decisions. It was a very lonesome existence. My life was a big void, and I was at loose ends."

Anybody who visited Mr. Pray several years ago could have seen the poignancy of these remarks. Memories of his Margaret brought sudden tears. An illness and hospitalization further complicated his loneliness.

But this was a man too interested in life to get lost in self-pity. When he returned home from the hospital, he learned about a federally funded Baltimore county program called "Lunch Plus," which was meeting at Catonsville's Salem Lutheran Church. For people over 60, the program featured a lunch "plus" a program organized by the Catonsville Community College.

"I used the same cookbooks as my wife, but the meals never came out the same," he said with a laugh. So he began attending the lunch program about a year ago. The oldest one in the group, he had no difficulty joining the mealtime conversations and even put on a few personal talk shows.

Then a college spokesman described the tuition-free courses available to the elderly. When he mentioned art, Mr. Pray thought he'd give it a try. By this time, he was beginning to establish a new life at 84.

"I had a happy marriage, a satisfying marriage," he recalled. "When you have that association and companionship, it seems sufficient. But I was too old to consider a second marriage, as some of my friends had done soon after their first wives died. Now they don't do much but eat, sit around, play cards and watch television."

"With me, I'm free again, not tied down, seeking a new direction. Everything was an experience to me. What amazed me so was the way I was received by the students. I expected a little ridicule, but was amazed that everybody wanted to help me."

Mr. Pray enrolled in three art courses last year and made the dean's list. His first assignment in his "art in history" course was to prepare a 50-minute talk on arts of the early twentieth century, a period he could recall from experience. Unfortunately, he had mistaken "50" minutes for "15."

After he ran out of his prepared notes, he decided just to tell the students what it had been like to live in those days. The class applauded him at the end, and from then on, he was "George" to everyone.

His daughter bought him a pair of blue jeans and he became an enthusiastic student. Some of the changed life style occasionally took him aback, but his sense of humor and natural tolerance helped him adjust. "Modern art" never quite made it with him, though.

"I paint what I see," he said, "but they paint like Picasso up there. I'm not creative in the sense that Picasso was, but I don't think he was a great artist. A lot of it was a hoax on the public; he must have laughed."

"Art is what it does for you, not what the artist tried to convey, because who knows? Most people like to associate something to it, to relate to it with something they're familiar with. So much of it I don't relate to."

Lest such remarks hint at stodginess, be it noted that Mr. Pray has painted a graphic female nude that seems to embarrass him just slightly. Inspired by the sprawling student model in front of him during that class, he had finally reached over and patted the shapely bottom of one of his attractive fellow students. She smiled, and the rest of the class applauded.

Having exhausted all the advanced painting courses last year, Mr. Pray will be taking a United States history course this term and pursue independent work with his painting.

"I look forward every day to going up there," he said. "I'll be going three mornings a week, then on to Lunch Plus, then I'll probably do some painting up there on campus. The distances and views are just great."

This activity plus his outside work for a church decorator and his personal calligraphy projects will undoubtedly keep him busy.

He praised the Catonsville Community College for its emphasis on programs for "senior citizens." An ardent supporter of the college's efforts, he has even become an adviser and spokesman for that institution's programs for the elderly. Last week he spoke to faculty members about the special needs of such students.

"I always thought of myself as an introvert," he concluded. "I was an only child and spent a lot of time by myself when I was growing up in New York State and Baltimore. But the people at the college are really bringing me out. I never thought I'd address the faculty, but they told me I could do it, and I did. They have helped me; they have developed me."

Throughout this review of various projects, one question that persists is whether the "intellectual" quest for the elderly reaches enough of those who have had relatively little experience with "mind-life" programs during their working years. The New York and San Diego projects summarized here are probably attractive to persons who have had such experiences; Elderhostel and Cleveland probably appeal to those from a mixture of backgrounds. The Senior Center Humanities Program, begun in 1976 by the NCOA (National Council on Aging, Washington, D.C.) is an attempt to reach persons from more limited backgrounds. Funded by the National Endowment for the Humanities, about 35,000 persons have already enrolled in one or more of 8 carefully prepared and tested courses through some 300 agencies across the country. These are mainly "senior centers" and have already been described in Chapter 10. The courses, each 8 weeks, have titles such as First Impressions of the New Land, Down on the Farm, Saving the Land, and A Family Album, and they revolve around a period of history and a style of life known to the participants. Reading materials are carefully collected and distributed in book form at no cost. Volunteers from the community usually do the teaching, but increasingly attempts are being made to use the participants as leaders and teachers. Numerous spin-offs have been created by the program, such as artistic and volunteer activity. Churches, libraries, nursing homes, and day care centers have become sponsors. Recorded tapes of the materials are available to blind students. One library system (Tacoma, Washington) has placed these readings on remote access telephone for use by the "elderly blind, developmentally disabled, shut-in and hospitalized."

The NCOA Senior Center Humanities Program provides many opportunities for those from a broad spectrum of socioeconomic and educational backgrounds. Based outside of traditional educational environments, it also provides a natural focus for other types of leisure activity (perhaps especially in the arts) and for more active participation in the full life of the community.

CHAPTER 16

Mass Media Activity Experiences

The history of the "old old" in America encompasses the total growth of the mass media, roughly in segments of 20 years. The two decades from 1900 to 1920 were periods of what the Lynds called "talking or listening to talk."[1] 1920 to 1940 witnessed the spread of radio and motion pictures. The 1940's and 1950's were the backdrop to the most widespread of all modes of communication up to that moment in human history—the development and acceptance of television. The 1960's and 1970's brought refinements such as color TV; the elderly responded with a devotion to this miracle of communication that even exceeded the commitment of younger generations.

Thus, in both transportation and communication, in one lifetime, there were some millions of persons whose experiences moved from what might be termed the "oatmeal box to Magnavox"—from crude homemade radio sets constructed with "cat's whiskers" from Woolworth's to the sophisticated gadget which enables us to see a television show, record it automatically for later viewing, record and play speech and music on cassettes, or use the 21-inch screen for showing home movies. If, indeed, as some tell us, this communications system is still in its infancy, the fact remains that the present achievement has been a primary symbol of the whole range of technological change that the youth of our time take for granted. My mother, born in a Lithuanian preindustrial village, would see jet planes overhead in Los Angeles and remark with authority that it was, of course, impossible for people to fly; or, while enjoying a TV show, she would remark that voices could never be heard over long distances without wires.

By now there are more radio sets than people in the United States. As to television, about 99% of homes have at least one set, with two or more sets in over 60% of homes. The approximately 700 TV stations are served by three major networks which share revenues of almost 3 billion dollars per year.

---

[1]Max Kaplan, *Leisure in America: A Social Inquiry.* New York: John Wiley & Sons, 1960, p. 122.

169

Several hundred noncommercial stations are served by the Corporation for Public Broadcasting and the Public Broadcasting Service. While the commercial networks are constantly being criticized for excessive violence, poor service to children, and low intellectual quotient, the public stations have in recent years been criticized for dullness and lack of innovation.

Research about "ageism" is bound to turn increasingly toward images of the elderly on television. As Ghita Levine noted in her *Baltimore Sun* column of January 22, 1978, "Programming shows fewer old people than their proportion in real life. Most of the older people on TV are men, when in reality elderly women far outnumber men."

While commercial TV has far and away attracted greater interest than public channels among the elderly, public stations have devoted proportionately larger portions of time to discussions or portrayals of the elderly. Cable TV, potentially a useful tool by which any group of citizens can reach the public, has not been used by the public to the degree that had been anticipated. For example, the summary of 30 Senior Center programs did not uncover one that took advantage of cable TV, and a recommendation for such a program to a Florida retirement community was not implemented (Chapter 10).

THE TORONTO STUDY

A comprehensive study of mass media use by the elderly was conducted in Toronto (1973) by the Canadian Radio-Television Commission.[2] As the preliminary discussion pointed out, in Canada (and only slightly less so in the U.S.A.) watching TV, listening to the radio, and reading newspapers and magazines took up a very large portion of retirees' time, yet their needs and preferences have been ignored. We know more about their habits in clubs and church groups. A carefully constructed interview of 616 persons was completed, about evenly distributed between the sexes and corresponding to the distribution of those in Toronto who fell into the five-year spans after 65 years. Bearing out our comments of Chapter 4, 58% of those interviewed viewed their health as good or excellent, and 27% as adequate. Therefore—assuming a close connection of health to general mood—25% said they never were in "low spirits," 34% "rarely," 30% "sometimes," and only 11% "frequently or always." Over a fourth of all answers about overall leisure activity were media-related. "Still more striking, 56% of the sample included at least one media-oriented activity in their compilation of most gratifying leisure pursuits." Below are summarized some additional highlights of the survey.

"Mental stimulation," "companionship," and "relaxation" were given as major sources of enjoyment, especially through TV and reading. The total use of mass media was "relatively unaltered" by age, with problems of hearing

---

[2]*Reaching the Retired: A Survey of Media Habits, Preferences, and Needs of Senior Citizens in Metro Toronto.* September, 1975; M. Adams, Project Coordinator.

and eyesight of concern only to octogenarians. Both a TV set and a radio were owned by 92%, and 46% having cable TV represented a higher rate than that in the general Toronto population. About three hours of daily viewing was claimed by nine of every 10 elderly—slightly below the general public, the bulk of use was in the evening (90%), and persons of ethnic background (except for the Jewish group) watched less than those limited to English. Health played no part in the amount of viewing, nor whether the person lived alone. News and public affairs, nature, and musical variety programs were favorites; least enjoyed were westerns and soap operas. Only 2% had ever watched "New Directions," a program designed for the elderly, and only a small number of Toronto's total audience listened to radio, using it more in the morning, except for the more educated segment of elderly. Receipt of a daily newspaper bore a marked relationship to income, however, the elderly spent about twice the time (1¼ hours daily) reading the daily newspaper than the national average.

Of the various media covered by the Toronto study, television was judged by the elderly as the most entertaining and relaxing, and the best source of companionship. Most regarded the newspaper as the best source for information. Greater dissatisfaction was registered against radio and TV for not supplying practical information (on health, pensions, etc.); others wanted more general education, culture, information on indoor hobbies, and religion. The importance of the "companionship" offered through mass media was evident from a listing of "loneliness" as the most acute problem of the elderly, even ahead of finances or health.[3]

IMPACT OF THE MASS MEDIA

The primary concern of numerous studies on the mass media (especially the motion picture and TV) has related to its impact on the person, or the resultant behavioral consequences. In the early years much effort went into drawing correlations of crime or violence in motion pictures with subsequent crime or emotional disturbance among children. About the most conclusive finding was that the children most affected were those with existing "predispositions" in those directions. It has also been accepted by now that the perception of crime and violence on the screen, as viewed by children, is not necessarily the perception of adults.

Conversely, a new issue at the present time is whether or not the perception of death—on or off the screen—by the elderly is different than earlier in their lives. The issue is more widespread than the issue of death. When, as the Toronto studies verified, a primary meaning of television for the elderly is *social companionship,* then the program itself is of relatively minor concern. McLuhan's "the medium is the message" is relevant, with the medium in this case becoming a substitute for other people, and the living room or the

---

[3]These summaries are found in pp. 117–124 of the Toronto report.

bedroom becoming the "global village," at least for the duration of the program. The soap opera becomes a powerful influence because, even more than companionship, the "village" now takes on drama, intrigue, suspense, conflict, victory, and frustration. This is quite enough. Yet more can be done if this experience in vicarious human drama becomes a lesson in creative theater that is acted, directed, and promoted.

Viewing the mass media as a whole, the elderly have become a major topic of discussion in recent years. Hardly a week goes by without a major study in a syndicated column or on one of the TV networks. As this chapter was being written, Charles Collingwood narrated a special called "The Retirement Revolution," with Dr. Ginny Boyak of the Andrus Gerontology Center as his resource and numerous shots of retirees in Des Moines. Several pilot films have been shown, directed specifically to the elderly.

With all this there seem to be some marked issues and gaps. The issues are illustrated by a script being prepared for CBS that a free-lance TV writer submitted to me for reaction. My advice was to discard the series of ten programs if it followed the proposed outline—namely, a series of "problems," depictions of loneliness, financial difficulties, rejection by family, and other familiar topics. My view was that there is, indeed, an ongoing need to educate the nation on all of these matters. But the greater need at the present time is for the mass media to correct the broad image that Dr. Robert Butler has called ageism, discussed previously. Specific issues can be attached and, if well done, can have repercussions in legislation. One such was a documentary on the loss of pension benefits as workers moved from one job to another. Over the longer time frame, the mass media are most influential in affecting moods and attitudes.

The mass media, as well as literature, provide fundamental responses and mirrors, rather than innovations. Thus, in the long run, they will report and dramatize the actual changes that take place. Even the TV soap operas, presently a fanaticism for many millions (including university students) did not embrace a topic such as homosexuality until it had become a commonly discussed issue.

When one considers the influence of such journals as *Commentary* or the *New York Review of Books* on public opinion, an observation is in order for a journal of substance to deal with issues concerning aging and adulthood. No such journal presently exists. *Retirement Living* (formerly *Harvest Years*), and *Modern Maturity* serve other purposes. The AARP might sponsor such a monthly magazine, or the Office of Aging. A more appropriate sponsorship—because it would be freer of bureaucratic decisions—would be a publication issued by an independent group, free to probe in depth and to seek out an intelligent minority among the vast potential of 27 million elderly and the many more who are interested.

Most pertinent, perhaps, would be a journal that is the organ of a national organization of elderly that presently does not exist. As with courses offered by the Institute for Lifetime Learning (part of AARP) and the Humanities Program of the National Council on the Aging, such an organization would combine all the possibilities for serving an intellectually-oriented segment of retirees. Included in its range of activities could be theme-oriented travels, conferences (regional, national, international), research, publications, and preretirement consultations. The membership would need to determine its policy toward a program of social action. Such an organization could spearhead the new body of opinion about the capacities of the elderly.

CHAPTER 17

Physical Activity Experiences

Several kinds of physical activity need to be identified in connection with leisure for all ages: exercise, to help preserve or improve the body, and sports, games, and general movement (such as walking for whatever reason).

Exercise per se is not recreational, although it may be enjoyable. It becomes part of a game, as in tennis, and when elements of social stylization enter, as in the presence of rules, traditions, a social selection of teammates or colleagues, special spaces (playing fields, tracks, parks, etc.), and a time frame.

The distinction between games and sports is not clear. James Michener, the writer, provided a distinction in his *Sports in America:*

Sports. (1) an athletic activity requiring physical prowess or skill and usually of a competitive nature (baseball, football, tennis, Olympic field sports, fencing, boxing, etc.); (2) any form of activity carried on out of doors, often not of a competitive nature (hunting, fishing, horseback riding, sailing, birdwatching, etc.). . . .
Games. a competitive activity involving skill, chance or athletic prowess on the part of two or more persons who play according to a set of rules, for their own enjoyment or for the entertainment of spectators. . . .[1]

Especially when the spectator dimension is added to participation, sports and games are viewed by a very large proportion of the total population. In 1975, professional baseball attracted about 30 million fans, basketball almost 8 million, and football almost 11 million; college football drew 32 million, and horseracing, over 79 million.[2] The total comes to 160 million, or 70% of the total population.

This astounding figure may be considered in the context of a society in which most workers are no longer involved in physical labor. One characteristic of industrial societies is the increased proportion of persons in the service industries and the use of machines to do heavy work. Nevertheless, gerontologists need to be reminded that whatever the job, one loss that comes with

[1]New York: Random House, 1976, p. 23.
[2]From Table 361, "Selected Spectator Sports," in *The Statistical Abstract of the U.S.,* 1977, 97th edition. U.S. Department of Commerce, Bureau of the Census.

retirement is movement of some kind in any work—walking, climbing stairs, or just getting to and from the job. That movement, however, like a game, has been in a framework of meaning and purpose. Leisure for the retiree can provide the cultural setting in which physical activity goes on, but without the boredom that exercise qua exercise (such as jogging) often induces.

IMPORTANCE OF THE PHYSICAL

An ongoing pattern of physical activity is essential for mental as well as for physical health. Perhaps these cannot be clearly distinguished. For example, physical work, such as farming, has been isolated by Dr. Alexander Leaf in explaining the unusual longevity of certain Russian, Pakistani, and Ecuadorian persons (as in the reputed lifespan of Shirali Mislimon, 168 years, in the Soviet Caucasus). However, the serenity of the environment was accompanied by other factors mentioned by Dr. Leaf: heredity, mountain living, and prolonged sexual life.[3]

On the other hand, De Carlo reported from a 20-year study of twins that as far as "successful" aging goes, motor activity "did not significantly relate to physical health." Affective activity and mental health were more closely related to cognitive activity and intellectual performance. Yet the team of researchers also concluded that "individuals who engage in a high degree of activity with regularity will age more successfully than those whose whole engagement is of low degree and sporadic."[4]

At the sports conference held in connection with the Munich Olympics, Professor A. Wohl of Warsaw wrote of sport:

As a leisure-time occupation, it offers man a wide field in which he can express his personality; it enables him to experience the delight that accompanies the risks of the game.... In sport man finds possibilities of expressing his striving for perfection, for surpassing positions already reached in harmony with the slogan, "farther, higher, quicker;" in sport he finds the fascination of a struggle which is not debased and degraded, but perfected and humanized.[5]

Older persons should not be written off as participants, for in tennis, golf, and baseball the same dynamics operate as among younger persons, even if with less physical abandon or energy input. Indeed, games provide a major example of the leisure "role" that was discussed in Chapter 1 and, sometimes, of roles that are as clearly defined as those of the person's former work. All of Znaniecki's elements—circle, function, esteem, and "self"—are clearly specified. This may be one of the attractions of participation in games and perhaps, to the spectator as he critically cheers, jeers—at least, judges—the

---

[3]"Every Day is a Gift When You are Over 100," *National Geographic,* 143, No. 1 (Jan. 1973), pp. 93–119.

[4]T. J. De Carlo, "Recreation Participation Patterns and Successful Aging," *Journal of Gerontology,* 29 (1974), p. 421.

[5]A. Wohl, *Sport in the Modern World—Chances and Problems.* Scientific Congress, Munich, Aug. 21–25, 1972. Editors: O. Grupe, D. Kurtz, J. M. Leipel. Berlin, Heidelberg, New York, Springer-Verlag, p. 25.

effectiveness with which they are being performed. In the daily world we may be somewhat unclear about the roles of a politician or teacher. Not so with the football quarterback, or a basketball guard, or a goalie in soccer.

In each case his general function is clear, and precise observations can be made to evaluate how well he performs. Not only his success, but that of the whole group of players—if it is a team play—can be measured by its victories and defeats.

The game world is generally a conservative one. With minor variations, baseball is still the baseball I knew as a boy. Its roles, therefore, are so well ingrained and its inherent controls are so widely accepted that three strikes are an "out," whether the player is an Al Capone in Alcatraz, a Hank Aaron in Milwaukee, or a sandlotter anywhere.

The team, in sports and the arts, may have a "style" of its own, so that the role of the shortstop is not standardized, but it is still carried on within the general specification of how a shortstop differs in function from a second baseman. Deviations from this acceptable function can be accepted by the circle of players only to a point, even in an amateur or leisure framework. When the same role is performed professionally, as in Aaron's case, there are several trained umpires who are present to serve as authorities to interpret the rules and, in case of doubt, to pull out a rulebook for reference.

The satisfaction of games, in even the leisure context, is not to violate the rules or norms, but to see how successfully the roles of batter, pitcher, and so forth, can be played *within* the system of regulations. The amateur may be as proficient as the professional, but his role is executed more in the spirit of immediate satisfaction and fun and less in the professional spirit of accountability, commitment to win, and play for financial reward.

The communications among game players exist on two levels, the performance itself and the attitude or "spirit" that is brought into the situation. As to the first, there is no substantial difference between leisure (amateur) and work (professional) game playing: the communications are, in both cases, the vernacular and the symbolic. The former consists of cognitive exchange, "throw the ball," "serve the deck," "third down, four to go," which is understood by players and watchers alike; the latter is communication without words, such as advancing a base when the next player at bat hits a ball.[6]

There is an important element of normative behavior in the game that is even more pronounced in leisure games and sports, especially when these are manifestations or symbols of class consciousness. This is the element of mannerism, as in the fox hunt. "Sportsmanship" is the watchword, with the emphasis on how the action occurs.

In his well known satire, *The Theory and Practice of Gamesmanship*, Stephan Potter instructed us on how to take advantage of the slogan "the good gamesman is the good sportsman." He advised us that against a stupid but strong opponent who suspects you of being unsporting, "extreme sportingness" is the thing, and "the instant waiving of any rule which works in your favour is the procedure." But against the introvertive, cynical type, sportingness will simply be wasted.[7]

"Sportingness," seriously considered, is the set of values that have been brought into the play situation by such clichés as "the spirit is what counts, not

[6]Max Kaplan, *Leisure: Theory and Policy*. New York: John Wiley & Sons, 1975, pp. 295–297

[7]Stephan Potter, *The Theory and Practice of Gamesmanship*. New York, Holt, 1948. Bantam Edition, 1956.

the winning." The familiar argument that recreation for youths will keep them off the streets and reduce crime is usually advanced with an implied formative creation of "teamsmanship" (read as "citizenship") by virtue of the comradeship or collective concern with the game. In this sense, those who argue for games as ethical articulations believe in some mystique of transference. It is somewhat odd that the same theory of transference is not admitted when we turn to the subject of extramarital sex: we do not say, at least publicly, that such sex as a form of leisure produces a human warmth that carries over to one's family life.

As to the second side of games and sports, the roles of spectators, the increase in their numbers in the United States over the past 20 years did not reduce the numbers of participants in games and sports. For instance, while attendance at professional baseball increased in the two decades from 1950 to 1969, from about 17.5 to 27.5 million, participation in amateur softball rose from 8 to 19 million in the last decade alone, and the number of golfers grew from 3.25 to 9.5 million. Nor must we forget the additional millions who watch all these spectacles on television or listen to radio accounts.[8]

DYNAMICS OF THE PHYSICAL

Both in the United States and in other nations we are obviously dealing with a significant phenomenon. The standings of the Mets may affect the mood of the populace in Brooklyn as much as war victories affected ancient Sparta. The impact of sports on the life patterns of families during the football season on TV was illustrated several years ago by the many complaints received when NBC had the temerity to start a special production of *Heidi* before the Oakland Raiders and the New York Jets had finished their football game. Cities such as Green Bay are known nationally only for the team that represents them. In Europe soccer occupies a similar status and, if anything, attracts an even higher interest in sports, sometimes to the point of spilling over into international politics.

The role of the sports enthusiast, the "fan" or follower, is far from passive, and provides more evidence that the active-passive dichotomy is useless. His moods alter with the fortunes of the teams he supports. "*We* won today," not a paid team of workers hired by a firm in the business of making money from baseball or football. Neither management nor team usually has the slightest interest in the community, and members of the team are bought and sold purely as business investments. But the image of the team remains as an ongoing symbol to the public, with individual heroes who emerge now and then to lend an aura of worship, myth, and fantasy to the real world.

The practice of betting on teams and on such sports as horse races is hardly accounted for in official estimates of expenditures on leisure, but serves to provide people with a deeper commitment as an active public.

Finally, Dumazedier has spoken of fantasies that are played out in leisure,

---

[8]Table 21, *The Statistical Abstract of the U.S.,* 1970.

such as the amateurish guitar player who hears himself as Segovia.[9] This probably occurs as frequently in sports as in the arts. Indeed, except for the business aspect of professional sports (which includes a large coverage in special journals and in the daily press) the roles played by the public are substantially fantasy roles. An artificial competition is concocted between artificial teams (i.e., with no generic homogeneity) as if the end result—who wins today, or at the end of the season—will change the course of history. Because this fantasy is heavily institutionalized with its symbols, officialdom, rules and traditions, and characteristic dress and speech, it becomes the whole real world to many persons.

But to describe this as a world of fantasy is to speak as an observer; it is acted on and altogether becomes a reality in relation to other portions of a person's life. Leisure, for such an individual, is not a peripheral element. The Packer fan is most alive during the season; if he is unable to turn with equal fervor to other sports fantasies, then he finds that the rest of the year is simply an interlude. For him sports is an end, and he knows its regulations, scores, great figures, and history as well as he knows his religious books and rituals.

As all sports followers know, age is a basic handicap to full activity in contact sports and games. However, "old" for professional baseball, football, and basketball players is in their 30s or 40s. George Blanda, extra-point kicker for the Oakland Raiders, retired in his mid 40s, an extraordinary "elder" in his circle.

Among the differences between the "old old" and the "new old" that we have drawn earlier a differing attachment to games and sports can be suggested. The former were probably more directly involved in physically-oriented games and in outdoor sports. The latter group is more urbanized, educated, and sedentary in their former work. As time goes on, and as more Americans are less physical in work, we note the rise of "jogging" and subscriptions to organized courses in exercise. The "Fitness after Fifty Institute," part of the Center for the Study of Aging, Inc. (Albany, New York) distributes tapes on such topics as motivation, mental health, fitness training, relaxation, and prescriptions for exercise.

Through yoga others are finding a combination of exercise with the psychological benefits of contemplation and relaxation. The physical benefits are there, whether or not the claims made by the yoga enthusiasts are fully justified. In their volume *"Easy Does It" Yoga: For People Over 60,* Christensen and Rankin noted the lack of

regular and safe exercise that is inexpensive—does not require elaborate equipment or transportation and that can be done on a daily basis year round. Walking, swimming, bicycling, jogging and tennis are all good forms of exercise, but remain dependent upon too many outside factors. In warmer areas, such as Florida, the older citizens are able to get the benefits of fresh air and sunshine most of the year, but in many parts of the United States, persons over 60 are often housebound from 3 to 5 months of the year. . . . Yoga offers the potent alternatives of daily invigorating exercise and mental discipline to the elderly person in any physical condition. . . .[10]

_____

[9]J. Dumazedier, *Toward A Society of Leisure.* New York, The Free Press, 1967.

[10]Alice Christensen and David Rankin, *"Easy Does It" Yoga: For People Over 60.* Cleveland Heights: Saraswati Studio, 1975.

Swami Satchidananda, one of the major authorities on Yoga, claims he has worked with beginners in their 80s. David Ben Gurion started at 75. Classes are found throughout the world.

Walking, often the major recourse by the poorer elderly, can be pursued at one's own pace, and is the best exercise one can pursue. Dr. Paul Dudley White, the famous cardiologist, used to leave his cab a mile from the airport to walk the rest of the way. Many persons combine walking with birdwatching.

The bicycle and tricycle are solutions for many. In addition to the exercise, they provide a cheap and enjoyable mode of transportation. Mrs. Sydney Rea, 69, from San Mateo, California, wrote:

It's amazing how you rediscover the pleasure of seeing the flowers in people's gardens that otherwise are lost in a blur through a car window . . . smelling fragrances . . . hearing nature's sounds as you pedal around. The exercise is great, too. No maintenance, no exhaust fumes to pollute the atmosphere. I don't know of a more enjoyable way to get around quickly and easily.[11]

Among the games often associated with the elderly, shuffleboard is noticed most often. Its physical requirements are mild and, as in other games for the elderly, provides some exercise in a framework of interest rather than routine commitment. Only one or two steps are required to release the "pigeon." A large club in St. Petersburg, founded in 1924, has 3,000 members for its 107 courts. Nationally shuffleboard players total 300,000. The game goes back to Scottish curling of the 13th century. National championships are held annually.

Lawn bowling balls are made so that they curve to break as much as 4 feet in the course of 80 feet. Origins of the game can be traced to Greece and Rome. King Henry VII tried to ban it in 1511 because of the prevalence of gambling. Contrary to shuffleboard the game has become identified with the upper class but that is changing.

More physically demanding games can be successfully pursued by older men, as illustrated by a softball club in St. Petersburg that has often been mentioned in the national mass media. As its title implies, the Three-Quarter Century Softball Club has a minimum age of 75, divided into the Kids and Kubs. Formed in 1930, base running was at first prohibited to prevent "dying on the bases," but this preventative measure was quickly discarded. As a 76-year-old second baseman, Frank Warton, noted in a story of April 18, 1976 (*St. Petersburg Times*): "If these fellas didn't have softball, I don't think they'd survive. They can't wait until the next game comes around." John Maloney, pitcher in the organization until his death at 97 in 1974, was asked in the same article if he didn't worry about toppling over dead some day on the field; he replied that this would be "just dandy. I live from one season to the next. I want to die right out there on the mound."

Camping provides an ambience for physical activity that has been introduced to the elderly in recent years, with unending possibilities for combining the purely physical with other activities in natural settings.

A *New York Times* editorial of May 12th, 1972 referred to one of the

[11]*Harvest Years,* March 1972.

"glorious sights" of summer: watching a busload of men and women in their 70s and 80s leaving the steaming city streets for a vacation in the country. The need for a change and anticipation are "lifegiving and ageless." An organization called Vacations for the Aging has provided more than 50,000 two-week holidays in the past 12 years, with camps in New York, New Jersey, and Connecticut.[12] The program includes boating, fishing, arts and crafts, square dancing, and a chance to "dream outside themselves." In 1972 5,820 persons participated, 224 more than the year before. Twenty camps were used for the purpose, all interdenominational. The project began in 1949 with the first camp session for 40 women, all over 60. Leaders of 16 women's philanthropic organizations in New York City joined with the Educational Alliance, affiliated with the National Jewish Welfare Board. Three years later men were admitted into the summer program. Other organizations arrange camping sessions as well, such as PCOP, the Philadelphia Center for Older People, a center that began in 1949.

---

[12]The project is conducted through private donations by Vacations for the Aging, 225 Park Avenue South, New York, New York.

CHAPTER 18

Social Activity Experiences

There are some persons we like to be with. We like them as *people*. There need be nothing vital to talk about, no "content," no chess game, no political agreements, no conversation of any consequence. Classical models of such relationships are the family, a pair of lovers, a social gathering. With the presence of content, even for a moment—entertainment, serious talk—the pure form of sociability has been replaced. Friends have become debaters, jesters, sages, teachers, audiences.

Georg Simmel's insights still remain unsurpassed:

> Inasmuch as in the purity of its manifestations, sociability has no objective purpose, no extrinsic results, it entirely depends on the personalities among whom it occurs. But precisely because everything depends on their personalities, the participants are not permitted to stress them too conspicuously. *Tact,* therefore, is here of such peculiar significance.[1]

We have here a relationship in which each person acts *as if* all are equals. Normal social roles—banker, artist, rich man, father—are suspended. This is not a "lie"; it becomes one only when the ostensibly self-contained phenomenon is a deception played for ulterior purposes.

The significance of sociability as leisure experience is that it covers a wide range of commitment and self-revelation. One can be with people he likes and say nothing of depth. On the other hand, in conversation which has no ulterior purpose, persons can delve into areas of thought, feeling or auto-biography of the utmost importance, especially in the company of strangers. By its nature, such conversation can "free" one, stimulate, lead to self-discovery, promote a self-confidence, or threaten one for the moment and for a long time afterward.

---

[1]*The Sociology of Georg Simmel.* Editor, Kurt H. Wolff. Glencoe, Ill.: Free Press, 1950, p. 45.

THE AGE FACTOR

The uniqueness of being an older person is perhaps most applicable to social forms of leisure. First, a crucial element in the fullest expression of sociability is its unhurried character. Flexibility in time is its charm—all that is interesting can hardly be confined to a precise 26 minutes, as on television.

Loneliness is a second characteristic of many older lives. Writing of sociable communication, I noted its difficulty:

> . . . because of the problem some persons have in maintaining or developing a theme of conversation or a fear of becoming involved with others, of feeling insecure in discussion, of hesitation in revealing one's position when controversial subjects enter the conversation, of revealing ourselves as unknowledgeable, as of saying the wrong thing.[2]

In these respects many older persons can be said to have an advantage over others. Their accumulated experience here comes to the fore. Obviously, among the 27 million over 60, there will be found a due proportion of bumblers, braggarts, fools, and dullards, the mainstream of "average persons" who get along, and those who can hold their own on any level of insight, intelligence, and worldly experience.

There are, however, patterns or values in American life that make deep friendships difficult. For instance, observing bazaars in Yugoslavia, Israel, Iran, Hungary, and other cultures, one is impressed by the close personal relationships that seem to exist among those who are thrown together day after day, selling their wares. In these older societies, the giant or extended family unit has served to prevent loneliness at any age. An American wife of an Iranian official informed me that she has no time to read, for her husband's relatives are over continually to keep her company. In our country the migration to cities was in part a move to achieve some sense of privacy. Both the car and television, miracles of physical and psychological mobility, are also private in their orientation. Friendship in the U.S. is also limited, compared to many European patterns, as by the suspicion of two men who are close friends; the holding of hands between them is entirely prohibited. The search for close friendship may be a major reason for many persons to prefer residency in nursing homes or retirement communities. However, one characteristic complaint that is heard, especially in such places, is the prevalence of gossip that results from the importance of minutiae. As one respondent noted in a study of friendships many years ago among the Golden Age Group in a city library:

> Hardly anyone's worthy of secrets. The minute you displease them they gossip and tell what you disclosed and more besides. . . . I make friends and leave them all the time. Some stay on but that's because they want to, not because I want them. I could leave any of them at any time.[3]

Yet, our interviews in Florida during the past ten years have uncovered a closeness among retirees in such diverse settings as mobile home com-

---

[2]Max Kaplan, *Leisure: Theory and Policy.* New York: John Wiley & Sons, 1975, p. 308.
[3]Malcolm Arth, "American Culture and the Phenomenon of Friendship in the Aged," San Francisco: Fifth International Congress of Gerontology, August 7–12, 1960.

munities, a number of nursing homes (such as the Jewish Towers, Tampa), and in Sun City Center. The Florida advantage of warm weather is conducive to developing opportunities for social relationships.

It is clear that the phenomenon of loneliness and the place of "sociability" as a form of leisure in dispelling it provides an area for more research than has been given to it so far.

Illustrations of sociability among the elderly are endless. The excerpt below from one informal report, written for the elderly, will suggest other devices. Helen Alpert set the basis for her report:

These days, friend and family relationships are transient and fleeting, pummeled by cultural pressures caused by "super-industrialism," "technocracy," "the technotronic society," "the corporate state," etc. Although we may not fully comprehend them, they're easy to understand when they invade our neighborhood—the nice next-door couple gets transferred across the country; the older couples up the street sell their house and move; families down the block who once stayed put are always off travelling; or (this is happening with frightening frequency) blight creeps into the street, shops and residents leave, and urban relocation is but one jump ahead of the bulldozer.

In Columbus, Ohio, there is a group called SOLO, "Shooing Our Loneliness Organization." Members enjoy speakers, travelogs, picnics, theater, dinners—and each other. In many cities, "phone pals" chat with each other every evening. Pennsylvania and New York were forerunners in initiating the now popular "telephone reassurance" as a daily way to check and cheer the aged, lonely, handicapped, shut-in. Last month in a mass move New York City set up club-like quarters in a nearby house for hundreds of men and women in lonely rooms who spent their days aimlessly adrift in the downtown bus terminal.

Churches and synagogues over the country have opened their doors for afternoon meetings of both sexes. Even a tiny town like Clarence, New York (pop. 2,014), has an ecumenical project that recruits all residents for richer living; following a questionnaire on how to improve town life, merged action put house numbers on homes to speed fire, police, and medical emergency calls; recreational, social and educational programs were launched (16 events in June alone); and work is ongoing to raise funds for a concert shell for the town's concert association. Every resident is involved, from Girl Scouts to the elderly. Help is neither wanted nor sought from the local, state or federal government.[4]

Mrs. Alpert closed with the story of a little girl playing alone in the sand. A neighbor called over the fence, "Where's your mother?" "She's asleep." "Where's your little brother?" "He's asleep, too." The neighbor asked, "Aren't you lonesome, playing all by yourself?" "No," replied the child, "I like me." This touches on the problem of many Americans who cannot say, "I like me," for they are surrounded with too few opportunities to explore themselves.

ISSUES FOR GERONTOLOGISTS

The issue of the degree to which we should encourage individuality and privacy strikes deeply into a judgment that contemporary gerontologists and leisure leaders must confront. Is it our purpose to encourage individualism, as in provisions for reading rooms or in taping oral histories? Or do we count ourselves as failures unless we have organized everyone in

---

[4]Helen Alpert, "Why Be Lonely?" Reprinted from *Harvest Years,* Feb. 1972 edition. Reproduced by permission.

sight? Even in the latter case, is the social event to be evaluated by the proportion of those present who have "participated"—that is, *said* something?

Dealing with this issue takes us into the dynamics of *informal* social relationships which have been studied far less by social scientists than have the structured, ritualized phenomena of audiences, families, or congregations. An analogy comes to mind here with a comparison made some years ago by the social psychologist, Kurt Lewin. Comparing Germans and Americans, he drew a picture of personality levels and observed that the American could quickly open a conversation, penetrating the first layer; then he had little to ask or say. The German took a longer time to open up, but then he was more willing to explore deeply.

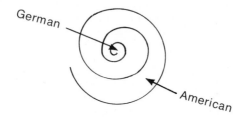

If a comparison were to be made of social "penetration" between older and younger persons within our culture, the former seem to combine the Germanic and American characteristics. There is little difficulty in starting a conversation with older persons, and they are willing to move quickly into their histories, likes and dislikes, political beliefs, or almost anything one cares to explore.

Again, ageism raises its head if we inquire about the extent to which these characteristics of the elderly have become part of leisure philosophy and programming. We have sold them short, substituting card games because it is easier—for us as well as for them. Thus, this is similar to the way in which we have underestimated the ability of our youth, and denied them the opportunity for cross-generational exchange. Even the oral history projects which abounded during the Bicentennial year in all parts of the country were generally one way. The older person was asked to narrate his life, which was all to the good. But older people should also listen to youth.

One of the dramatic historical places and symbols in the United States is Ellis Island. It was here that more than half the immigrants entering the United States in the 30 years after 1890 passed through and underwent medical examinations. In spite of its historical importance to millions of Americans, the federal government spends little more than one million dollars annually to maintain the property, which is in shambles.[5] One has to see

---

[5]*Ellis Island,* National Park Service, U.S. Department of the Interior, pamphlet, based in part on details from Ann Novotny, *Stranger at the Door,* Riverside, Conn.: Chatham Press, 1971.

the motion picture *Godfather 2* to get an idea of what the main reception room at Ellis Island looked like. The millions of records of immigrants—in these days of *Roots*—are spread across the country, many lost for all time. Since no federal agency has attempted to bring order out of this historiographic disaster, the responsibility can be undertaken by collective action of the elderly—all of whom, without exception, were immigrants or descendants. However, the task of gathering these records and cataloguing them should be accompanied by a massive "recall," assisted by thousands of young people who, within the federal job programs reinstituted by the Carter administration, could serve as interviewers. Youth would learn something about American history. Looking back at the 1930's they might get insights into the depression years in a way that few written accounts, aside from William Manchester's *The Glory and The Dream,* have captured in detail.[6]

Benefits to the elderly would be apparent on many levels. From such programs and cooperative historical adventures social activities could reach some depth, our national archives would be enriched, and everyone among our elderly, especially the "old old," would be recognized as a participant in the national drama. Out of it might even come a collective vision that would contribute to goals for the future of the nation. If young people need to develop a sense of history, the elderly are needed to develop a vision of the future; no one group is more entitled to an opinion and a vision.

---

[6]*The Glory and the Dream, A Narrative History of America, 1932–1972.* New York: Bantam Books, 1974.

CHAPTER **19**

Spiritual Activity Experiences

It is a moot point to some as to whether contemplation about one's place in the world should be placed in the category of leisure. Yet our characterization in Chapter 3 pointed the way, for it spoke of the "whole range" of human experience, not only of entertainment, play, or relaxation. No direct lines are, in fact, to be drawn from a specific form of activity to the classification "leisure," and the concept would be impoverished if it excluded experiences of the mind, emotion, imagination, perception, or contemplation. When looking at a flower is the observer not an integral part of the encounter? Can we remain content with putting only an event itself into some statistical table as a physical act, but remain ignorant of or unconcerned with its meaning? If so, social science has come to a low point of reality. As I advocated in Chapter 5, we need to protect ourselves from that prospect by moving explicitly into less measurable but equally essential levels of life or experience.

The academic tradition prefers to center on the term "value" for such discussions. What are some issues that relate philosophy, even theology, to leisure? How do these relationships refer more specifically to older persons? One would expect to find a mature discussion on the first of these among theologians.

SOME VIEWS

Gordon Dahl, a leading Lutheran spokesman, asserted that "To put it sharply, most middle-class Americans tend to worship at their work, to work at their play, and to play at their worship."[1] He identified the aspect of the leisure ethic, which

. . . is based upon a radical affirmation of personal freedom, based upon the inherent dignity and uniqueness of every human being. It presupposes a pluralistic

---

[1]Gordon Dahl, *Work, Play and Worship in a Leisure-Oriented Society.* Minneapolis: Augsburg, 1972, p. 12.

186

system of values and promotes a wide diversity of life styles. It compels the integrity, but dispels the permanence, of human relationships and replaces narrow group loyalties with more ecumenical attitudes and interests. It prefers immediate satisfaction over promises of future happiness. And it advances the interdependence of men and groups instead of their independence and competition.[2]

Specific relationships between such leisure values and Christianity were discussed in *Religion and Leisure in America,* written in 1954 for the National Council of Churches by Robert Lee. A decade later came Rudolf Norden's *The Christian Encounters the New Leisure,* with its thesis that God calls his followers to leisure as well as to work. As Harold D. Lehman summarized this view, and affirmed his own position:

> We dare not dichotomize life, as though it is necessary to honor God with our work, but when leisure time comes we have somehow earned the freedom to make our own choices as if God doesn't matter. . . . The totality of our commitment to Christ knows no off-bound areas of time or of activity.[3]

Another writer on leisure and religion, William R. H. Stevens, simultaneously affirmed the position of the Churches of Christ, reflected the Catholic position of Josef Pieper, and paralleled his contemporary, Harvey Cox, in the view that

> The essential spirit of leisure is that of celebration and of saying "yes" to life, a joyfulness in the midst of the created world. It enjoys life. Instead of fleeing from life in the world, the man of leisure literally relishes his life in the world. . . . To say that genuine leisure is essentially joyful does not mean that leisure may have nothing of sadness, pain, suffering, or loneliness. Real joy is a condition of the spirit deeper than the mere fleeting experience of pleasurable sensation.[4]

In my own volumes of 1960 and 1975, I sought to explore the relation of values to leisure in a more academic sense.[5] In a series of short prescriptions addressed to the religious community, I asked "What goals, what visions do we want so that we can more hopefully—if not always successfully—achieve them with the help of our new abundance and technology? . . . The church, whatever its tradition, could do well to look at leisure. . . ."[6]

Again, addressing a Minnesota conference, largely composed of ministers on leisure and religion, I was led to the general observation:

> Thus, as economic scarcity has given way to the expectation of widespread abundance, Christianity seems to have cooperated with the profane institutions in the physical/psychological/cultural/theological relocation of Heaven to earth. Paradise has achieved instant visibility and attainability by the dispensers of television specials and sports, by Florida winter vacation, and by whatever content the impatient person wishes to associate with his heavenly guest. Perhaps the church could not meet the

---

[2]Ibid. p. 90.

[3]Harold D. Lehman, *In Praise of Leisure.* Scottsdale: Herald Press, 1974, p. 137.

[4]William R. H. Stevens, *Are We Ready for Leisure?* New York: Friendship Press, 1966, pp. 31–32. Used with permission.

[5]Max Kaplan, *Leisure: Theory and Policy.* New York: John Wiley & Sons, 1975, Chapter 11; *Leisure in America: A Social Inquiry.* New York: John Wiley & Sons, 1960, Chapter 14.

[6]_____, "Christian Leisure," in *The Upper Room Disciplines.* Nashville, 1972, pp. 229–235.

challenge. After all, can the pulpit's vague visions match the pragmatic paradisiac palpitations provided by *Peyton Place?*[7]

THE AGE FACTOR

What has all this to do, more specifically, with the elderly?

First, it is surely true that "spiritual" forms or aspects of leisure are not limited to the special philosophies or programs of churches, Christianity, or religious institutions as a whole. Yet it is also true that what these institutions have to say about leisure is germane to issues of values. Religious institutions should be one primary source and proponent of "spiritual activity experiences" in leisure.

Secondly, there has existed an image that, in the "ages" of life referred to in Chapter 1, older persons can be expected to be the more conservative or religious in the traditional sense. Perhaps the familiar contrast between the "active" and the "contemplative" life is relevant, with the second close to Erikson's association of *wisdom* with the integrity of old age.[8]

The sociologist Robert N. Bellah has traced the specific historic roots of *vita activa* and *vita contemplativa,* from Aristotle and Plato to Thomas Jefferson, Abe Lincoln, and Hannah Arendt. He quoted Jacques Maritain's singular comment about the United States as a social framework for both activist and contemplative lifestyles:

> . . . contemplation is particularly important to this continent. Is it not a universally repeated commonplace that America is the land par excellence of pragmatism and of the great undertakings of human activity? There is truth in this, as in most commonplaces. Whitman celebrates the pioneers in a manner which is certainly characteristic of the American soul. But, in my opinion, there are in America great reserves and possibilities for contemplation. The activism which is manifested here assumes in many cases the aspect of a remedy against despair. I think that this activism itself masks a certain hidden aspiration to contemplation. . . . On the other hand, the tendency, natural in this country, to undertake great things, to have confidence, to be moved by large idealistic feelings, may be considered . . . as disguising that desire and aspiration of which I spoke.[9]

Maritain's judgment, in my view, goes to the heart of our subject. The "old old" generation came to this country when it was in its formative stage. There was enough work for all, throughout the year and throughout a lifetime. Without denying the ability or propensity for that generation to engage in contemplation that could be serious and productive, in spite of its

---

[7]M. Kaplan, "Leisure, Human Values and Religion," for conference of same title, co-sponsored by the University of Minnesota, Department of Physical Education and Recreation and the Leisure Education Resource Center of the National Lutheran Campus Ministry, Minneapolis, April 1976.

[8]Erik H. Erikson, "Reflections on Dr. Borg's Life Cycle," *Daedalus,* 105, No. 2 (1976), pp. 22–23.

[9]Jacques Maritain, quoted in Robert N. Bellah, "To Kill and Survive or to Die and Become: The Active Life and the Contemplative Life as Ways of Being Adult," *Daedalus,* 105, No. 2 (1976), p. 73. Reproduced by permission.

primary commitment to building a nation rather than thinking about it, the "new old" has the tools for more serious contemplation: time, a more democratic, educational base, a milieu of widespread literacy. On the other hand, as I noted in the Minnesota conference, these "new old" also matured in a period when our humanist intellectual community was busy attacking technology, subscribing to the gloom of the Heilbronners, Elluls, Illiches, Mumfords, Sorokins and Toynbees. I asked: "Has vision for the future died with the H. G. Wells, the Sydney Webbs, and the Edward Bellamys? Have humanistic philosophers been silenced by our computer-oriented futurologists—the Herman Kahns and the Club of Rome?"[10]

In the mid-1970's, as a reaction to the gloom that followed Vietnam and Watergate, among all age groups, there was a noticeable rise in optimism. The danger is that our efforts to overcome or to counteract "ageism" will center on activism—i.e., that the elderly are performing their "natural" (nonageistic) role when they are *active:* working, moving about, or going through the motions of agelessness. This is as dangerous a fallacy as ageism itself.

Without subscribing to the theological coloring, I agree with several sentences that Maritain added to his statement noted earlier:

> To wish paradise on earth is stark naiveté. But it is surely better than not to wish any paradise at all. To aspire to paradise is man's grandeur; and how should I aspire to paradise except by beginning to realize paradise here below? The problem is to know what paradise is. Paradise consists, as St. Augustine says, in the joy of the Truth. Contemplation is paradise on earth, a crucified paradise.[11]

One cannot tell how many older persons are now spending time "contemplating." It is a nonsensical question to put to our social scientists for, in typical fashion, they would "define" the term, play the game of creating "scales" of depth or intensity, and then use a questionnaire spelled out in a scale of seven choices. It is necessary to encourage older persons to think, evaluate their past, comment on the human drama they have seen and lived, generalize from it, preach at us, open visions for us, spell out the aspirations they see as needed for their children and grandchildren.

The author of *The House by the Sea,* May Sarton, wrote:

> "Poor old man sitting in the sun doing nothing," we might think. But the old man on a park bench may actually be very busy *doing* nothing because he is *being* something. He may, to use a haunting phrase of Florida Scott-Maxwell's, be "blind with insight." Self-exploration is a natural organic way toward understanding the universal.[12]

There are tangible ways of encouraging thought, contemplation, and vision for the generations that have earned the right to free-floating, assumptive, historically-enriched opinions or perspectives of their world. One can envision formal "graduation" from work careers, sponsored by universities, with appropriate "commencement" exercises for and by the elderly. Yet,

---

[10]Kaplan, Minnesota Conference, op. cit.
[11]Maritain, quoted in Bellah, op. cit.
[12]May Sarton, *The House by the Sea: A Journal,* November 1974–August 1976. New York, Norton, 1977.

universities have not moved toward such a vision, in which potential "graduates" would qualify for the certificate with extensive narratives and interpretations of earlier phases of their lives, and from which they would themselves organize the types of courses described in Chapter 15.

One can visualize a series of regional and national conferences in which retirees would not ignore such issues as necessary legislation, but would devote themselves to cultural interpretations.

In all of this, what is the difference from "intellectual" leisure activity experiences? The use of the category "spiritual activity experiences" here is comparable to a historical category I employed in my 1975 volume— "cultivated society," in contrast to the more familiar term "postindustrial." In both cases, I propose that the intellectual or academic tradition, with its essentials of rigor and evidence, has limitations. "Spiritual" opens us to the interdisciplinary, fusionary, holistic prospect of leisure that invites emotional, unforced, free, adventuresome levels of experience. "Religious" elements, whether defined by a John Dewey or a papal spokesman, can be present, but do not limit the larger "spiritual" horizons of leisure.

PURPOSES

Two other arguments can be made for the encouragement and analysis of contemplation among the elderly. One emanates from the retiree's passage through society as he crosses from work to retirement, the potential passage from *egoism* to *altruism*. The second is the spirit of this passage as a potential for what Henri Bergson has called the *elan vital*.

The first is a duality that is central to classical Judaic philosophy, which rejects the doctrine of original sin as its cornerstone. The side of man's nature that is associated with self or egoism is balanced by the tendency toward other-orientation, selflessness, or altruism. Altruism "represents a reaching out for others through whom we find our fulfillment. This is the psychological foundation of love experience, from the most primitive to the most exalted, and it goes far beyond the confines of the family where we find it most frequently."[13]

Egoism, according to the proponents of this balance, is needed for self-expression, to develop individuality, to drive one in resisting difficulties, to realize (in Maslow's terms) some degree of "self-actualization." In the leisure context we find frameworks for such individual strength as games or achievement in the arts.

Altruism, the balancer, finds its function in such leisure forms as civic volunteerism or in travel that opens one to other cultural values. The balance, according to Judaism, is not the mere presence of both, but the inevitability of

---

[13]Ben Zion Bokser, "Rabbinic Judaism and the Problem of Egoism," in L. Bryson, L. Finkelstein, and R. M. MacIver, eds. *Conflicts of Power in Modern Culture.* New York: Harper & Row, 1947, p. 417.

one in the presence of the other: "Without the evil impulse, one could do no evil; but neither could he do good."[14]

What retirement provides is the possibility of the balance between egoism and altruism, not in a limited time framework, but in the perspective of the full life. Retirement in this sense is a freedom from those drives that persisted as the person sought (perhaps *fought*) his way through the frustrations and competitions of his work situations, not only in such areas as the business world, but in the politics of the campus and the conflicts of the art community or other characteristic clusters of values. Preretirement counselors can raise such issues as: What were the inherent tensions in each of the fields from which our subjects went into retirement? Did retirement entirely remove these encounters of egos in the roles that pervaded the business or the art world? When the Xerox Company provides a "sabbatical" to selected employees to work in the nonprofit setting of a community project, does the employee return to his job with a new attitude toward the goals that typically dominate work situations?

The broadest question is whether the leisure role for the retiree can be one which, devoid of work conflicts, tensions, or the necessity for individual assertion, becomes the occasion for achieving the human balance. Altruism, then, is not a *function* of leisure in such a case, but its characteristic. One does not set out to read for the blind in his free time with the avowed intention to do "good." It is not a duty that one fulfills, or a reward one seeks, but a life that finds its proper balance between the "I" and the "thou," or between "self" and "selflessness."

In this crystallization of the whole person through leisure the goal is not specific. It is the process becoming primary—the "becoming," as we noted earlier in the Confucian concept of the passage to adulthood. For the question now turns to the purpose or goal to which we wish to put the Judaic balance of ego and altruism. It would seem that leisure can provide the instrument for achieving this balance. Freed of the conflict with our fellow man that too often consumes us in work, we can now turn to roles that are cooperative rather than competitive, contemplative rather than combative.

---

[14]Nofet Tzufim, Warsaw, 1929; in Bokser, Ibid. p. 420.

CHAPTER 20

Touristic Activity Experiences

In a 1960 volume I had this to say about two types of travelers:

First there are those we may call "comparative strangers." These persons travel physically, but in reality they never, or seldom, leave their own familiar ideas and judgments. They find security wherever they may be in what is called *ethnocentrism*, the application of one's own standards to other situations: their own are always superior to those of others. They view, but do not understand. As Walter Lippmann wrote, these are persons "who do not see first and then define, they define first and then see."

A second group may be called "empathic natives." These persons seek, as best they can, to put themselves in the place of those whom they visit. They become native as much as their backgrounds, study, and empathy permit. What they take from their own environments are not particulars but universals. They sincerely wish to perceive and to understand. Like the explorer or trader, the soldier or the priest, these travelers depend on preparation and knowledge.[1]

MOTIVATIONS FOR TRAVEL: PATTERNS

Where do the elderly fall into these categories? That is, are they traveling now—for status ("the thing to do,"), out of curiosity, to fulfill their aspirations of earlier years, to relieve boredom? We can argue that the organizer or leader need not worry about such motivations. Travel, like other activities, is its own rationale, and pervading this experience there will be a multitude of meanings. Yet, the organizer does have a responsibility beyond simply making the trip possible. His function is to create a situation whereby the elderly in his groups are a minimum of "comparative strangers," wherever they go.

If, in contrast, the traveler is to be, as far as possible, an "empathic native," a case can be made for preparation and follow-up. The uniqueness of older persons for travel is manifold. They bring to travel experience, far more than the young, a lifetime of observations that are bound up with both negative and positive elements—biases, past judgments or knowledge of the

---

[1]Max Kaplan, *Leisure in America: A Social Inquiry.* New York: John Wiley & Sons, 1960, p. 216.

peoples and places visited, a freedom in meeting strangers, a more explicit celebration than the young of the opportunity, an unbounded energy that often finds unexpected release from the neighborhood, the nursing home, the community center, or the family. Note the first paragraph of a report in the *New York Times* of July 17, 1977:

> The bus broke down an hour after leaving the city—an electrical failure the driver couldn't repair. For four hours the 47 of us sat on Interstate 84 near Brewster, N.Y. I was fuming—but not my fellow passengers. They were singing, dancing the hustle by the roadside, shouting answers to a trivia quiz. Of course, they were much older than I.[2]

We have not only a new segment of travelers, the elderly, but remarkable opportunities to bring new understanding and meaning into the travel experience. Before the present era of tourism, the major travelers throughout history had been the explorer-adventurer, the businessman, the soldier, and the missionary. Then, after World War II brought long distance travel into the consciousness of the middle classes, several segments began to emerge: the young, the black, the post-pilgrim (returning to battle scenes or graves), and the vacationer of any age. Now a group of elderly emerges, bringing new business to the travel agent, a new type of traveler to the host nation or area and, mainly, a new vitality into their own lives.

If the sociology of leisure as a whole can be considered as a young field, 20 years old, then the sociology of tourism—one of its offshoots—is even younger, between 10 and 15 years. Oddly, the economics of tourism is older than either, although even now in the late 1970's there are relatively few solid contributions of economics to *general* issues of leisure. As a UNESCO research team pointed out, sociologists are inclined to view tourism from the view of society's decline, economists, from the view of future possibilities and growth.[3] If both alarm as well as optimism pervade the studies of tourism, the attitude relates to the welfare of the host nations, for many studies emanate from their concerns about protecting their cultures while simultaneously profiting from tourist "transients." A summary of some recent studies is in order to suggest the present and potential leisure roles of the older person as tourist.

Four types of tourists were noted by the sociologist, E. Cohen: (1) "organized mass tourists"; (2) "the individual mass tourist"; (3) "the explorer"; and (4) "the drifter." His first group is comparable to those whom I earmarked earlier as the "comparative strangers." In Cohen's view, they are least willing to give up their own values. His "drifter" corresponds to my category of "empathic native," immersed completely in the new environment. Of the remaining two types, highly institutionalized, the "explorer" is the potential trailblazer.[4]

In respect to Cohen's typology, the elderly of our time may be expected to deinstitutionalize themselves just as, in the case of retirement communities,

---

[2]Paul Grimes, "Old Folks Hop a Travel Bandwagon," Section 10.

[3]"The Effects of Tourism on Socio-Cultural Values," Paris: UNESCO, December 18, 1975, manuscript.

[4]E. Cohen, "Toward a Sociology of International Tourism," *Social Research*, 39, 1972, pp. 164–182.

they have on occasion gone further than the visions sold to them by commercial developers. For example, the current lifestyle in Port Charlotte, Florida, with its library, adult education program, and convention center, far exceeds the original facilities constructed, such as golf courses and marinas.

Cohen's category of the organized mass tourist applies to one "who buys a package tour as if it were just another commodity in the modern mass market."[5] He wants everything planned in advance—care of luggage, tickets to events, good hotels, transportation details, sympathetic guides, palatable food. The "drifter," on the other hand, "has no fixed timetable and no well-defined goals of travel."[6]

In considerable detail Cohen analyzed the elements of "institutionalized" tourism—well standardized, controlled, predictable, and "phony," to provide an illusion of participation in the host society without actually doing so. All this is sold as an advantage, with advance conditioning via the breezy literature of tourist-oriented guidebooks. The "drifter," more than the "explorer"—both are relatively free of packaging—is willing to immerse himself in the culture being visited.

A number of studies have centered on the purposes of tourism, with references to "curiosity," escape, a search for "authentic experience." MacConnell even spoke of sightseeing as a "form of ritual respect for society," absorbing some of the "social functions of religion in the modern world."[7] Yet, more important for the purposes of public policies, a new concern of developing nations are two other issues: (1) the "encounter" between tourists and natives; and (2) the social consequences of this encounter.

The degree to which the tourist is prepackaged, according to most research, determines the nature of contacts between traveler and native, rather than the length of the visit. Such a pre-planned track is called the "migratory trail" by Aerni—one on which an impersonal contact is developed with such roles as waiter, guide, or handicrafts salesman, rather than "people-to-people" relationships. The harm, according to Aerni, is that the tourist brings home the conclusion that he really has experienced, and knows, the culture.[8] The transitory nature of the relationship was observed in a UNESCO report:

> The encounter between tourist and host is brief, lasting theoretically a maximum of three to four weeks, and in many cases only a few hours. Language, reception facilities and the very concept of tourism itself all contribute to limiting this encounter. In reality, a feeling of uncertainty on the part of the tourist arriving in a new country causes him at first to avoid contacts with the result that these will only take place at the end of his trip. . . . While for the tourist this encounter is not only brief but also a unique event in the year, for the host it is simply one of a series of encounters that follow one another almost throughout the whole year, all of them equally brief and superficial.[9]

[5]Ibid. p. 167.

[6]Ibid. p. 168.

[7]D. MacConnell, "Staged Authenticity: Arrangements in Social Space in Tourist Settings," *American Journal of Sociology,* 79 (1973), p. 589.

[8]M. J. Aerni, "The Social Effects of Tourism," *Current Anthropology,* 13 (1972), p. 162.

[9]UNESCO, op. cit. p. 10.

The "inequality" of the relationship between host and visitor has been observed by several scholars; it is based on economic inequality, but tends to disappear as the host recognizes the tourist's lack of assurance. A genuine cultural exchange is handicapped by the lack of spontaneous relationships.

In recent years the issue that has concerned nations the most, especially developing areas—and the question that has been put to these nations by the World Bank as they apply for loans to prepare for expanding tourism—is the sociocultural impact upon host countries. In a document written for the Bank, Raymond Noronka summarized the current scholarship on this point: the results of touristic contact "are generally destructive of indigenous traditions and lead to the homogenization of cultures. . . ." These studies give "little consideration of the host culture's ability to resist, or to take advantage of tourism and convert it to the attainment of its own ends."[10]

Noronka found little "hard" data to support these conclusions, for they fail to distinguish between the normal consequences of social change (such as industrialization) and those changes attributable to tourism. Nevertheless, he cited the following sociological insights:

1. There are fewer resentments when tourists and hosts are of similar cultural backgrounds.

2. The resentment of tourists is generally directed to specific groups of individuals (such as the hippie) or to the impersonality of mass tourism.

3. Host people tend to stereotype all tourists, disregarding their national origins.

4. Increased numbers of tourists produce more institutionalization.

On this, Onha wrote:

> There is a minimum of individuality permissible which has to be combined with a maximum of illusion: the tourist has to be "sold" the idea that he is seeing something different, and that what he sees is both "authentic" and the most important facets of the place (including the culture of the people) he is visiting. . . . Soon, one country becomes much like, and can therefore be substituted for, another.[11]

To this we may add R. Schawinsky's observation that 50% of information about a culture to be visited is passed on by previous visitors, and 30% by brochures and travel guides.[12]

From this theoretical background we turn to some developments in the present travel scene for the elderly.

THE ORGANIZATION OF TOURISM FOR THE ELDERLY

There are, first, the thousands of "trips" that are a normal aspect of programs in Senior Centers, churches, schools, and nursing homes

---

[10]R. Noronka, *Review of the Sociological Literature on Tourism*. Washington, D. C.: World Bank, April 30, 1975, unpublished.

[11]Ibid.

[12]Ibid.

everywhere. A bus is engaged or is available to take a group shopping, or to a theater, sporting event, picnic, and the like.

Second, there are the more ambitious trips, requiring more time and more cost to either the sponsoring organization or to the traveler. Again, there is no single pattern. Here is a report of a program begun by one woman with initiative:

This widow of 70 had got the idea after noting that many older people never got around to traveling because they had no one to encourage them to go places, and no one with whom to go.

So she started a list of all the retired people in her area. Next, she contacted the local bus company and asked about rates for chartering buses for one-day trips to points of interest. Then she divided the number of seats on a bus into the charter rate, and discovered that charter fares per person were considerably lower than regular fares.

She decided to launch the club with a one-day trip to Atlantic City. She chartered a bus seating 55 people. Then she sent out a letter to everyone on the mailing list describing the excursion. She said those going would meet the night before at her house so that they'd all get acquainted. Then they'd leave at 9 a.m. next day, stop en route for morning coffee, and arrive at Atlantic City by 11 a.m.

They'd be able to stroll the boardwalk, go shopping, see the sights, and all get together for a big luncheon at 2 p.m. at a major hotel. Then there would be time for more strolling and sight-seeing and they'd board the bus for home at 5 p.m., with a guarantee that they'd all be back at their homes by 6:30 p.m. That first trip was such a success that Mrs. Thompson found herself with a new career. Every week she planned a trip somewhere. Her club was open to all persons past 60 who felt that they could afford to take occasional inexpensive bus trips. Members were encouraged to call on older people who were stay-at-homes and urge them to enrich their years by joining the club.

Mrs. Thompson handled all arrangements, such as chartering buses, making hotel reservations, choosing restaurants, planning side trips, and keeping tab of expenses. All trips were made in chartered, comfortable buses. Members shared the expenses, and traveling costs were kept to a minimum. . . . popular trips were to Atlantic City, Philadelphia, Washington, D.C. and to New York City to attend Radio City Music Hall . . . one- and two-week jaunts to Florida, Chicago, and even to the Thousand Islands of the St. Lawrence River. . . .[13]

As to tourism on a larger scale, the most significant development in the past decade has been the ambitious and successful entrepreneurship of the elderly for themselves. The fraternity of commercial travel agents—as is still the case in the television industry—was asleep to trends. Thus, the prime "movers," literally, have been the AARP-NRTA and such groups as B'nai B'rith, Senior Centers, church groups and schools. The AARP-NRTA has over 10 million members, and has its own travel service in New York City and its own waiting rooms at Kennedy Airport. Its 1976 tours included Majorca (eight days for $458, including accommodations, air fare, and two meals daily), and a South American trip of a full month ($1,895).[14] The NRTA Journal for March-April, 1977, listed the following travel brochures: Europe,

[13]From Robert Peterson's column "Life Begins at 40," March 24, 1973. Reproduced by permission of the author.

[14]NRTA brochure, 1976.

world tours, Africa, short and long cruises from the East Coast, Hawaii, the Orient and India, South Pacific cruises from West Coast ports, Alaska, South America, and Mexico.

Mr. Robert Dunn, Vice President for Marketing of Grand Circle (a travel agent that serves only members of AARP-NRTA), indicates that, from 190 elderly travelers in 1955, 30,000 are now served annually.[15] Every kind of work and educational background is found among them. A very high proportion of "repeaters" are found among these groups, often as many as 17 or 18 out of a group of 25 to 30. Some will be on their tenth trip, some on their thirtieth. "We never lose them," said Mr. Dunn. The first tour that is usually preferred is the familiar "grand tour" to such places as England, France, Switzerland, Italy, and Holland.

Among the benefits that Mr. Dunn noted is the knowledge that age is no barrier to travel. (Careful preparations are made to provide medical care in all phases of every trip.) Furthermore, these travelers, since they are in groups, lose their fear of incapacity in other languages. Not only is the trip of great value to those who are lonely in their home environment, but it creates friendships throughout the country "that last indefinitely."

Grand Circle has occasionally arranged specialized tours, centered around museums, operas, gardens, and other interests. These are usually most successful if a local garden club, for example, arranges for the trip. Otherwise, it is difficult to attract sufficient garden (or opera) enthusiasts who can all travel at a given period of time. Since the AARP chapters can take the initiative, the travel agent has not gone far in these directions. However, what Grand Circle has introduced with increasing success since 1974 are the "extended vacation" tours, whereby a member can spend six weeks in one place in a comfortable hotel with room and bath and kitchenette in the center of a city. Nightly entertainment is prearranged but can be ignored if the traveler prefers. All of this, including transportation, can be provided for $449 from New York (1977 rates). Such extended vacations are presently offered in Sorrento, Tangiers, the French Alps, the French Riviera, Hawaii, Guadalajara, and Florida.

Another new travel plan is the London Sojourn of 21 days, during which the member is taken on walking trips, visiting the Houses of Parliament and other places of interest. Again, the visitor can go his own way.

As to intergenerational travel Mr. Dunn noted, first, that by its charter, Grand Circle tours are only for AARP-NRTA members. However, an exception was made for tours in which a grandchild, 17 years or older, could travel for the same rates, especially to Hawaii. Increasingly, couples travel together; in the past, many men would not go.

Based on such evidence as reports from hotel managers in the host nations, Mr. Dunn believed that elderly Americans are not "ugly Americans," for they exhibit a willingness to accept the local customs and traditions and are

---

[15]In telephone conversation with the author, July 28, 1977.

not inclined to compare those conditions with their own. In respect to the Eastern European countries—trips are made to all of them, including the USSR—the American elderly are usually glad they went, but will not go a second time. They return more convinced than before of the political freedoms they enjoy. In this sense, the elderly travelers are significant "missionaries" on an international level.

Mr. Dunn verified the research studies noted above—that, aside from visits by some tour groups or individuals to hospitals or homes for the aged, there is little person-to-person contact with older persons of host countries. He believed that language is one explanation; another is that the American is usually at a hotel that is unavailable in terms of cost to most European elderly.

Future plans for the AARP-NRTA tours will include an expansion of "extended vacation" trips and the possibility of tours to China.

Within a membership of elderly travelers—thousands annually, in addition to the 30,000 arranged for by Grand Circle for AARP-NRTA—we may expect a wide range of interests and aspirations for each trip. Many, perhaps most, will go with a sense of immediate enjoyment and a fun orientation. One tour manager was quoted in the *Times* report as saying: "Seniors are beautiful that way. They're not deadbeats. And they just love bus rides. They don't want anywhere where they're going just to sit in the sun and rock. They want dancing and they want fun and games. They want to hop and jump. . . ."[16]

The extended vacation experience for an AARP excursion to Miami Beach included an on-site swimming pool, shuffleboard, table tennis and hourly shuttle-bus service to nearby shopping malls. Almost every evening there was something special (and free)—a movie, bingo, a "sing-along," a game night, or a party. Package excursions included deep-sea fishing charters, trips to race tracks and jai alai matches, a trip up the Intercoastal Waterway, bus tours to Walt Disney World, and a cruise to the Bahamas.

Putting together the experiences and programs of AARP-NRTA with the broader observations of scholars in this area, what does this tell us about older tourists? For instance, does their role in this form of leisure suggest possibilities for new tourist-host relationships?

POTENTIALS

We immediately confront a paradox. On the one hand—or so we are told—older persons who travel want guarantees of comforts, and prepackaging or, to use the language we have been quoting, a maximum of "institutionalization." On the other hand, older persons share with youth an ease in communication and in spontaneous adjustment, as we saw in the *Times* report on the bus breakdown.

Again, there is a uniqueness that takes us back to the distinction between "old old" and "new old." The first was defined earlier in this volume as those

---

[16]Grimes, op. cit.

whose roots went directly back to the Old Country. Their memories were often unpleasant, for they had come here to escape the famines, the pogroms, the wars, the lack of opportunity. The 30 million or more who arrived in the several decades before and after the turn of the century were not (to put it mildly) those whose image of themselves was contented and satisfied in their homeland. During the decades they were raising us in the U.S.A.—their sons and daughters—they could hardly afford to return as tourists to Germany, Poland, or Italy and, if they could, a common statement was that they left the Old Country for good, and had no interest in reviving those memories.

The "new old," on the contrary, has matured in a socioeconomic milieu and intellectual environment during which our appetite to be "explorers" has been whetted—by television and movies, by more reading, by the wars of our century. The automobile has made us into a nation of perpetual wanderers, and among more adventuresome "empathic natives" abroad, there are applicants for international AAA drivers' licenses. Thus, the larger proportion of "new old" among the American elderly may produce a generation with unique qualities for affecting a dramatic change for world tourism. Note these possibilities:

1. Alex Haley's book, *Roots,* has confirmed the desire of the "new old" elderly to explore their past.[17] We may expect, in the decades ahead, that this *personal* searching will be equal to the generalized entertainment tour among all ages of travelers.

2. There could be dividends for democracy if the State Department, or other agencies (foundations, colleges, municipal recreation departments, etc.), would realize the potential effectiveness of older persons as "missionaries" who can mingle easily with people in the host countries. The U.S. State Department might consider a cooperative with AARP-NRTA and other tour sponsors whereby such contacts are facilitated. If, as Mr. Dunn noted, the typical European older person does not frequent the hotels in which Americans stay, then other places in the community might provide far more suitable environments for such meetings than hotels. Up to now the initiative that has taken place has been by the tour organizer. I would argue that our federal offices take new initiatives in concert with the officials of the host nations. There is room for imaginative experiments by American gerontological centers through consortium grants.

3. High school juniors have been selected by such travel agents as the Council for Student Travel to live in homes abroad for a summer, or to develop "exchanges" between European and American homes. A comparable plan might be considered for elderly persons, especially those who prefer to avoid institutionalized tours. My first trip to Europe, in 1955, was for the Council. In exchange for my transportation I led a daily discussion aboard ship about various aspects of American life and institutions. Comparable discussions took place on the return trip, with some 400 young people from West Germany, Austria, and the Scandinavian area. The substitution of older

---

[17]Alex Haley, *Roots.* New York: Doubleday, 1976.

persons would be equally fruitful for international relations and, with a realistic and updated perception of the term "student," might be considered by the same Council.

4. Finally, ways must be found by which subsidies for wide travel can be provided to the masses of elderly who are too poor to travel. Over 17% are presently classified as being below the official poverty line. In economic terms, obviously, the entire discussion above—except for local trips within the community—has been addressed to the middle or upper class of elderly. At this time in history travel subsidies may seem far-fetched, when the country is going through a major reform in the administration of welfare. Yet this may be precisely the time for a discussion of priorities—not of food, shelter, and health vis-à-vis tourism—but of subsidized travel between age groups, or with the elderly as missionary (yes, "propaganda") instruments compared to other goodwill expenditures by the Department of State or other international agencies of the federal government. One can ask, for example, whether our elderly might not become an integral element in the "Voice of America"? Such a project could be integrated with the historical project advocated at the close of Chapter 18 so that, as part of their recollection of coming to this country as immigrants, groups of elderly could simultaneously be sent to their original homeland to sharpen their recollections and to contact members of their families.

We may conclude that whatever freedom the elderly travelers effectuate from the "institutionalized" patterns of Grand Circle or other sponsorships has to come from them. These sponsors will, short of outright subsidy, arrange packages and print glossy brochures to attract members. The scheduling problems described by Mr. Dunn may be real, yet many tours for younger people are arranged around special interests that ensure maximum benefit to the traveler. With more flexibility in their time schedules than among younger persons, retirees could probably be found to study exemplary urban renewal projects (Rotterdam, Skopje), classic parks (Vienna, Versailles), great ballet and theater (London, Munich), Roman impacts (Trier), or famous cathedrals and mosques (Istanbul, Chartres). True, those wishing to go to Miami will still be there; the agents for ageism will see to it. But, there are wider horizons. . . .

Summary: Social Roles in Activity Experiences

The concepts of social circle, function, status, and "self" will be summarized rather loosely by the activities treated in Section 4. Within each form of leisure there are characteristic role components. For example, the social circle of the club is distinct from that of the athletic team. The purpose of the interpretations below is to move us toward a greater capability for counseling persons—i.e., for matching personal qualities with the demands, skills, and satisfactions inherent in the activity experience. Rather than separate the discussion below by types of activity, as in Chapters 13 to 20, the summary that follows will be informal.

There are major distinctions between the social roles of elderly persons who engage in theater, music, painting, filmmaking, or other arts. A further distinction is usually made between "public" and "participants." Yet, cutting across the arts and the degree of involvement, major emphases in aesthetic experience are on the components of function and reward. A criterion of success in both is the degree to which the "social" functions" are maintained, but which are increasingly blended with the "aesthetic" function. In the latter, attention is given to inherent experiences in the arts *as art*—the development of the sonata subjects in a symphony, or the resolution of themes in a drama. The social functions consist of external factors, such as the aspect of friendships, reputation, gossip, response of the public, a way to spend an evening, an opportunity to dress.

The component *social circle* referred to the total context by which we are affected in leisure activity. The most explicit circles are those of fellow tourists on a joint trip (Chapter 20) and the companions in a party, club, or social gathering (Chapter 18). The former is often a rapid transformation from 20 or 30 strangers who are, perhaps, all members of AARP in units spread across the land, to a close-knit primary group that will travel through cathedrals and airports of half a dozen countries over several weeks. Indeed, the rapport that is established between them may be as important as the quality of hotels or the impressiveness of the Vatican. The tour director's job, in good part, is to foster a healthy interpersonal relationship. On the other hand, the social group of the women's club or of an AARP chapter in St. Louis is usually well established by the time one becomes a tour participant. As many studies of social organization have observed, a major reason for joining is to "belong," to share, to be with others whom one enjoys; the program or content may be central, but it may also be incidental.

As to *function*, aesthetic, civic, and intellectual activities may provide useful examples. One paints, helps pass a law, studies a language, acts, volunteers in a hospital, attends a lecture. The content, hopefully, is self-sufficient and satisfying. If the others in one of these situations are pleasant to be with or work with, so much the better (it is like marrying into a family of relatives who can also be friends), but the force of the activity can overcome a dissatisfaction with other people. Note that these activities can often be done quite alone or in small groups.

The emphasis on *rewards* or *esteem* can be found in all activities; as nonwork experiences, the rewards are psychic, emotional, even physical— one "feels better" after exercising or engaging in yoga. A reward from watching a TV show may be "keeping up with the world." Participating in the preparation for a church bazaar may be its own reward, vaguely expressed in such phrases as being a "good person" or "Christian." From such experiences there may be a general purpose in living, difficult to define and sometimes embarrassing to articulate.

Similarly, the affirmation of *self* cuts across all activities. Some experiences are more visible than others, and evoke more response from others. Participation in the arts is especially useful; others can watch us do our thing on stage or canvas, or read our writings. Touristic activities lend themselves to oral reporting, one of the anticipations of that particular leisure adventure.

It may be too much to conclude that we have here a basis for counseling. Those who need response can be steered into socially approved and visible activity; travel opportunities can be reserved for those with a threshold for new visions of the world. We will, in fact, see some of these principles emerging in Chapter 22.

Another approach is to concentrate on the continuity from the values of one's work career to the values of a leisure role. This is an approach used in the case study for counseling that I suggest later. Still another use for such analysis might be to provide a full palette for evaluating recreational programs in the VA hospital, the retirement community, or nursing home.

These considerations lead us into the next section, policies for the elderly, which begins, but does not end, with matters of facilities and budgets.

Policies

INTRODUCTION

If we think of social action as a process, there are five major components that do not necessarily proceed in a rational order, but that are inevitably present:

1. The recognition of data or facts—not always in numerical form. The "society," or parts of it, becomes aware, from the facts, that something needs attention, that a "problem" has emerged.

2. These facts are put into some perspective or meaningful relationship, which may be a set of religious beliefs, or a political position. Fundamentally, a set of goals is present from which to judge and act on the facts.

3. Action of some kind is determined—a law, a decree, an agreement by parents about something a child should do.

4. Implementation is created—a set of actions to carry out the decision, such as appropriation of funds by Congress.

5. A formal or informal evaluation, which may include a review of the original data as well as the philosophy, the decision, and the implementation. In recent years there has been a trend toward specifying or structuring evaluations into grant proposals to governmental or foundation sources.

Within this total process, the structure of this volume is evident. Broadly speaking, the data or facts constitute Section 1. Section 2 asked, What do these facts mean? How do they contribute to a view of the elderly? Section 3 moved outside of the actor and turned to several types of sponsors, communities, institutions, even whole cultures, which provided settings or environments within which the elderly could act out their new leisure roles. Section 4 then described a set of decisions and implementations made by older persons to be involved in aesthetic, civic, intellectual, and other activities.

We turn now in Section 5 to persons who serve as the connecting links between the elderly clients or participants and to the agencies that serve them: program leaders, counselors, trainers, and researchers. The fundamental responsibility for all such persons, no matter what their specific roles, is to be as fully informed as possible about each of the steps in the process—facts, philosophy, decisions, implementations, and evaluations. Indeed, they may not be aware that they are functioning in all stages of the process as they specialize in one role. For example, the "social director" of a nursing home has absorbed a battery of materials about what the elderly are; if this is a Catholic-sponsored home, she accepts the philosophy of the church as it applies to a nursing home, and accordingly sets up an atmosphere and program that is pertinent.

Each chapter below will consolidate the 20 earlier chapters for specific purposes of the program leader, emphasizing those discussions that are most applicable. One of the perennial issues is that of bridging the gap between the theoretical and the practical. These bridges constitute a "no man's land." Claudine Donfut of Paris and I tried to provide some bridges when we prepared a special issue of *Society and Leisure.*[1] The remainder of this chapter is drawn from our introduction to this volume.

The methodology of research into leisure as a specific dimension of gerontology raises again the familiar issue of bridges from theory or research to policy and implementation. For on the one hand, when research is done about youth, or tourism, or recreation patterns in the outdoors, we may gather our data, publish them, and hope that somehow, in the short or the long run, these findings will be read and used by policy-makers. Of course, the role of the scholar varies among the cultures, and in some he is closer to policy-making by virtue of his position in a national academy of science, or his employment (permanently or as occasional consultant) by an agency of tourism, the mass media, a ministry of culture, or some other active enterprise. In some situations, as in the U.S.A., many social scientists are members of university faculties—a situation they seek and enjoy precisely because they are freer to engage in "fundamental" or value-free research.

Yet, in the gerontological aspect of leisure research, there are several unique elements. The profession has its own theoreticians, but it is primarily a complex of persons and agencies who are responsible for governmental programs, nursing homes, and

---

[1]Max Kaplan and Claudine Attias-Donfut, eds., *Educational and Leisure-Time Activities of the Elderly.* Special issue, *Society and Leisure,* 5, No. 4 (1975); Prague: European Center for Leisure and Education.

a variety of other "real" situations. Those who create policy or administer programs are not unaware of theoretical studies on aging or on leisure; like policy or program makers in all fields, they rely heavily on experience, common sense, or intuition, aided (often spasmodically) by the professional journals, which they may (or may not) read, and the conferences which they may (or may not) attend. Their need for the help of the scientists of leisure is real, with the rapidity of changes they confront.

We need not here enter into the familiar problem of values in social science on a theoretical or abstract level, for this perennial issue cannot help but emerge in many ways throughout the discussion of the bridging. It is, of course, a problem that permeates all social sciences, not merely the inquiry into leisure or into the matter of aging. However, the leisure scientists and the gerontologist have available, at this period of history, a remarkable set of circumstances: to further the investigation of interplay between "pure" and "applied" knowledge, funds are often available for research; there is a receptive audience; many observations exist about social change; there are possibilities of designed experiments in laboratory-like settings such as nursing homes; most of all, there is a new challenge to interdisciplinary research inherent in the issue of objective-subjective life, or put another way, in the transformation from societies marked by quantitative abundance to a concern with quality and meaning. Most significant, the transition from the roles of work to nonwork demands increasing attention by both scientists and by administrators.

But even to put "scientists" and "administrators" side by side again reminds us (1) of the need to develop principles of the transition from the world of research to the world of action, (2) to recognize the important cultural differences that affect such transitions, especially since this volume is addressed to a world audience, and (3) to pinpoint at least one unique segment of our readership in respect to potential impact.

There is by now a special field, almost a new discipline, often referred to as "policy sciences." As more and more academic persons have been brought into consultation by governmental and private sectors, there developed a clear need to conceptualize the role of the consultant or researcher vis à vis policy. In the business world, a familiar issue is "RD" or the relation of research to development. This, indeed, is a basic issue for all industrial managers. Can some of these principles not be adopted for the leisure/gerontology rapport? It had been the intention of the editors to submit the full manuscript to several authorities of world status, who would come from neither leisure nor gerontology, to assess the volume as a contribution to "policy science." Time did not permit this climax. Instead, we have been granted permission by the American Sociological Association to reprint in full a statement by Dr. James Coleman, Professor of Social Relations, Johns Hopkins University. The "Coleman Report" has recently taken its place in the U.S.A. as a major assessment of research into the education of minority groups—grants often funded by federal agencies. We leave it to the reader to apply Coleman's observations to leisure and gerontology.

Partial information available at the time an action must be taken is better than complete information after that time.

The criteria of parsimony and elegance that apply in discipline research are not important; the correctness of the predictions or results is important, and redundancy is valuable.

It is necessary to treat differently policy variables which are subject to policy manipulation, and situation variables which are not.

The ultimate product is not a "contribution to existing knowledge" in the literature, but a social policy modified by the research results.

The research problem enters from outside any academic discipline and must be carefully translated from the real world of policy or the conceptual world of a client without loss of meaning.

The existence of competing or conflicting interests, together with the time-coupling of research to policy, requires special self-corrective devices, such as the commissioning of more than one research group, under the auspices of different interested parties, and independent review of research results, using an adversary or dialectical process.

The canons of scientific method, and the values implied by those canons, govern the execution of policy research. Values from the world of action govern the formulation of policy research problems. The transmission of policy research results back into the world of action may be governed by either set of values, depending on conditions.

The values governing transmission of research results back into the world of action and thus the conditions of that transmission are determined by conditions of acceptance of the policy research problem.

If policy research results are transmitted back, without open publication, to an interested party, then those results will ordinarily not be acted upon nor will they be openly disclosed to others, unless it benefits his interests.

Those stages of policy research that lie in the world of action, formulation of the research problem, posing conditions for communication of the research results back into the world of action, and making policy recommendations based on the research results, should be governed by the investigator's personal values and appropriately include advocacy. Those stages that lie within the disciplinary world, execution of the research and statement of research results, should be governed by disciplinary values and do not appropriately include advocacy.

"There are no social or humanitarian values in the disciplinary world," said Coleman in explaining the last principle. Disciplinary values such as objectivity, the search for truth, and an interest in expanding the borders of knowledge "do not recognize the existence of action, nor even the world of action—except as subject-matter for study—but only of knowledge." In effect, the researcher must separate his disciplinary from his personal values and use the proper set in the proper phase of the policy research process or his work "loses its value for all interested parties."

In Coleman's eyes the "greatest barriers" to the use of social science information in public policy are rooted in the very nature of the American political process.

Probably because of the fragmentation of power, the principal deliberations in the formulation of policy are often deliberations about what strategies will generate enough support to enable passage of legislation, rather than deliberations about social consequences of the legislation.

Policy decisions are often made during "bursts of last-minute activity . . . as legislative log-jams break."

"So long as such timing characterizes policy formation in government, the fruitful use of policy research appears limited." Yet, the dangers inherent in a more authoritarian government which would be required to make policy formation rational "seem sufficiently great to outweigh the benefits that would arise from more adequate use of policy research," Coleman reasoned.[2]

Dr. Coleman's observations come out of the American experience. Yet there are cultural differences which undoubtedly influence the relationships of theory to policy. Even a cursory approach must note such conditions as the following:

a. The ideological: historical-political differences in attitudes toward the elderly, as seen in legislation, the provision of public housing or recreational facilities, or traditional attitudes on being "young," "old," "active," "inactive," etc. Even the nature or definition of leisure or of gerontological "problems" will differ.

b. The differences in the status of social scientists within the decision-making process of a given society. An illustration is the presence of "academy of science" in some nations, as distinct from a university research program. The presence of theorists close to policy bodies does not itself suggest close communications, for even within university structures there is often a "social distance" between such groups as sociologists and social workers, or between theoretical and clinical psychologists. All are familiar with the prestige of "outside" consultants. But certainly, the relationship of theory to policy cannot be understood without the social organization of respective roles.

c. The degree of *crisis* in which the issue of retirement is a central element. Crises relating to the elderly and leisure may

---

[2]Reprinted from *APA Monitor* (Feb. 1973), p. 6. Used by permission.

result from an election of public officials, or the physical (and therefore, the political) concentration of the elderly, or public debate on a new tax to support adult education; even a momentary "crisis" may emerge from the showing of a television program about the elderly.

These examples illustrate, but do not exhaust the place of cultural differences in a discussion of theory/policy.

Finally, a discussion of theory/policy does well to note at least one potential readership of this volume: students preparing for the profession of gerontology. In many nations "gerontologists," especially those in the social or nonmedical levels, come from a wide range of backgrounds. To some degree, the professionalism of this field will depend upon a systematic training. In the U.S.A. this tendency is already clear, usually within the university framework. But whatever the sponsorship, "principles" and "program" are *both* essential for the student. These may find their ultimate synthesis in proposals for clubs, vacations, transportation facilities, accessibility to entertainment, community centers, the development of participation in planning activities among the elderly themselves, and so forth. Nor will these attempts at interrelating principles to programs lose sight of larger issues that subsume both, namely, the broad purposes of gerontology itself, as in the relative values of social integration vis-à-vis individuality.

Further, this conjunction of both levels enters the teaching process. The student, even though he may not enter into subsequent programs of research, has been made sensitive to the importance of concepts, hypotheses, and other aspects of the scientific undertaking; he develops criteria for judging a leisure (or any other) program; his techniques for whatever program he organizes for the elderly will, hopefully, proceed on more than intuition, common sense, and personal relations, important as these always remain.

CHAPTER 21

Programming Policies

Principles and *policies* lead directly into *programs*. We speak of "moral" and "legal" principles or policies. It is important that students of leisure policy and program—what *should* be done and *how* it should best be done—become conscious of principles, goals, rationales, and objectives. All of these move us roughly in the same direction of reexamining the assumptions behind our professional conduct. If we do not, the danger is that we, like the public at large, may fall victim to common stereotypes about what the elderly can or cannot do. The real issue is that in addition to choosing from what exists in their environment, providing they know about them, *what else* might older persons do if larger alternatives were available?

A second reason for examining basic policies is that we are forced to consider whether these should come from a random scrambling, based on intuition, experience, or present knowledge, or whether they should be related to some systematic scheme of thinking. Otherwise there can be an unending list, but without any internal order or relationship. The goal in methodology is not to formulate a *complete* list of policies but to present *representative* suggestions that provide some illustrations of relationship.

Those who become involved in planning programs with the elderly are invariably attached to a sponsoring institution or agency, some of which have been described in the preceding section. Yet not only are there many differences between such units as VA hospitals, Senior Centers, Elderhostels, private nursing homes, etc., but each of these settings, as noted earlier for persons and culture, is in some respects like "all others," in other ways like "some others," and in some ways like "no others." The more objective differences consist of such gross matters as the medical regime and traditions that permeate the VA hospital, or the educational traditions that dominate an adult education program. The objective nature of these regimes is reflected in, or results from, different purposes, clienteles, funding sources, or schedules. The *subjective* differences consist of the personalities and local conditions that give each environment its own "feeling" or "atmosphere."

But the one factor that brings all of these agencies and institutions into a common framework is the presence of elderly persons, and even though these

209

elderly occupy various roles—as patient, prisoner, student, teacher, resident, etc.—the fact of age underlies all else. When "ageism" is at its height, life is simpler for those in command, for they impose a certain program and treat the elderly like children. As we show greater respect to older persons, as *people* rather than as *categories*, the job of leadership becomes more sensitive, flexible, creative, and elusive. In the same raw sense that dictatorships are "easier" to run than democracies, a nursing home leisure program that is all *laid out* or *hung up* on the bulletin board ("7:00 P.M.: singing, 8:00 P.M.: movie") is predictable for all concerned. Putting it another way, the more control there is at an objective level over the program, the fewer decisions remain for either the leader or the older population. The "philosophy" is then settled a priori by those in the higher echelons, who may be M.D.'s, psychiatrists, wardens, school principals, municipal recreation supervisors, priests, or recreation leaders. Some objective controls exist in every situation, of course, in such matters as amount of available space for a meeting, or weather conditions for a picnic.

We may submit the proposition, then, that ultimate freedom never—well, hardly ever—exists for the program leader. His job is to know the "realities" of the objective situation, to know (or suspect, or want to find out) the level of subjective aspirations, desires, and potentialities of the elderly, and to find *a creative resolution between the two.* The first will be easier than the second, and the danger is that the realities of budgets and space and time limitations will be clear, while the human potential is not and, therefore, easier to minimize or neglect. Worse, the leader may surrender too easily to what seem to be clear limits, as in the case of budgets, failing to seek ways of improving these conditions.

Three sets of principles for programming are presented below, from the more general to the more specific.

PRINCIPLES: THEORY

The first set of principles is derived from a number of theoretical propositions about leisure in general that appeared in an early chapter of my 1975 volume.[1] For our present purpose I will select those propositions that are most relevant to the elderly, state them *verbatim,* and follow with a policy statement and some relevant questions.

1. *Proposition:* The amount of free time useful for some leisure choices is dependent on the arrangement of this time, especially in the difference between fragmentary and bulk time.

Policy: Plan leisure experiences that take advantage of "bulk time"–i.e., stretching over a number of days or even weeks (continuing education, tours, volunteerism, etc.).

Question: Are some persons more willing than others to become involved

---

[1]Max Kaplan, *Leisure: Theory and Policy.* New York: John Wiley & Sons, 1975, Chapter 3.

in extended activities? Are there ways of taking short-time activities and transforming them to longer periods (for example, short trips in town before going out of town)?

2. *Proposition:* Specific time periods—such as seasons, days of the week, or hours of the day—are often associated with characteristic leisure activities.

Policy: Take advantage of "special" hours, days, birthdays, national holidays in planning, as with any aged group; time symbols are important to all of us.

Question: Can the anticipation of birthdays, etc., be a vital instrument in developing a "future orientation" for the elderly, without diminishing respect for memories and sentiment relating to the past?

3. *Proposition:* Time carries different images, meanings, and associations at various stages in the life of a person as well as in various types of activities.

Policy: Leisure planning is based in part on the perception of an "hour," an "evening," or a "week," and on how these perceptions are affected by age.

Question: Can we assume that the "days fly by" for the elderly, or do these "drag" for those who are bored? Can we look at activities as instruments for making the time go by rapidly? Is this what we want to do?

4. *Proposition:* New aspirations in living and leisure have a significant impact on the amount of free time one wants.

Policy: One useful evaluation of a leisure program is the willingness of older persons to stretch the day, getting them up earlier or staying up later.

Question: Is the tendency among many older persons to shrink the day explainable by economic reasons (saving a meal) or, in part, by an anticipation of boredom? If the latter, can leisure programs be useful? How?

5. *Proposition:* Selection in leisure is generally determined by a complex of purposes, and it is the configuration of such purposes that determines the use of a specific experience.

Policy: Leisure programming need not proceed from a clear consensus among the elderly as to their objectives, even though they should be involved in the planning; the leadership can steer them toward agreement, not by ignoring conflicts but arriving at a perspective that goes beyond the differences.

Question: Does this suggest that a major clue to the leader's success is a rapport with the elderly, earned by developing trust, and the ability to pick up "cues" as to the "right moment" to move a discussion forward?

6. *Proposition:* The original anticipation of meaning brought to a leisure experience may, under capable leadership, be modified toward more depth and personal growth.

Policy: While the values of the leadership are not to be imposed upon the elderly, or used as a criterion, the possibilities of new experiences, or behavioral change, are not to be ignored; explicit policies of "behavioral modification" are to be viewed only with the greatest care, in favor of change that may come about through new experience.

Question: Are techniques of behavioral modification ever useful in working with the elderly? Is the technique of "deepening" leisure experience (for example, from a superficial to a more committed attitude toward group singing) any different with older persons than with anyone else?

8. *Proposition:* Like the child who learns to enjoy the water after he knows how to swim, many of us—in whatever the original situation that led us to it—use a leisure experience first and then assess the experience for subsequent decisions.

Policy: The elderly, like all of us, will often enjoy a new experience without a prior security that this will be the case; the leader need not convince persons beforehand, but should feel free to use secondary or indirect techniques as motivation.

Question: How can the leader provide a favorable environment or "setting" from which the elderly will be made inclined to attempt a new experience?

9. *Proposition:* The nature of one's use of leisure experiences includes a variety of elements, such as use-length, time of day (week, month, year), exposure, companionship, sequence in relation to past and future experiences, required skills, and challenges; therefore, the meanings that are associated with, or that derive from, a given experience also exist on many levels of analysis.

Policy: Many meanings may be anticipated by various persons engaged in the same activity; this may be considered an advantage to leadership rather than an index of disorganization.

Question: What questions does this raise for evaluating a program or activity? Does this open a major theoretical consideration in working (a) with a variety of persons within an elderly group, (b) with a mixture of age generations?

12. *Proposition:* The major function of a leader in leisure activity is to insure that the participant uses the experience to obtain a maximum benefit that may go beyond the limited expectation or meaning he brought to it.

Policy: Same as proposition.

Question: Is there a danger that a leader can "oversell" or overpredict the beneficial impact of an activity?

17. *Proposition:* The choice of leisure activities inside or outside of the home provides a major clue to relationships between family members and is useful as one modality for affecting the roles and character of family life.

Policy: Leisure activities of the elderly can be a source of major impact on relationships with husband/wife or with children; a balance between independence and interdependence can be achieved through leisure.

Question: But what should such a "balance" be in a situation where there is contact between the generations? Are there some activities (for example, picnics, family gatherings, etc.) which are more useful than others for interdependence?

19. *Proposition:* Since the first objective limitation on choice of leisure is the absence of alternatives, the major policy criterion of community and regional planning concerns the physical provision of opportunities for many tastes, skills, and interests.

Policy: A realistic plan for leisure in any setting should be based on a complete knowledge of all the available alternatives that exist in the community; in this sense, one role of the recreation director is to serve as a resource person who works within a network of services.

Question: Should it, therefore, be a legitimate responsibility of the leader to work with others on the community level, even if this takes time from the specific content?

22. *Proposition:* Leisure can be used as a social device to maintain and to nurture social and ideological pluralism as well as to provide an integrative or assimilative vehicle among subcultural groups.

Policy: Where the elderly are part of an ethnic group, a valid leisure objective can be to use this background as one base for activity, as in study of a cultural heritage or art experiences.

Question: Many subcultures and members of ethnic groups live together in nursing homes; what lessons come out of this experience for social techniques of developing harmonious patterns?

23. *Proposition:* We may expect to see more use of leisure devoted to volunteer activity for significant tasks in the study of community and regional issues, accompanied by programs of transformation by various methods, in many cases as a full commitment of time.

Policy: Volunteerism in community agencies can be a major commitment for the elderly; the trend is for the elderly to select their own commitments rather than for them to be selected by agencies.

Question: What type of preparation is needed by the leaders who will be serving the elderly as resources for information about the community?

26. *Proposition:* One large differentiation of leisure meanings among all cultures is related to social roles of men and women.

Policy: Same as proposition.

Question: What are some trends in general on the leisure choices of men and women, and how do they apply to those in their 60s and up?

42. *Proposition:* The crucial element within the social system for the development of a philosophy of meaning for the new leisure is education at all levels.

Policy: Same as proposition.

Question: One distinction between the "old" and the "new" retiree is the greater amount of formal education among the latter. What are some implications for leaders in the field of leisure?

PRINCIPLES: SOCIAL CHANGE

The next set of principles derives directly from the discussions in the earlier chapters of this volume, and moves us a little closer to "objectives" for realistic programming in a broad range of situations. Realism, as viewed here, is forward looking.

Principle 1: Flexibility

Leisure in the coming decades will increasingly be predicated upon greater flexibility between work and nonwork. Two subprinciples result:

a. We will increasingly consider "free" time during retirement years as a continuity of "free" time during the work life. This continuity, however, is affected by the presence, respectively, of the work and the retirement roles as a positive bond or strength upon which the gerontologist can build. The implication for policy is that leisure policy—private and public—deals with all ages; leisure of the child and adult is preparation for preretirement and, therefore, of concern to gerontology.

b. *Increasingly, during the half-century span from one's twentieth to the seventieth year, the person will decide how "old" he wants to be in respect to lifestyle.*

Already, we see students who at the age of 20 have chosen to die intellectually; simultaneously, larger numbers of the middle-aged and elderly attend formal classes and take more active roles in the community. Cases of voluntary disengagement among the elderly are balanced by voluntary engagement in community programs such as SCORE. On the other hand, the recent growth of 3,000 to 4,000 communes in the U.S.A., with an average life span of three to four years, is an attempt by young people to live a prelaunderette, preelectronic, preindustrial mode of life which is a negation of the activism often associated in the symbols of our society with youth.

Indeed, it is this symbolic dimension that will be of special interest in the turquoise model of which Johnston writes.[2] Recall that both work and leisure have provided powerful symbols on the levels of social class and of age. Recall also that the common symbolic association in the present U.S.A., with some factual justification, is of the elderly and the poor. A third symbolic component provides the formula "old-poor-inactive."

The productivity level of today already makes possible the elimination of poverty among all persons, young or old, black or white. It is a political problem, not an economic one—one of priorities, not resources. And increasingly, therefore, as we look several decades ahead, the political process will be based on moral issues. It is one consequence of a society of abundance, and may, frankly, be an expression of hope more than of fact. Yet the present revolutions among the youth, women, and blacks, or the environmental movement which cuts across all populations, gives credence to this forecast.

Thus, the reduction of poverty and of biological age limitations opens the door to freer choice of lifestyles, whether symbolized by degrees of activity, leisure actions, or an internal and psychological security.

Principle 2: Alternatives

Increasingly, in future decades, the gerontologist will need to be concerned with the provision of a wide range of leisure alternatives from which an increasingly sophisticated generation of elderly will make their own choices and refashion existing facilities and resources. This moves gerontology toward a political role. Again, several subprinciples emerge:

a. There will be an emphasis on *people*, not *programs*.

---

[2]Dennis F. Johnston, "The Future of Work: Three Possible Alternatives," *Monthly Labor Review*, Washington, D.C.: U.S. Department of Labor, May 1972.

b. We will see the creation of networks, or "interfacing," between recreational, athletic, educational, medical, and library resources, so that the enlargement of resources will not result from larger budgets but from the maximum use of existing facilities through well planned coordination.

Principle 3: Dynamics

The familiar division of *indoor-outdoor* activity, presently the basis of Federal services, grows out of the "program" and "facility" emphasis of the recreation profession, and will give way to categories that relate to people rather than geography. Such categories as autonomous-dependent will emphasize *types of people,* or *movement-immobility* will emphasize degrees of *potential action.* A dynamic theory for programming will result for gerontology, rather than a static set of prescriptions. Several subprinciples emerge:

a. Gerontologists will increasingly enlarge their perspectives and techniques to enable them to concentrate on processes rather than on age categories and characterization, leading to a specialty in *intergeneration* dynamics. Even the Rapoports have not sufficiently grappled with this dimension of the problem.[3]

b. Programs in leisure—reaching all ages—should leave *quantitative measures of the activity* for a more *qualitative observation of the experience.*

Principle 4: Functions

The present search for precision in measuring the impact of leisure experience should, without surrendering the importance of accuracy in science, absorb an equally significant concern for opening experiences to a multitude of "impacts." The drama-oriented observer (such as the poet Kenneth Koch in Chapter 13) will be relied upon as much in programming and evaluation of experiences for the elderly as the numbers-oriented psychologists or sociologist. Simultaneously, leisure programs will have innumerable functions and no functions. Emerging from this position are two subprinciples:

a. The least recommended type of leisure programming is that which is designed to "fill the day."

b. The most recommended type of leisure programming is that which is designed to "fulfill the person" through experiences that operate on various levels of skills, insights, temporal patterns, combinations of individual and collective participation, and integrations of past experiences with creative or unfolding adventures.

---

[3]Professor Billy Gunter, sociologist, University of South Florida, Tampa, is presently at work on this issue.

CHAPTER 22

Counseling Policies

The fundamental objective of all personal counseling is to help the person know himself with greater insight and candor. This applies to such matters as choice of work, marital partner, or home to buy. There are other types of counseling, such as in the matter of investments, but even here the bottom line goes further than the trend in stocks or in business, involving the investor's goals, degree of patience, family, and financial status.

Even as a consultant to organizations—another term for counselor—I have found that the same need is invariably present: to help the Veterans' Administration, or the Polish Ministry of Tourism, or the Lincoln Center for the Performing Arts (1) to know their objectives, and (2) to know themselves within the larger situation. The second takes us into the dynamic or operational level, but it is subordinate to the goals.

It would be convenient if by now it could be said that the general discipline of counseling has agreed on a body of principles that applies to all situations, or a body of concrete procedures that applies to marital, vocational, or emotional issues. Alas, such is not the case; even a summary of "principles" and "truths" that are used to help people would have to include the psychiatrist, psychoanalyst, psychologist, fortune teller, Aunt Minnie, the guru, established and commercial religions, Professional Listeners in California, the Planned Parenthood Association, a variety of TM groups and offshoots, today's astrology prescriptions, and the fortune cookies of last night's Chinese meal.

If such a melange of advisers is available on such solid matters as jobs, health, and the stock market, how hopeless must be the accumulated "wisdom"—folk, academic, vernacular, profit-oriented—concerning the relatively esoteric matter of *leisure*. What shall I do tonight? Where should we go for vacation this year? What will I do in retirement?

There is no doubt that on personal matters, including leisure, most counselors are amateurs—our friends, family, the local newspaper. There are pseudocounselors with vested interests, such as the army of salesmen in the travel office with ideas on where to go, or the TV barkers with tips on what to buy. I turn to the more systematic, professionally-oriented segment of thought. Our procedure will be, first, to review a new volume, *Leisure Counsel-*

ing, which contains the views of 31 authorities, a cross section of current thinking without special reference to the elderly. Second, we will turn to a prominent program that deals directly with preretirement, and third, we will discuss some advice from one authority as he deals directly with those already retired. Last, my own approach toward effective counseling of the elderly will be presented.

SOME CURRENT THINKING

Leisure Counseling, An Aspect of Leisure Education has as its objectives:

1. to organize resources from journals, speeches, and conference proceedings regarding the philosophy, rationale, and practice of leisure counseling;
2. to identify needs and examine priorities and directions in the area of leisure counseling;
3. to draw implications for education and research related to this area of service.[1]

The four sections of this work include philosophy and background, techniques and approaches, audiences and group settings, and education and training. Within this range specialized discussions are addressed to serving female psychiatric patients, adult psychiatric and alcoholic patients, youths, inmates of correctional institutions, probationers and parolees, the developmentally disabled, and university students. Although Patsy Edwards, describing her private firm, Constructive Leisure, Inc., mentioned counseling for preretirees, neither she nor anyone else in the volume dealt in any substantive way with the elderly. Yet the general discussion may be relevant to our own interest here, in spite of the explicit emphases on rehabilitative or therapeutic concerns.

In an introductory chapter, Richard Stracke, who works in a Kansas City VA Hospital, discussed the transition that took place by 1966 from the hospital-therapy orientation for leisure counseling to "recreation and life in general."[2] Discussions turned to such matters as "What's important to you? Recreation is where you find it. What's your hex appeal? How's your sense of humor? Are you fun to be with? Games kids play." Superficial as these may seem, they indicated a turn from illness to "wellness." One session with psychiatric patients was called "recreation-leisure planning," and a second, "community recreation resources."

Stracke noted four types of settings for leisure/recreational counseling:[3]

1. The community recreation resources group, directed to special populations, as in institutions: "informational, unstructured, elective attendance group."
2. Recreation and leisure topics group, and "informational but entertaining and intellectually stimulating groups composed of those persons desiring to broaden personal recreational interests: films, speakers, workshops, discussions."

---

[1]From Arlin Epperson, P. A. Witt, and G. Hitzhusen, eds., *Leisure Counseling, An Aspect of Leisure Education,* 1977, p. ix. Courtesy of Charles C Thomas, Publisher, Springfield, Illinois.
[2]Ibid. p. 35.
[3]Ibid. p. 39.

3. Recreation counseling, oriented to activities and facilities.

4. Leisure counseling, "formal intellectual discussion designed for those who need to explore life patterns and attitude changes. . . ."

Stracke advocated an involvement with the last, leisure counseling, for the therapeutic recreator or counselor cannot reach the masses. Pursuing this position, Professor Gerald Fain has turned to a way of "translating" needs into action.[4] He viewed the role of the leisure counselor as one of helping to bridge the gap between the "real" world of the person's situation and the "ideal" world of what he would like to do. Both the real and the ideal must be examined closely to test the person's insights about himself, as well as the nature of his specific behavior. For these purposes Fain has worked with the following "constructs": games, art, mobility, immobility, sociability, altruism, and egocentricity.[5]

Analyzing this construct in the course of counseling, Fain concluded: "We must in part abandon the idea of adapting activity for the individual's needs and begin to think in terms of helping the individual create the activities he needs."[6] In this sense, he observed, some elderly persons should be directed to a vocational counselor, for they need more work to realize self-fulfillment, meaning, and enjoyment.

An "empirical strategy" for leisure counseling based on psychology was presented by Professor George E. McKechnie, now of Berkeley. His approach developed from Fain's use of the real-ideal construct, and he used his own LAB (Leisure Activities Blank) for psychological assessments. The LAB lists 120 activities; for each the subject notes his degree of past participation and plans for future use. Through the use of factor analysis, based on a sample of 288 persons over 20 years of age, McKechnie felt that he could develop "covariations" that lead to predictions as to the kinds of persons most likely to select those areas. For example, of those who went into intellectual activities (concerts, civic organizations, travel, bridge, etc.) high scorers turned out to be relatively "active, alert, energetic, farsighted, healthy, imaginative, insightful, optimistic, outgoing, planful, poised, tactful, verbally fluent." Low scorers, on the other hand, were inclined to be "awkward, defensive, evasive, inert, meek, retiring, silent, simple, sensitive, and unintelligent."[7] Other "high-order" profiles are:

Glamour sports, easy living, and ego recognition (tennis, sailing, skiing, motorcycling, etc.). Such persons seek status and recognition by winning, hoping to be heroes, identifying with "action."

Sports, adventure, and clean living activities (baseball, bowling, jigsaw puzzles, child-related activities, etc.). Such persons are action-oriented, demonstrating "achievement, dominance, and an almost sensuous pleasure in using

---

[4]Ibid. Chapter 3.

[5]Edwinia Hubert, "Leisure Interest Inventory," Ph.D. Thesis, University of North Carolina, 1969.

[6]Fain, op. cit. p. 49.

[7]Ibid. p. 69.

one's body at its optimal level of performance." These are opportunistic and sociable persons.

Slow living activities (dining out, gardening, moviegoing, reading, visiting friends and museums, window-shopping, letter writing). Participants in these were in the process of relaxing from "full, active, perhaps hectic lives, who are heavily involved in their career or in family-raising." These activities served as a "refreshing respite and a well-earned reward." Since the elderly are heavily involved in this category, McKechnie's observation is useful:

> Slow living activities are implicitly heterosexual, and the eroticism and interest in persons of the opposite sex characteristically displayed by high scorers is causally related. Many of the pastimes, i.e., sunbathing, social dancing, and visiting friends, afford the opportunity for sitting back, observing other persons, and perhaps making new acquaintances or reviving old ones. Having arbitrary rather than fixed points of initiation and conclusion, they also allow for varying duration and, if necessary, a quick get-away.[8]

The important task of seeking to match types of persons with types of leisure, undertaken by McKechnie, was also pursued in a more traditional manner by Willoughby Walshe, a doctoral candidate at New York University. There is solid proof, she maintained, "that people's personalities do, in fact, dictate the leisure activities they pursue. Financial recompense is certainly not the spur and is not a factor that affects personality variables!"[9] Noting that the use of the "four temperaments" (personality "profiles," to use contemporary jargon) go back to the Greeks, Immanuel Kant and W. Wundt, Walshe relied on the more recent work of Rudolf Steiner and Karl A. Lund in her application of the "melancholic," "phlegmatic," "sanguine," and "choleric" types as predictive factors in leisure selections. Each was summarized by her in their "pure" state; the subtleties of their dynamics were stressed, for each has three "stages." Certain characteristics play against this, thus allowing new patterns to evolve continually out of the basic configuration."[10] She developed an association of personality needs and temperaments.

Choleric: with dominance, physical activity, creativity.
Sanguine: with creativity, new experience, and social interaction.
Phlegmatic: with relaxation, mental activity, security, and belonging.
Melancholic: with security and belonging, recognition, and service to others.

Interestingly, Walshe went the whole way and matched specific activities with these temperaments:

Choleric: archery, baseball, flight, shooting, etc.
Sanguine: bargain sales, carving, chorus, clubs, etc.
Phlegmatic: card games, chess, cooking, flower arranging, etc.
Melancholic: antiques, autographs, philosophy, religion, etc.[11]

---

[8]Ibid. p. 80. Courtesy of Charles C Thomas, Publisher, Springfield, Illinois.
[9]Ibid. p. 88.
[10]Ibid. p. 96.
[11]Ibid. pp. 101–102.

One of the most discussed contributions in leisure counseling was summarized in the anthology by Robert P. Overs, Sharon Taylor, and Katherine Adkins, all of the Creative Workshop, a project within the Milwaukee School System. The one-year research project on avocational counseling was frankly designed to parallel the principles of vocational counseling. The program began in 1968 by classifying 800 specific activities under nine headings. Psychological dimensions or components of each activity were developed as a reference for counselors of handicapped persons. Each major category, such as Games, was further divided into subgroups (Active Games, Target and Skill Games, etc.), each numbered for quick reference. In 1973–1974, a research and demonstration program emphasized the structure of counseling—the process of time, for example, as separate from the dynamics of interpersonal relationships in counseling. One hundred ten handicapped persons were the experimental subjects.

A useful caveat was noted in the Milwaukee report:

> . . . a selection process does occur and people referred to an avocational counseling service will be those whose characteristics are such that the common pool of knowledge is not sufficient for their needs. Those who deviate from the population mean of the referral source, either above or below, in intelligence, talents, interests, emotional makeup, or life situation are most likely to be referred for counseling.[12]

The actual counseling steps consisted of: (1) finding out why the person is seeking counsel and what he expects from it; (2) reviewing his previous avocational pursuits; (3) interpreting the past and current attitudes, and the consequences for future activities; and (4) reaching concrete choices of one or more new activities, with implemental help from the counselor in getting started. A variety of exploratory tools were used, such as oral discussion, readings, films, sorting of cards, and role playing.

One unique position taken by the Milwaukee group was the value of contacts outside the office, not only with the client through telephone calls, but also with friends of the client or other key individuals—"gatekeepers to avocational opportunities." There was a median of 3.62 collateral contacts per client; telephone calls to clients ranged in number from 1 to 30.

Another unique contribution of the Milwaukee group was an attempt to classify activities according to a variety of criteria and demands, from simple to complex, concrete to abstract, terminal to ongoing, low to high involvement, sedentary to active, indoor to outdoor, spectator to participant, little to much equipment, less to more expensive, more to less popular. The apparent complexity in combining all these variables for the client was simplified by "avocational interest inventories" which, as in the work of McKechnie and Walshe, developed a profile of the person that made wholesale dislikes and propensities available to both counselor and client.

In all counseling, one issue is how far the service should extend. When is the "patient" freed from the therapist? The Milwaukee group believed that the counseling process should go into the behavioral stage. Thus, 119 handi-

---

[12]Ibid. p. 109. Courtesy of Charles C Thomas, Publisher, Springfield, Illinois.

capped clients were given direct assistance in becoming involved with community organizations; 25 visits to activities were made by counselors with their clients; 72 clients were followed up for one to six months after counseling was "completed." Based on a careful tabulation of responses to the new experience, it was concluded that the two criteria of success in avocational experiences were "interpersonal relationships . . . and displays of skill, accomplishments, and competence by the individual participants."[13]

The volume edited by Epperson, Witt, and Hitzhusen contains theoretical discussions that are substantive, but generally supplement the range of topics summarized above. James M. Montagnes, Director of the Institute of Reality Therapy in Ontario, argued for the need for the counselor to become one with his client, to make a value judgment about the client's choices as well as a plan. Professor Scout L. Gunn of the University of Illinois applied some principles of "transactional analysis" and Gestalt to leisure counseling through the analysis of play.

From this assortment of general principles and methods that are currently in use by academics and practitioners, we now turn to some programs that are addressed directly to the elderly.

Title IV of the Older Americans Act funded several research and demonstration programs. Among these, Drake University's Des Moines Retirement Opportunity Planning Center has served about 500 older workers annually through information services, individual counseling, and group discussions. The University of Massachusetts has compared groups that did and did not receive literature as part of their preretirement planning. The University of Oregon has studied success in the retirement of about 650 persons as related to counseling, retirement benefits, and personal characteristics. This study will be summarized here.[14]

The Oregon research compared workers from four plants which had preretirement programs for eight or more years with plants that had no program. Careful screening reduced the number of plants to be studied to 65; these, in turn, were then screened further through detailed questionnaires. It was found that smaller companies had no programs, putting the responsibility on the individual. Of course, wide variations in "program" were found; 48% dealt only with such matters as rights and benefits under the company's plan.

Criteria included programs of five years or longer, mandatory retirement, counseling on company time, a minimum of six hours in counseling, a maximum of 60-year age average for employees, and the keeping of records on the program. Leisure activities were among the seven areas considered (others were benefits, personal financing, health, housing, postretirement work, and legal matters).

Geographical comparisons led the Oregon investigators to conclude that companies in the western U.S. began their retirement programs somewhat

---

[13]Ibid. pp. 128–132.

[14]Mark Greene, *Counseling, Retirement Adjustment, and the Older Employee.* Eugene: University of Oregon, Graduate School of Management and Business, 1969.

later than eastern companies. Of the twelve companies studied, ten used company time, four used the group approach, four used the individual session, and four used both arrangements; all were voluntary; half invited spouses (one third to one half attended); most programs commenced at age 55; length of counseling varied from five to twenty hours; in only one plant did the union participate. Leisure issues usually received one to three hours in western companies, one to four hours in the eastern.

The eight companies finally chosen were matched (4:4) on the basis of industry, size, and geographic location. Four were medium-sized plants (1000 to 5000 employees), and four had over 5000. All were in southern California: two insurance firms, four in communications, and two in aviation and aerospace. A stratified sample of workers was selected in the large plants, the entire population in others. With some refusals for interviews, 648 persons were interviewed.[15]

Some specific results in relation to leisure indicate a significant difference between the number of activities of those persons who had participated in preretirement counseling as compared to those who had not. This, indeed, was the largest correlation among all the topics investigated. The report noted: ". . . we might be so bold as to speculate that his attendance in a pre-retirement counseling program will manifest itself more vividly in his participation in a variety of activities after retirement."[16]

However, no significant difference could be detected between those matched on such matters as intensity of participation in activities, degree of enjoyment, or change of activities. The research did not find explanations for this discrepancy.

On a more general level, the researchers found that the important variables in adjustment to all areas of retirement were income, health, and the degree of activity that was engaged in *before* retirement. Almost no support was found for the "disengagement" theory of retirement—i.e., a gradual withdrawal from the life of the community.[17] Generally, the effect of counseling was apparent: "even an exposure to preretirement which was seen as not particularly helpful still produces better results than no participation in a program at all."[18] A disappointment was found among employees who did *not* enter into a preretirement program and who liked to say, "When I retire, I'm going to take up all the activities which I have always wanted to do, but have always been too busy to do."[19] The evidence is that self-fulfilling prophecy will not materialize as well without the counseling. However, little difference was found between persons in this regard who entered a counseling program before or after retirement.

[15]Material on research methods will be found in more detail, Greene, Ibid., Chapter 22, pp. 17–37.
[16]Ibid. p. 149.
[17]Ibid. p. 238.
[18]Ibid. p. 243.
[19]Ibid. p. 244.

More direct advice to leaders will be found in Appendix C, prepared by Professor Howard Rosencranz of the University of Connecticut's Program in Gerontology.

"HOW-TO-DO-IT"

We turn next to a sample of counseling that is directed to the elderly en masse, in one of the increasing number of how-to-do-it books. One of the most recent, and best, is by Peter A. Dickinson, founding editor of *Harvest Years* (now, *Retirement Living*) and the *Retirement Letter*. He has lectured widely, and serves as retirement consultant to major corporations. *The Complete Retirement Planning Book* has three sections of information, advice relating to money, place of residence, and legal matters. A final section is titled "Time—The Money of Your Life." In this section Dickinson covers a wide range of topics, including relaxation, self-expression, recognition, participation, adventure, learning, contemplation, activity, and security. Each discussion includes some general comments followed by specific suggestions and alternatives. A portion of an introductory discussion is reproduced below as a sample of his style.[20]

Whatever we do, we should stress the *quality* of time, rather than its *quantity*. Free yourself! Realize that you're a unique person with unique interests and abilities. Take a close look at yourself to see *who* you are and *what* you really want.

In finding *you*, you'll realize that your likes and dislikes rarely change. Your leisure activities depend more on your *personality* than on your age, sex, or social status. You *are* what you *were* and what you *will be*. Your *past* is the key to your *present* and the clue to your *future*. If you weren't a joiner, you aren't going to become one at any age. Successful retirement and successful leisure depend on cultivating or renewing old interests and developing new ones. Ask yourself:

- What did you *like* to do as a youngster?
- What did you *like* to do in your spare time?
- How did you *like* to earn money?
- What have you always *wanted* to do?
- *Why* you like to do things and with whom?
- Do you like to do things alone or with other people?
- Do you prefer playing for fun or playing to win?
- Do you want recognition or money?

Dr. Joseph H. Peck, author of *Let's Rejoin the Human Race*, says: "It is my firm belief that every man was born to follow some latent ability and the desire to follow some destiny; 90 per cent of us, however, lose sight of this goal somewhere between the ages

---

[20]Peter A. Dickinson, *The Complete Retirement Planning Book*. New York: E. P. Dutton, 1976, pp. 223–224. Copyright © 1976 by Peter A. Dickinson. Reprinted by permission of the publisher.

of fifteen and thirty." Dr. Peck feels that although we may lose this "spark of greatness" during our working years, it lies smoldering in our subconscious, and we can rekindle it if we take stock of ourselves before we reach retirement. He adds: "As soon as you step down from your life's work, you must be born again. That's the meaning of leisure."

"To be born again" doesn't mean painting gallery pictures or writing best-selling novels—we "create" when we do our "own thing." "He's a true artist" or "she makes an art of whatever she does" applies to arranging flowers, setting a table, painting a garage, or repairing a staircase. And some gerontologists feel that an aging person resembles an aging tree—while the trunk may grow more rigid, the tree still grows offshoots that reach into the world to seek nourishment.

Reaching out doesn't depend on formal education. An English schoolmaster once said that the mark of an educated man was determined by three things: Could he entertain another? Could he entertain a new idea? Could he entertain himself?

Although the past guides the future, the future leads the way. Look to the future for new directions and activities. It's never too late to learn; wisdom and experience will help you pick and choose. And when trying something new, measure your progress in the light of *your past*—not that of someone else.

Variety, Balance for Full Satisfaction

No single activity satisfies forever. Plan a balanced program to nourish your mind, train your hands, limber your body, and lift your spirit. Seek *continuity*—activities you can return to time and time again. Identify with them and feel they're a part of you. They should be *varied enough* so you never get bored, but they should offer you a sense of accomplishment.

Seek *various activities:* noncompetitive as well as competitive sports; solitude as well as companionship; contemplation as well as information; creativity as well as entertainment. Well-chosen activities should replace work satisfactions and status. You'll find these in activities that: (1) serve others as well as yourself; (2) allow you to participate rather than just observe; (3) are more service than social; (4) are a means toward an end rather than an end in themselves; (5) are more art than games; (6) are more exploring than stagnating. Choose activities that involve you with others and yet let you maintain your independence.

THE COUNSELING INTERVIEW: A CASE

Finally, my own approach to counseling for preretirement purposes or for leisure in general is based on the view presented in this volume that the roles of the elderly occur in an enlarged leisure context, not qualitatively different from their experience as younger persons. What is therefore avoided is any kind of test or questionnaire that considers the elderly as a horizontal group and treats them as a separate subculture. Rather, the approach is longitudinal, based not on comparisons with other persons but upon the unique history and essence of each person.

Counseling, as undertaken here, is a joint endeavor by the counselor and client; the interaction becomes one of colleagues. It proceeds through several clear stages that are discussed openly as the relationship commences, and consists of:

I. A broad summary of the person's life and work career. This would subsume such basic data as education, place of residence, family situation, and so on.

II. As the individual speaks, the counselor makes notes on the career in addition to taping the session. At the close of the client's statement, a list of major "themes" from his life are discussed—those recurring characteristics that might hold a clue to leisure patterns during those years. Examples might be: travel as part of the job, reading, contacts with people. This list is then discussed by counselor and client for modification and addition.

III. Then the client turns directly to his/her leisure activities during the work years. The categories used in Chapters 13 to 20 provide the base for a somewhat systematic discussion, to help obtain a profile of activities and attitudes. We attempt, of course, to draw connections between the themes of the work life and the simultaneous patterns of leisure.

IV. Only then do we turn to retirement: the person's attitudes, fears, plans, hopes, and so on. These are discussed within the realistic setting that has already been defined, consisting of such information as the person's income.

V. The last stage consists of:

A. Leisure selections.

B. "Probes" into these experiences.

C. Evaluations of the experience, especially if it is new for the person, in the light of all prior considerations.

Below is the case of a university professor who had just retired the week of the interview. It will become apparent that he is not in need of counseling; however, he agreed to proceed through stages I to IV, and enjoyed the opportunity of a self-review.

From a research point of view, rather than a service or counseling standpoint, it is commonly heard in scientific circles that one or a few cases cannot be the basis of a science—in this case, counseling. Nevertheless it can be important to suggest hunches, ideas, connections and, ultimately, hypotheses. One case—not important? Imagine the excitement throughout the scientific world if our space cameras were to photograph *one* living creature on Mars, with three heads, a tail, and four legs! Of course, successive pictures might modify the "data"—perhaps something with four heads and six legs. . . .

The hypothesis to which the case below leads is an old one, based on the impression that there are connections between occupational values and the ease of retirement. One might want to compare the case of an educator with that of a recent retiree from the communities of business, the arts, clergy, military, science, manufacturing, farming, or others. Researchers in occupational sociology and psychology have already delved into such matters; Harold Wilensky in the United States and Stanley Parker of England have related leisure to work or occupation more fully than others in the field.[21]

---

[21]Harold Wilensky, "Emerging of Life Styles: A Microscopic Prediction about the Fate of the Organization Man," read to the Research Committee on Leisure, 7th World Congress of Sociology, Varna, Bulgaria, September 1970; Stanley R. Parker, *The Future of Work and Leisure,* London: MacGibbon and Kee, 1971. Also see Ethel Shanas and R. J. Havighurst, "Retirement in Four Professions," *Journal of Gerontology,* 8 (1953), pp. 212–221; L. Germant, "What 84 Retired Professors Say about Retirement," *The Gerontologist,* 12 (1972), pp. 349–353; and Alan Rowe, "Scientists in Retirement," *Journal of Gerontology,* 21 (1972), pp. 113–118, and 22 (1973), pp. 335–345.

Professor C. W. (Lance) Hunnicutt, who has given permission to use his real name, retired from the College of Education, University of South Florida, Tampa. He and Mrs. H. moved to a condominium apartment on Longboat Key, north of Sarasota, with her 99-year-old mother.

L. H. was born in California. Early in their childhood he and his sister were orphaned; both parents died of tuberculosis. He had one form or another of respiratory illness during childhood and early adulthood. The children were raised by relatives in California.

During his freshman year at Whittier College, for reasons of health, he transferred to the University of Arizona, Tucson, where he earned a B.S. in Chemistry (1930) and an M.A. in Chemistry and Education (1931). The latter degree was completed during his first year as principal of the Scottsdale, Arizona, Elementary School (1930–1938). During one summer he developed tuberculosis, which fortunately was arrested within a month or so, and he was able to avoid jeopardizing children or job. The years at Scottsdale helped shape L. H.: early marriage, the Depression, "warrants" instead of paychecks, extreme wealth amid stark poverty—which included child malnutrition— culture contrasts, with efforts at bilingual teaching among the many Chicanos and even the trilingualism of Yaqui Indian children, a school growth which doubled the number of teachers, and winter visitors who temporarily ballooned enrollments during the winter months.

Doctoral work at Stanford University (1938–1940) opened new dimensions to education and determined that his future would be in universities. Mrs. H. supported them both by secretarial work at $65 a month. In the first winter he was invited to teach three undergraduate courses during the following summer at the University of North Carolina. He had always been happy teaching children, but distressingly timid in public speaking before adults; he worried as to which pattern would characterize his *college* teaching. Acting on advice he planned his first class as a seminar in supervision for a dozen or so, and at 8:00 A.M. walked in to find fifty-odd teachers, principals, and supervisors of all ages in a room designed for twenty. They, in turn, were jolted not to see the Alabama State Superintendent of Schools, who had been specified as instructor in the advance publicity (and for whom L. H. was an unwitting substitute). It was a proverbial baptism of fire. The summer went very well.

Years later, at a national conference, the former dean announced, "Hunnicutt, do you know you were the reason I left North Carolina?" "Heavens, no—give!" It seems that he had gotten permission from the university president to invite the young man across the continent to teach and be watched with a view to his starting a program in Elementary Education there a year later (all a total surprise to the naive young L.H.). When the dean reported his satisfaction to the president and suggested an immediate decision, he was told that with war probably coming (August 1939), they should not hire new people or start any new programs. "So I said, 'To hell with it' and went to Colorado."

This is but one of several examples of how his life was decided by others, totally without his knowledge.

On his return to California, he was invited to spend the full quarter in Santa Barbara as part of the Stanford University curriculum research team. (Mrs. H. of necessity kept her job in Palo Alto.) He lived in the Stanford apartment with Professor Paul Leonard, who later became president of San Francisco State College and then of the American University in Beirut. In Santa Barbara he had a part in developing the kind of schooling that is still magnificent by today's standards—an experience useful throughout his professional life. He also helped to write three books, and he had coauthored a journal article before his return to Stanford at the end of the year. Several of his friends among the doctoral students at Stanford achieved national and international recognition.

By June L. H. had completed doctoral course work and qualifying examinations; he was scheduled to be a consultant for five weeks in the Drake University-Des Moines Public Schools Workshop in Progressive Education, and then return to Santa Barbara as a country curriculum coordinator, where he would presumably complete his dissertation.

In September, however, with the gracious release by Santa Barbara, he accepted an unexpected "one-year" appointment to Syracuse that was to last 27 years (1940–1967). Fortune favored him. Almost immediately he became part of one of the great educational experiments of all times, the New York City Experiment, with an experimental group of 60,000 and a control group of 600,000 children. Here he built lasting friendships with city and state leaders (and incidentally completed a dissertation on schedule). The experiment was superbly planned and executed, with persuasive results. The City board voted a step-by-step commitment, and national recognition began (e.g., *Time*). But less than two weeks later came Pearl Harbor, and almost all went out the window. Schools in New York and elsewhere would never again have such opportunities.

His Syracuse position was as head of elementary education, then a fourth-year graduate program for already certified teachers. In due course, elementary education there became one of the quality programs of the country. In each small area, by the mid-1950's, there was at least one person of national eminence. At that time L. H. stepped out of directing the laboratory to head 18 graduate assistants, helping children, students, and even medical faculty. Two of the first three presidents of the International Reading Association had taken their doctorates with him.

L. H. created an arithmetic team that created a unique diagnostic laboratory. A group of three, including L. H., initiated the Psychological Services Center of the University. He was also instrumental in creating the University Nursery School, used by the colleges of Education, Medicine, and Home Economics, and in creating the undergraduate program for preparing elementary school teachers. He was also the founding president (two years) of the New York State Association for Supervision and Curriculum Development (an important affiliate of the national organization). At the time, it was the only educational organization that brought together leaders of New York City Schools with those outside the city. It was easy to create significant programs with the superb talent then at work in Columbia and New York Universities and in the great city system, and in the State educational systems and major universities outside New York City. L. H. later was to have responsibilities in the national organization.

In 1952 came the well paid opportunity to spend four quarters as visiting professor at Stanford University, filling in for the man who had been his major professor, but who was now on sabbatical leave in the Philippines. So the family (now including a daughter and three sons) uprooted and trekked across country. Here he discovered the joy of a visiting professorship with no administrative or committee responsibilities—freedom to teach and *write*. From this came several books. The next year was even more wonderful—a year with the family in the Orient under a Stanford-University of the Philippines contract to help create doctoral programs there. At the time, college faculty members throughout the country could only earn doctorates at great expense in Europe or America. Then on around the world to Egypt, Europe, and Syracuse—and to the immediate sudden death of Mrs. H. Meeting contract deadlines as senior author of a text series was essential therapy.

Years later, when asked by a new dean for a report, he was to discover that he had been author or senior coauthor of three dozen books and between seven and eight dozen articles or yearbook chapters. "I found to my amazement, that starting in 1939 there wasn't a year that went by without something of mine being published." This continued for more than a third of a century.

Some offbeat experiences covering but a few years at a time included a series of educational movies with Coronet Films, a consultancy with an architectural firm in planning school buildings, and the role of secretary to the Handwriting Foundation Committee, which met quarterly in interesting parts of the country.

But the one role that had more chance than any others of bettering many lives covered a five-year span, 1965–1970. Under the Alliance for Progress, he spent nearly a fourth of his time in Central America helping a team representing each country prepare a uniform series of social studies texts that are now used in all elementary schools of the six countries. (Other teams treated mathematics, science, reading, and language arts.) These books met several goals: they provided materials in *many* rural schools which had previously tried to teach without any texts, greatly improved information and methodology, a common base of attitudes and information for the next generation that might diminish suspicions and antagonism between neighboring countries, and the preparation of a cadre of authors who have continued to write for children after the project ended.

About 1960, L. H. began to consider seriously his future years. Retire in Syracuse and live on there? Retire in Syracuse and *move* to a geographic area he preferred? Or try to work and sink roots for a final decade in an area he would choose for retirement? He took extensive lecture assignments in California and Arizona to consider possibilities, and then a semester off in Florida for writing. Florida became his choice. In 1967 he was invited to help create a doctoral program in the College of Education of the vigorous new

University of South Florida, Tampa, and retired ten years later, at age 70, with the goal achieved.

Following the narrative of this career, the interviewer then pinpointed several "themes":

1. The centrality of "mind-life."
2. Constant association with creative colleagues.
3. Innovative or experimental programs and experiences.
4. Ongoing contact with significant institutions of higher learning.
5. Ongoing creation in the form of writings, hence a form of "immortality."
6. Experiences in organizing.
7. The presence of criteria for "success" in the job, both objective and subjective.
8. Illness as a career factor.
9. Contact with all ages.
10. Comparative freedom in his job.
11. The juxtaposition of isolation (as in writing) and sociability (committee work, teaching).

L. H. did not disagree with these themes from his career. His leisure activities during his work life took advantage of these factors. His avocational reading tended toward scientific subjects, with subscriptions to such journals as *Scientific American, Natural History* and *International Wildlife.* The family could never afford wide travel, yet they visited 18 national parks one summer. Other trips included the Philippines and Central America. He had little time for civic interests; sports participation was never a "big deal." The television set was off more than on. Social visits were mostly with campus colleagues and neighbors, usually in the Hunnicutt home.

In respect to what L. H. now intends to do, the "values of a lifetime" remain his guide. He doubts that he will ever be bored. He may write; he may not. He may join a former colleague in organizing new materials for high school students to continue his productivity and, more important, to afford him a chance to spend six months in Spain. Music continues to be an interest. Professionally, he once directed research on children's tastes; personally, he was a pianist, but "not good." He now plans to become active in the planning of an innovative nursing home in Sarasota; formerly he had little time to engage in civic activities.

L. H. has purchased a season's ticket to see the new AFL Buccaneers in Tampa, traveling the 50 miles to the games or watching them on TV.

He is "religious" in the humanistic sense and characterizes himself as an agnostic. This results less from his scientific interests than from finding that as an adult he "did not care" about the afterlife. He had been born into a Quaker family; the first choir he sang in as a boy was a Methodist, and later he joined the Unitarian church in which to raise his children.

Coming to an assessment of his professional life, he was invited to rate his "life performance" on a scale of 1 to 10. "Is there any reason you would rate yourself as less than 10?" "Oh, yes. I know of associates who did so much more.

I never was very good at comparing myself with people who were doing less. I was never anywhere near a Dewey or a Thorndike. But I guess, in all fairness, of the influential educators of my generation I probably was up in the top 5%."

As to whether he foresaw any difficulties in his retirement: "I don't know if I'm going to have a problem or not. I haven't the least idea if I'm going to be bored a year from now. I have taken golf up seriously for the first time in the last six months. I intend to keep up with swimming and with fishing that I enjoyed greatly when I was a kid. I'm simply keeping doors open to see. I'm presently tied down here, and can't do any traveling, but that won't last forever."

Did he believe in preretirement or postretirement counseling? "Well, I suppose. But I don't know what anyone could have done for me. There are people who are ignorant and don't know about it. I've read a great deal about it in the past few years."

Wouldn't he like to know more about resources in the community? "Right, and I intend to find out. Now I'm enjoying no deadlines. I've lived with deadlines all my life."

Did he feel that many people of our generation, educated or not, needed the security of numbers, as in a retirement community? "To me, age is much less important than people themselves. The problem is one of stereotypes; I think of people who were mentally alive and doing things. . . . I think I can find people with good minds. They don't necessarily have to have been college graduates. Let's put it another way. Perhaps the best educated man that I ever had personal contact with was George W. P. Hunt of Arizona, who never went beyond the sixth grade, but was truly a great man. He was the one who almost single-handedly set up the Arizona constitution when it became a state so that any kid anywhere has a chance to go clear through graduate school for free. He had such great respect for education that his study, from floor to ceiling, was filled with books. You could pick out any book at random and you'd find his marks. He was really educated. And so you'll find people with minds, alertness, interested in things, without having to tie in with professors."

CHAPTER 23

Training Policies

In the introduction to a report, *Translating Aging Research into Training*, the Southern Regional Education Board noted:

> At present there is little training and education in the field of aging. . . . While there has been some progress and there are high quality programs in a few locations, most states do not have any appreciable amount of training of any type related to problems of aging.[1]

In addition to formal curricula for the preparation of gerontologists, there is a broad range of "targets" for training in this field, including the preparation of community volunteers, preretirement training, and in-service training for agency staff members. By the mid-1970's, over 30 American universities and colleges had a curriculum for careers in gerontology. The University of Michigan, in the days of Clark Tibbitts and Wilma T. Donahue, was the pioneer. According to the *New York Times,* June 19, 1977, 1,277 schools now have one or more courses in the field, about triple of five years ago. Also in this article Dr. James Birren, Director of the Ethel Percy Andrus Gerontology Center of the University of Southern California, predicted that by the year 2000 there wouldn't be a college or university in the country without a gerontology program; "they'll have to."

Many programs of this type have been funded by the Older Americans Act under Titles III, IV, and V. There is no clear consensus about a preference for professional "gerontologists" as compared to social workers, nurses, or others who can apply their special backgrounds to the elderly under appropriate supervision. A comparable question can be raised as to whether there is need, within the field itself, for a special curriculum on leisure or recreation for the elderly, or whether someone already in the recreation field with sensitivity to older persons can do a creditable job.[2] My mind is open on this issue; more experience is needed in observing those who have a background in traditional recreation curricula, and those who come from a broader gerontology

---

[1]Sponsored by the Southern Regional Education Board, supported by HEW, December, 1972, p. iv. This is a quotation from James Birren, "Training," *Background and Issues* series by the White House Conference on Aging, March 1971.

[2]Robert Lindsey, *The New York Times,* June 19, 1977. "Gerontology Is Still a Very Young Science," IV, 9:1.

background, before definitive conclusions can be reached. Should a community recreation department engage a gerontologist? Should a nursing home take on a recreation graduate? A middle ground is presently being sought in both types of training. There is, however, more to the ideal curriculum than the best of these two backgrounds. I propose that we translate the directions of this volume into training needs, and see where we arrive. The fields of both recreation and gerontology contain valuable insights and skills; there may be facets of the issue that neither touches adequately.

Five roles of the potential leader will concern us: as *persons, organizers, colleagues, scholars,* and *researchers.* Within each role we can apply the components that were noted in Chapter 1—social circle, function, status, and self.

AS PERSONS

The most essential qualification for the leader of leisure programs among the elderly is to be a person of substance. Conceptions of such a person will vary widely, but what is broadly meant here is someone to whom older people will respond as a human being, with qualities that go beyond special expertise in the professional field. I make no claim to insights beyond those that are current in the tradition of humanism. We cannot expect superpersons, but we can look for and train toward such factors as:

—a reasonable knowledge of oneself, both strengths and limitations;

—a reasonably healthy person, physically and emotionally;

—a reasonably intelligent person, however that is defined;

—an indisputably honest person, with himself/herself and others;

—a reasonably informed person who keeps up with national and world affairs by going beyond the 6:00 P.M. TV news, and who reads good newspapers, magazines, and books;

—a person who likes people of all ages, not only the elderly;

—one who is sufficiently secure to respect the views of others;

—one who is constantly growing, rather than stagnant.

Many of these qualities are difficult to measure or evaluate by traditional psychological testing methods. A group of children or retirees will soon know whether our mythical leader is such a whole person, without need of tests or scales.

One method by which the training faculty can move toward attracting or producing such men and women is by *themselves* to seek to be whole persons. The university student can also judge the faculty as people, and often accepts them as "role models" for the profession they want to enter.

A second approach is for the training program to allow enough *time* for the graduate student to grow in directions outside the prescribed curriculum; attendance at a concert may be as valuable a university experience as the same evening spent in reading a technical article. There is little logic in a professor's teaching that a program with retirees should be flexible if her own teaching is pedestrian and inflexible; the dull instructor has little business advocating a program for retirees that is "interesting."

A third approach in preparing whole persons is to provide enough access, through electives, for experiences in humanities courses that may have little apparent relation to the profession—in languages, the arts, literature, history, the social sciences, and so on.

A fourth approach is to eliminate all examinations, oral or written, in the university gerontology and leisure program. Examinations are relics of medievalism, and provide protection for professors who are insecure in themselves or in their judgment of colleagues and schools. Graduate students who are preparing to conduct leisure experiences along the lines advocated in this volume should be considered as young colleagues by the faculty, given tasks by joint agreement, and judged on the same level of observation as professional colleagues would be judged on the job. Assignments can be creative, and will reveal very shortly whether they have been fruitful for the student or called forth a serious effort. Some 40 years of university teaching can hardly fail to produce some observation about students. I learned long ago that many students have been so ruined mentally that they are afraid of freedom; the better students—those whom we want in the field—will work far harder when they are treated with respect. The leader, as a whole person, is himself proficient in one or more leisure activities, in any of the realms discussed in Section 4. He need not be an expert in many of them, nor will this be expected by the elderly.

AS ORGANIZERS

The next role we prepare the student to fill is that of organizer. A more accurate French word is *animateur* (which can be roughly translated as a "moving spirit, life-giver.")

Several principles are appropriate to this role. A general rule that is often followed successfully with children in recreational situations is to let them act on the assumption that they are making decisions. In actuality the leader is guiding them toward desirable ends. Conversely, in working with the elderly, a technique is sometimes required whereby they act on the assumption that the leader is making the decision, but in truth they are deciding. This difference arises from the reality that in many situations, older persons *want* to be led, partly because little things in institutional frameworks grow to monumental proportions, and squabbles become a common occurrence. The desire for the leader to settle arguments and "decide" that the picnic will be on Saturday rather than on Sunday is partly a gesture of confidence in the leader, and partly a need to withdraw from the decision making that has plagued them all of their lives. Decisions are ready-made, just as the grass is cut, the meals are prepared, and someone else washes the dishes.

The sensitive leader "decides" with full knowledge of his group's traditions, needs, and material circumstances. This sensitivity is part of being the "whole person" discussed above, one who respects older persons. All too common are leaders who have been heard referring to the residents of the nursing home as "idiots," as "stupid," as "children." On a slightly higher level perhaps, they speak of their "children."

A second principle of organization is operative when a relationship exists in which a democratic milieu is present among the elderly residents, or club members, or participants in a given activity. Involvement in decision making is accepted by all, with the professional person looked upon as a resource. Such a situation was present in a meeting I was permitted to attend in San Diego, when the Board of the Institute for Continued Learning met in the home of a member to discuss their educational programs (also see Appendix B). Sitting with them was Doris Brosnan, who is engaged by the University to serve as its liaison with the group. I discerned no trace of condescension on her part toward them and no subservience by them. Everyone had a chance to be heard. In this case she served as chairperson for the meeting.

A contrast to the San Diego experience was one in St. Petersburg, when some students and I attended a meeting of an upper middle class nursing home in which an open conflict emerged between the residents and the manager. He had removed some furniture from the lobby because (as he maintained), too many residents sat around every evening just to gossip "about who was going out with whom," "what they were wearing," etc. The residents did not dispute these motivations for use of the lobby. They objected because he had not openly discussed the problem with them, and they objected to what they called the "institutionalization" of what they thought should be a pleasant "residential hotel" situation.

The adequate leisure leader is a one-man or one-woman network, capable of meshing his/her leadership and available facilities with those of other leaders, facilities, and programs in the community. Such a person must, therefore, be alert to what goes on in communities in general and this one in particular. This type of leader has no hesitation in communicating as an equal with sources of power and services in the community.

AS COLLEAGUES

The leader of leisure activities or programs is often one figure in a team, whether the setting is that of a community center, park, VA hospital, prison, school, industrial Y, or church. There are unique issues involving relationships and communications.

First, respect the motivations, objectives, and programs outside of your own and be ready to recognize or emphasize the common elements rather than the differences. It was no secret, some years ago, that the VA hospitals were often scenes of antagonism between the occupational therapists and the recreation departments. There were overlapping and philosophical disputes that had been fed by the respective training institutions that had prepared these professionals. As a "consultant" (i.e., an outsider), I had the freedom they were sometimes lacking from within to discuss these situations. Rare, indeed, is the situation in which complete harmony exists between the disciplines that are found in a large institution. Even on a modest playground one may hear rumblings between those trained in recreation or in physical education. (Are there not similarities here to other fields and university preparations—attitudes between sociologists and psychologists, clinical and experimental psychologists, musicologists and performing musicians, or colleges of education vis à vis all other colleges of a university?)

Second, learn to be articulate, not only for obvious reasons in all aspects of one's profession but, in this case, to represent your field among professionals of other areas. I need hardly comment critically about the number of college graduates in many fields who can neither talk before the public nor write intelligently. The lack is particularly acute among recreational students, for their field already suffers from an image of nonintellectuality within the university, aided and abetted by the flow of inanities heard almost every time Howard Cosell interviews an athletic hero.

The leader of "leisure" programs is, ostensibly, concerned with the arts, visits to other cultures, educational activity—"culture" as a whole. This is all the more reason for an ability to verbalize our purposes. As opposed as I am to written examinations, so am I in favor of written reports in relation to creative experiences within the training experience.

Finally be open to alliances and programming relationships with colleagues who are doing different things. One of Arthur Koestler's major theses in *The Act of Creation* is that many creative insights derive from the integration of two seemingly separate fields.[3] Perhaps somewhat the same can be said of whole programs that converge. Recall the pride of those older Bostonians as they combined their concerns for conserving trees and historical markers. The result was an innovative series of projects far beyond the usual volunteering stint.

AS SCHOLARS

What is the ideal blend of institutional and rational action? This question can be applied to all aspects of life. Yet here, assisting older persons to live creative lives, the issue is persistent, and never goes away. It is apparent that we don't know so much. Gerontology is a young field, the systematic study of leisure is a new field, and the situation is like two infants trying to relate to each other.

On the other hand, the range of knowledge represented in the various theoretical disciplines and practicing professions is immense. The actuality of the Renaissance man who can truly be said to know all the services and all the humanities is impossible in our time. He cannot have heard all the music known to literate musicians, or read all the books known to literature spe-

---

[3]Arthur Koestler, *The Act of Creation.* New York, Dell Publishing Co., Laurel Edition, 1964.

cialists, or performed all the experiments of chemistry, physics, and psychology.

Two issues, then, become paramount: (1) having a grasp of the *kinds* of knowledge that are necessary to perform our role of leaders well; and (2) knowing the *sources* for such knowledge, whether these be books, research reports, information retrieval systems, or knowledgeable persons.

As to types of knowledge, basic readings should be known from the fields of gerontology, leisure, and recreation. Beyond that there are no prescriptions, but a wide selection of books and professional journals in the social sciences. The student should become an inveterate browser for materials that should be in the library as staples for constant reference, and for monographs or journals that are published occasionally. An example of the first might be the three volumes issued by the University of Chicago in the late 1950's and early 1960's, and the latter might be the *Daedalus* issue of Spring 1976, devoted to the theme "Adulthood."

As important as reading is the ability to organize the material gathered; this should be systematically kept and should be *immediately available*.

I do not apologize here for suggesting some simple methods for organization, for few students, on any level, keep materials carefully. My own system consists of file folders and cards, each subdivided as follows:

Files, with drawers devoted to:

Correspondence—persons

Correspondence—organizations

Articles—by others

Articles—my own

Materials on aging—with guide folders to delineate major and minor headings

For example, in writing this book, this set of files is organized according to the chapters in this book. If I clip a newspaper story about a retiree going to school, it goes immediately into the file marked 15, corresponding to the chapter. A magazine article on artistic activity among retirees goes into number 13. Each item—monograph, clipping, etc.—is marked with the chapter number so that after use it will go back where it belongs.

Card Box, with cards in three colors:

White—bibliographical listing, noting author, title, publisher, date, and occasionally a comment on the card

Brown (or green, etc.)—quotations, always noting the full source (author, book, page, etc.)

Blue—my own ideas, fragments, reminders of things to read, etc.

These cards are, of course, divided by headings which are organized precisely like the file material. Each card, in the upper-right corner, carries its number, such as III-2. In both the files and the cards, "III-2" is taken from the outline of the subject, or the writing underway (term paper, article, book, lecture). If the outline of the subject is changed at times as the student's perceptions of the subject grow, then he faces the need to adjust his files, which means the subject headings and the reallocation of every item in every category. The present volume, for example, has gone through many such changes; about a year elapsed before I felt comfortable with the outline as the instrument for what needed to be said. Many hours were, therefore, spent in renumbering and reallocating every item in the cards and the file. These were useful to me, giving me repeated chances to become acquainted with the material.

Most important to the student or to the more experienced scholar is developing, using, and modifying the outline. One's thinking becomes more systematic, and the subject begins to fall into clear categories or relationships. The alternative is to have notes scattered through one's home or office—ideas or references are found, or lost, on the backs of envelopes, and disorganized piles of newspaper clippings become easy to forget.

Drawers of cards used and developed in writing my 1975 volume are similarly organized. The difference is that after the book was published, I could eliminate cards, clippings, etc., that were included in the book itself. Yet these files presently include considerable material that was not used; further, they continue to provide a repository for material that now comes to my attention and that can still be used for articles, lectures, or eventual revisions of the book.

There are other techniques that each scholar uses to ease his path. A few odds and ends:

1. My files are open to examination by my students, and we spend time in seminars on problems of organization.

2. I have a box of cards for keeping track of materials I lend, and promise to keep this record faithfully. I am a failure at this and frequently lend materials that never come back.

3. Left undiscussed is the crucial matter of how one arrives at the "outline" of the subject, the skeleton upon which the materials and the writing is based. The answer—if there can be one—would tell one how to think. Everyone goes about it his own way; each book has its own history. As to the leisure leader who may never write anything but whose materials will help in his professional work, there are only general suggestions that may be useful.

The outlines and materials that the student accumulates from his graduate courses represent lifetime products of more experienced scholars and practitioners. The young worker in the field may be inclined, within the first few months or years in the profession, to think that he/she knows all the answers, and that the faculty was all wrong. I have come across young people in their 20s who were already self-proclaimed experts, and even a few who announced their availability as "consultants." Advice: rely on the experience of others who have been in it longer. This should not hinder an innovative, questioning spirit.

Gradually move toward an integration of published materials, what you were taught, experiences in the field, discussions with colleagues, and your own research or intuition. Eventually, even as a young composer never really leaves the traditions of Bach and Beethoven, but develops his own sounds, so the gerontologist leisure leader develops his own *professional* lifestyle. This comes more quickly to some than to others, but never quickly enough for such persons as the young lady, perhaps 20 years old, who sat in my office and remarked, "Professor Kaplan, I'd like to do what you're doing, to combine several fields. What book should I read?"

AS RESEARCHERS

Research is a primary commitment of the scholar—the creation, verification, and modification of knowledge. With careers, curricula, and libraries of materials on research available in the social sciences, no more is needed here than some broad commentaries and a few specific suggestions.

Throughout this volume there have been explicit and implicit cues. On almost every topic that has been raised there are potential topics for research. As in any field, several kinds of experiences are needed by those who claim to do research:

1. Sufficient acquaintance with the field to deal adequately with its theoretical issues.

2. Sufficient skills to design, pursue, or understand the techniques of research, as in the gathering and treatment of statistical data, and in interviewing.

3. Ability to interpret, summarize, communicate findings in the development of hunches, observations, or "hypotheses." And, perhaps more, to apply common sense and cut through jargon.

Traditionally, especially in our country, there has been a separation between those who are expert in theory or research and those who apply the findings toward policy—i.e., the distinctions between sociologist/social worker, or psychologist/counselor. There is no need here to invoke the perennial arguments as to whether the former can, as they claim, represent an "objective" approach, leaving "values" to others. My own predilections are on the side of a Gunnar Myrdal and a Robert Friedrichs, rather than of Lundberg or other positivists. However, the introduction to this section has already noted my position on the importance of "bridging" and, perhaps, the need to reexamine what Professor Dror of Israel and others have called the "policy sciences."[4] Gerontology has the professional advantage of being a young field, and hence, open to innovations. Its interdisciplinary nature invites theory and application to come more closely together on a day-to-day basis.

Below are listed several types of research directions or studies that will continue to need close attention:

1. Studies on the carry-over to retirement from work skills, values, and attitudes.

2. Economic studies, as in the California Senate Bill (1977) on the place

---

[4]Yehezkel Dror, *Design for Policy Sciences.* New York, Elsevier, 1971; *Ventures in Policy Sciences.* New York, Elsevier, 1971.

of retirees in "leisure sharing" attempts to enlarge employment opportunities, and the impact of removing mandatory retirement for government employees and raising the retirement age in private industry upon older workers. Will the elderly want to continue working, or will they, rather, want the alternative of work or leisure? And, in either case, what does this mean to the gerontology profession, program planning, and the nature of evolving "lifestyles?"

3. Improved methods and conceptualization of preretirement counseling.

4. Longitudinal and laboratory studies in the perception of time—more familiar in the areas of physics and philosophy, less so in the fields of psychology, sociology, and gerontology.

5. Relations between national cultural patterns or values on "ageism," and methods for changing ingrown attitudes through the use of mass media or other agents of change.

6. Studies are needed on the dynamics of all types of activities—aesthetic, civic, intellectual, etc.—as they apply to the elderly: functions, meanings, requisite skills, prospects of personal growth, and so on.

7. Impact studies on the mass media image of the elderly, together with the application of new electronic devices that will soon be on the market to permit a scheduling of the experience within the time frame of the viewer.

This list could be infinitely expanded. There will always be a necessity for the "needs" of the elderly within a given community or geographical area as a basis for programming and the allocation of personnel and funds. Two such state surveys are described briefly below, North Carolina and Florida.

Vira R. Kivett, School of Home Economics, University of North Carolina, is the author of *The Aged in North Carolina: Physical, Social and Environmental Characteristics and Sources of Assistance.*[5] This study of Guilford covered 469 persons over the age of 65 in urban (52.6%) and rural (47.4%) areas. The median age of those studied was 72. Almost 79% had worked in skilled manual operations, or were farmers and housewives. Over 53% were married. Of every five, four were fully retired. Most were in lower economic and educational categories, based on Hollingshead's "two-factor index of social position." Data were obtained on housing, work, income, health, life satisfaction, service use and needs, and activities.

Eighty per cent reported some "leisure time" each day, ranging from 43.8% among those having most of the day free to 12% for those who said they had little time. There were high correlations of much free time with older age, never having married, and being a male. Favorite activities, in rank order, were church, time with friends, radio, reading, and "sit and think." Commercial theater, cards, and table games were least popular. Only 1% were members of political groups; 18% were in church-related groups. In all choices race was comparatively unimportant. Two thirds spent time with friends and neighbors every week.

---

[5]Chapel Hill: North Carolina Agricultural Station, 1976.

The Florida report of May, 1973 is titled *Assessment of Needs of Low-Income Urban Elderly Persons,*[6] and covers Dade, Pinellas, and Palm Beach counties. It was part of Florida's In-Step Project, funded by the Office of Aging and the OEO. The questionnaire was issued to 1657 persons over the age of 60; 118 questions were put directly to persons by the interviewers. As in North Carolina the data covered a broad range of issues but, in respect to leisure, only the area of social relations was studied, with the conclusion:

> Most elderly persons interviewed appeared to have relatively frequent and satisfying social interaction with their children and their friends and neighbors. They were satisfied with their level of activity and their general social relations. A substantial minority of respondents, however, were found to have a very real problem of social isolation. . . . One person in four either did not know any of his neighbors, or never visited with those they did know. . . . One-fifth of the respondents said they did not get out of their homes as often as they would like to, and almost as many said they often felt lonely. For many respondents, these low levels of social interaction have come about gradually and without choice—when their spouse died, when their friends moved away, or as they simply came to feel that people "just didn't care."[7]

Offices of aging of most or all states have collected data, primary or secondary, surveying leisure needs and preferences. A wide range of data is available among the federal agencies. Special attention is called to the *National Clearinghouse Thesaurus on Aging.*[8] This is the "retrieval vocabulary to the data base; it represents the standardized list of terms used in indexing the literature collected." Although information retrieval is available to individuals, on a "time available basis," priority of the service goes to national and state agencies and Title VII nutrition projects. In the first edition, data areas are: (1) low-income elderly; (2) impaired, noninstitutionalized elderly; (3) minority elderly; and (4) services for the elderly. The scope of leisure data (index #550) includes: "Leisure activities, use of free time, vacations, travel, participation in senior citizen centers; recreation programs, daily living routine."

The full list of activities for which data is available follows:

> activity participation, crafts, cultural activities, daily activities, entertainment, gardening, hobbies, housekeeping, leisure, leisure activities, mass media, movies, newspapers, parks, radio, reading, recreation, recreation centers, recreation programs, senior citizen centers, senior citizen clubs, shopping, sports, television, travel, vacation expenses, vacation trips.[9]

Canadian Research

As noted in Chapter 7, research on the international level is highly important, even for policy considerations within our own country. As an illustration of effective national studies we turn to Canada, specifically the

---

[6]Bureau of Research and Evaluation, Division of Planning and Evaluation. Department of Health and Rehabilitative Services, State of Florida, Tallahassee, 1973.

[7]Ibid. p. 160.

[8]1st ed., Washington, D.C.: Office of Human Development, Administration on Aging, p. 4. Under Section III, "Display." HEW Publication No. (OHD) 76–20083.

[9]Ibid.

second volume of a background study concerning the housing needs of older persons, prepared under a Part V grant. Its full title is *State of the Art: Research on the Elderly, 1964–1972.*[10] Its two sections deal with "quantity" and "quality" of Canadian research. Under the second, the following comments will suggest, especially to Canadian students, fertile areas for needed research.

From the inventory of available lifestyle surveys, it can be concluded that such general research has been conducted in five provinces—Alberta, British Columbia, Manitoba, Quebec, and especially Ontario. However, only two surveys are province-wide, the rest being narrower in scope, and even these two are not probability samples drawn from the province's entire populace of elderly. There is, therefore, justification for conducting lifestyle surveys in every province in order to gain a complete and representative picture of the living patterns and perceptions of senior citizens in each of the provinces. For an even more comprehensive understanding of the lifestyle and general attitudes of Canada's collective community of elders, a national probability survey would be in order. And, of course, the ultimate, most desirable, and conceivably most instructive research approach to total comprehension would be a longitudinal national survey examining the changing lifestyles and opinions of a probability sample of senior citizens drawn from across the country.

Less grandiose suggestions for additional lifestyle surveys underscore the need for future community studies of ethnic minorities, rural elderly and widowed aged women, since relatively little survey information exists on these samples. Also missing from much of the survey literature on life patterns is a deliberate stress on and exploration of religious and political opinions among the elderly. And lastly, the consumer patterns and preferences of senior citizens are subjects almost entirely excluded from academic survey research, and even market research tends to neglect these topics since opinions of various strata of senior citizens are generally lumped together without any conceptual gradation in the single age category "55 and over."

Having discussed the themes of firstly clinical-experimental, and secondly survey research, the next topic for consideration is the quality of *gerontological research undertaken since 1964 by graduate students in Canadian universities.* It will be recalled that a total of 58 masters theses and 3 doctoral dissertations related to aging are reported. When these theses are classified according to theme, the results indicate that: 39% focus on lifestyle (particularly, family, social psychological and financial aspects); 34% concern institutionalization (particularly Homes for the Aged); 15% deal with services (particularly health and home care services); and only 11% treat the subject of senior citizen housing (particularly urban housing need).

Some general conclusions are that academic interest in the subject of aging is considerably less than overwhelming, averaging about eight Canadian gerontological theses per year, and that interest in researching problems of senior citizen housing is exceptionally weak with only seven such theses appearing since 1964. It is also interesting to note parenthetically that no single Canadian textbook dealing with gerontology or geriatrics is known to exist. Indeed, in all the 1200 recorded Canadian references on aging since 1964, only one is a published book, and this merely a handbook for senior citizens. In sum, the lack of Canadian texts on aging addressed to either students or general readers interested in the subject is astounding.

---

[10]Environs Research Group Limited. Ottawa: Central Mortgage and Housing Corporation of Canada, October 1972.

Epilogue

What has this section, and the volume as a whole, had to say about "leisure: lifestyle and lifespan?"

That the increased longevity in years has been more than a postponement of death; with a longer life have come changes in our lifestyles, accompanied by better health, increased education, urban living, transformations in work, and a host of other social changes. The two phenomena are entwined. For example, when England raised its requirements for compulsory education to 17 years, it had to rethink all the years of schooling up to 17. The woman at 50, knowing that she will probably live into her mid-70s, plans differently—perhaps lives differently—in respect to the future, and her 50s take on different meaning. Put it another way—the social forces that keep us alive longer do not function in a vacuum. Biological and social facts mingle; medical research that eliminates some diseases of aging has been aided by electronic advances that also contribute to television. Leisure roles of the elderly, so goes the argument of the volume, are more than the content of the new years of life; the quality, variety, range and depth of that leisure becomes a major focus or framework of those years.

The simplicity of these connections hides their importance. Perhaps this is one reason that the case has not been examined more extensively by gerontologists, busy as they have been with issues of health, housing, income, protective legislation, transportation, and other immediate problems. Indeed, given the increasing interest in leisure among both the general public and social scientists, one can express some surprise that not a single volume along these lines has appeared in gerontological circles since the pioneering anthology, *Aging and Leisure: the Meaningful Use of Time.*[1]

What any one book can do is limited. This work has attempted to provide broad perspectives, especially in Sections 1 and 2, some settings within which leisure takes place for the elderly (Sections 3 and 4), and conclusions for professional behavior (Section 5). A balance has been sought between general

---

[1]Robert Kleemeier, ed., New York: Oxford University Press, 1961.

243

ideas and concrete examples, as well as between traditional and emerging issues. Since its intended audience has been the professional student and practitioner, future editions will no doubt reflect the accuracy of their discontents, and gain therefrom.

As I began, so may I close on a personal note. Upon retirement, coinciding almost exactly with the completion of this book, I look forward with my peers to new social changes, to new adventures of the mind, perhaps to growth and to contributions by my generation that have been barely suggested in these pages, leading perhaps to a revolution in the lifestyles of older persons that is beyond our present imagination.

Appendix A

PORTIONS OF SCRIPT: FREE STREET TOO[1]

DB: I wish I could emigrate too. What is the future here? I ask you what will the future bring? But I must think of my family . . . and I can't do housework.

HM: Bless you, Herr Bremmer. Look, automatic focus.

DB: Bless you, Hilda—and bless the little Leica.

(Music: "Over There")

AB: Armistice!

EH: I was only 8; I don't remember much.

DB: It was a truly joyous celebration.

AB: The streets were filled with people.

DR: My girlfriend and I were at a concert at Orchestra Hall. . . When we came out, the world had gone crazy.

AB: I didn't get home until 5 A.M. My parents didn't know where I was.

BS: We had saved the world for democracy.

HM: After the war it was terrible in Germany. Runaway inflation. . . You had to spend all your money as soon as you were paid on Friday because by Monday all the prices were double.

LK: I was stationed at Bar Harbor, Maine as a radio technician. While I was

---

[1]From *To Life,* Free Street Theater, Chicago. Copyright 1976 by the Free Street Theater. Used with permission.

245

there we conversed with President Wilson who had gone to Europe to discuss the League of Nations.

ER: It was the war to end all wars. The next one was to keep the world safe for peace. But there's been no peace. It's a farce.

(Tape: James sings)

> Colors of gray
> That's what I see
> I was once power
> Now weakness is me
> Now I must stand
> People listen to me
> Time causes changes
> That we must learn to see.
> Don't kill the eagle
> Please let it be
> It's just a bird
> That longs to be free

EH: "Over There"....We sang that song for two wars. The first one I barely remember. The second time around—I remember that time.

ER: Mama, what difference does it make if it's over over there if it's not over over here?

EH: What do you tell a seven-year-old boy?

AB: You tell him the truth.

EH: And whose truth is that?
I have always seen the world through my own eyes and I don't think I've been blind. . . . When I came back from a visit to Europe in 1955 I stopped at a counter to buy something or other and I saw that the clerk waited on everyone else before me. I thought to myself, "Well, I'm home." I have not been blind.
I have seen the drinking fountains at Lookout Mountain, Tennessee with their labels: white, colored, dogs.
I have also seen my father—born five years out of slavery—I have seen him defend his integrity as an independent landowner.

EH: When the city council of my hometown—Monmouth, Illinois—held a meeting to determine whether they should establish segregation laws, my father led the opposition. He told the city fathers 'You cannot and will not do this!'—and they didn't. That man is one of my truths, one that I grew up with.
I didn't even know that there was a "race problem" until I went to Detroit. . . . I saw that truth then.

To me America is a land of opportunities. Just look at all the opportunities I have made. I have been a beautician, a librarian, a teacher. I have worked for families that showed me real consideration and affection and for families that told their children that they should not display their affection for me.
Whose truth?

DB: Life is a paradox.

WH: Life is life. You just live it.

EH: I have never been disillusioned. I've been disappointed, yes . . . and at times I have been angry—I've been plain mad. But I don't think I've been disillusioned; I see too well for that.

ER: Etoria, what did you tell your son?

EH: I don't remember. Richard's question has a longer life than my answer.

DB: That's the mark of a good question.

BS: I think your life has been the answer.

DR: I've always been an accompanist—first on the piano and then in my life. I have no regrets about this; in fact I prefer it this way. Amelia Earhart I'm not: no solo flights, please.
Now don't get the idea that I'm the shy retiring type—do I look like a shrinking violet? I've always been a rebel.

(Ed stands to testify to this fact. Dorothy stops him with a look or chord)

DR: When I think of the headaches and heartaches I gave my parents. . . .

(Leo stands and pounds on the piano)

LK: Dorothy, I am not spending good money paying for your music lessons just so you can play Tin Pan Alley for your friends. Learn the classics!

DR: My father—he burned all my popular sheet music . . . I just turned around and bought it all over again.

LK: Foul ball!

DR: My mother was a saint (if there are Jewish saints). She never raised her voice. In fact the only thing she ever said to me was—

HM: I have only one wish for you, Dorothy. I hope that some day you have a daughter just like you.

DR: And I did—three of them. Those girls were impertinent enough to be born during the Depression!

Mainly it's people. I like working with and being with people: I'm an accompanist and I've had my share of fabulous experiences . . . I've accompanied many famous opera stars for rehearsals—Geraldine Farrar, and Chaliapin. I even accompanied Harold F. McCormick, the industrialist, privately.

(Ed stands again to protest)

There was nothing to it! He was a whistler; he loved to whistle the classics. He used to send his chauffeur-driven limousine to my house to pick me up. It was a sensation in my neighborhood. I was driven away to a palace with crystal chandeliers and butlers behind every chair.
People. . . . That's always been my great love. People and the piano.

BS: You could have been a great concert artist.

DR: Maybe . . . but I didn't want that . . . it was too much work. I was cursed—and blessed—with a talent for sight reading. I could read anything. I didn't have to perspire—and I didn't want to. I'm lazy. I hate housework too. I keep the place clean but I'm not compulsive about it. I'm a lazy, liberated, loving woman—excuse me for living.

(She dashes off a few bars of Bach's "Italian Concerto")

AB: Dorothy . . . Dorothy! *(Dorothy stops playing)* I know you were just kidding, just using an expression—weren't you?

DR: What are you talking about?

AB: What you just said, "Excuse me for living."

DR: I've said that all my life—or most of it.

AB: Shame on you!

DR: ? . . . . . Excuse me for living.

AB: You said it again.

DR: It's a habit.

AB: Get out of that habit! *(Everyone laughs)* I'm really serious. Oh, I know I sound like a fishwife—but why should anyone have to make excuses?

AB: I don't want to be one of those people who say, "Oh, I wish I had done this or that. I don't have any regrets. I want to do it now. Let's go! Come on, Dorothy, bless yourself.

(Music: "Life Is Just a Bowl of Cherries")

AB: Good! That's it. Yes it is! Life is a bowl of cherries. So come on, Bertha—you regret not being able to sing, well, here's your chance. Creative energy knows no age. Get it on, girl!!

BS: Life is just a bowl of cherries
Don't take it serious
Life's too mysterious
You work, you slave,
You worry so
But you can't take your dough
When you go, go,

AB: Gentlemen!

BS: So keep repeating
It's the berries
The strongest oak must fall
The sweet things in life
To you were just loaned
So how can you lose
What you've never owned
Life is just a bowl of cherries
So live and laugh at it all.

LK: I am Leo Kallis.

AB: Anne Binyon.

EH: Etoria Hunt.

DB: David Bush.

HM: Hilda McLean.

ER: Ed Rawson.

DR: Dorothy Rawson.

BS: Bertha Schlan.

LK: I am a human being.

AB: An American.

EH: A teacher.

DB: A successful father.

HM: A fighter.

ER: A kid who loves trains.

DR: An accompanist.

BS: On my way.

LK: I am 80 years young.

AB: 77.

EH: 66.

DB: 74.

HM: 63.

ER: 77.

DR: 70.

BS: 74.

LK: I am.

AB: I am.

EH: I am.

DB: I am.

HM: I am.

ER: I am.

DR: I am.

BS: And I am.

Appendix B

COURSES: INSTITUTE FOR CONTINUED LEARNING, SAN DIEGO[1]

G—2   AUTOBIOGRAPHICAL EPISODES

Mondays—10:00 A.M.

This is a continuing group of writers, would-be writers and recorders interested in bridging generation gaps with true tales or experiences that (put together chronologically some day) may be worthy of publication. While some writers are already launched, emphasis (and illustration) will be on beginning (maybe as Ben Franklin did). A sheet on how to listen and criticize constructively will be provided, together with bibliography. We're all programmed by history but then we can also make a bit of it.

G—4   BIO-MED, MUSEUM, AND SCIENCE

Tuesdays—10:00 A.M.

The purpose of this group is principally to disseminate scientific information in non-technical form, as well as to correct prevalent misconception, misinformation, and superstitions. The appeal is to the lay person who has not had the opportunity to delve into these subjects before, as well as to the scientifically trained. The subject matter ranges widely from human physiology to oceanography, geology, physics, psychology, etc. The program will include trips to

---

[1]From the catalogue of the Institute for Continued Learning, San Diego, 1976. Reproduced by permission of Doris R. Brosnan, Coordinator.

museums, institutions, etc., conducted by specialists on staff, and will include discussion of exhibits and behind-the-scenes visits to workshops. This is the start of our fourth year, the first two having been held in New York City.

G—8 ENERGY SOURCES, PROSPECTS, CURRENT PROBLEMS

Thursdays—10:00 A.M.

A subject of vital interest to everyone. Nothing in this country is of more crucial importance at the present time, and it behooves all of us to become thoroughly familiar and informed in the subject when world policy decisions of crisis proportions affecting our future for generations to come, are about to be made. The group will delve into sources, the impact of the crisis, the national energy program, the economics of oil, and world money, current problems, the technology involved with oil, coal, gas, and uranium, a time-table for expanded energy availability, geothermal electricity production, and utilization of solar energy. Non-technical and geared to the layman.

G—10 POSSIBLE FUTURE PATHS OF MAN

Tuesdays—1:30 P.M.

We will become a discussion group and workshop. A new provocative topic will be introduced at each session, the participants will be asked to examine and share their responses. This program is not for the spectator but for those who are seeking to involve themselves. IT IS FOR THOSE TRYING TO UNDERSTAND SOME OF THE DIRECTIONS AND CHANGES THE FUTURE MAY BRING, with the realization that the keys to opening doors rest inside each one of us. This is an experimental-type program designed to fit the avant-garde attitude of ICL. Warning: this is not for those who desire to maintain or justify the status quo. Hopefully, those in the program may find themselves questioning that which previously they had accepted.

G—12 SHARING FOREIGN TRAVEL ADVENTURES

Fridays—10:00 A.M.

A continuation of last year's popular study group in which we travel the world via slides and lectures by ICL's many travellers. Accent is on geography and culture, not just scenery. Scheduled are: Hawaii, Alaska, Scandinavia, and a dual session by many participants giving a Grand Tour of Europe. New members are urged to contact the coordinator if they have travel adventures to share.

G—21 LIFE PROBLEMS

Tuesdays—1:30 P.M.

A workshop to assist in resolving some of the minor problems in everyday living. Meetings will be held weekly. Limited enrollment.

G—22 SCIENCE AND RELIGION

Mondays—10:00 A.M.

This will be a discussion group having the objective of learning as much as we can about the physical universe from the point of view of both science and religion, and resolving the conflicts between the two points of view, if any.

G—23 WORLD TROUBLESPOTS—BEHIND THE HEADLINES

Tuesdays—10:00 A.M.

The group will discuss in depth the current world trouble spots, such as the Middle East, South Africa, China, Ireland, Southeast Asia, Panama, Yugoslavia after Tito, etc. Everyone will be asked to participate.

G—24 CREATIVE WRITING

Mondays—1:30 P.M.

Participants will be encouraged to write poetry, short story, plays, etc., as creative expression of their experiences and philosophies. The group will be a supportive workshop offering suggestions on ways to enhance and perfect individual writings. Please bring some work to first meeting to read aloud.

G—25   PLAY READING

Mondays—1:30 P.M.

Participants will read aloud and analyze conflict, character development, dramatic impact, etc., of a number of plays, including
Shakespeare, if desired. We will consider the philosophy of the
dramatist within the context of the historical milieu of his time, as
well as the impact on the contemporary playgoer. Current productions at the Old Globe Theatre will also be considered. Please
come prepared to take part in Jean Anouilh's RING AROUND THE
MOON for the first meeting.

G—26   BOOK DISCUSSION

Wednesdays—10:00 A.M.

Classics which have contemporary values will be covered. At opening
session members will choose for each quarter a category such as
SOCIAL COMMENTARY, THE CLASSICS, or whatever. Participants will select books to be read and each will serve as reviewer and
discussion leader of one work. Please read and come prepared to
discuss Machiavelli's THE PRINCE, for the first meeting. Second
meeting will consider Jung's THE UNDISCOVERED SELF.

G—27   HISTORY OF SAN DIEGO

Wednesdays—10:00 A.M.

The group will cover the period from the European discoveries up to
the Gold Rush. The Fall Quarter will include a field trip. The group is
expected to continue in the Winter and Spring Quarters. Members
will participate in discussions, giving 20-minute reports. Slides are
available and will be shown.

G—28   DESTINY OF THE HUMAN RACE

Tuesdays—1:30 P.M.

This group, as a continuing endeavor, will seek to identify and
elucidate major factors—amenable to human control—tending to
predetermine in some manner and degree the future of man of the
planet earth. During the Fall Quarter attention will be focused upon
one such factor, namely the theory of evolution (not evolution itself).

Aspects of theory dealing with both the origin of living species and the origin of the universe will be considered.

G—29 ART: WHAT'S HAPPENING TODAY?

Thursdays—1:30 P.M.

In layman's language, a series of four illustrated talks by leader will explain major art trends since 1950. You are not expected to remember dates, nor to "love" today's art, but you will see the vast changes in the art concept during the past 25 years and the influence of modern technology. With congenial friends we will discuss and explore the California art scene, visit museums and galleries in the greater San Diego area.

The wide-ranging ICL program summarized above was formally incorporated in 1974–1975, although parts of it had begun several years ago.

Appendix C
PRE-RETIREMENT EDUCATION

The selection to be reproduced in this section, by Professor Howard Rosencranz of the University of Connecticut's Program in Gerontology, serves as the first essay in Pre-Retirement Education: A Manual for Conference Leaders, *designed for administrators and conference leaders.* [1]

Recognition of the need to prepare for retirement from the labor force can be attributed to at least two categories of current understandings. The first of these can be found among social science contributions of the last two decades, particularly in sociological literature. Students of work and social role emphasize the significance of occupation in establishing status and maintaining life styles of incumbents. Loss of work, through unemployment or retirement, is considered to be equally critical. This loss frequently requires alteration of self-concept and a restructuring of social relationships as well as economic adjustments.

The second category of understandings which stresses the need for and importance of pre-retirement education is more directly associated with those persons who have already retired. Many of the most enthusiastic advocates of PRE are retirees who say that this stage of life must be planned for and anticipated. "Retirement should not just 'happen' to people" becomes the major theme.

And at still another level there is agreement that the accelerating rate of social change in the American social system has placed new competency demands on older people.

The brief comments above, in a sense, are addressed to the "why" of pre-retirement education. As an introduction to the material in this volume, the journalistic mode might be pursued to round out the picture—What is it?, Who?, When?, How?, and Where?

---

[1]Storrs, Conn.: University of Connecticut, Program in Gerontology, 1975, pp. 11–14. Reproduced by permission of the author.

What? Very simply, Pre-Retirement Education may be defined as *the acquisition of information, understandings, and appreciations which serve to facilitate personal adjustment after retirement from the labor force.* This definition is sufficiently broad to include all the forms that PRE can take. Nor does it restrict its delivery because of sex, age, or content factors. In the above definition, inclusion of the word "appreciations" recognizes that attitudes of the pre-retiree are important in the retirement process. The connotation is also present which suggests that realistic anticipation of changed conditions, statuses, and relationships is required by the pre-retiree.

Certain experts in the area of pre-retirement education still quarrel over the differences between 'counseling' programs and 'planning' programs for retirement. The former emphasize the processes of attitude change, while 'planning' gives emphasis to information acquisition (Kasschau, 1974). Actually, while these distinctions may have historical value, this author holds the view that these differences are largely methodological or differences in format. It would seem that opportunities for both processes are requisite to any adequate PRE program.

Who? If one asks the question, "Who should be the recipient of PRE?", it would be difficult to list exclusions either by income category, general social category, or occupational groupings. Most persons about to retire would benefit from PRE. However, it must also be recognized that there are persons whose needs are greater.

Research on retirement process and adjustment consistently reveals the paradox that those persons who enjoy working most and who frequently have options for working beyond age sixty-five, also represent the persons who are more equipped to enjoy retirement. The converse appears to be also true. It does seem that previous life style, coping patterns, educational level, and financial status constitute the variables for retirement satisfaction differences. Taken all together, there is a differential "consciousness" among pre-retirees for the need for PRE.

In 1970, in the State of Connecticut, there were approximately 70,000 males and about 45,000 females between the ages of fifty-five and fifty-nine in the labor force. For the next older pre-retirement age bracket, ages sixty to sixty-four, the comparable figures were 48,000 males and 30,000 females. This is the pre-retirement population in Connecticut.

Using demographic data and retirement research literature, the *typical* pre-retiree can be described. Though there is no "average" person except through the process of delineating modalities, when this is done a profile emerges. The Retiree—

1. is more apt to be a male than a female.
2. is more likely to be employed as a craftsman, kindred worker, or operative than self employed or professional.
3. has an educational level of 10–11 years of formal schooling.
4. is married with children who have left the "nest."
5. is a home owner.
6. has assets of $17,000–$19,000 mostly tied up in home.

7. may repress worries about retirement particularly relating to income and health, but at the verbal level he is looking forward to more "free" time to fish, play golf, garden, and do "nothing."
8. says he will be happy to stop working and in so doing stop fighting traffic to get back and forth, be able to stop worrying about company policies, unemployment, and the "rat-race"—by which he means many of the dissatisfactions with life that he attributes to work.
9. is conscious of and concerned about cost-of-living and inflation patterns yet he probably has not computed a) what his retirement income will be, and b) what adjustments he and his wife will have to make because of reduced retirement income.
10. does not fully appreciate the effects of his retirement on wife and family.

And typically, this retiree *has not* had access to a structured pre-retirement program.

"How many pre-retirees receive formal exposure to PRE?" Estimates, probably overestimates, indicate that fewer than one-third receive any meaningful form of PRE. Vermel and Biedeman (1961) found that thirty-two per cent of American companies offered some sort of pre-retirement education. However, in many instances offerings were limited to simple explanations of pension benefits. Though based on small returns, a recent survey by the Connecticut Department on Aging among over 300 Connecticut manufacturing corporations produced findings similar to the national picture (DOA, 1974).

When? "When should Pre-Retirement Education be offered?" Ideally, as in Europe where the phrase "Preparation for the Third Age" is incorporated in prevailing educational philosophies, it should begin early in life. This broad perspective gives attention to life-long preparation for the post-retirement period.

More realistically, perhaps, in terms of the present developments in the United States, PRE should be available prior to the actual occurrence of retirement. In this volume we have singled out the age period of fifty-five to sixty-four years because:

1. This is when a 'psychological readiness' becomes apparent. While all workers do not overtly verbalize retirement apprehensions, in the career patterns of most persons, this is the age period when thinking about retirement starts to take place.
2. Early retirement patterns indicate that more people are retiring before age sixty-five.
3. Long term, as opposed to short term, planning has greater pay-off.

It may well be expected that in the years ahead formal schooling programs at very early ages will incorporate materials in their curricula dealing with older, post-retirement-age living. There are several examples of this at the present time. It is also a possibility that future work and career patterns will be drastically altered so that "sabbaticals" will allow leisure or non-work periods during late and middle-age. Such programming might provide a kind of transition into retirement that now is not available. In the meantime, pre-retirement education seems most plausibly directed toward persons in those years after age fifty-five and before the final year(s) of work.

How? "How is pre-retirement education provided?" This is a question of delivery and method. It is also related to the final consideration "Where?"

The figure that follows presents pre-retirement education in its broadest spectrum indicating: 1) the forms in which it can appear, and 2) the dissemination points at which it may occur. While a certain relativity is present in this conceptual classification, as well as overlap, these are the available forms of pre-retirement education today.

The PRE format which has increasingly become the standard format is emphasized in Figure 1 as the Lecture-Discussion model. This format is associated with Woodrow Hunter (1968), Drake University (1969), and other advocates of PRE. While a complete description of the Lecture-Discussion model appears in other sections of Part One, certain features which contribute to its successful application should be mentioned.

1. It provides a small group experience with personal contact for participants with both expert information sources and with fellow pre-retirees facing the same future stage of the life-cycle.
2. It is less costly than in depth person to person counseling yet possesses similar inter-personal ingredients for problem solving.

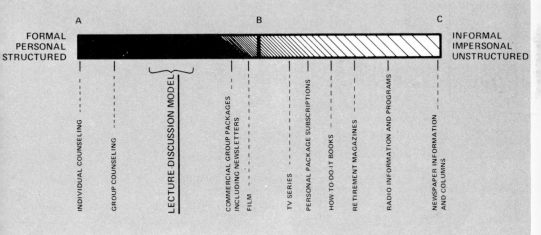

Howard Rosencranz, in *Pre-Retirement Education: A Manual for Conference Leaders.* Storrs, Connecticut: University of Connecticut, Program in Gerontology, 1975.

3. It is an adaptable format sufficiently flexible to meet identified needs of participants.

4. It allows sponsorship within a variety of organizational contexts.

Where? To ask "Where should PRE take place?" is a question similar to the question "Whose responsibility is it to provide PRE?"

Until recently the responsibility for providing pre-retirement education was considered to be that of the employer. Many successful programs, indeed, have been conducted by large companies for their own employees. There are other examples of successful programs jointly sponsored by management and unions. But such sponsorship has not been universal for several reasons:

1. Some companies are too small to generate retirees in sufficient numbers to warrant company programs.
2. Some corporate and personnel managers do not think PRE is important.
3. Some companies lack economic and education resources to launch programs.
4. Some companies have tried forms of PRE with unsuccessful effects.

Newer sponsorship patterns include the utilization of public educational structures for augmenting the delivery of PRE. Legislative allocations in the State of Connecticut for pre-retirement education have been used to develop programs and for training conference leaders. This places Connecticut among one of the first states in the country to partly assume PRE as a public responsibility. Similarly, as one outgrowth of the 1971 White House Conference on Aging, the Federal government has stimulated alternate delivery forms of PRE by the funding of demonstration projects.

Following selections in Part I describe three contexts within which PRE is now being delivered in Connecticut: 1) the *Corporate Context,* 2) the *Community College Context,* and 3) the *Adult Education Context.* These are likely to be the main PRE access "settings" as increased programming occurs in the future. Additionally, it can be expected that in different communities existing voluntary organizations, church groups, and other community agencies will continue to recognize local community needs by providing this special kind of mid-life education.

REFERENCES

Connecticut State Department on Aging, Memorandum No. 54, (Mimeo.), May 22, 1974.

Drake University Pre-Retirement Planning Center, (Manpower Project, U.S. Department of Labor), Annual Report, Des Moines, Iowa, August, 1969.

Kasschau, Patricia L., "Reevaluating the Need for Retirement Preparation Programs", Industrial Gerontology, Winter, 1974, pp. 42–59.

Wermel, M. and G. Biedeman, "Retirement Preparations Programs, A Study of Company Responsibilities", California Institute of Technology, Los Angeles, April, 1961.

Hunter, Woodrow W., Preparation for Retirement, University of Michigan, Ann Arbor, 1968.

Bibliography

LEISURE—GENERAL

Abrams, John. "Cybernetics and Automation." *Leisure in Canada,* Montmorency Conference on Leisure, September 1969, pp. 59–79. Fitness and Amateur Sport Directorate, Department of National Health and Welfare, Ottawa.

Allardt, E., et al. "On the Cumulative Nature of Leisure Activities." *Acta Sociologica,* 3, Fasc. 4 (1959).

Anderson, Nels. "Time on Their Hands." *Man's Work and Leisure.* Glencoe, Ill.: Free Press, 1961, pp. 182–204.

Berger, Bennett M. "The Sociology of Leisure: Some Suggestions." *Work and Leisure,* ed. Erwin O. Smigel. New Haven: College and University Press, 1963.

Brightbill, Charles K. *Man and Leisure: A Philosophy of Recreation.* Englewood Cliffs, N.J.: Prentice-Hall, 1961.

———. "Leisure—Its Meaning and Implications." *Leisure—The Heart of Living.* New York: National Recreation Association, 1963*a*.

———. *The Challenge of Leisure.* Englewood Cliffs, N.J.: Prentice-Hall, 1963*b*.

———. *Educating for Leisure–Centered Living.* Philadelphia: Shackpole Company, 1966.

Charlesworth, James C., ed. *Leisure in America: Blessing or Curse?* Philadelphia: American Academy of Political and Social Science.

Corbin, H. D., and W. J. Tait. *Education for Leisure.* Englewood Cliffs, N.J.: Prentice-Hall, 1973.

Cox, Harvey. *The Secular City.* New York: Macmillan, 1965.

———. *The Feast of Fools.* Cambridge: Harvard University Press, 1969.

de Grazia, Sebastian. *Of Time, Work, and Leisure.* New York: Twentieth Century Fund, 1962.

Dever, John Preston. "Toward an Ethical Understanding of Leisure in a Technological Society." Unpublished Ph.D. Thesis, Louisville, Southern Baptist Theological Seminary, 1968.

Dumazedier, Juffre. *Sociology of Leisure.* New York: Elsevier, 1974.

———. *Toward a Society of Leisure.* New York: Free Press, 1967.

Edwards, Patsy. *Leisure Counseling Techniques.* Los Angeles: University Publishers, 1975.

Farina, John. "Towards a Philosophy of Leisure." *Leisure in Canada,* Montmorency Conference on Leisure, September 1969, pp. 3–15. Fitness and Amateur Sport Directorate, Department of National Health and Welfare, Ottawa.

Glasser, Ralph. *Leisure: Penalty or Prize?* London: Macmillan, 1970.

Goode, William J. "Outdoor Recreation and the Family to the Year 2000." *Trends in American Living and Recreation,* Washington, D.C.: Outdoor Recreation Resources Commission, 1962, Study Report 22, pp. 101–112.

Grodzins, Morton. "The Many American Governments and Outdoor Recreation." *Trends in American Living and Recreation.* Washington, D.C.: Outdoor Recreation Review Commission, 1962. Study Report 22, pp. 61–80.

Heckscher, August. "The New Leisure." *Adult Leadership,* 14 (1966), pp. 258–260, 281–283.

261

Hoffer, Eric. "Leisure and the Masses." *Parks and Recreation,* IV, 3 (March, 1969), pp. 31–34, 60–65.

Huizinga, Johann. *Homo Ludens, A Study of the Play Element in Culture.* Boston: Beacon Press, 1950.

Jephcott, P. *Time of One's Own.* Glasgow: University of Glasgow Social and Economic Studies, 1967, Occasional Papers, No. 7.

Kaplan, Max. *Leisure in America: A Social Inquiry.* New York: John Wiley & Sons, 1960.

———. "The Uses of Leisure." *Handbook of Social Gerontology,* ed. Clark Tibbitts. Chicago: University of Chicago Press, 1960, pp. 407–443.

———. *Leisure: Theory and Policy.* New York: John Wiley & Sons, 1975.

———, and Phillip Bosserman, eds. *Technology, Human Values, and Leisure.* Nashville: Abingdon Press, 1972.

Kelly, John. "Work and Leisure: A Simplified Paradigm." *Journal of Leisure Research,* 4, No. 1 (1972), pp. 50–62.

Kraus, Richard. *Recreation and Leisure in Modern Society.* 2nd edition, Santa Monica: Goodyear, 1978.

Larrabee, Eric, and Rolf Meyersohn, eds. *Mass Leisure.* Glencoe, Ill.: Free Press, 1958.

Lee, Robert. *Religion and Leisure in America.* New York: Abingdon Press, 1969.

Linder, Staffan Burenstam. *The Harried Leisure Class.* New York: Columbia University Press, 1970.

Lundberg, George A., Mirra Komarovsky, and Mary A. McIllnery. *Leisure: A Suburban Study.* New York: Columbia University Press, 1934.

Mead, Margaret. *The Changing Cultural Patterns of Work and Leisure.* Washington, D.C.: U.S. Government Printing Office, U.S. Manpower Administration, 1967. (Seminar on manpower policy and program, January 1967.)

Merrill, Lynch, Pierce, Fenner and Smith, Inc. *Leisure: Investment Opportunities in a $150 Billion Market.* New York: Merrill, Lynch, Pierce, Fenner and Smith, 1968.

Miller, Norman P., and Duane M. Robinson. *The Leisure Age: Its Challenge to Recreation.* Belmont, Cal.: Wadsworth, 1963.

Murphy, James F. *Concepts of Leisure.* Englewood Cliffs: Prentice-Hall, 1974.

Narasimham, P. S. *Hours of Work.* Geneva: International Labor Organization (I.L.O.), Leisure and Welfare Section, 1976.

Nash, Jay B. *Philosophy of Recreation and Leisure.* Dubuque: William C. Brown, 1953.

———. *Recreation: Pertinent Readings.* Dubuque: William C. Brown, 1965.

Neulinger, John. *The Psychology of Leisure.* Springfield, Ill.: Charles C Thomas, 1974.

Norden, Rudolf F. *The Christian Encounters the New Leisure.* London: Concordia Publishing House, 1965.

Parker, Stanley. *The Future of Work and Leisure.* London: MacGibbon and Kie, 1971.

Pieper, Josef. *Leisure: The Basis of Culture.* New York: Pantheon Books, 1964.

Riesman, David. *The Lonely Crowd.* New Haven: Yale University Press, 1950.

Roberts, Kenneth. *Leisure.* London: Longmans, 1970.

Rosenberg, B., and D. M. White, eds. *Mass Culture.* Glencoe, Ill.: Free Press, 1957.

———. *Mass Culture Revisited.* New York: Van Nostrand Reinhold, 1971.

Shaffer, Helen B. *Leisure in the Great Society.* Washington, D.C.: Editorial Research Reports, 1964.

Smigel, Erwin O., ed. *Work and Leisure: A Contemporary Social Problem.* New Haven: College and University Press, 1963.

Soule, George. *Time for Living.* New York: Viking Press, 1955.

Southern California Research Council. *The Challenge of Leisure: A Southern California Case Study.* Claremont: Pomona College, 1967, Report 15.

Staley, Edwin J., and Norman P. Miller, eds. *Leisure and the Quality of Life.* Washington, D.C.: American Alliance for Health, Physical Education, and Recreation, 1972.

Stevens, William P. H., Jr. *Are We Ready for Leisure?* New York: Friendship Press, 1966.

Stone, Walter L. "A Sociologist Discusses the New Meaning of Recreative Use of Leisure." *Parks and Recreation,* II, 4 (April, 1967), pp. 22, 56–59.

Szalai, Alexander, ed. *The Use of Time: A Cross-National Comparative Study of Daily Activities of Urban and Suburban Populations in Twelve Countries.* The Hague: Mouton, 1971.

Toffler, Alvin. *The Culture Consumers.* Baltimore: Penguin Press, 1965.

———. *Future Shock.* New York: Random House, 1970.

Veblen, Thorstein. *The Theory of the Leisure Class.* New York: Mentor, 1953.

Wilensky, H. L. "The Uneven Distribution of Leisure." *Social Problems,* 9 (1960–62), pp. 32–56.

LEISURE AND AGING

Adler, Joan. *The Retirement Book.* New York: William Morrow, 1975.

Agutter, Margaret. *Leisure.* London: National Council of Social Service, 1963.

Alpaugh, Patricia K., V. Jayne Renner, and James E. Birren. "Age and Creativity: Implications for Education and Teachers." *Educational Gerontology,* 1 (1976), pp. 17–40.

American Association of Retired Persons. *Preparation for Retirement.* Washington, D.C.: American Association of Retired Persons, 1968.

———, and National Retired Teachers Association. *Your Retirement Hobby Guide.* Washington, D.C.: American Association of Retired Persons and National Retired Teachers Association, 1969.

Anderson, John E. "Psychological Aspects of the Use of Free Time." *Free Time: Challenge to Later Maturity,* ed. Wilma T. Donahue, Woodrow Hunter, Dorothy H. Coons, and Helen K. Maurice. Ann Arbor: University of Michigan Press, 1958, pp. 29–44.

———. "The Use of Time and Energy." *Handbook of Aging and the Individual: Psychological and Biological Aspects,* ed. James E. Birren, Vol. I. Chicago: University of Chicago Press, 1959, pp. 769–796.

———. "Comments on Chapter 10 by John E. Anderson." *Aging and Leisure: A Research Perspective into the Meaningful Use of Time,* ed. Robert W. Kleemeier. New York: Oxford Press, 1961, pp. 422–28.

———. "Aging and Educational Television: A Preliminary Survey." *Journal of Gerontology,* 8 (1962), pp. 447, 449.

Andrus, Ethel Percy. "Education as the Retired See It." *Adult Leadership,* 9 (1960), p. 23.

Arnstein, George E. "Of Leisure, Education, and the Older American." *The Home Study Review,* 4 (1963), pp. 15–23.

Arth, Malcolm J. *American Culture and the Phenomenon of Friendship in the Aged.* San Francisco: Fifth International Congress of Gerontology, August 7–12, 1960.

Arthur, Julietta K. *Retire to Action: A Guide to Voluntary Service.* Nashville: Abingdon Press, 1969.

"The Arts and the Aging: Forging a New Link." *Aging International,* III, No. 4 (1976), pp. 6–11.

Atchley, Robert C. "Retirement and Leisure Participation: Continuity or Crisis?" *Gerontologist,* 11 (1971), pp. 13–17.

———. *The Social Forces in Later Life: An Introduction to Social Gerontology.* Belmont, Cal.: Wadsworth, 1972.

———. *The Sociology of Retirement.* New York: Schenkman, 1975.

Avedon, E. M. "Outdoor Facilities for the Aged or Disabled." *Parks and Recreation,* I, 5 (1966), pp. 426–429.

Bates, Barbara, ed. *Leisure and Aging: New Perspectives.* Washington, D.C.: American Alliance of Health, Physical Education and Recreation, 1977.

Baxt, George. "What Are You Going to Do with the Rest of Your Life?" *Mainliner,* (1976).

Bell, Tony. "The Relationship Between Social Involvement and Feeling Among Residents in Homes for the Aged." *Journal of Gerontology.* 22 (1967), pp. 19–22.

Binstock, Robert. "Interest Group Liberalism and the Politics of Aging." *Gerontologist,* 12 (1972), pp. 265–281.

Birren, James E., ed. *Handbook of Aging and the Individual: Psychological and Biological Aspects.* Chicago: University of Chicago Press, 1959.

———, ed. *The Psychology of Aging.* Englewood Cliffs, N.J.: Prentice-Hall, 1964.

———, ed. *Contemporary Gerontology: Issues and Concepts.* Los Angeles: Gerontology Center, University of Southern California, 1970.

Bolles, Richard. *The Three Boxes of Life.* Berkeley: Ten Speed Press, 1976.

Born, Ted J. "Variables Associated with the Winter Camping Location of Elderly Recreational Vehicle Owners in Southwestern Arizona." *Journal of Gerontology,* 31 (1976), pp. 346–351.

Botwinick, J. *Cognitive Processes in Maturity and Old Age.* New York: Springer, 1967.

Boyack, Virginia, ed. *Time on Your Hands: Discussions for Those Concerned with Exploring the Significance of Opportunities and Resources Available for Senior Adults.* Los Angeles: University of California, Ethel Percy Andrus GerontologyCenter, 1973.

Boyd, R. R., and C. G. Oakes. *Foundations of Practical Gerontology.* Columbia, S.C.: University of South Carolina Press, 1969.

Bromley, D. B. *The Psychology of Human Aging.* Baltimore: Penguin Books, 1966.

Brotman, Herman. "The Changing World of Pre-retirement Planning—Present Pre-Retirement Population and Its Needs." Des Moines: Drake University, National Conference on Pre-Retirement Planning, October 1, 1974.

Brown, J. Paul. *Counseling with Senior Citizens.* Englewood Cliffs, N.J.: Prentice-Hall, 1964.

Buckley, Joseph C. *The Retirement Handbook: A Complete Planning Guide to Your Future.* New York: Harper and Row, 1967.

Bultena, G., and V. Wood. "The American Retirement Community: Bore or Blessing?" *Journal of Gerontology,* 24 (1969), pp. 209–218.

Burgess, Ernest W., ed. *Aging in Western Societies.* Chicago: University of Chicago Press, 1960.

———. *Retirement Villages.* Ann Arbor: University of Michigan, Institute of Gerontology, 1961.

Burrill, Roger H. "Recreational Therapy for the Aged Psychiatric Patient." *Mental Hygiene,* 50 (1966), pp. 297–303.

Butler, Robert. *Why Survive? Being Old in America.* New York: National Publications Center, 1975.

———. *Living History: Program for the Acquisition of Tape-Recorded Memoirs of History.* Commission on History of the American Psychiatric Association, October 1970.

Canadian Conference on Aging. *Background Papers.* Ottawa: Welfare Council, 1966.

Canadian Council on Social Development, Division on Aging. *Learning Opportunities for Older People.* Toronto: Canadian Council on Social Development, 1970.

Canadian Radio-Television Commission. *Reaching the Retired: A Survey of the Media Habits, Preferences and Needs of Senior Citizens in Metro Toronto.* Toronto: Prepared for the Communications Committee, Toronto Area Presbytery, United Church of Canada, by Environics Research Group Limited, 1973.

Canadian Welfare Council. *The Aging in Canada 1966.* Ottawa: Canadian Conference on Aging and Special Committee of the Canadian Senate on Aging, 1966.

Carlson, Avis. *In the Fullness of Time: The Pleasures and Inconveniences of Growing Old.* New York: Henry Regnery, 1977.

Carp, Frances M. *A Future for the Aged: Victoria Plaza and Its Residents.* Austin: University of Texas Press, 1966.

———. "Retirement Travel." *Gerontologist,* 12 (1972), pp. 73–78.

———. "A Senior Center in Public Housing for the Elderly." *Gerontologist,* 16 (1976), pp. 243–249.

Cavan, R. S. "Self and Role in Adjustment During Old Age," ed. A. M. Rose. *Human Behavior and Social Processes.* Boston: Houghton Mifflin, 1962.

Christensen, Alice, and David Rankin. *"Easy Does It" Yoga: For People Over 60.* Cleveland Heights, Ohio: Saraswati Studio, 1975.

Clark, Frederick L. *Work, Age, and Leisure.* London: Michel Joseph, 1966.

Clark, Margaret, and Barbara G. Anderson. *Culture and Aging: An Anthropological Study of Older Americans.* Springfield, Ill.: Charles C Thomas, 1967.

Cleveland Public Library. *National Survey of Library Services to the Aging.* Washington, D.C.: U.S. Department of Health, Education and Welfare, Bureau of Libraries and Educational Technology, 1971.

Collingwood, T. "Recreation Leader as a Therapeutic Agent." *Therapeutic Recreation Journal,* 6, No. 4 (1972), pp. 147–52.

Comfort, Alex. *A Good Age.* Fairfax, Va.: National Publication Center, 1976.

Continuing Choices: A Comprehensive Handbook of Programs for Work with Older Adults. New York: National Council of Jewish Women, 1975.

Coons, Dorothy, and Helen K. Maurice. "Activity Programming." *Retirement Villages,* ed. E. W. Burgess. Ann Arbor: University of Michigan, 1960.

Coplan, Kate, and Edwin Castagna. *The Library Reaches Out.* Dobbs Ferry, N.Y.: Oceana Publications, 1965.

Corrick, Frank. *Preparing for Your Retirement Years.* New York: Pilot Books, 1973.

Council of Social Agencies. *Elderly Library Centers Project: Final Report.* Newport, Vt., Orleans County: The Council, June 30, 1971.

Crabtree, Arthur P. "Education—The Key to Successful Aging," *Adult Education,* 17 (1967), pp. 157–165.

Crandall, Mae. *Recreation for Nursing Home Residents.* Raleigh, N.C.: Association of Nursing Homes, 1964.

Cranford, Charles B. *Demonstration Program: A Leisure and Recreation Program for Older Americans.* Washington, D.C.: U.S. Administration on Aging, 1968, Publication No. 11.

Crosson, Carrie. "Art Therapy with Geriatric Patients: Problems of Spontaneity." *American Journal of Art Therapy.* 15 (1976), pp. 51–56.

Culver, Elsie Thomas. *New Church Programs with the Aging.* New York: Association Press, 1961.

Cumming, E., and W. E. Henry. *Growing Old: The Process of Disengagement.* New York: Basic Books, 1961.

Cunningham, David A., et al. "Active Leisure Time Activities as Related to Age Among Males in a Total Population." *Journal of Gerontology,* 23 (1968), pp. 551–556.

Curtin, Sharon K. "Aging in the Land of the Young." *Atlantic,* 230, 1 (July, 1972), pp. 68–78.

———. *Nobody Ever Died of Old Age.* Boston: Little, Brown, 1973.

Dancy, Joseph, Jr. "Manuscript A: The Black Elderly." Prepared for Institute of Gerontology, Ann Arbor, University of Michigan-Wayne State University, 1974.

Davis, Richard. "TV and the Older Adult." *Journal of Broadcasting*, 15, No. 2 (1971).

———. "A Descriptive Study of Television in the Lives of an Elderly Population." Unpublished Ph.D. Thesis, Los Angeles, University of Southern California, 1972.

deBeauvoir, Simone. *The Coming of Age*. New York: G. P. Putnam's Sons, 1972.

De Crow, Roger. *New Learning for Older Americans: An Overview of National Effort*. Washington, D.C.: Adult Education Association of the United States, 1975.

Department of Health, Education, and Welfare. *Are You Planning on Living . . . the Rest of Your Life?* Washington, D.C.: U.S. Printing Office, Superintendent of Documents, 1972, OHD/AOA 73-20803.

Dickinson, Peter A. "Your Leisure Time." *Harvest Years*, 5 (1965), pp. 17–32.

———. *The Complete Retirement Planning Book*. New York: E. P. Dutton, 1976.

Dixon, J. C. *Continuing Education in the Later Years*. Gainesville: University of Florida Press, 1963.

Donahue, Wilma T., ed. *Education for Later Maturity*. New York: Whiteside, 1955.

———, Woodrow W. Hunter, Dorothy H. Evans, and Helen K. Maurice, eds. *Free Time, Challenge to Late Maturity*. Ann Arbor: University of Michigan Press, 1958.

———, and Clark Tibbitts, eds. *The New Frontiers of Aging*. Ann Arbor: University of Michigan Press, 1957.

Donfut, Claudine. *Vacances: Loisir Du 3ᵉ Age?* Paris: Documents d'Information et de Gestion, 1972.

Emerson, A. R. "The First Year of Retirement." *Occupational Psychology*, 33 (1959), pp. 197–208.

Evaluation of the Effectiveness of Congregate Housing for the Elderly: Final Report. Washington, D.C.: U.S. Department of Housing and Urban Development, Office of Policy Development and Research, 1976.

Farhurst, Janet Perry. "Developing A Sense of Community." *Nursing Homes*, (1972), p. 16.

Florida Citizens' Committee for the Humanities. *The Youth-Age Syndrome*. Pensacola: University of West Florida, 1973.

Florida Council on Aging. *Successful Retirement: Proceedings of Regional Conference— September 18–19, 1968*. Port Charlotte: Florida Council on Aging and Port Charlotte Cultural Center, 1969.

Folson, D. K., and C. M. Morgan. "The Social Adjustment of 381 Recipients of Old-Age Allowances," *American Sociological Review*, 2, 2 (April, 1972), pp. 223–229.

Ford, Phyllis M. *Leisure and the Senior Citizens*. Bloomington: Indiana University, Department of Recreation, School of Health, Physical Education and Recreation, 1962.

Fox, E. "Does It Have to Be Bingo?" *Nursing Homes*, 19 (1970), pp. 17–19.

Friedman, E. A. "The Work of Leisure." *Free Time: Challenge to Later Maturity*, ed. Wilma T. Donahue, Woodrow W. Hunter, Dorothy H. Coons, and Helen K. Maurice. Ann Arbor: University of Michigan Press, 1958.

Gaitz, Charles M. *Strengths and Weaknesses of the Elderly*. Washington, D.C.: National Council on Aging, Regional Training Institutes, 1969.

Germont, L. "What 814 Retired Professors Say About Retirement." *Gerontologist*, 12 (1972), pp. 349–353.

Gerontological Society Committee on Research and Development Goals in Social Gerontology. "Work, Leisure, and Education—Toward the Goal of Creativity. Flexible Life Styles." *Gerontologist*, 9, No. 4 (1969), pp. 17–36.

Gould, Elaine and Loren. *Crafts for the Elderly*. Springfield, Ill.: Charles C Thomas, 1971.

Grabowski, Stanley, ed. *Education for the Aging: Living with a Purpose as Older Adults Through Education. An Overview of Current Developments*. Syracuse: Erie Clearing House in Adult Education, 1974.

Grant, Roy. *Sing Along—Senior Citizens*. Washington, D.C.: National Publications Center, 1973.

Gray, Robert M., and David P. Moberg. *The Church and the Older Person*. Grand Rapids: Aerdmans Publishing Company, 1962.

Greene, Mark R. *Preretirement Counseling, Retirement Adjustment and the Older Employees*. Eugene: University of Oregon, Graduate School of Management and Business, 1969.

Gross, Selma Woodrow. *Opening the Door to Creative Experience for the Aging Through an Art Program*. Baltimore: City Commission on Problems of the Aging, 1963.

Guadagnolo, Frank. "1000 Handmade Ashtrays—Meaningful Leisure?" *Leisure and Aging: New Perspectives*, ed. Barbara Bates. Washington, D.C.: American Alliance for Health, Physical Education, and Recreation, 1977.

Guide for Senior Citizens to Groups, Clubs, and Centers in the Chicago Area. Chicago: Mayor's Office for Senior Citizens, 1972.

Guinan, St. Michael, Sr. "Aging and Leisure." *Canada and the World,* (1972).

Gunn, Scout Lee. "Labels That Limit Life." *Leisure and Aging: New Perspectives,* ed. Barbara Bates. Washington, D.C.: American Alliance for Health, Physical Education, and Recreation, 1977.

Hand, Samuel E. *A Review of Physiological and Psychological Changes in Aging and Their Implications for Teachers of Adults.* Tallahassee: Florida State Department of Education, 1968.

Hansen, Curtis C. "R.S.V.P.: Needing and Being Needed." *Leisure and Aging: New Perspectives,* ed. Barbara Bates. Washington, D.C.: American Alliance for Health, Physical Education, and Recreation, 1977.

Hardie, E. A. "Therapeutic Recreation for the Institutionalized Ill Aged: A Rationale." *Therapeutic Recreation Journal,* 4, No. 3 (1970).

Hardy, R. E., and J. G. Gull. *Organization and Administration of Service Programs for the Older American.* Springfield, Ill.: Charles C Thomas, 1975.

Harris, Lou, and Associates. *The Myth and Reality of Aging in America.* Washington, D.C.: Survey for National Council on Aging, 1975.

Havighurst, Robert J. "Social and Psychological Needs of the Aging." *Annals of the American Academy of Political and Social Science:* 279 (1952), pp. 11–17.

——. "Flexibility and the Social Roles of the Retired." *American Journal of Sociology,* 59, No. 4 (1954), pp. 309–311.

——. "The Leisure Activities of the Middle Aged." *American Sociological Journal,* 63, No. 2 (1957), pp. 152–162.

——. "The Significance and Content of Leisure Activities from Age Forty to Seventy." Cleveland: Gerontological Society, Inc., 1957 Conference.

——. "The Nature of Values of Meaningful Free Time Activity." *Aging and Leisure,* ed. R. Kleemeier. New York: Oxford University Press, 1961, pp. 309–343.

——. *Developmental Tasks and Education.* New York: David McKay, 1965.

——. "The Future Aged: The Use of Time and Money." *Gerontologist,* 15, No. 1 (1975), pp. 10–15.

——. "Education through the Adult Life Span." *Educational Gerontology,* 1 (1976), pp. 41–51.

——, and Betty Orr. *Adult Education and Adult Needs.* Chicago: Center for the Study of Liberal Education for Adults, 1956, 1960.

Health and Welfare Council. *Proceedings, Second Biennial Leadership Training Conference on Recreation and Leisure for Older People.* Louisville: Health and Welfare Council, February 4, 1958.

Hecksher, A., and de Grazie, Sebastian. "Executive Leisure." *Harvard Business Review,* 37, 4 (July–August, 1959), pp. 6–16, 144–156.

Heidell, Beth. "Sensory Training Puts Patients 'In Touch'." *Modern Nursing Home,* (1972), pp. 39–43.

Hendrickson, Andrew, and George F. Aker. *Education for Senior Adults.* Tallahassee: Florida State University, 1969.

Henley, Barbara, L. Zeitz, and G. Reader. "Uses of Free Time by Ambulatory Chronically Ill Elderly Patients." *Journal of American Geriatrics Society,* 10 (1962), pp. 1081–1091.

Heron, W. "The Pathology of Boredom." *Scientific American,* 196 (1957), pp. 52–56.

Heymon, Dorothy, ed. *Community and Junior Colleges: Education and Training for Work with the Elderly.* Durham: Duke University, Center for the Study of Aging and Human Development, 1975.

Hill, Robert B., *A Profile of the Black Aged.* New York: Research Department, National Urban League, 1971.

Hiltner, Seward, ed. *Toward a Theology of Aging.* Fairfax, Va.: National Publications Center, 1975.

Hitzhusen, G. "Recreation and Leisure Counseling for Adult Psychiatric and Alcoholic Patients." *Therapeutic Recreation Journal,* 7, No. 1 (1973), pp. 16–22.

Hixon, Leroy E. *Formula for Success.* Long Beach, Cal.: National Retired Teachers Association, 1968.

Hoar, Jere. "A Study of Free-time Activities of 200 Aged Persons." *Sociology and Social Research,* 45, No. 2 (1961), pp. 157–163.

Hoffman, Adeline M., ed. *Daily Needs and Interests of Older People.* Springfield, Ill.: Charles C Thomas, 1970.

Houle, Cyril. *Continuing Your Education.* New York: McGraw-Hill, 1964.

——. *Residential Continuing Education.* Syracuse: Publications in Continuing Education, 1971.

Howe, Irving. *World of Our Fathers.* New York: Harcourt, Brace, Jovanovich, 1976.

Hoyt, G. C. "The Life of the Retired in a Trailer Park." *American Journal of Sociology,* 49 (1954), pp. 361–370.

Huber, R. T., G. A. Myren, and S. Sweeney. *Community College Services for Senior Citizens.* Ann Arbor: University of Michigan, Institute of Gerontology, 1971.

Hunter, W. *Guidelines for Preretirement Educa-*

tion Programs, Ann Arbor: University of Michigan, Institute of Gerontology, 1971.

Hunter, Woodrow W. *Preparation for Retirement,* 3rd ed. Ann Arbor: University of Michigan, Institute of Gerontology, 1976.

Hutchinson, Enid. *Learning and Leisure in Middle and Later Life.* London: Pre-Retirement Association, National Institute of Adult Education and National Old People's Welfare Council, 1970.

Incani, A., B. Seward, and J. Sigler. *Coordinated Activity Programs for the Aged: A How-to-Do-It Manual.* Fairfax, Va.: National Publications Center, 1975.

Indiana Commission on the Aging and Aged. *Counseling of the Older Person.* Indianapolis: Commission on the Aging and Aged, Governor's Sesquicentennial Conference on Aging, 1966.

Institute of Lifetime Learning. *Demonstration Pilot Project of Comprehensive Library Services for the Aged in Selected Communities in Kentucky.* Washington, D.C.: U.S. Office of Education, Bureau of Librarians and Learning Resources, 1973–1974, 2 vols.

International Association of Machinists and Aerospace Workers. *A Handbook for Conducting Pre-Retirement Sessions in the IAM.* Washington, D.C.: IAM, 1968.

International Center of Social Gerontology. *International Course in Social Gerontology, Proceedings.* 1st: Lisbon, March 16–20, 1970; 2nd: Florence, May 24–28, 1971; 3rd: Dubrovnik, May 15–19, 1972. Paris: International Center of Social Gerontology.

————. *Leisure and the IIIrd Age.* Paris: International Course, Dubrovnik, May 15–19, 1972.

International Federation on Aging. *On Defense of the Ageing and Ageing. Mankind's World Problem.* Nairobi: International Conference on Social Welfare, July 14–20, 1974.

Jacobs, Bella, ed. *Senior Centers: Realizing Our Potential.* Washington, D.C.: Eighth National Conference of Senior Centers, 1975.

Jacobs, H. Lee, W. Dean Mason, and Earl Kauffman. *Education for Aging: A Review of Recent Literature.* Syracuse: ERIC Clearinghouse on Adult Education, 1970.

Jacobs, J. *Older Persons and Retirement Communities.* Washington, D.C.: National Publications Center, 1975.

Johnson, A. C., and E. A. Prieve. *Older Americans: The Unrealized Audience for the Arts.* Madison: University of Wisconsin, Graduate School of Business, Center for Arts Administration, 1976.

Johnstone, John W. C., and Ramon J. Rivera. *Volunteers for Learning: A Study of the Educational Pursuits of American Adults.* Chicago: Aldine, 1965.

Kalish, A., ed. *The Dependencies of Old People.* Ann Arbor: University of Michigan, Institute on Gerontology, 1969.

Kaplan, Max. "Uses of Leisure." *Handbook of Social Gerontology,* Clark Tibbitts. Chicago: University of Chicago Press, 1960, pp. 407–443.

————. "Implications of Leisure Theory for Gerontology." *Leisure and the IIIrd Age,* Conference, Dubrovnik. Paris: International Centre for Social Gerontology, 1972, pp. 49–63.

————. "Aging and Leisure." *International Encyclopedia of Psychiatry, Psychology, Psychoanalysis and Neurology.* B. Wolman, ed. New York: Van Nostrand, 1977.

————. "Arts and the Elderly." Minneapolis: National Council for the Arts and Aging and National Council on Aging, October 18, 1976.

————, and Claudine Attias-Donfut. *Educational & Leisure-Time Activities of the Elderly.* Special issue, *Society and Leisure,* Prague: European Center for Leisure and Education, 5, No. 4 (1975).

Kart, Cary S., and Barbara B. Manard. *Aging in America: Readings in Social Gerontology.* Port Washington, N.Y.: Alfred Publishing, 1976.

Kimmel, Douglas C. *Adulthood and Aging.* New York: John Wiley & Sons, 1974.

Kleemeier, Robert W. "Moosehaven: Congregate Living in a Community of the Retired." *American Journal of Sociology,* 59, No. 4 (1954), pp. 347–351.

————, ed. *Aging and Leisure: A Research Perspective Into the Meaningful Use of Time.* New York: Oxford University Press, 1961.

————. "The Use and Meaning of Time in Special Settings." *Social and Psychological Aspects of Aging, Aging Around the World,* ed. Clark Tibbitts and Wilma T. Donahue. New York and London: Columbia University Press, 1962, pp. 913–918.

————. "Leisure and Disengagement in Retirement." *Gerontologist,* 4 (1964), pp. 180–184.

Klevins, Chester, ed. *Materials and Methods in Adult Education.* Canoga Park, Cal.: Klevins Publications, 1972.

Knowles, Malcolm S. *The Modern Practice of Adult Education: Andragogy versus Pedagogy.* New York: Association Press, 1970.

Kreps, Juanita M. *Lifetime Allocation of Work and Leisure.* Washington, D.C.: U.S. Government Printing Office, 1968, Social Security Administration, Research Report No. 22.

———. "Loaf More, Retire Later." *Journal of the Association of Retired Persons International,* 5, No. 2 (1969), pp. 5–7.

———. *Lifetime Allocation of Work and Income: Essays in the Economics of Aging.* Durham, N.C.: Duke University Press, 1971.

Krippene, Arleen. "Today's Facts About Senior Sex." *Harvest Years,* 7 (1967).

Kuhlen, Raymond G., ed. *Psychological Backgrounds of Adult Education.* Chicago: Center for the Study of Liberal Education for Adults, 1963.

Kurasik, Steve. "Why Recreation in Hospitals, Nursing Homes, and Homes for the Aged?" *Journal of the American Geriatrics Society,* 14 (1966).

Labouvie-Vief, Gisela. "Toward Optimizing Confidence in Later Life." *Educational Gerontology,* 1 (1976), pp. 75–92.

———, and Judith N. Gonda. "Cognitive Strategy Training and Intellectual Performance in the Elderly." *Journal of Gerontology,* 31 (1976), pp. 327–332.

Lakin, Martin, and Melvin Dray. "Psychological Aspects of Activity for the Aged." *American Journal of Occupational Therapy,* 12 (1958), pp. 172–175.

Lamb, Tony, and Dave Duffy. *The Retirement Threat.* New York: St. Martin's Press, 1977.

Lambert, C., M. Goberman, and R. Morris. "Reopening Doors to Community Participation for Older People: How Realistic?" *Social Service Review,* 38 (1964), pp. 42–50.

Lehman, Harvey C. *Age and Achievement.* Princeton: Princeton University Press, 1953.

Lerner, Joseph. "Recreational Activities for the Aging." *Journal of the American Geriatrics Society,* 12 (1964), pp. 323–327.

Lewis, C. A., Jr., et al. "Implications for Leisure and Old Age." *Nursing Homes,* 22 (1973), pp. 16–18.

Linden, M. E. "Preparation for the Leisure of Later Maturity." *Free Time: Challenge to Later Maturity,* ed. Wilma T. Donahue, Woodrow W. Hunter, Dorothy H. Evans, and Helen K. Maurice. Ann Arbor: University of Michigan Press, 1958.

Lindsey, John R. "Recreation as Part of the Environment." *Nursing Homes,* 16 (1967), pp. 18–23.

Long, Huey B. *Are They Ever Too Old to Learn?* Englewood Cliffs, N.J.: Prentice-Hall, 1971.

Long, Irene. "Human Sexuality and Aging." *Social Casework,* 57 (1976), pp. 237–244.

Lucas, Carol. *Recreation in Gerontology.* Springfield, Ill.: Charles C Thomas, 1964.

Lundegren, H., P. Farrell, and G. Godbey. "Leisure and Aging." Unpublished, presented by Penn State University at NRPA Congress, Boston, October 17, 1976.

Martin, Alexander Reid. "Urgent Need for a Philosophy of Leisure in an Aging Population." *Journal of the American Geriatrics Society,* 10, No. 3 (1962), pp. 215–224.

———. *Leisure Time—A Creative Force.* Washington, D.C.: National Council on Aging, 1974.

Mathiasen, Geneva, ed. *Flexible Retirement.* New York: G. P. Putnam's Sons, 1957.

Maves, Paul B. "Aging, Religion and the Church." *Handbook of Social Gerontology,* ed. Clark Tibbitts. Chicago: University of Chicago Press, 1960, pp. 698–749.

———, and J. L. Cedarleaf. *Older People and the Church.* Nashville: Abingdon-Cokesbury, 1949.

McCluskey, Howard Y. *Education.* Washington, D.C.: U.S. Government Printing Office, 1971. Background paper, 1971 White House Conference on Aging.

———. *Education and Aging.* Ann Arbor: University of Michigan, Institute of Gerontology, 1971.

McLeish, John. *The Ulyssian Adult: Creativity in the Middle and Later Years.* New York: McGraw-Hill, 1976.

Meir, Golda. *My Life.* New York: G. P. Putnam's Sons, 1975.

Mering, Otto von, and F. L. Weniger. "Social-Cultural Background of the Aging Individual." *Handbook of Aging and the Individual,* ed. James E. Birren. Chicago: University of Chicago Press, 1959.

Merrill, Toni. *Activities for the Aged and Infirm.* Springfield, Ill.: Charles C Thomas, 1962.

———. *Social Clubs for the Aging: Including Twenty-four Programs for Nine Clubs.* Fairfax, Va.: National Publications Center, 1972.

Miller, Dulcy B. "Nursing Home Setting: How the Administrator Relates to the Recreation Program." *Parks and Recreation,* 11, 1 (1967), pp. 39, 53–54.

Miller, Harry L. *Teaching and Learning in Adult Education.* New York: Macmillan, 1964.

Miller, Norman P., and Duane M. Robinson. *The Leisure Age: Its Challenge to Recreation.* Belmont, Cal., Wadsworth Publishing, 1963.

Miller, Stephen J. "The Social Dilemma of the Aging Leisure Participant." *Aging in America: Readings in Social Gerontology,* ed. C. S. Kart and B. B. Manard. Port Washington, N.Y.: 1976, pp. 264–285.

Monk, A., and Ayns, A. G. "Predictors of Voluntaristic Intent Among the Aged." *The Gerontologist,* 14, No. 5 (1974), pp. 425–429.

Moody, H. R. "Philosophical Presuppositions of Education for Old Age." *Educational Gerontology,* 1 (1976), pp. 1–16.

Morgan, Ann, and Geoffrey Godbey. "The Effect of Entering an Age-Segregated Environment Upon the Leisure Activity Patterns of Older Adults." Manuscript, Pennsylvania State University, 1977.

Mulac, Margaret E. *Leisure—Time for Living and Retirement.* New York: Harper and Row, 1961.

———. "Retirement and Leisure." *Leisure and Aging: New Perspectives,* ed. Barbara Bates. Washington, D.C.: American Alliance for Health, Physical Education, and Recreation, 1977.

Murphy, James F. "Leisure, Aging and Retirement: Changing Patterns and Perspectives." *Leisure and Aging: New Perspectives,* ed. Barbara Bates. Washington, D.C.: American Alliance of Health, Physical Education, and Recreation, 1977.

Myran, Gundar A., Robert Huber, and Sean A. Sweeney. *Senior Citizens Services in Community Colleges.* East Lansing: Michigan State University, November 1971; Research and Report Series, Report No. 5, Kellogg Community Services Leadership Program.

National Clearing House on Aging. *Thesaurus.* Washington, D.C.: U.S. Department of Health, Education, Welfare, Office of Human Development, Administration on Aging, July 1975.

National Conference on Aging. *Senior Centers Today: New Opportunities, New Challenges.* Washington, D.C.: National Council on the Aging, 1967. Selections from NCOA's Fourth National Conference of Senior Centers.

National Council of the Churches of Christ in the U.S.A. *The Task Force on Leisure; Report of the First Meeting, October 24 and 25, 1965.* Princeton: Princeton Theological Seminary, 1966.

National Council on the Aging. *Community Action and the Elderly Poor: The Role of the Organizer.* Washington, D.C.: National Council on the Aging, 1969.

———. *Senior Centers: Realizing Our Potential,* ed. Bella Jacobs, Washington, D.C.: NCOA Proceedings, Eighth National Conference of Senior Centers, 1975.

National Federal Employees. *Sunset Years: Plan for Your Retirement Living.* Washington, D.C.: National Federal Employees, 1971.

National Institute of Senior Centers. *Senior Centers: A Focal Point for Delivery of Services to Older People.* Washington, D.C.: National Council for Aging, 1972.

National Jewish Welfare Board. *Jewish Community Center Program Aids: A New Look at the Jewish Older Adult.* New York: National Jewish Welfare Board, 1966.

National Urban League. *Double Jeopardy—The Older Negro in America Today.* Washington, D.C.: U.S. Government Printing Office, 1966. Hearings before Special Committee on Aging, U.S. Senate, Long-Range Program and Research Needs in Aging and Related Fields.

New Jersey Division on Aging. *Uses of Free Time for Senior Citizens. A Report of the Conference April 6, 1961.* Trenton: Trenton State College, 1962.

Niemi, John A. *Mass Media and Adult Education.* Englewood Cliffs, N.J.: Educational Technology Publications, 1971.

Nystrom, Eleanor P. "Activity Patterns and Leisure Concepts Among the Elderly." *American Journal of Occupational Therapy,* 28, No. 4 (1974).

Olmstead, Alan H. *Threshold: The First Days of Retirement.* New York: Harper & Row, 1975.

Ontario Department of Social and Family Services. *Conference on University Education Related to Aging and the Teaching of Professional Skills in the Field of Gerontology,* ed. Crawford Lawrence. Toronto: Department of Social and Family Services, 1965.

Ontario Ministry of Community and Social Services. *Measures of Leisure Time Activities of Men in Their Early Fifties.* Toronto: Ministry of Community and Social Services, Homes for the Aged, Office on Aging Branch, June 1972.

Palmore, Erdman B., ed. *Normal Aging: Reports from the Duke Longitudinal Study, 1955–1969.* Durham: Duke University Press, 1974.

———. *Honorable Elders: A Cross-Cultural Analysis of Aging in Japan.* Fairfax, Va.: National Publications Center, 1975.

———. "The Effects of Aging on Activities and Attitudes." *Aging in America: Readings in Social Gerontology,* ed. C. S. Kart and B. B. Manard. Port Washington, N.Y.: Alfred Publishing, 1976, pp. 252–263.

Peery, Johnette. *Exercises for Retirees.* Milwaukee, Ore.: North Cloehames Print Shop, 1976.

Peterson, David A. "Educational Gerontology: The State of the Art." *Educational Gerontology,* 1 (1976), pp. 61–73.

Philadelphia Health and Welfare Council, Inc. *To Brighten the Later Years.* Philadelphia: Health and Welfare Council, 1961.

Phinney, Eleanor, ed. *Library Trends: Library Services to the Aging.* Urbana: University of Illinois, 1973.

Piscopo, John, and Charles A. Lewis. "Preparing Geriatric Fitness and Recreational Specialists." *Leisure and Aging: New Perspectives,* ed. Barbara Bates. Washington, D.C.: American Alliance of Health, Physical Education and Recreation, 1977.

Planning for Your Retirement: A Design for Active Living. Albany: State Education Department, Bureau of Continuing Education, 1970.

Poe, William D., and H. Lawrence Rice. "Friendship Manor: A Community Geriatrics Model." *Journal of the American Geriatrics Society,* 24 (1976), pp. 283–284.

Pullias, Earl V. "Problems of Aging: Some Psychological Principles." *Leisure and Aging: New Perspectives,* ed. Barbara Bates. Washington, D.C.: American Alliance of Health, Physical Education and Recreation, 1977.

Quigley, John L., and Alexandra Walcott. "Recreation Renews Interest in Life." *Hospitals* (November 1, 1972), pp. 52–57.

Racklis, David. Developing Transportation Services for Older People. Washington, D.C.: National Council on Aging, 1970.

Rapoport, Rhona and Robert (with Ziona Strelitz). *Leisure and the Family Life Cycle.* London, Boston: Routledge & Kegan Paul, 1975.

Releasing the Potential of the Older Volunteer. Los Angeles: Andrus Gerontology Center, 1976.

Retirement Council. *101 Ways to Enjoy Your Leisure.* Stamford: Retirement Council, 1964.

Rich, Thomas A., and Alden S. Gilmore. *Basic Concepts of Aging: A Programmed Manual.* Washington, D.C.: U.S. Government Printing Office, Superintendent of Documents, 1972.

Rivas, Armando. *Manuscript B: The Spanish Speaking Elderly.* Ann Arbor: University of Michigan-Wayne State University, 1974.

Rose, Arnold M., and Warren A. Peterson, eds. *Older People and Their Social World.* Philadelphia: F. A. Davis, 1965.

Rosencrantz, Howard, ed. *Pre-Retirement Education: A Manual for Conference Leaders.* Storrs, Conn.: University of Connecticut, Program in Gerontology, 1975.

Rowe, Alan. "Scientists in Retirement." *Journal of Gerontology,* 21 (1972), pp. 113–118; 28 (1972), pp. 335–345.

Sainer, Janet S., and Mary L. Zander. *Serve: Older Volunteers in Community Service: A New Role and a New Source.* New York: Community Service Society, 1971.

Schalinske, William. *Aging and Mass Communication.* Unpublished Ph.D. Thesis, Columbus, Ohio State University, 1968.

———, and I. Strodel. "Age-Dependency of Leisure-Time Activities." *Human Development,* 14 (1971), pp. 47–50.

Schramm, W., and R. T. Storey. *Little House: A Study of Senior Citizens.* Stanford: Stanford University, Institute for Communication Research, 1961.

Scott, Wilfred C. "The ABC's of Retirement Planning." *Ontario Welfare Reporter,* 14, No. 3 (1967).

Scudder, Delton L., ed. *Organized Religion and the Older Person.* Gainesville, Fla.: University of Florida Press, 1958, Eighth Annual Southern Conference on Gerontology.

Sessoms, H. Douglas. "Aging: Its Implications for the Recreation Center." *Colloquium on the Physical Health and Recreation Implications of Aging.* Lafayette, Ind., Purdue University, October 1969.

Shanas, Ethel. *Aging in Contemporary Society.* Special issue, *American Behavioral Scientist,* 14, No. 1 (1970).

———, et al. *Old People in Three Industrial Societies.* New York: Atherton Press, 1968.

———, and Robert J. Havighurst. "Retirement in Four Professions." *Journal of Gerontology,* 8 (1953), pp. 212–221.

Sheehy, Gail. *Passages: Predictable Crises of Adult Life.* New York: E. P. Dutton, 1976.

Shimmel, B., and F. M. Tobin. "Sexuality and Aging." *Leisure and Aging: New Perspectives,* ed. Barbara Bates. Washington, D.C.: American Alliance of Health, Physical Education and Recreation, 1977.

Shore, Herbert. "A Resident-Directed Adult Study Program in a Home for the Aged." *Geriatrics,* 14 (1959), pp. 52–55.

Smaridge, Nora. *Choosing Your Retirement Hobby.* New York: Dodd Mead, 1976.

Smith, Robert M., George F. Aker, and J. R. Kidd, eds. *Handbook of Adult Education.* New York: Macmillan, 1970.

Staff Guide for Volunteer Resources. Harrisburg: Department of Public Welfare, Commonwealth of Pennsylvania, August 1968.

Staley, E. J., and R. H. Singleton. *How To Retire and Love It.* Fairfax, Va.: National Publications Center, 1976.

Stone, Ken, and Richard A. Kalish. "Of Poker, Roles and Aging: Description, Discussion and Data." *Aging in America: Readings in Social Gerontology,* ed. C. S. Kart and B. B. Manard. Port Washington, N.Y.: Alfred Publishing, 1976, pp. 286–301.

Streib, Gordon F., and A. Schneider. *Retirement in American Society: Impact and Process.* Ithaca: Cornell University Press, 1971.

Strong, E. K. *Change of Interest with Age.* Stanford: Stanford University Press, 1931.

Stough, Ada B. *A Rural County Cares for Its Aging (Aiken County, Minn.), #17. Patterns for Progress in Aging.* Washington, D.C.: U.S. Government Printing Office, 1964.

Sunderland, Jacqueline Tippett. *Older Americans and the Arts: A Human Equation.* Washington, D. C.: National Center for Older Americans and the Arts and John F. Kennedy Center for Performing Arts, 1973.

Teaff, Joseph D. "Leisure and the Aging Process: Policy Alternatives." *Leisure and Aging: New Perspectives,* ed. Barbara Bates. Washington, D.C.: American Alliance of Health, Physical Education and Recreation, 1977.

Terrell, William R., and Ronald K. Bass. "Accountability in Adult Education: The Result of Planning and Salesmanship." *Educational Gerontology,* 1 (1976), pp. 93–98.

Tibbitts, Clark, ed. *Handbook of Social Gerontology.* Chicago: University of Chicago Press, 1960.

———, and Wilma T. Donahue, eds. *Aging in Today's Society.* Englewood Cliffs, N.J.: Prentice-Hall, 1960.

Tisseyre, J. P. *Troisième Âge: Vivre ou Survivre?* Paris: Sefa, 1975.

Townsend, P. *The Last Refuge: A Survey of Residential Institutions and Homes for the Aged in England and Wales.* London: Routledge & Kegan Paul, 1962.

Transition: A Guide to Retirement. Washington, D.C.: U.S. Government Printing Office, Superintendent of Documents, 1972.

Tuckman, Jacob. "Factors Related to Attendance in a Center for Older People." *Journal of the American Geriatrics Society,* 15 (1967), pp. 474–479.

Tuckman, J., and I. Lorge. *Retirement and the Industrial Worker: Prospect and Reality.* New York: Columbia University Press, 1953.

Tunstall, Jeremy. *Old and Alone.* London: Routledge & Kegan Paul, 1966.

Union of American Hebrew Congregations. *Aging and Retirement.* New York: Union of American Hebrew Congregations, 1956.

———, Committee on the Aging. *Judaism, The Synagogue and the Aging.* New York: Union of American Hebrew Congregations, 1962.

United Community Services. *A City-Wide Study of Leisure Time Services: Self-Appraisal Project for the City of Omaha, Nebraska, 1959.* Omaha: United Community Services, 1959.

United Community Services of Metropolitan Boston. *Profile for Planning; An Approach to Measuring Need for Leisure Time Services in Metropolitan Boston.* Boston: United Community Services of Metropolitan Boston, 1962.

Use of Volunteers in Public Welfare. New York: Family Service Association of America, 1963, National Study Service for New York City Department of Welfare.

Verhoven, Peter J. "Recreation and the Aging." *Recreation and Special Populations* ed. Thomas A. Stein and H. Douglas Sessoms. Boston: Holbrook Press, 1973.

Vickery, Florence E. *Creative Programming for Older Adults.* New York: Association Press, 1972.

Wallis, Gwyneth. *Guide to Activities for Older People.* London: Elek Books, 1970.

Webber, Irving L. "The Organized Social Life of the Retired: Two Florida Communities." *American Journal of Sociology,* 59, No. 4 (1954), pp. 340–346.

Weisman, Celia B. *The Future Is Now: A Manual for Older Adult Programs in Jewish Communal Service Agencies.* New York: National Jewish Welfare Board, 1976.

Welford, A. T. *Aging and Human Skill.* London: The Nuffield Foundation, Oxford University Press, 1958.

Wermel, N. J., and S. Gelbaum. "Work and Retirement in Old Age." *American Journal of Sociology,* (1945), LI, no. 1, pp. 16–21.

Wheeler, Harvey. "The Rise of the Elders." *Saturday Review* (December 5, 1970).

Williams, Arthur. *Recreation in the Senior Years.* New York: Association Press, 1962.

Williams, Jill. "Over Sixties Keep Fit at Waxter Center." *Aging,* 258 (1976), pp. 15–16.

Williams, Wayne R. *Recreation Places.* New York: Reinhold Publishing, 1958.

Wolcott, Jean. "There's Only Me, Now." *Leisure and Aging: New Perspectives,* ed. Barbara Bates. Washington, D.C.: American Alliance of Health, Physical Education and Recreation, 1977.

Woodruff, Diana S., and James E. Birren. *Aging: Scientific Perspectives and Social Issues.* New York: Van Nostrand, 1975.

Woods, J. H. *Helping Older People Enjoy Life.* New York: Harper & Row, 1953.

Yates, Elizabeth. *Call It Zest—The Vital Ingredient After Seventy.* Washington, D.C.: National Publications Center, 1977.

Youman, E. Grant. *Leisure-Time Activities of Older Persons in Selected Rural and Urban Areas of Kentucky.* Lexington: University of Kentucky, Agricultural Experiment Station, 1962.

Your Retirement Hobby Guide. Washington, D.C.: AARP and NRTA, 1969.

Zborowski, Mark. "Aging and Recreation." *Journal of Gerontology,* No. 3 (1962).

Zeiger, Betty L. "Life Review in Art Therapy with the Aged." *American Journal of Art Therapy,* 15 (1976), pp. 47–50.

INFORMATION RESOURCES

Journals

Adding Life to Years. Institute of Gerontology, University of Iowa; 26 Byington Road, Iowa City, Iowa. Monthly. $1.00 per year. Recognized as an example of an outstanding small publication, containing information relating to programs in Iowa. Also offered are scholarly, timely editorials of national interest and reviews of current publications.

Aging and Human Development. Greenwood Periodicals, Inc.; 51 Riverside Avenue, Westport, Conn. 96880. Quarterly. $20.00 per year. A relatively new journal directed to the psychosocial aspects of gerontology. Articles presented cover human development. Book reviews are also offered.

Aging and Work (formerly *Industrial Gerontology*). Volume 1, number 1 of new title, Winter 1978. Quarterly. $30.00 annually, $8.00 per issue.

Aging International. International Federation on Ageing (French, English, German); 1909 K Street, N.W., Washington, D.C. 20049, U.S.A.

American Association of Retired Persons News. Bulletin. American Association of Retired Persons; 1225 Connecticut Ave., N.W., Washington, D.C. 20036. Monthly. Membership, $2.00 per year. Provides information on national developments, local association activities, and other items of practical value to members.

American Journal of Public Health. American Public Health Association, Inc.; 1015 18th Street, N.W., Washington, D.C. 20036. Monthly. $20.00 per year.

American Psychologist. The American Psychological Association, Inc.; Prince and Lemon Streets, Lancaster, Pa. 17604. Monthly. $10.00 per year.

Canada's Mental Health. Mental Health Division, Department of National Health and Welfare, Ottawa. Frequently carries book reviews or articles on sociopsychological aspects of importance to community organizations and the aged.

Current Literature on Aging. National Council on Aging; 1828 L St., N.W., Washington, D.C. 20036. Quarterly. $3.00 per year. A subject guide to selected publications in the field of aging and related areas.

Directory of Senior Citizens Clubs and Groups in Ontario, 1967 and 1968. Prepared in Community Programs Division, Dr. E. M. Dutton, Special Adviser. Ontario Department of Education, 559 Jarvis Street, Toronto 5, Ontario.

Dynamic Maturity. American Association of Retired Persons; 1909 K St., N.W., Washington, D.C. 20036. Bimonthly. $2.00 per year.

Geriatrics. Lancet Publications; 4015 West 65th Street, Minneapolis, Minn. 55435. Monthly. $21.00 per year.

Gerontologia. Albert J. Phiebig, Inc. (U.S. Representative of S. Karger); P.O. Box 352, White Plains, New York 10602. Bimonthly. $25.00 per year.

Gerontologist. Gerontological Society; #1 Dupont Circle, Washington, D.C. 20036. Quarterly. $10.00 per fiscal year.

Human Development. Albert J. Phiebig, Inc. (U.S. Representative of S. Karger); P.O. Box 352, White Plains, New York 10602.

International Journal of Aging and Human Development. Baywood Publishing Company, Inc.; 43 Central Drive, Farmingdale, New York 11735. Quarterly. $25.00 per year.

International Senior Citizens News. Older People Around the World—Official Quarterly Publication of the ISCA.

International Social Security Review. International Social Security Association; The General Secretariat, 154 Rue de Lausanne, Geneva, Switzerland. Quarterly. $7.00 per year.

Journal of the American Geriatrics Society. American Geriatric Society, Inc.; The Williams and Wilkins Co., 428 E. Preston St., Baltimore, Md. 21202. Monthly. $10.00 per year. A magazine format which contains articles oriented to clinical geriatric medicine, case reports, review articles, editorials, news and notices, book reviews, and also includes commercial advertising. Articles cover subjects related to etiology, preventive diagnosis and treatment of diseases of the aging and aged, rehabilitation, and other problems relating to health care of the older patient.

Journal of Gerontology. Gerontological Society; #1 Dupont Circle, Washington, D.C. 20036. Quarterly. $26.00 per year. Contains scholarly articles, signed book reviews, and the "Current Publications in Gerontology and Geriatrics" section.

Modern Maturity. American Association of Retired Persons; 406 E. Grand Ave., Ojai,

Calif. 93023. Bimonthly. $2.00 per year. A publication offering articles of interest to persons over 55 years of age. Items covered include current news, recipes and nutrition, medical information, and other information of interest to this age group.

National Retired Teachers Association Journal. National Retired Teachers Association; 701 North Montgomery Street, Ojai, Calif. 93023. Bimonthly. Membership $2.00 per year.

The Ontario Welfare Reporter and *Newsletter,* the latter the paper of the Section on Aging. Both from Ontario Welfare Council, 22 Davisville Avenue, Toronto 7, Ontario.

Retirement Living. New York: Harvest Years Publishing Company, 1969.

RSVP Newsletter. Community Service Society; 105 E. 22nd Street, New York, New York 10010.

U.S. Government Publications

Adult Development and Aging Abstracts. Experimental Issue, No. 5, 1969. HEW, Public Health Service, National Institutes of Health.

Aging. U.S. Department of Health, Education and Welfare, Superintendent of Documents, Washington, D.C. 20402. Monthly. $2.50 per year. A publication for the Administration on Aging. Includes short articles on items of interest in the field, education programs, news items, actions of various agencies and organizations, and reviews of literature in the study of aging.

Bureau of the Census. *Some Demographic Aspects of Aging in the United States.* Washington, D.C.: U.S. Government Printing Office, Current Population Reports, Series P-23, No. 43.

Commission on Aging. Cranford, Charles B. *Demonstration Program: A Leisure and Recreation Program for Older Americans.* Washington, D.C.: U.S. Administration on Aging, No. 11.

Department of Labor Bulletin 489. Reported in "Problems of Idleness in Old Peoples Homes." *Monthly Labor Review* (December 1929), Bureau of Statistics.

Department of Labor/Manpower Administration. *America's Volunteer.* Washington, D.C.: U.S. Government Printing Office, April 1969, Monograph No. 10. $0.50.

Extending the Human Life Span: Social Policy and Social Ethics. Washington, D.C.: U.S. Government Printing Office, Superintendent of Documents, 1977, 18 P 8: NS 1.2:L62, S/N 038-000-00337-2.

HEW, Public Health Service, National Institutes of Health. *Adult Development and Aging Abstracts.* Experimental issue, No. 5, 1969. Chief, Scientific Information Centers Branch, National Institute of Child Health and Human Development, National Institutes of Health, Bethesda, Maryland 20014.

Individual Retirement Account (IRA) Plan for Your Retirement. Washington, D.C.: U.S.

Government Printing Office, Superintendent of Documents, 1977, 109 p 8. X3 P 38/2:2 R 31/2 S/N 040-000-00381-9.

Institute of Public Administration. *Planning Handbooks—Transportation Services for the Elderly.* Washington, D.C.: Administration on Aging, November 1975.

Mandatory Retirement: The Social and Human Cost of Enforced Idleness. Washington, D.C.: U.S. Government Printing Office, Superintendent of Documents, 1977, 139 P 8 Y 4 AG 4/2:R 31/2, S/N 052-070-04191-9.

Office of the Aging. "Recreation and Creative Activity." In *Aging in the Modern World—An Annotated Bibliography,* Washington, D.C.: Office of the Aging, 1963, pp. 144–149.

Senate. *Developments in Aging: 1976, Part 2—Appendices, 95th Congress, 1st Session, Report 95–88, April 7, 1977.* Reports by National Endowments on Services to the Elderly.

Senate, Special Committee on Aging. *Research and Training in Aging.* Washington, D.C.: U.S. Government Printing Office, 1971.

Senate Special Committee on Aging, Subcommittee on Retirement and the Individual. Hearing on "The Federal Role in Encouraging Pre-Retirement Counseling and New York Life Time Patterns." July 25, 1969.

Senate Subcommittee on Long-Term Care. *Nursing Home Care in the United States: Failure in Public Policy.* November 1974, first of 12-volume series.

Social Security Administration, Office of Research and Statistics. Kreps, Juanita M. *Lifetime Allocation of Work and Leisure.* Washington, D.C.: U.S. Government Printing Office, 1968, Research Report No. 22.

White House Conference on Aging, Washington, D.C., 1961. Free time activities: recreation, voluntary service, citizenship participation; a statement of needs, values, and importance of free time activities to individual and social well-being of senior citizens together with recommendations from the 1961 White House Conference on Aging. Reports and guidelines from the White House Conference on Aging. Washington, D.C.: U.S. Department of Health, Education, and Welfare, Special Staff on Aging, 1961.

White House Conference on Aging, Washington, D.C., 1961. Background paper on free time activities: recreation, voluntary services, citizenship participation. Prepared under direction of the Committee on Free Time Activities: Recreation, Voluntary Services, Citizenship Participation. Washington, D.C.: National Advisory Committee, 1961.

White House Conference on Aging. *Roster of Participating National Organizations with Programs in the Field of Aging.* Washington, D.C.: U.S. Government Printing Office, 1971.

White House Conference on Aging. *Section Recommendations on Education, 1971.* With related recommendations from other sections and special concerns sessions. Washington, D.C.: U.S. Government Printing Office, 1972.

Organizations

ACTION. 806 Connecticut Ave., Washington, D.C. 20525. Federal agency that administers Peace Corps, VISTA, SCORE, Foster Grandparent Program, RSVP, etc.

Action for Independent Maturity (A/M). 1909 K Street, N.W., Washington, D.C. 20049. A section of AARP for persons between 50 and 65.

Administration on Aging. U.S. Department of Health, Education and Welfare, Washington, D.C. 20201.

American Alliance for Health, Physical Education and Recreation. 1201 16th St., N.W., Washington, D.C. 20036.

American Association of Retired Persons, 1909 K Street, N.W., Washington, D.C. 20049.

American Geriatrics Society. 10 Columbus Circle, New York, New York 10019.

Australian Council on the Ageing. Box 1817 Q, Melbourne, Victoria 3001, Australia.

Avocational Counseling Research, Inc. Box 267, Sussex, Wisconsin 53089; (414)-252-3219, Dr. Robert P. Overs, Executive Director.

Centre Internationale de Gerontologie Sociale. Administrator, J. P. Dartique-longue, 3 Place des États-Unis, 75116 Paris, France.

Constructive Leisure, Inc. 511 N. La Cienega Blvd., Los Angeles, Cal. 90048. Patsy B. Edwards, Director.

Educational Facilities Laboratories, Inc. 850 Third Ave., New York, New York 10022. Funded by National Endowment for the Arts to provide information about arts for the elderly, children, and handicapped.

Elderhostel. New England Center for Continuing Education, University of New Hampshire, Durham, N.H. 03824.

European Centre for Gerontological Documentation and Research. Administrator, Emile Van de Vorst, 363 B Chausée de Waterloo, B-1060 Bruxelles, Belgium.

European Federation for the Welfare of the Elderly (EURAG). Administrator, E. Pumpernig, Moserhofgasse 47, A-8010 Graz, Austria.

Gerontological Society. 1 Dupont Circle, Washington, D.C. 20038.

Hospital Audiences. 1540 Broadway, New York, New York 10031.

International Center of Social Gerontology, 3 Place des Etats-Unis, Paris, France 75116.

International Federation on Ageing, 1909 K Street, N.W., Washington, D.C. 20049. President, Bernard E. Nash, U.S.A.; Bulletin, *Aging International.*

International Senior Citizens Association, Inc. Administrator, Mrs. Marjorie Borchardt, 11753 Wilshire Blvd., Los Angeles, Cal. 90025.

National Center for Voluntary Action. 1785 Massachusetts Ave., N.W., Washington, D.C. 20036.

National Center on Black Aged. Suite 402, 1424 K Street, Washington, D.C. 20005.

National Council of Senior Citizens, Inc. 1511 K Street, N.W., Washington, D.C. 20005.

National Council on the Aging. 1828 L Street, N.W., Washington, D.C. 20036.

National Center on the Arts and the Aging. National Council on Aging, Inc., Jacqueline T. Sunderland, Coordinator, 1828 L Street, N.W., Washington, D.C. 20036.

National Endowment for the Arts. Washington, D.C. 20506.

National Institute of Senior Centers. 1828 L Street, N.W., Washington, D.C. 20036 (National Council on Aging).

National Retired Teachers Association (NRTA) and American Association of Retired Persons (AARP). 1909 K Street, N.W., Washington, D.C. 20049.

Retired Senior Volunteer Program (RSVP). ACTION, 806 Connecticut Ave., Washington, D.C. 20525.

World Association for the Senior Citizens Union (WASCU). President, Jan Olivier, AMTA, Box 22, Geneva 3, Switzerland.

Name Index

Subject Index

Page numbers followed by (t) indicate tables.
Page numbers in *italics* indicate illustrations.

283